Windows NT Workstation 4

Second Edition

201 West 103rd Street, Indianapolis, Indiana 46290

Luther Stanton

MCSE TestPrep: Windows NT Workstation 4, Second Edition

International Standard Book Number: 0-7357-0008-7

Library of Congress Catalog Card Number: 98-87706

Printed in the United States of America

First Printing: November, 1998

00 99 98 4 3 2 1

Trademarks

All terms mentioned in this book that are known to be trademarks or service marks have been appropriately capitalized. New Riders Publishing cannot attest to the accuracy of this information. Use of a term in this book should not be regarded as affecting the validity of any trademark or service mark.

Warning and Disclaimer

Every effort has been made to make this book as complete and as accurate as possible, but no warranty or fitness is implied. The information provided is on an "as is" basis. The author and the publisher shall have neither liability nor responsibility to any person or entity with respect to any loss or damages arising from the information contained in this book.

EXECUTIVE EDITOR
Mary Foote

ACQUISITIONS EDITOR
Nancy Maragioglio

DEVELOPMENT EDITOR
Scott Warner

MANAGING EDITOR
Sarah Kerns

PROJECT EDITOR
Clint McCarty

COPY EDITOR
Molly Schaller

INDEXER
CJ East

TECHNICAL EDITORS
Clyde Jenkins
Phillip Lawerance
Marc Savage

BOOK DESIGNER
Barb Kordesh

COVER DESIGNER
Sandra Schroeder

PROOFREADER
Megan Wade

PRODUCTION
Jeannette McKay

Contents at a Glance

Table of Contents

About the Author

Luther Stanton is currently employed as an Internet Application Developer with Elite Systems, Inc., a Microsoft Solution Provider based in Atlanta, GA. He and his wife also own WebWorks Southeast, an Internet presence provider focused on designing and hosting dynamic, data-driven Web sites for small and medium sized businesses.

Luther and his wife Heidi reside in Locust Grove, GA, approximately 40 miles southeast of Atlanta. He has over five years of system development and deployment experience and is currently a Windows NT Workstation 4.0 and Server 4.0 MCPS. He has co-authored and served as technical editor on various other Microsoft Certification study guides by Que and New Riders Publishing.

He can be reached at lstanton@wwse.net.

Acknowledgments

At first glance, when you pick up a book in a bookstore, you page through the contents, perhaps look at the index, and decide if you should make the purchase. During that entire process, most readers rarely stop to consider what went into making the book. Not just the print, paper, and cover art, but rather the work behind that print, paper, and art. After eight weeks of working with New Riders Publishing to put this book together I took a step back to look at what went into this book and how I got to this point. As many authors do, I wish to take a small bit of your time and real estate in this work to give thanks to a few people who helped to get me where I am and make this book possible.

I think one of my single biggest influences growing up was my grandfather. It was his guidance, love, and friendship that sparked my interest in electronics that eventually led to my career choice of engineering. It was also he and my grandmother who bought my first computer, a Commodore VIC 20.

My mother and sister also had a big influence on making me the person I am today. The lessons, advice, and love they provided while I was growing up have been invaluable. They taught me to always strive to do my best and never give up. Without their influence, many of my accomplishments would not have been possible.

No book would be possible without a lot of hard work from the people at New Riders Publishing. Thanks to Mary Foote, who got me started working with New Riders Publishing, and Scott Warner, the development editor, who ensured the chapters were checked for consistency and technical accuracy. And a big thanks goes out to Nancy Maragioglio, the acquisitions editor. Nancy is one of the best people I have had the pleasure of working with. No book would ever make it to the shelf without the hard work and dedication of people like Nancy.

And most of all a well-deserved thanks goes to the person who has sacrificed the most during the eight weeks of developing this work, my wife Heidi. Heidi was cutting the lawn on the weekends and maintaining our house and business while I was busy typing away. She never complained once about the countless hours I spent in front of the computer or the short weekends when the only time I could spare was a quick trip out for dinner. Without her love, support, and understanding, I would not have been able to complete the book.

Tell Us What You Think!

As the reader of this book, *you* are our most important critic and commentator. We value your opinion and want to know what we're doing right, what we could do better, what areas you'd like to see us publish in, and any other words of wisdom you're willing to pass our way.

As the Executive Editor for the Certification team at Macmillan Computer Publishing, I welcome your comments. You can fax, email, or write me directly to let me know what you did or didn't like about this book—as well as what we can do to make our books stronger.

Please note that I cannot help you with technical problems related to the topic of this book, and that due to the high volume of mail I receive, I might not be able to reply to every message.

When you write, please be sure to include this book's title and author, as well as your name and phone or fax number. I will carefully review your comments and share them with the author and editors who worked on the book.

Fax: 317-581-4663

Email: `certification@mcp.com`

Mail: Mary Foote
Executive Editor
Certification
Macmillan Computer Publishing
201 West 103rd Street
Indianapolis, IN 46290 USA

Introduction

The *MCSE TestPrep* series serves as a study aid for people preparing for Microsoft Certification exams. The series is intended to help reinforce and clarify information with which the student is already familiar by providing sample questions and tests, as well as summary information relevant to each of the exam objectives. Note that this series is not intended to be the only source for student preparation, but rather a review of information with a set of practice tests that can be used to increase the student's familiarity with the exam questions. Using this series with the *MCSE:Training Guide* series can increase the student's likelihood of success when taking the exam.

Who Should Read This Book

The Windows NT Workstation 4 book in the *MCSE TestPrep* series is intended specifically for students preparing for Microsoft's *Implementing and Supporting Microsoft Windows NT Workstation 4* (70–073) exam, which is one of the core exam electives in the MCSE Microsoft Windows NT 4 Track program.

How This Book Helps You

This book provides a wealth of review questions similar to those you will encounter in the actual exam, categorized by the objectives published by Microsoft for the exam. Each answer, both correct and incorrect, is explained in detail in the "Questions, Answers, and Explanation" section for each objective. The "Further Review" section provides additional information that is crucial for successfully passing the exam. The two full-length practice exams at the end of the book will help you determine whether you have mastered the facts necessary to successfully complete the exam.

How to Use This Book

When you feel like you're fairly well prepared for the exam, use this book as a test of your knowledge. After you have taken the practice tests and feel confident in the material on which you were tested, you are ready to schedule your exam. Use this book for a final quick review just before taking the test to make sure that all the important concepts are set in your mind.

Hardware/Software Recommendations

MCSE TestPrep: Windows NT Workstation 4 is meant to help you review concepts with which you already have training and experience. In order to make the most of the review, you need to have as much background and experience as possible. The best way to do this is to combine studying with working on real networks using the products on which you will be tested. This section gives you a description of the minimum computer requirements you need to build a good practice environment.

The minimum computer requirements to study everything on which you are tested include one workstation running Windows NT Workstation 4, and one server running Windows NT Server—both of which must be connected by a network.

Windows NT Workstation requirements:

- Any computer on the Microsoft Hardware Compatibility List
- 486DX 33MHz or better (Pentium recommended)
- A minimum of 12MB of RAM (32MB recommended)
- 200MB (or larger) hard disk
- 3.5-inch 1.44MB floppy drive
- VGA (or Super VGA) video adapter
- VGA (or Super VGA) monitor
- Mouse or equivalent pointing device
- Two-speed (or faster) CD-ROM drive
- A Windows NT compatible Network Interface Card (NIC)
- Presence on an existing network, or use of a hub to create a test network

Windows NT Server requirement:

- Any computer on the Microsoft Hardware Compatibility List
- 486DX2 66MHz or better (Pentium recommended)
- 16MB of RAM (64MB recommended)
- 340MB (or larger) hard disk
- 3.5-inch 1.44MB floppy drive
- VGA (or Super VGA) video adapter
- VGA (or Super VGA) monitor
- Mouse or equivalent pointing device
- Two-speed (or faster) CD-ROM drive
- A Windows NT compatible Network Interface Card (NIC)
- Presence on an existing network, or use of a hub to create a test network
- Microsoft Windows NT Server

What the Implementing and Supporting Microsoft Windows NT Workstation 4 Exam (70–073) Covers

The *Implementing and Supporting Microsoft Windows NT Workstation 4* certification exam measures your ability to implement, administer, and troubleshoot information systems that incorporate Windows NT Workstation version 4. It focuses on determining your skill level in seven major areas:

- Planning
- Installation and Configuration
- Managing Resources
- Connectivity
- Running Applications
- Monitoring and Optimization
- Troubleshooting

The *Implementing and Supporting Microsoft Windows NT Workstation 4* certification exam uses these categories to measure your ability. Before taking this exam, you should be proficient in the job skills discussed in the following sections.

Planning

The Planning section is designed to ensure that you understand how to create an unattended installation of Windows NT Workstation 4, developing strategies for sharing and securing resources such as users' home directories and shared applications, as well as selecting the appropriate file system.

Objectives for Planning

- Create unattended installation files.
- Plan strategies for sharing and securing resources.
- Choose the appropriate file system to use in a given situation. File systems and situations include:

  NTFS
  FAT
  HPFS
  Security
  Dual-boot systems

Installation and Configuration

The Installation and Configuration section of the NT Workstation exam measures your knowledge on installation, basic setup, and configuration of Windows NT Workstation 4 on an Intel platform. You are tested on various items such as removing existing Workstation installations, configuring server based installations for enterprise environments, installing hardware components, and using the Control Panel to configure the machine.

Objectives for Installation and Configuration

- Install Windows NT Workstation on an Intel platform in a given situation.
- Set up a dual–boot system in a given installation.
- Remove Windows NT Workstation in a given situation.
- Install, configure, and remove hardware components for a given situation. Hardware components include:

  Network adapter drivers
  SCSI device drivers
  Tape device drivers
  UPS
  Multimedia devices
  Display drivers
  Keyboard drivers
  Mouse drivers

- Use Control Panel applications to configure a Windows NT Workstation computer in a given situation.
- Upgrade Windows NT Workstation in a given situation.
- Configure server-based installations for wide scale deployment in a given situation.

Managing Resources

The Managing Resources section measures your skills in areas such as creating and managing users and local group accounts; setting permissions on NTFS partitions, folders, and files; and installing and configuring printers.

Objectives for Managing Resources

- Create and manage local user accounts and local group accounts to meet given requirements.
- Set up and modify user profiles.
- Set up shared folders and permissions.
- Set permissions on NTFS partitions, folders, and files.
- Install and configure printers in a given environment.

Connectivity

The Connectivity section of the Windows NT Workstation 4 certification exam concentrates on configuring an NT Workstation computer to communicate with other computers and network operating systems.

Objectives for Connectivity

- Add and configure the network components of Windows NT Workstation.
- Use various methods to access network resources.
- Implement NT Workstation as a client in a NetWare environment.
- Use various configurations to install NT Workstation as a TCP/IP client.
- Configure and install Dial-Up Networking in a given situation.
- Configure Microsoft Peer Web Services in a given situation.

Running Applications

The Running Applications section of the Windows NT Workstation 4 certification exam measures your skills in configuring applications to run in the Windows NT Workstation environment.

Objectives for Running Applications

- Start applications on Intel and RISC platforms in various operating system environments.
- Start applications at various priorities.

Monitoring and Optimization

The Monitoring and Optimization section focuses on your abilities to use various NT Workstation tools to monitor system performance and utilization as well as modify the tunable parameters of Windows NT Workstation for optimal performance.

Objectives for Monitoring and Optimization

- Monitor system performance by using various tools.
- Identify and resolve given performance problems.
- Optimize system performance in various areas.

Troubleshooting

The Troubleshooting section of the Windows NT Workstation 4 certification exam measures your knowledge of troubleshooting problems with NT Workstation 4 such as, but not limited to, printing, installation, resource access, and the boot process.

Objectives for Troubleshooting

- Choose the appropriate course of action to take when the boot process fails.
- Choose the appropriate course of action to take when a print job fails.
- Choose the appropriate course of action to take when the installation process fails.
- Choose the appropriate course of action to take when an application fails.
- Choose the appropriate course of action to take when a user can not access a resource.
- Modify the registry using the appropriate tool in a given situation.
- Implement advanced techniques to resolve various problems.

CHAPTER 1

Planning

OBJECTIVES

Create unattended installation files.

Plan strategies for sharing and securing resources.

Choose the appropriate file system to use in a given situation. File systems and situations include:

- **NTFS**
- **FAT**
- **HPFS**
- **Security**
- **Dual-boot systems**

Planning is a key element in the implementation of any new operating system. Microsoft emphasizes this fact by devoting an entire section of the exam to testing your knowledge on planning for a Windows NT Workstation 4.0 implementation. A planning session answers questions such as what file system to use, how to set up security for users and applications, and whether or not Windows NT Workstation is the best operating system, given your requirements and objectives.

This chapter focuses on planning an installation of Windows NT Workstation. Microsoft expects you to master the following elements: planning the unattended installation of Windows NT Workstation 4.0, planning how to most effectively share and secure resources, and planning the appropriate file system to use on your Windows NT Workstation.

PRACTICE QUESTIONS

CREATING UNATTENDED INSTALLATION FILES

1. **Which Microsoft tools can assist you in automating the rollout of Windows NT Workstation to 35 newly purchased machines? Select all that apply.**

   A. SYSDIFF.EXE

   B. WINDIFF.EXE

   C. UNATTEND.SIF

   D. Uniqueness database file (UDB)

   E. Answer file (UNATTEND.TXT)

2. **This is a scenario question. First you must review the scenario, then review the required and optional results. Following that is a solution. You must pick the best evaluation of that solution.**

   Scenario:
   ABC has decided to roll out 100 copies of NT Workstation 4.0 and Microsoft Internet Explorer 4.0 to the users in the engineering department. The hardware platforms are identical.

   Required Result:
   Automate the text mode portion of the Windows NT Workstation installation.

   Optional Results:
   Automate the GUI portion of Windows NT Setup.

   Automate the installation of Office 97.

   Proposed Solution:
   ABC completed the following steps in order:

   1. Create a single answer file using the Setup Manager application on the Windows NT Resource Kit CD.
   2. Create a baseline system by installing Windows NT Workstation using the answer file created in step 1.
   3. Install Office 97 and run SYSDIFF.EXE to create a difference file.
   4. Install NT by using the answer file and apply the difference file immediately after NT is installed.

   The system administrator of ABC performed no other tasks.

   Evaluation of Proposed Solution:
   This implementation achieves the following objectives:

   A. Only the Required Result

   B. The Required Result and both Optional Results

   C. The Required Result and one Optional Result

   D. Both Optional Results

   E. Neither the Required Result nor the Optional Result

3. **Which switches enable you to run Windows NT Workstation 4.0 Setup with an unattended text file and a uniqueness database file (UDB file) during installation?**

   A. `/u, /UDF`

   B. `/u, /UDB`

   C. `/auto`

D. `/ox, /s`

E. `/o, /b`

4. **What are the three steps required for using SYSDIFF.EXE to install additional applications after installing the base operating system?**

   A. Create a snapshot file, create a difference file, and apply the difference file.

   B. Create a baseline file, create a modification file, and apply the modification file.

   C. Create a snapshot file, create an installation file, and apply the installation file.

   D. Create a baseline file, create a difference file, and apply the difference file.

5. **This is a scenario question. First you must review the scenario, then review the required and optional results. Following that is a solution. You must pick the best evaluation of that solution.**

Scenario:
ABC deploys Windows NT Workstation to 25 new machines, identically configured, in a Windows NT domain environment for the sales department.

Required Result:
Automate the NT Setup to minimize user intervention.

Optional Results:
Ensure a machine account is created in the ABC domain during the installation.

Automate the configuration of user-specific information for each workstation.

Proposed Solution:
ABC generated an answer file with a text editor. The answer file's [UserData] section appears as:

```
[UserData]
OrgName = "ABC"
ProductID = "123-4567890"
```

The [Network] section appears as:

```
[Network]
InstallServices = ServiceList
InstallAdapters = AdapterList
InstallProtocols = ProtocolList
```

The ServiceList, AdapterList, and ProtocolList appear elsewhere in the answer file with the correct values to achieve all results.

The UDB file appears as:

```
[UniqueIds]
User1 = UserData, Network
User2 = UserData, Network
...
User25 = UserData, Network

[User1-UserData]
FullName = "James Schmidt"
ComputerName = "ABCSALES1"
[User1-Network]
JoinDomain = "ABC"

[User2-UserData]
FullName = "Daryl Tritt"
ComputerName = "ABCSALES2"
[User1-Network]
JoinDomain = "ABC"

...

[User25-UserData]
FullName = "Alex Left"
ComputerName = "ABCSALES25"
[User1-Network]
JoinDomain = "ABC"
```

Evaluation of Proposed Solution:
This implementation achieves the following objectives:

A. The Required Result only

B. The Required Result and both Optional Results

C. The Required Result and one Optional Result

D. Only one Optional Result

E. Neither the Required Result nor any Optional Results

6. **Which of the following statements best describes the use of the uniqueness database file (UDB) during the unattended installation of Windows NT Workstation 4.0?**

A. Specify information for installing applications after Windows NT Workstation is installed.

B. Specify user- and machine-specific information to answer the prompts raised during the GUI phase of Setup.

C. Specify user- and machine-specific information to the Windows NT Setup program during the text mode portion of Setup.

D. Specify user- and machine-specific information for both the GUI phase and text mode phases of Windows NT Setup.

E. Specify common information for both the GUI and text mode phases of Windows NT Setup.

7. **This is a scenario question. First you must review the scenario, then review the required and optional results. Following that is a solution. You must pick the best evaluation of that solution.**

Scenario:
ABC deploys a Windows NT Workstation upgrade to 25 users in a Windows NT domain environment. Ten of the workstations have Windows 3.1 installed, and 15 have Windows NT Workstation 3.1 installed.

Required Result:
Automate the NT Setup to minimize user intervention.

Optional Results:
Retain the settings and current configuration on the Windows NT Workstation 3.1 machines.

Retain the settings and current configuration on the Windows 3.1 machines. Ensure the machines have domain accounts created during the installation and join the domain "ABC."

Proposed Solution:
Create a single answer file and a uniqueness database file. The answer file is created with the Setup Manager application included with the NT Workstation Resource Kit. The answer file contains all the correct entries to install the Windows NT Workstation with the configuration required by ABC. Ensure the NtUpgrade and Win31Upgrade keys in the [Unattended] section in the answer file are not present. Create a UDB file with only the following entries:

```
[UniqueIds]
WINNT = Unattended
WIN31 = Unattended, Network

[WINNT-Unattended]
NtUpgrade = Yes

[WIN31-Unattended]
Win31Upgrade = Yes

[WIN31-Network]
JoinDomain = "ABC"
CreateComputerAccount = boba,
➥password
```

Launch the NT installation with the `/u` and `/udf` switches to specify the location of the answer file, the unique ID to use for that particular installation, and the location of the uniqueness database file.

Evaluation of Proposed Solution:
Which of the following results does this solution achieve?

A. The Required Result only

B. The Required Result and both Optional Results

C. The Required Result and one Optional Result

D. Only one Optional Result

E. Neither the Required Result nor the Optional Results

8. You need to automate the installation of NT Workstation 4 and Microsoft Office 97 on 15 desktop computers and 18 identically configured laptop computers. The desktop machines have two hardware configurations. The laptop computers are identically configured. What are the minimum installation files you will need?

A. Three answer files and three UDB files

B. One answer file and 33 UDB files

C. One answer file and 1 UDF file

D. Three answer files and one UDB file

E. Thirty-three answer files and one UDB file

9. Select the statement that best describes the function of the Windows NT 4.0 Application Pre-Installation Tool (SYSDIFF.EXE) during an automated installation of Windows NT Workstation?

A. Specify which difference file should be applied to install applications after Windows NT Workstation is installed.

B. Create a snapshot and difference file for installing applications after Windows NT 4.0 or Windows 95 is installed. The difference file contains the Registry setting changes from the baseline NT system. After the difference file is created, it must be run on the specific workstation to install the desired applications.

C. Specify user- and machine-specific information to the Windows NT Setup program during the text mode portion of Setup.

D. Create a snapshot and difference file for installing applications after Windows NT 4.0 is installed. The difference file contains the Registry setting changes from the baseline NT system, and after the difference file is created, it must be run on the specific Workstation to install the desired applications.

E. Create a snapshot and difference file for installing applications after Windows NT 4.0 is installed. The difference file contains the Registry setting changes and directory changes from the baseline NT system. After the difference file is created, it must be run on the specific Workstation to install the desired applications.

10. Select the statements best describing the function of an answer file during an automated installation of Windows NT Workstation.

A. Specify information for installing applications after Windows NT Workstation is installed.

B. Specify common platform-type information to answer the prompts raised during the GUI phase of Setup.

C. Specify common platform-type information to the Windows NT Setup program during the text mode portion of Setup.

D. Specify user- and machine-specific information for the text mode phase of Windows NT Setup.

E. Specify user- and machine-specific information for the GUI phase of Windows NT Setup.

ANSWER KEY

1. D-E
2. A
3. A
4. A
5. D
6. B
7. E
8. D
9. E
10. B-C

ANSWERS & EXPLANATIONS

CREATING UNATTENDED INSTALLATION FILES

1. Which Microsoft tools can assist you in automating the rollout of Windows NT Workstation to 35 newly purchased machines? Select all that apply.

D. Uniqueness database file (UDB)

E. Answer file (UNATTEND.TXT)

1. CORRECT ANSWER: D-E

The answer file is a text file that enables you to automate both the text and GUI modes of Windows NT setup. During the installation of Windows NT, the setup program extracts the information from the answer file to supply information required during the text and GUI phases of Setup. This information can range from the type of SCSI driver to load to the User Name and Product ID (CD-KEY). The answer file is not dynamic. One answer file will be required for each specific hardware platform type. Additionally, unique user information cannot be supplied. If you are installing ten copies of Workstation, there is no method to supply ten unique machine names with a single answer file, you would need ten answer files.

The uniqueness database file, or UDB file, enables the administrator to insert dynamic information into a single answer file. A UDB file can never be used alone; it must be used with an answer file. The UDB overcomes the problem of specifying unique user information such as a username and a machine name. Many of the parameters specified in the answer file for the text mode portion of Setup, such as SCSI and video drivers, cannot be contained in a UDB file and require the use of multiple answer files.

Although SYSDIFF.EXE is often associated with the automated installation of NT Workstation, it is not used to assist in the installation of Windows NT Workstation. SYSDIFF.EXE is an application that enables the administrator to perform additional configuration, such as installing an application, after NT Workstation is installed.

For more information on using answer and UDB files, see the "Further Review" section.

2. Proposed Solution:

ABC completed the following steps in order:

1. **Create a single answer file using the Setup Manager application on the Windows NT Resource Kit CD.**
2. **Create a baseline system by installing Windows NT Workstation using the answer file created in step 1.**
3. **Install Office 97 and run SYSDIFF.EXE to create a difference file.**
4. **Install NT using the answer file, and apply the difference file immediately after NT is installed.**

The system administrator of ABC performed no other tasks.

A. Only the Required Result

2. CORRECT ANSWER: A

Because the hardware platforms are identical, by creating a single answer file, the text mode portion of Windows NT Setup will be completely automated, accomplishing the Required Result.

To use SYSDIFF to install the Office 97 application, SYSDIFF must be run twice. First, SYSDIFF must be run on a freshly installed Windows NT installation to create a snapshot file. Then SYSDIFF must be run after Office 97 is installed to create the difference file. If the snapshot file is not created first, SYSDIFF cannot be used to automate the installation of Office 97.

Automating the GUI portion of Setup requires a mechanism to specify user- and machine-specific information, such as User Name and Machine Name, on all 20 machines. This could be accomplished using 20 different answer files, or one answer file with a UDB file. Because neither was specified, the GUI portion of Windows NT Setup can not be automated on the 20 machines.

3. Which switches enable you to run Windows NT Workstation 4.0 Setup with an unattended text file and a uniqueness database file (UDB file) during the installation?

A. `/u`, `/UDF`

3. CORRECT ANSWER: A

Windows NT Setup uses the `/u` switch to specify the name and location of the answer file. The syntax for this switch is

```
/u:FILE
```

where the following is true:

`FILE` is the filename, with an optional drive letter and path designation.

The `/udf` switch specifies the location and name of the UDB file, as well as which Unique ID within the UDB file should be used. Although the file is termed a UDB file, the actual switch to use the file is `/udf`. The syntax for this switch is

```
/udf:ID[,filename]
```

where the following is true:

`ID` is the unique id to be used from the UDB file. The ID must be listed in the [UniqueIds] section of the UDB file.

filename is the filename of the UDB file to be used. An optional path and drive letter can also be specified.

4. What are the three steps required for using SYSDIFF.EXE to install additional applications after installing the base operating system?

A. Create a snapshot file, create a difference file, and apply the difference file.

4. CORRECT ANSWER: A

Using SYSDIFF to automate the installation of applications requires three steps:

- **Create a snapshot file:** This file is created on a base workstation with only Windows NT installed. For best results, the answer file or the method that will be used to build all the workstations should be used.
- **Create a difference file:** The difference file is created by running SYSDIFF on the same machine used to generate the Snapshot File after the desired applications are installed.
- **Apply the difference file:** After the difference file is generated, the file must be applied to each workstation after completing the automated Windows NT installation.

See the "Further Review" section for additional information on the valid command line switches used with SYSDIFF.EXE.

5. Proposed Solution:
ABC generated an answer file with a text editor. The answer file section for the [UserData] section appears as:

```
[UserData]
OrgName = "ABC"
ProductID = "123-4567890"
```

The [Network] section appears as

```
[Network]
InstallServices = ServiceList
InstallAdapters = AdapterList
InstallProtocols = ProtocolList
```

The ServiceList, AdapterList, and ProtocolList appear elsewhere in the answer file with the correct values to achieve all results.

5. CORRECT ANSWER: D

By creating the answer file and accompanying UDB file, the user-specific information will be automated during the configuration. The UDB must contain the section [UniqueIds]. As the question illustrates, the UDB file created by ABC contains the Unique Ids named User1 through User25. The values for the [UniqueIds] USER1 key specify which sections should be included in the answer file for that ID. In the above example, the UDB file should contain the UserData and Network sections for each ID. These sections are titled [<UniqueID>-UserData] and [<UniqueID>-Network], where <UniqueID> is the corresponding value in the [UniqueIds] section. When the setup application is launched, the administrator can specify the IDs on the command line with the `/udf` switch as follows:

5. The UDB file appears as:

```
[UniqueIds]
User1 = UserData, Network
User2 = UserData, Network
...
User25 = UserData, Network

[User1-UserData]
FullName = "James Schmidt"
ComputerName = "ABCSALES1"
[User1-Network]
JoinDomain = "ABC"

[User2-UserData]
FullName = "Daryl Tritt"
ComputerName = "ABCSALES2"
[User1-Network]
JoinDomain = "ABC"

...

[User25-UserData]
FullName = "Alex Left"
ComputerName = "ABCSALES25"
[User1-Network]
JoinDomain = "ABC"
```

D. Only one Optional Result

```
/udf:ID, filename
```

where the following is true:

ID is the unique id to be used from the UDB file. The ID must be listed in the [UniqueIds] section of the UDB file.

filename is the filename of the UDB file to be used. An optional path and drive letter can also be specified.

When the corresponding ID on the command line is specified, Setup automatically appends the sections specified for that ID in the answer file. For the USER1 ID, the answer file would look as follows:

```
[UserData]
OrgName = "ABC"
ProductID = "123-4567890"
FullName = "James Schmidt"

ComputerName = "ABCSALES1"

[Network]
InstallServices = ServiceList
InstallAdapters = AdapterList
InstallProtocols = ProtocolList
JoinDomain = "ABC"
```

Therefore, because the machines will not join the domain without user intervention, the Required Result will not be accomplished.

Although there is an entry in each [Network] section specifying the domain to join in the UDB file, the key that specifies an account should be created is not included. Because Windows NT Workstation requires a machine account in the domain prior to joining the domain, the first Optional Result will not be accomplished. This could be accomplished by specifying the following key/value pair in the [Network] section of the answer file or UDB file:

```
CreateComputerAccount = <userid>,<pwd>
```

where the following is true:

userid is any user account with the right to create machine accounts within the domain.

pwd is the password for the user account.

This key could be included either in the answer file, if all accounts should be created with the same User ID and password, or in the UDB file [Network] section if different accounts are to be used to create the machine account.

The second Optional Result will be achieved because all user-specific information is included in either the answer file or the UDB file. This example also illustrates how information common to every machine in a specific section, in this case the [UserData] section, can be included in the answer file, and how unique information can be included for the same section in the UDB file. In other words, Setup will combine information in the same section from the answer file and the UDB file during installation.

6. Which of the following statements best describes the use of the uniqueness database file (UDB) during the unattended installation of Windows NT Workstation 4.0?

B. Specify user- and machine-specific information to answer the prompts raised during the GUI phase of Setup.

6. CORRECT ANSWER: B

The UDB file is used to supply the Windows NT setup program with user- and machine-specific information during the GUI phase of Setup. The specific information required by Setup during the text mode phase of Setup cannot be specified in a UDB file, only in an answer file. If Setup requirements dictates that different information for specific platforms is required during the text mode phase of Setup, you will have to create and apply multiple answer files.

7. Proposed Solution:

Create a single answer file and a uniqueness database file. The answer file is created with the Setup Manager application included with the NT Workstation Resource Kit. The answer file contains all the correct entries to install the Windows NT Workstation with the configuration required by ABC. Ensure the NtUpgrade and Win31Upgrade keys in the [Unattended] section in the answer file are not present. Create a UDB file with

7. CORRECT ANSWER: E

Neither upgrade will retain the original settings. To maintain the existing configuration, the Win31Upgrade key must be specified with a value of Yes for the Windows 3.1 machines, and the key NtUpgrade must be specified with a value of Yes for the Windows NT 3.1 machines. Although it appears that in the example this is the case, both keys are extracted from the answer file during the text mode portion of Setup. Because the UDB can only be used to specify answers to Setup during the GUI phase of Setup, neither key specified in the UDB will be included in the answer file. To perform an upgrade on both platform types, two answer files would need to be specified. Therefore, the neither Optional Result is achieved.

only the following entries:

7.
```
[UniqueIds]
WINNT = Unattended
WIN31 = Unattended

[WINNT-Unattended]
NtUpgrade = Yes
[WIN31-Network]
JoinDomain = "ABC"
CreateComputerAccount = boba,
➥password
```

Launch the NT installation with the `/u` and `/udf` switches to specify the location of the answer file, the unique ID to use for that particular installation, and the location of the uniqueness database file.

E. Neither the Required Result nor the Optional Results

Additionally, because each Workstation entering the domain requires a unique machine name, only the first Windows 3.1 machine completing the installation will be brought into the domain. A [UserData] section would need to be included for every Windows 3.1 computer being upgraded specifying a key/value pair for a unique machine name. Notice, however, the key/value pairs in the [WIN31-Network] section are correct to create a machine account in the domain using the User Account "boba" with a password of "password." Because the Windows NT Workstation 3.1 machine already has an account in the domain, it is not necessary to create another account during an upgrade.

Because Setup is not able to bring the machines into the domain, the setup is not completely automated. The Required Result is not achieved.

8. **You need to automate the installation of NT Workstation 4 and Microsoft Office 97 on fifteen desktop computers and eighteen identically configured laptop computers. The desktop machines have two hardware configurations. The laptop computers are identically configured. What are the minimum installation files you will need?**

D. Three answer files and one UDB file

8. CORRECT ANSWER: D

Each hardware platform requires a separate answer file to provide Setup with the specific information required during the text mode phase of Setup. One UDB file can be used to specify all user- and machine-specific information, such as username and machine name, during the GUI portion of Setup for all hardware platforms.

9. **Select the statement that best describes the function of the Windows NT 4.0 Application Pre-Installation Tool (SYSDIFF.EXE) during an automated installation of Windows NT Workstation.**

E. Create a snapshot and difference file for installing applications after Windows NT 4.0 is installed. The difference file contains the Registry setting changes and directory changes from the baseline NT system. After the difference file is created, it must be run on the specific Workstation to install the desired applications.

9. CORRECT ANSWER: E

SYSDIFF.EXE is used to create a snapshot and difference file to install applications after Windows NT is installed. SYSDIFF.EXE can only be used on Windows NT Workstation (or Server) 4.0. It will not work on earlier versions of Windows NT or Windows 95/98. The difference file created by SYSDIFF contains the Registry and directory changes between a baseline system created with the desired answer and UDB files and the same system with the applications installed.

10. Select the statements best describing the function of an answer file during an automated installation of Windows NT Workstation.

B. Specify common platform-type information to answer the prompts raised during the GUI phase of Setup.

C. Specify common platform-type information to the Windows NT Setup program during the text mode portion of Setup.

10. CORRECT ANSWER: B-C

The answer file is used to supply the setup program with common answers for both the text mode phase and the GUI phase of Windows NT Setup. If unique information is required for any of the key/value pairs used during the text mode portion of Setup, such as SCSI drivers or different HALs, multiple answer files must be created. If user- or machine-specific information needs to be created during the GUI mode of Setup, a UDB file or multiple answer files must be utilized.

FURTHER REVIEW

CREATING UNATTENDED INSTALLATION FILES

The Windows NT Workstation Setup application normally prompts the user for information about the current installation. Examples of some of the parameters the user must supply are:

- File system type (NTFS or FAT)
- Computer name
- Network options, such as protocols to install or domain membership
- Video hardware and resolution
- Time zone information

Instead of accepting manual input, the Windows NT Setup application can retrieve the information for these parameters through various text files that are created prior to beginning the setup. When Setup is launched, command-line switches specify the locations of these files. These files can automate portions of or the entire setup process, eliminating the need for a user to be present at each machine during setup.

After setup is complete, Microsoft has also provided a tool to automate the installation and configuration of any additional applications, such as productivity suites.

The two key tools for automating the installation are answer files and uniqueness database files (UDB files). The tool for installing additional applications is SYSDIFF.EXE.

Understanding Answer Files

Answer files eliminate the need for an administrator to sit at a particular computer and manually reply to the prompts of the Setup program. Windows NT Setup uses an answer file (sometimes called an unattended answer file) to provide specific information about setup options. An answer file is a plain ASCII text file. The name and path to the answer file is specified with the `/u` switch when starting Windows NT Setup. You can use the same unattended answer file across a number of installations. If you use an unattended answer file only, however, it is difficult to completely automate the setup process because of the unique information required to install Windows NT Workstation, such as machine name, domain memberships, and applicable network information, such as IP address or DNS hostname.

To circumvent this problem, one option is to create an answer file for each computer and specify the unique name and path when starting setup on each machine. This drastically increases the management effort required during the installation and can lead to errors during the installation.

Another option is to selectively automate portions of the setup. For those parameters that require unique responses, you can force the installation program to pause for user input. However, this approach reduces much of the benefit of automating the setup process.

The best solution to the problem of providing unique information in the unattended answer file during the installation process is to create what is called a uniqueness database file or UDB file. A UDB file is a text file that enables you to supply the information that must be unique for each computer or each user. Uniqueness database files are used with an unattended answer file to provide a complete installation of Windows NT Workstation without any user intervention during the setup process. The uniqueness database file provides the capability to specify per-computer parameters for a truly unique automated installation.

Uniqueness Database Files (UDB Files)

A UDB file is used to merge or replace sections of the answer file during the GUI portion of the Windows NT Setup process. For the installation of Windows NT Workstation 4, you can use one unattended answer file for the information that applies to all installations and one or more UDB files to specify the settings intended for a single computer or for a group of computers. It is possible to have one UDB file that contains settings for multiple computers or users within it. The name and path to the UDB file is specified with the `/UDF` switch when starting Windows NT Setup.

Windows NT Application Pre-Installation Tool (SYSDIFF.EXE)

In addition to installing Windows NT Workstation, you might need to install other applications. If those applications do not support a scripted installation, you can use the SYSDIFF.EXE utility to install the additional applications on the destination computers. SYSDIFF.EXE requires three steps:

- Create a snapshot file
- Create a difference file
- Apply the difference file

SYSDIFF.EXE is also alternatively used to:

- Create an INF file
- Dump the contents of a difference file

After creating the difference file, you can use SYSDIFF.EXE to apply the difference file, which contains the Registry edits and directory modification between a baseline system and the same machine with the desired applications installed, after completing the automated installation of Windows NT. SYSDIFF.EXE is not limited to only installing applications immediately after the installation of Windows NT 4.0. SYSDIFF.EXE can be used to create applications packages to be installed on existing Windows NT 4.0 installations.

Creating Answer Files

The answer file is a simple text file that can be created or edited with any text editor such as Notepad.exe. A sample answer file, named unattend.txt, is included with the Windows NT Workstation CD. You can use it as a template for creating or customizing your specific unattended installation file. You can also use the Windows NT Setup Manager, a graphical application included with the Windows NT Workstation Resource Kit CD, to create an unattended answer file.

The format of an answer file is very similar to the INI files used by Windows 3.1. The answer file consists of headings, enclosed with braces, such as

```
[Unattended]
```

Within each section are key/value pairs, such as

```
NtUpgrade = Yes
```

Table 1.1 lists some of the common headings and their uses. The NT Workstation Resource Kit and

Microsoft's Technical Information Network contain a wealth of information on using answer files as well as the sections and key/value pairs that can be used to automate an NT installation.

TABLE 1.1 COMMON SECTION HEADINGS IN AN ANSWER FILE AND THEIR USES

Answer File Section Heading	*Typical Use*
[Unattended]	This section is used during text mode Setup and can be modified only in the answer file; there is no valid entry in the UDF. This section specifies parameters such as the installation type (upgrade/fresh), installation path, and file system type (NTFS/FAT).
[DisplayDrivers]	This section contains a list of display drivers to be loaded by the text mode Setup process.
[GuiUnattended]	This section is used to specify settings for the GUI portion of Setup. It can be used to indicate the time zone and to hide the administrator password page.
[Network]	This section is used to specify network settings, such as network adapters, services, and protocols. If this section is missing, networking won't be installed. This is the section used to specify the domain or workgroup to join, as well as to create a computer account in the domain.
[UserData]	This section is used to provide user-specific data such as username, organization name, computer name, and product ID.

Creating UDB Files

The UDB is also a simple text file that can be created and edited with any text editor. Like the answer file, it consists of sections containing keys and values. The first section must always be the [UniqueIds] heading. This section contains a list if the unique IDs contained within the UDB file, as well as which sections should be merged into the answer file during setup. The [UniqueIds] section of a UDB file containing three unique IDs, SALES1, SALES2, and SALES3 would look like this:

```
 [UniqueIds]
SALES1 = UserData, Network
SALES2 = UserData, Network
SALES3 = UserData
```

In this example, the UDB should contain [UserData] and [Network] specific sections for the SALES1 and SALES2 unique IDs and only a [UserData] section for the SALES3 ID.

The number and name of the remaining section headings in the UDB file are determined by the content of the [UniqueIds] section. For each key/value pair specified in the [UniqueIds] section, there must be a corresponding section heading titled [<UniqueId>-Section]. Continuing with the preceding example, the Network Section for the SALES1 ID would look like this:

```
[SALES1-Network]
key = value
key = value
...
key = value
```

where the following is true:

`key` is any key allowed in the answer file for the specific section.

`value` is any valid value for the given key.

It is important to note that the UDB file's contents are not used to replace values in the answer file, but rather the contents are merged to create the unique answer file for the installation.

The UniqueID value you want to use to create the unique answer file must be specified with the `/UDF` switch as follows:

```
/UDF:ID,[filename]
```

where the following is true:

`ID` is the unique ID value to use within the UDB file.

`filename` is the path and name of the UDB file to use.

Using SYSDIFF.EXE

The first step in using SYSDIFF.EXE is to complete an installation of Windows NT Workstation on a sample system. This computer's hardware configuration should be identical to the systems on which you intend to install Windows NT Workstation. Also, the installation method on this machine should be identical to the method you will use during the rollout. After the operating system is installed, use sysdiff to take a snapshot of that reference machine by using the this command:

```
Sysdiff /snap [/log:log file] snapshot file
```

where the following is true:

`log file` is the name of an optional log file that can be created by sysdiff.

`snapshot file` is the name of the file that will contain the snapshot of the system.

This process creates the snapshot file, which is referred to as the original configuration. The original configuration is the baseline system to compare with the changed system. In addition to being an identical hardware platform, the Windows NT root directory (d:\winnt, for example) must be the same on the reference machine and the target machines that will have the difference file applied.

After the snapshot has been taken, install all desired applications on the baseline machine. After the applications have been installed, apply the second step of sysdiff, which is to create the difference file. The difference file is created by using this command:

```
Sysdiff /diff [/c:title] [/log:log file]
snapshot file difference file
```

where the following is true:

`/c:title` is the title for the difference file.

`log file` is the name of an optional log file that can be created by sysdiff.

`snapshot file` is the name of the file that contains the snapshot of the system. This file must be created from the same snapshot file created with the `/snap` command. If you use a file created on another system, sysdiff will not run.

`difference file` is the name of the file that contains the changes made when the snapshot was created, as well as the current configuration of the system.

This mode uses the snapshot file (the original configuration) created in the first step to determine the changes in the directory structure and the Registry entries created by the application installations.

The final step in the sysdiff process is to apply the difference file to a new installation as part of the unattended setup. This is done with the following command:

```
Sysdiff /apply /m [/log:log file]
➥difference file
```

where the following is true:

`/m` applies the changes made to the menu structure map to the Default User profile structure, rather than to the currently logged on user. Otherwise, these menu changes would be made only to one user account, not globally to the system, and that one user account might not even exist on the destination workstation.

`log file` is the name of an optional log file SYSDIFF.EXE uses to write information regarding the process. This is good to use for troubleshooting if SYSDIFF.EXE fails during the application process.

`difference file` is the file created by the `/diff` command. The Windows NT root must be the same (d:\winnt, for example) as the system that created the difference file. This means that all the unattended installs you perform using this difference file must have this system root in the same location.

You do not have to run this command as part of the unattended installation. You can run it at any time after Windows NT Workstation is installed. To fully automate the installation of Windows NT and your applications, you might want to have this command run as part of the install.

Because this difference file contains all the files and Registry settings for the applications you installed, it can be quite large (depending on how many applications you install). Applying such a potentially large package as part of the installation can add a significant amount of time to your setup process. One way to alleviate this problem is to create an INF file from this difference file.

An INF file created from the difference file contains only the Registry and the initialization file directives. It is, therefore, significantly smaller than the difference file itself. The command to initiate the INF portion of the installation is as follows:

```
Sysdiff /inf /m [/u] sysdiff_file oem_root
```

where the following is true:

`/m` applies the changes made to the menu structure map to the Default User profile structure rather than to the currently logged on user. Otherwise, these menu changes would be made only to one user account, not globally to the system, and that one user account might not even exist on the destination workstation.

`/u` indicates that the INF is generated as a Unicode text file. The default is to generate the file by using the system ANSI codepage.

`Sysdiff_file` is the path to the file created by the /diff process.

`Oem_root` is the path of a directory. This is where the OEM structure required for the INF is created and where the INF is placed.

This command creates the INF file, as well as a OEM directory structure that contains all the files from the difference file package. You should create this directory under the I386 directory (if installing x86 machines) on the distribution server. If the directory is not under the I386 directory, move it so that it is.

The initial phase of Windows NT installation is DOS-based and cannot copy directories with path names longer than 64 characters. Make certain that the directory length under the OEM directory does not exceed 64 characters.

To use an INF file after it has been created, you must add a line to the file Cmdlines.txt under the OEM directory. This line is used to invoke the INF that you created. The format of the command is as follows:

```
"RUNDLL32
➥syssetup,SetupInfObjectInstallAction
➥section 128 inf"
```

where the following is true:

section specifies the name of the section in the INF file.

inf specifies the name of the INF file. This needs to be specified as a relative path.

Using an INF file rather than the entire difference file package can save you time in your unattended installation.

You can use the `/dump` option to dump the difference file into a file that you can review. This command enables you to read the contents of the difference file. The syntax of this command is as follows:

```
Sysdiff /dump difference file dump file
```

where the following is true:

difference file specifies the name of the difference file that you want to review.

dump file specifies the name you want to give to the dump file.

After creating the dump file, you can view it with a text editor such as Notepad.

Table 1.2 summarizes the command line switches available with SYSDIFF.EXE and their functions.

TABLE 1.2 AVAILABLE COMMAND LINE SWITCHES FOR USE WITH SYSDIFF.EXE

Switch	*Function*
`/snap`	Instructs the difference tool to create a snapshot file of a base system that will be used as the basis for comparison in generating the difference file.
`/diff`	Creates the difference file containing the directory and Registry changes between a baseline system (the information contained within the snapshot file) and a system configured as required by the administrator.
`/apply`	Applies the contents of the difference file; for example, applies directory and Registry changes to a target workstation.
`/dump`	A debugging switch that generates a user-friendly version of the contents of a SYSDIFF-generated difference file.
`/inf`	Prepares a Windows NT distribution point for all applications that will be pre-installed. The output will be an .inf file listing the changes to be made, an OEM directory containing the required files to complete the changes, and a modified CMDLINES.TXT file to enable the changes to be applied.
`/log`	Creates a log file of SYSDIFF actions during the execution of SYSDIFF with the `/inf`, `/snap`, or `/diff` switches.

PRACTICE QUESTIONS

PLAN STRATEGIES FOR SHARING AND SECURING RESOURCES

1. **This is a scenario question. First you must review the scenario, then review the required and optional results. Following that is a solution. You must pick the best evaluation of that solution.**

   Scenario:
   You are an administrator of a LAN with 200 users. You have been asked to create home directories for every user. You want to achieve the following objectives:

   Required Result:
   Ensure that users can access their home directories from anywhere on the network.

   Optional Results:
   Minimize the administrative requirements in managing the new home directory structure.

   Ensure maximum security for the users' home directories.

   Proposed Solution:
   Create a folder named UserData on a FAT volume. Within this folder, create a home directory for each user and share this directory with Full Control permissions for only that user. No other permissions will be assigned to the directory.

   Evaluation of Proposed Solution:
   This solution accomplishes which of the following:

   A. The Required Result only

   B. The Required Result and both Optional Results

   C. The Required Result and one Optional Result

   D. Only both Results

   E. Neither the Required Result nor the Optional Results

2. **Select each advantage of using locally installed applications over shared network applications.**

   A. Less network traffic.

   B. Less space is required on the system hard disk.

   C. Better performance.

   D. Centralized control.

   E. Accessibility is not tied to server availability.

3. **This is a scenario question. First you must review the scenario, then review the required and optional results. Following that is a solution. You must pick the best evaluation of that solution. Note that question 6 also deals with the same scenario.**

   Scenario:
   You are an administrator of a LAN with 30 users. You have been asked to install Microsoft Office 97 for all LAN users.

Required Result:
Ensure that users can access the applications from anywhere on the network.

Optional Results:
Create data folders that are accessible to only certain groups of users.

Minimize the amount of management and maintenance required on the design structure.

Proposed Solution:
Create a folder named "sharedapps" on a server NTFS formatted volume with NTFS and share permissions of Everyone Full Control. Install the Microsoft Office 97 application in the "sharedapps" directory. Create a folder on the same server volume named userdata with NTFS and share permissions of Everyone Full Control. Within the "userdata" folder, create subfolders with the required department names. Each of these folders is shared with Full Control NTFS permissions for the respective groups.

Evaluation of Proposed Solution:
This solution accomplishes which of the following:

A. The Required Result only

B. The Required Result and both Optional Results

C. The Required Result and one Optional Result

D. Only both Optional Results

E. Neither the Required Result nor the Optional Results

4. Which statement best describes the benefits of using local (that is, on the user's machine) user home directories over centrally (that is, on the server) created home directories?

A. Local home directories enable the user to access his or her files from anywhere on the network, do not generate any excess network traffic, and do not occupy server disk resources.

B. Local home directories enable the user to access his or her files regardless of server availability and provide a better chance of data recovery in the event of a workstation disk failure.

C. Local home directories enable users to access their data from anywhere on the network, provide a better chance of data recovery in the event of a workstation disk crash, and do not utilize server disk resources.

D. Local home directories enable the user to access his or her files regardless of server availability, limit the amount of network traffic generated in accessing the data, and free server disk resources.

E. Local home directories limit the amount of network access and increase the possibility that the data will be recovered in the event of a workstation disk failure.

5. This is a scenario question. First you must review the scenario, then review the required and optional results. Following that is a solution. You must pick the best evaluation of that solution.

Scenario:
You are an administrator of a LAN with 30 users. You have been asked to create home directories for every user. You want to achieve the following objectives:

Required Result:
Ensure that users can access their home directories from anywhere on the network.

Optional Results:
Minimize the administrative requirements in managing the new home directory structure.

Ensure maximum security for the users' home directories.

Proposed Solution:
Create a folder named "UserData" on a server volume NTFS volume. Share this folder with the permissions Everyone Full Control. You create a folder for each user within the "UserData" folder with NTFS permissions set to Full Control only for that user.

Evaluation of Proposed Solution:
This solution accomplishes which of the following:

A. The Required Result only

B. The Required Result and both Optional Results

C. The Required Result and one Optional Result

D. Only both Optional Results

E. Neither the Required Result nor the Optional Results

6. **This applies to the same scenario as number 3.**

Scenario:
You are an administrator of a LAN with 30 users. You have been asked to install Microsoft Office 97 for all LAN users.

Required Result:
Ensure that users can access the applications from anywhere on the network.

Optional Results:
Create data folders that are accessible to only certain groups of users.

Minimize the amount of management and maintenance required on the design structure.

Proposed Solution:
Create a folder named "sharedapps" on a server FAT formatted volume with share permissions of Everyone Full Control. Install the Microsoft Office 97 application in the "sharedapps" directory. Create a folder on the same server volume named "userdata." Within the "userdata" folder create subfolders with the required department names. Each of these folders are shared with Full Control permissions for the respective groups.

Evaluation of Proposed Solution:
This solution accomplishes which of the following:

A. The Required Result only

B. The Required Result and both Optional Results

C. The Required Result and one Optional Result

D. Only both Optional Results

E. Neither the Required Result nor the Optional Results

7. **This is a scenario question. First you must review the scenario, then review the required and optional results. Following that is a solution. You must pick the best evaluation of that solution.**

Scenario:
You are an administrator of a LAN with 30 users. You have been asked to create home directories for every user.

Required Result:
Ensure that users can access their home directories from anywhere on the network.

Optional Results:
Minimize the administrative requirements in managing the new home directory structure.

Ensure user data is backed up on a regular basis.

Proposed Solution:
Create a folder named UserData on an NTFS volume. Create a folder for each user within the UserData folder with NTFS permissions set to Full Control only for that user. Set the share permissions for each individual user's folder to Full Access only for the specific user.

Evaluation of Proposed Solution:
This solution accomplishes which of the following:

A. The Required Result only

B. The Required Result and both Optional Results

C. The Required Result and one Optional Result

D. Only both Optional Results

E. Neither the Required Result nor the Optional Results

8. Select all the advantages of using shared network applications (that is, application executables stored in a central location on the server) over locally installed applications (that is, applications installed on the user's local machine).

A. Less network traffic.

B. Less space is required on the system hard disk.

C. Better performance.

D. Centralized control.

E. Accessibility is not tied to server availability.

9. Which statement best describes the benefits of using centrally (that is, on the server) created home directories over local (that is, on the user's machine) user home directories?

A. Server-located home directories enable the users to access their files from any location on the network, increase management of server disk resources through the use of NT disk quotas, and are more likely to be backed up on a regular basis.

B. Server-located home directories enable the user to access files from anywhere on the network and have a better response time than locally created directories.

C. Server-located home directories enable the user to access files from any location on the network and are more likely to be backed up on a regular basis.

D. Server-located home directories can regulate the amount of server disk resources used through Windows NT quotas, enable users to access data from anywhere on the network, and provide a better chance of data recovery in the event of a workstation disk failure.

E. Server-located home directories minimize the amount of network traffic generated through file access, provide access from anywhere within the network, and are more likely to be backed up on a regular basis.

10. **This is a scenario question. First you must review the scenario, then review the required and optional results. Following that is a solution. You must pick the best evaluation of that solution.**

Scenario:
You are an administrator of a LAN with 20 users. You have been asked to create home directories for every user.

Required Result:
Ensure each user can access their home directories from anywhere on the network.

Optional Results:
Minimize the administrative requirements in managing the new home directory structure.

Ensure maximum security for the users' home directories.

Proposed Solution:
Create each user's home directory on his or her workstation. Each workstation has only FAT volumes.

Evaluation of Proposed Solution:
This solution accomplishes which of the following:

A. The Required Result only

B. The Required Result and both Optional Results

C. The Required Result and one Optional Result

D. Only one Optional Result

E. Neither the Required Result nor the Optional Results

ANSWER KEY

1. C
2. A-C-E
3. B
4. D
5. B
6. C
7. C
8. B-D
9. C
10. E

ANSWERS & EXPLANATIONS

PLAN STRATEGIES FOR SHARING AND SECURING RESOURCES

1. **Proposed Solution:**
   Create a folder named "UserData" on a FAT volume. Within this folder, create a home directory for each user and share this directory with Full Control permissions for only that user. No other permissions will be assigned to the directory.

   C. The Required Result and one Optional Result

1. CORRECT ANSWER: C

By creating the users' home directory structure on the server, the users will be ensured access from anywhere on the network as long as they have connectivity to the server where the directories reside. The Required Result has been accomplished.

Because each directory is shared with Full Control permissions only for the appropriate user, users will only have access to their directories when accessing the server through a share. If a user is able to gain access to the server, he will be able to access other users' home directories. Because users are typically not allowed to access a server, either through physical security or account rights (see Chapter 3, "Managing Resources," for more information on account rights), it can be assumed the data will be secure. If the server partition were formatted with NTFS rather than FAT, this would not be an issue, even if a user were to access the server locally. The second Optional Result is achieved with the proposed solution.

Because a share will have to be created and maintained (with other than default permissions set) for 200 users, the administrative requirements are definitely not minimized. Therefore, the first Optional Result is not met.

However, with a FAT volume, no other method would ensure the second Optional Result is met. If the "UserData" folder were shared instead of each user's directory, every user would have full access to all folders beneath the share due to the fact the FAT can only support share level permissions. If NTFS were used instead of FAT, the "UserData" folder could be the share point. Each subfolder would need to have the NTFS permissions set for only the corresponding user.

2. Select all the advantages of using locally installed applications over shared network applications.

A. Less network traffic.

C. Better performance.

E. Accessibility is not tied to server availability.

2. CORRECT ANSWER: A-C-E

By installing applications locally, the users will not be required to use the network to access the applications, thereby reducing the amount of network traffic generated. Because hard disk access is typically quicker than network access, the user will see improved performance while executing the application. Lastly, the user will not be dependent upon server availability to use the application.

On the downside, upgrades to locally stored applications will require "touching" every copy of the application installed on the workstations. If the applications were server-based, any upgrades or maintenance would only need to be performed in one location.

3. Proposed Solution:
Create a folder named "sharedapps" on a server NTFS formatted volume with NTFS and share permissions of Everyone Full Control. Install the Microsoft Office 97 application in the "sharedapps" directory. Create a folder on the same server volume named "userdata" with NTFS and share permissions of Everyone Full Control. Within the "userdata" folder, create subfolders with the required department names. Each of these folders is shared with Full Control NTFS permissions for the respective groups.

B. The Required Result and both Optional Results

3. CORRECT ANSWER: B

By creating the group's home directory structure and application directory structure on the server, the users will be ensured access from anywhere on the network as long as they have connectivity to the server where the directories reside. The Required Result has been accomplished.

Because each group's private directory is assigned the Full Control NTFS permission for the respective groups, each group will have access to its folder when accessing the folder structure through the single parent directory share. Because the share is created on an NTFS partition, the data in the other group's directories will be secure even if other groups are able to gain local access to the server.

Because only one share needs to be created and maintained, the administrative requirements are minimized. As new users are added to the network, a directory will have to be created with the appropriate permissions set. Therefore, the first Optional Result is met.

4. Which statement best describes the benefits of using local (that is, on the user's machine) user home directories over centrally (that is, on the server) created home directories?

D. Local home directories enable the user to access their files regardless of server availability, limit the amount of network traffic generated in accessing the data, and free server disk resources.

4. CORRECT ANSWER: D

By locating users' home directories on the local workstation, users will not be tied to the availability of the network and the server as they would be if the directories were placed on a network file server. Users are only required to access their local hard disk to retrieve data. If the data resided on a network file server, additional network traffic would be generated when the data in the home directories was accessed. Additionally, Windows NT Workstation (and Server) 4 does not provide a means to limit the amount of content that can be placed in a folder. If the directories were placed on the server, excessive amounts of disk resources on the server would be required. By placing the home directory on the local workstation, the disk space requirement is distributed among all the workstations.

One drawback of placing users' home directories on the local workstation is that each user becomes responsible for backing up and restoring the data in the event of a disk or system crash. If the data was placed on the server, the folders could be included in the server backup that should be run on a regular basis.

5. Proposed Solution:
Create a folder named "UserData" on a server volume NTFS volume. Share this folder with the permissions Everyone Full Control. You create a folder for each user within the "UserData" folder with NTFS permissions set to Full Control only for that user.

B. The Required Result and both Optional Results

5. CORRECT ANSWER: B

Because the directory structure is created on the server, users will have access to their home directories from anywhere on the network as long as they can connect to the server. The Required Result is realized.

Because only one share needs to be created and maintained, administrative requirements will be minimized. The first Optional Result is accomplished.

With NTFS permissions assigned, each user will be able to access only her own home directory although the user will be able to see all the home directories. The second Optional Result is achieved.

6. **Proposed Solution:**
   Create a folder named "sharedapps" on a server FAT formatted volume with share permissions of Everyone Full Control. Install the Microsoft Office 97 application in the "sharedapps" directory. Create a folder on the same server volume named "userdata." Within the "userdata" folder create subfolders with the required department names. Each of these folders is shared with Full Control permissions for the respective groups.

   C. The Required Result and one Optional Result

6. CORRECT ANSWER: C

Because the application folder structure is placed on the server, users are able to access the applications from anywhere on the network, provided they have server connectivity.

Because each department's folder is individually shared with permissions that only allow access for a specific group, the data will be secure. The first Optional Result is achieved. However, if a user is allowed local access to the server, the user will be able to access the data in any folder. The only way to avoid this is to place the application data on an NTFS formatted volume and restrict access by using NTFS permissions. Because users are typically not given local access to a server, it can be assumed that the data will remain secure.

Creating the shares on a FAT formatted volume will require a share to be created and maintained for each department since FAT supports only share-level permissions. If an NTFS volume was used for the data, a single share point could have been created at the "UserData" folder, and NTFS permissions could have been applied to the individual department folders. Since creating and maintaining individual shares requires more administrative work than does creating a single share, the second Optional Result is not achieved.

7. **Proposed Solution:**
   Create a folder named "UserData" on an NTFS volume. Create a folder for each user within the "UserData" folder with NTFS permissions set to Full Control only for that user. Set the share permissions for each individual user's folder to Full Access only for the specific user.

   C. The Required Result and one Optional Result

7. CORRECT ANSWER: C

Because the home directory folder structure is placed on the server, users are able to access the applications from anywhere on the network provided they have server connectivity. The Required Result has been realized.

Placing users' home directories on the server will help to ensure the users' data will be backed up when the server itself is backed up. When home directories are placed on the user's workstation, it becomes the responsibility of the user to ensure that the data is backed up on regular intervals. The second Optional Result is achieved.

It would have been more effective to share the "UserData" folder and allow the NTFS permissions on each folder to restrict access. If the "UserData" folder were used as the share point instead, only one share would need be created and maintained, regardless of the number of users. Therefore, the first Optional Result was not accomplished.

8. Select all the advantages of using shared network applications (that is, application executables stored in a central location on the server) over locally installed applications (that is, applications installed on the user's local machine).

B. Less space is required on the system hard disk.

D. Centralized control.

8. CORRECT ANSWER: B-D

Installing applications on a centrally accessible location on the server will ease the space requirements on workstation disk resources. Typically, applications will only install a small stub on the workstation to allow the user to launch the application from a network location.

When it is necessary to perform maintenance or an upgrade on an application, it only requires one change to an application residing on a network share. If the applications were installed locally, it would require the "touching" of every machine to complete application maintenance or upgrade.

When accessing and using an application, the user will be required to communicate over the network. This leads to an increase of network bandwidth utilization compared to locally stored applications.

Because hard disk access times are typically lower than network access times, the user might see a slight decrease in the performance of applications that are accessed through the network.

Lastly, because the server must be accessed to use any applications stored on the server, the availability of the applications will be tied to network and server availability.

9. Which statement best describes the benefits of using centrally created (that is, on the server) home directories over local (that is, on the user's machine) user home directories?

C. Server located home directories enable the user to access files from any location on the network and are more likely to be backed up on a regular basis.

9. CORRECT ANSWER: C

By placing the users' home directories on the server, you ensure that the users will be able to access the directories from anywhere on the network, provided they can connect to the server. Although the same could be said about home directories placed on a workstation and shared appropriately, creating and maintaining the number of shares required is not feasible. It a networked domain environment, the administrator should strive to not create share resources on the workstations. Creating workstation shares is a security risk. Additionally, Workstation can support only ten inbound simultaneous connections for any resources, except RAS connections, in which case only two are supported.

Any network file server should be backed up at period intervals. By placing the directories on a file server, it is much more feasible to include the home directory structure created in the file backup process.

There are two important drawbacks to maintaining home directories on a server. The first is extra network traffic. Because the users must access the directories across the network, each access will generate additional network traffic, possibly reducing the amount of bandwidth available to other applications. The second drawback is the amount of disk space required. Users can store a large amount of data in the file structure, requiring the administrator to increase the amount of disk resources available to the server. Windows NT Workstation (or Server) does not currently provide a means to limit the amount of content that can be placed in a directory.

10. **Proposed Solution:**
    Create each user's home directory on his or her workstation. Each workstation has only FAT volumes.

    E. Neither the Required Result nor the Optional Results

10. CORRECT ANSWER: E

Placing the users' home directories on the local workstation will allow the directory to be accessed only when the user is at her workstation. If she is using another machine on the network, she will not be able to access her home directory. The Required Result was not achieved.

Because the data is placed on a FAT formatted volume, any user with local access to the workstation will have access to the user's home directory. The second Optional Result was not met.

Placing the users' home directories on the local hard disk creates an additional administrative burden because the administrator might now have to visit every workstation to create home directories. Additionally, the home directories will not be backed up unless the backup strategy involves backing up all workstations. The first Optional Result has not been met.

FURTHER REVIEW

PLAN STRATEGIES FOR SHARING AND SECURING RESOURCES

When planning a Windows NT Workstation installation, you must consider how resources will be made available to users while remaining secure. To effectively share and secure resources for Windows NT Workstation, you must understand the built-in groups and what rights those give the users within them, as well as how sharing one folder affects the other folders in the hierarchy below it.

Sharing Home Directories

One of the issues that you have to resolve in the planning process is whether to give your users their own home directories on the server or on their local workstations. A home directory is used as a location in which users can store their own data or files. Typically, the user is the only account that has access to the user's home directory. Table 1.3 compares the methods of storing a user's home directory on the server versus the local workstation.

Typically, when you create home directories on the server for users, it is best to centralize those directories under one directory (for example, "UserData"). If you have two accounts—named LStanton and HStanton—your directory structure would appear as shown in Table 1.4.

TABLE 1.3 Storing Users' Home Directories on the Server Versus the Local Computer

Server-Based Home Directories	*Local Home Directories*
Are centrally located so that users can access them from any location on the network.	Available only on the local machine. If the user is a *roaming user*, information is not accessible from other systems.
If a regular backup of the server is being done, information in users' home directories is also backed up.	Often users' local workstations are not backed up regularly as part of a scheduled backup process. If the user's machine fails, the user cannot recover the lost data.
Windows NT does not provide a way to limit the size of a user's directory. Thus, if a lot of information is being stored in home directories, it uses up server disk space.	If a user stores a lot of information in his home directory, the space is taken up on his local hard drive rather than the server.
If the server is down, the user won't have access to her files.	The user has access to his files regardless of whether the server is up because the files are stored locally.
Some network bandwidth is consumed due to the over-the-network access of data or files.	No network traffic is generated by a user accessing his or her files.

TABLE 1.4 TYPICAL NESTED USER HOME DIRECTORY STRUCTURE

Directory	*Permissions*
\UserData	Everyone Full Control
\UserData\Lstanton	Lstanton—Full Control
\UserData\Hstanton	Hstanton—Full Control

By establishing a share at the "UserData" level, all users are allowed access to directories on a FAT partition. FAT partitions do not enable you to establish file and folder permissions. Thus, if Heidi wants to access Luther's directory, using this setup, you cannot prevent her from doing so. If you use share permissions only, you must share each user's directory individually at the folder level. It is easy to see the benefits of creating and maintaining the users' home directories on an NTFS formatted volume. (For a more thorough discussion of NTFS, FAT, and share permissions, see Chapter 3, "Managing Resources.")

Sharing Application Folders

Another resource for which you might have to plan is giving your users access to shared network applications. Shared application folders are typically used to give users access to applications that they run from a network share point. Another option is to have users run applications locally from the individual user's computer. Table 1.5 shows a comparison.

TABLE 1.5 SHARED NETWORK APPLICATIONS VERSUS LOCALLY INSTALLED APPLICATIONS

Shared Network Applications Applications	*Locally Installed Applications*
Take up less disk space on the local workstation.	Use more local disk space.
Easier to upgrade/control. Use network bandwidth.	To upgrade, the administrator must "touch" every machine locally.
	Use no network bandwidth for running applications.
Slower response time because applications are accessed from the server.	Faster, more responsive.
If the server is down, users can't run applications.	Users can run applications regardless of server status.

If you choose to use shared network applications, you must plan your server directory structure so that these folders can be shared in the most efficient and secure method. If, for example, you use a shared copy of Word, Excel, and PowerPoint, your directory structure might look something like that shown in Table 1.6.

TABLE 1.6 DIRECTORY STRUCTURE PERMISSIONS FOR SHARED NETWORK APPLICATIONS

Directory	*Group*	*Permission*
\appshare	Administrators AppManager AppUsers	Full Control Change Read
\appshare\word	Inherited from appshare	Inherited from SharedApps
\appshare\pwrpoint	Inherited from appshare	Inherited from SharedApps
\appshare\excel	Inherited from appshare	Inherited from SharedApps

In this example, you want all the members of the "AppUsers" group to be able to access these folders for running applications, but you do not want them to be able to change the permissions or delete any files from within these directories. A group (members of the "AppManager" group) is in charge of updates to these applications. That group, therefore, needs permission to modify the application directories but not to modify the permissions on the directory structure.

Because you are sharing the top-level folder (appshare), you do not need to share the lower-level folders word, excel, and pwrpoint unless you want them to be individually available to users. By giving administrators full control, you give them the ability not only to add files, but also to change the permissions on the directory structure. By giving the "AppManager" group the change permission, you are allowing them to upgrade the applications in these directories, as needed.

Sharing Common Access Folders

In the event that folders must be shared for common access by group membership, the discussion on users' home directories can be extended for common access folders. In this case, the permissions on the individual folders requiring restricted access should be set as they are in the home directory example, except individual user permission is replaced with the appropriate group access. As with the home directories, it is best to create the folder structure on an NTFS formatted partition to eliminate the need for creating and maintaining excessive shares.

PRACTICE QUESTIONS

CHOOSE THE APPROPRIATE FILE SYSTEM TO USE IN A GIVEN SITUATION

1. **This is a scenario question. First you must review the scenario, then review the required and optional results. Following that is a solution. You must pick the best evaluation of that solution.**

   Scenario:
   You are configuring a new machine with a 1.5GB hard disk for Windows NT Workstation.

   Required Result:
   Maximize the available space on the new hard disk.

   Optional Results:
   Maximize read/write performance on the hard disk.

   Minimize the amount of disk space required for file system overhead.

   Proposed Solution:
   Create a single partition on the disk and format the partition with NTFS.

   Evaluation of Proposed Solution:
   This solution accomplishes which of the following:

   A. The Required Result only

   B. The Required Result and both Optional Results

   C. The Required Result and one Optional Result

   D. Only both Optional Results

   E. Neither the Required Result nor the Optional Results

2. **Select all the advantages of the FAT file system over NTFS.**

   A. FAT is better suited for larger partitions.

   B. FAT requires less space than NTFS on the disk for file system overhead.

   C. FAT is better suited for recovery in the event of a system crash.

   D. FAT supports native compression.

   E. FAT can be accessed by other Microsoft operating systems in a dual boot configuration.

3. **This is a scenario question. First you must review the scenario, then review the required and optional results. Following that is a solution. You must pick the best evaluation of that solution.**

   Scenario:
   You are configuring a new machine with a 2GB hard disk to dual-boot between Windows NT Workstation 4 and Windows 98.

   Required Result:
   Maximize the amount of accessible space on the disk when using either operating system.

Optional Results:
Maximize the amount of space available to each operating system.

Maximize the security for files when they are booted into Windows NT Workstation.

Proposed Solution:
Create two partitions on the disk of 1GB each. Format the first partition with FAT32 and install Windows 98. Format the second partition with NTFS and install Windows NT Workstation 4.

Evaluation of Proposed Solution:
This solution accomplishes which of the following:

A. The Required Result only

B. The Required Result and both Optional Results

C. The Required Result and one Optional Result

D. Only both Optional Results

E. Neither the Required Result nor the Optional Results

4. **Which of these methods enable file compression on a FAT partition from within NT Workstation 4?**

A. Windows NT 4 does not support file compression on FAT formatted volumes.

B. Run the COMPRESS utility from the command line.

C. Run the COMPACT utility from the command line.

D. From the Properties context menu for the file, click the Compression check box.

E. Select the file in Explorer and select Compress from the File menu.

5. **Which statement best describes the advantages of using the NTFS file system over the FAT file system with Windows NT?**

A. NTFS requires less overhead than FAT for the file system, supports compression down to the file level, and has significantly better recovery features.

B. NTFS supports long filenames up to 255 characters in length, performs better than FAT on partitions larger than 400MB, and supports file, folder, and volume compression.

C. NTFS is inefficient for larger volumes, supports transaction logging, and security at the file level.

D. NTFS supports transaction logging, security at the file level, and compression at the volume level.

E. NTFS supports transaction logging, file-level compression, and security at the file level.

6. **This is a scenario question. First you must review the scenario, then review the required and optional results. Following that is a solution. You must pick the best evaluation of that solution.**

Scenario:
You are preparing a Windows NT Workstation machine to run an application that produces a graphics file in excess of 1GB in size. Your machine has two hard disks installed, a 400MB disk and a 9GB disk.

Required Result:
Maximize the disk performance for the graphics applications.

Optional Results:
Maximize the security of the graphics data file.

Maximize available disk space on each partition.

Proposed Solution:
Create a partition on each disk. Format each disk with NTFS. Install the operating system on the 400MB partition.

Evaluation of Proposed Solution:
This solution accomplishes which of the following:

A. The Required Result only

B. The Required Result and both Optional Results

C. The Required Result and one Optional Result

D. Only both Optional Results

E. Neither the Required Result nor the Optional Results

7. **You have a computer with a single partition on the hard disk that needs to dual boot between Windows 98 and Windows NT Workstation 4. The file system needs to support both long filenames and file-level security. Select the best file system for this workstation.**

A. NTFS

B. FAT32

C. FAT

D. HPFS

E. There is no file system that will support the requirements

8. **Heidi has a computer with a 400MB hard disk. She only requires permission to be set at the share level. She is planning to install Windows NT Workstation 4. What is the best file system for Heidi to use?**

A. NTFS

B. FAT32

C. FAT

D. HPFS

E. There is no file system that will support this configuration

9. **Which of these methods enable file compression on an NTFS partition from within Windows NT Workstation 4?**

A. Windows NT Workstation 4 does not support file compression on NTFS formatted volumes.

B. Run the COMPRESS utility from the command line.

C. Run the COMPACT utility from the command line.

D. From the Properties context menu for the file, click the Compression check box.

E. Select the file in Explorer and select Compress from the File menu.

10. **Jamie is running a dual-boot system with Windows NT Workstation 4.0 and Windows 3.11. The system has a single hard disk with one 800MB partition. She is running out of disk space and wants to**

use Windows NT compression. How can she enable compression and still be able to access the files with both operating systems? Select all the correct answers.

A. Use the Windows 3.11 shrink.exe utility.

B. Use the MS-DOS DoubleSpace utility.

C. She cannot use compression.

D. From the Windows NT command prompt, run compress.exe.

E. Right-click on one of the files in Windows NT Explorer; from the resulting context menu, select Properties. Click the Compress check box.

ANSWER KEY

1. C
2. B-E
3. C
4. A
5. E
6. C
7. E
8. C
9. C-D
10. C

ANSWERS & EXPLANATIONS

CHOOSE THE APPROPRIATE FILE SYSTEM TO USE IN A GIVEN SITUATION

1. **Proposed Solution:**
   Create a single partition on the disk and format the partition with NTFS.

   C. The Required Result and one Optional Result

1. CORRECT ANSWER: C

By formatting a large volume with NTFS rather than FAT, you will maximize the available space on the hard disk. Because of FAT's required structure, cluster sizes will increase as the volume size increases. If you have a cluster size of 32K on a FAT volume, a 1K file will actually occupy 32K of disk space. On a volume with a 2K cluster size, the same file will occupy only 2K of disk space. Because NTFS cluster size does not increase with volume size in the same manner as FAT cluster sizes do, you will maximize the amount of available disk space. The Required Result has been achieved.

NTFS also provides better read/write performance on larger volumes (over 400MB in size) as compared to FAT. Therefore, the first Optional Result is achieved.

NTFS does require more disk space overhead for the file system than FAT does on any size volume. Therefore, the second Optional Result is not achieved.

2. **Select all the advantages of the FAT file system over NTFS.**

   B. FAT requires less space than NTFS on the disk for file system overhead.

   E. FAT can be accessed by other Microsoft operating systems in a dual boot configuration.

2. CORRECT ANSWER: B-E

FAT is best suited for partitions that are 400MB or less when compared to NTFS. As mentioned in the explanation of question 1, FAT does require less disk space to store the file system itself. FAT does support transaction logging as NTFS does. Transaction logging enables NTFS to roll back or re-do incomplete disk operations in the event of a system crash or power outage. FAT does support compression through separate compression applications supplied by Microsoft or other vendors. NTFS contains compression native to the file system. Lastly, NTFS can be utilized only by Windows NT systems. Other operating systems, such as MD-DOS, Windows 95, and Windows 98 support FAT formatted volumes.

3. Proposed Solution:
Create two partitions on the disk of 1GB each. Format the first partition with FAT32 and install Windows 98. Format the second partition with NTFS and install Windows NT Workstation 4.

C. The Required Result and one Optional Result

3. CORRECT ANSWER: C

As with NTFS, FAT32 under Windows 98 will yield more available disk space on larger volumes, as it does not suffer the cluster size problems that FAT does on larger volumes. Therefore, formatting the Windows 98 partition with FAT32 and the Windows NT partition with NTFS maximizes the amount of disk space available to each operating system, realizing the first Optional Result.

FAT and FAT32 both support security only at the share level; NTFS supports security at the file level. By formatting the Windows NT partition with NTFS, you will maximize the security of files when booted into Windows NT. The second Optional Result is achieved.

Windows NT only supports FAT and NTFS, not FAT32. Windows NT will not be able to access the FAT32 formatted partition. Windows 98 only supports FAT and FAT32. Windows 98 will not be able to access the NTFS partition. Therefore, the Required Result is not met.

4. Which of these methods enable file compression on a FAT partition from within NT Workstation 4?

A. Windows NT 4 does not support file compression on FAT formatted volumes.

4. CORRECT ANSWER: A

Windows NT only supports file compression on NTFS formatted volumes. Third party utilities that provide compression on FAT partitions under operating systems other than NT are not compatible with NT formatted FAT volumes.

5. Which statement best describes the advantages of using the NTFS file system over the FAT file system with Windows NT?

E. NTFS supports transaction logging, file-level compression, and security at the file level.

5. CORRECT ANSWER: E

The FAT file system under Windows NT does not support file-level security; it supports only share-level security. There is no way to enable compression on FAT formatted volumes under Windows NT.

NTFS will support compression at the file level, as well as file-level security. Additionally, NTFS supports transaction logging, which provides a higher level of recovery in the event the disk transaction is interrupted.

Both NTFS and FAT under Windows NT support long filenames up to 255 characters in length.

6. **Proposed Solution:**
   Create a partition on each disk. Format each disk with NTFS. Install the operating system on the 400MB partition.

   C. The Required Result and one Optional Result

6. CORRECT ANSWER: C

Because FAT is better suited for volumes under 400MB in size, formatting the 400MB partition with NTFS will not maximize the available space on the partition due to the increased size of disk space required for file system overhead. The second Optional Result is not achieved.

NTFS supports security at the file level; therefore, formatting the 9GB partition, where the graphics files will be stored, as NTFS will maximize the security of the files. The first Optional Result is achieved.

On larger volumes, NTFS will provide better disk performance than FAT. Formatting the 9GB partition with NTFS will yield the best performance. The Required Result is achieved.

7. **You have a computer with a single partition on the hard disk that needs to dual boot between Windows 98 and Windows NT Workstation 4. The file system needs to support both long filenames and file-level security. Select the best file system for this workstation.**

   E. There is no file system that will support the requirements

7. CORRECT ANSWER: E

When dual booting a system on a single partition, that partition must be formatted with a file system that is accessible to both operating systems. The only file system that is accessible by both Windows 98 and Windows NT is FAT. However, FAT does not provide file-level security. The only file system listed in the options that does provide file-level security is NTFS. Therefore, there is no file system that can accomplish the stated requirements.

8. **Heidi has a computer with a 400MB hard disk. She only requires permission to be set at the share level. She is planning to install Windows NT Workstation 4. What is the best file system for Heidi to use?**

   C. FAT

8. CORRECT ANSWER: C

Because the only security requirement is share-level permissions, either NTFS or FAT could be used. FAT is a better file system for smaller partitions (under 400MB) due to smaller space requirements for the file system overhead. FAT is the best choice for the file system in this situation.

9. Which of these methods enable file compression on an NTFS partition from within Windows NT Workstation 4?

C. Run the COMPACT utility from the command line.

D. From the Properties context menu for the file, click the Compression check box.

9. CORRECT ANSWER: C-D

Compression on NTFS volumes can be enabled on file folders or volumes by using the Properties menu in Explorer or the command line utility COMPACT.EXE.

10. Jamie is running a dual-boot system with Windows NT Workstation 4 and Windows 3.11. The system has a single hard disk with one 800MB partition. She is running out of disk space and wants to use Windows NT compression. How can she enable compression and still be able to access the files with both operating systems? Select all the correct answers.

C. She cannot use compression.

10. CORRECT ANSWER: C

FAT formatted volumes cannot be compressed with Windows NT compression. Alternatively, using an MS-DOS-based compression program will render those files unreadable by Windows NT.

FURTHER REVIEW

CHOOSE THE APPROPRIATE FILE SYSTEM TO USE IN A GIVEN SITUATION

Windows NT 4.0 supports the use of either or all of the following file systems: NTFS, CDFS, and FAT. An important decision in planning your Windows NT Workstation environment is which file system to use. Which file system you use depends on the needs of your particular environment. Some of the issues to consider when choosing a file system are the following:

- Performance
- Partition size
- Recoverability
- Dual-boot capabilities
- Security
- File compression

Support for the HPFS File System

Prior to NT Workstation 4.0, NT provided support for the HPFS file system. The High Performance File System, or HPFS, is a file system most typically used with IBM operating systems. HPFS support was limited in the fact the NT could access data stored on an HPFS partition but could not format new partitions with HPFS.

Windows NT Workstation 4 no longer supports HPFS in any capacity. Prior to upgrading any prior version of NT with an HPFS formatted partition, the partition must be converted to NTFS (using convert.exe from the Windows NT Workstation prompt) or reformatted as a FAT partition during the installation of Windows NT Workstation 4.0.

Using the NTFS File System

NTFS is one of the two file systems supported by Windows NT, both Workstation and Server. The other is FAT, discussed later in this section. NTFS support has been present in both operating systems since their release. NTFS tends to be the preferred file system for use under Windows NT if your environment can support it (you don't need to dual boot, for instance). Only Windows NT provides NTFS support.

Benefits of NTFS

Using NTFS has many benefits, including the following:

- *Support for long filenames.* NTFS supports filenames up to 255 characters long.
- *Preservation of case.* NTFS is not case-sensitive, but it does preserve case for POSIX compliance.
- *Recoverability.* NTFS is a recoverable file system. It uses transaction logging to automatically log all file and directory updates so that, in the case of a power outage or system failure, this information can be used to redo failed operations.
- *Security.* NTFS provides the user with local security for protecting files and directories.

- *Compression.* NTFS supports compression of files and directories to optimize storage space on your hard disk.
- *Size.* NTFS partitions can support much larger partition sizes than FAT. Theoretically, NTFS can support partitions up to 16 exabytes in size. (An exabyte is one billion gigabytes.)

Using NTFS gives you better security and enhanced functionality compared to the FAT file system.

Limitations of NTFS

The main limitations of NTFS are compatibility with other operating systems and overhead. If you need to dual boot or if you have a partition size smaller than 400MB, use FAT rather than NTFS.

Using the FAT File System

Windows NT Workstation and Server 4.0 supports the FAT file system, which is named after its method of organization—the File Allocation Table. The File Allocation Table resides at the top, or beginning, of the volume. Two copies of the FAT are kept in case one is damaged.

Benefits of FAT

The FAT file system is typically a good option for a small-sized partition. Because FAT is required for DOS, it is also a good option for a dual-boot system with Windows 95 or Windows 3.*x*. The FAT file system on Windows NT has a number of advantages over using FAT on a DOS-based system. Used under Windows NT, the FAT file system supports the following:

- Long filenames up to 255 characters
- Multiple spaces
- Multiple periods
- Filenames that are not case-sensitive, but that do preserve case

The FAT file system has a fairly low file-system overhead, which makes it good for smaller partitions.

Limitations of FAT

Although the FAT file system is necessary for dual-boot configurations, there are some significant limitations to using it with Windows NT, including the following:

- *Inefficient for larger partitions.* There are two reasons that FAT is inefficient on larger partitions (over about 400MB). One reason is that FAT uses a linked list for its directory structure. If a file grows in size, the file can become fragmented on the disk and will have slower access time for retrieving the file because of fragmentation. The other reason is the default cluster size used on a FAT partition. For partitions up to 255MB, FAT uses a 4KB cluster size. For partitions greater than 512MB, however, FAT uses 16KB cluster sizes and up to 256KB cluster sizes for drives above 8192MB on Windows NT 4. Therefore, if you use FAT under Windows NT and have a partition that is 800MB and you have many smaller files (under 32KB) on the drive, you waste a lot of space on the drive due to the cluster size.
- *Has no local security.* The FAT file system does not support local security, so there is no way to prevent a user from accessing a file if that user can log on locally to the workstation.

- *Does not support compression under Windows NT.* Although the FAT file system supports compression by using DriveSpace or DoubleSpace, neither of those are supported under Windows NT. For this reason, there is no way to use compression on FAT under Windows NT.

Choosing Dual-Boot Scenarios

If you want to dual boot between Windows NT 4.0 and any other non-Windows NT operating system, you must use the FAT file system for universal access across all installed operating systems. The NTFS file system is accessible only by Windows NT; if you are dual booting with Windows 95, the NTFS partition will not be visible under Windows 95.

If you have a machine that you dual boot between Windows NT Workstation 4.0 and Windows 95 or Windows 98, you can use an NTFS partition if you choose to, even though it is inaccessible from within Windows 95 or Windows 98. You must make sure in doing this, however, that you do not format your active partition (your c: drive) or the partition that has the windows directory on it. Otherwise, you can't boot into Windows 95 or Windows 98.

If you choose to dual boot between Windows 95 or Windows 98 and Windows NT Workstation 4.0, any applications that you have installed under one operating system must also be installed under the other operating system.

Both Windows 98 and Windows 95 OSR2 provide support for the FAT32 file system. Windows NT Workstation 4.0 does not provide support for the FAT32 file system. Just as Windows 95 and Windows 98 cannot access a partition formatted with NTFS, Windows NT Workstation cannot access a FAT32 formatted partition.

CHAPTER SUMMARY

Both in real world rollouts of Windows NT Workstation and on the Microsoft certification exam, planning is an important first step. During the planning session, you must address such issues as

- Creating unattended answer files

  By properly combining the use of an answer file and a uniqueness database file, you can completely automate and customize the Windows NT Workstation 4 installation for ten machines on the local LAN or hundreds of machines in the enterprise.

  By following the installation with the application of a difference file created with SYSDIFF.EXE, you can concurrently automate the installation of any additional applications required in your environment.

- Plan strategies for sharing and securing resources

  You must determine where and how you will create user home directories—either on a centralized server or on the local workstations. Your choice might affect the availability of the directories for use or the performance of the network.

  Additionally, if shared applications are going to be used, you must determine where and how the directory structure will be created. Selecting a FAT formatted partition might cause excess administrative work in the creation and management of the chosen directory structure.

- Chose the appropriate file system to use in a given situation.

  File system selection, either FAT or NTFS, will determine the security of your users' files. This decision must be weighed with both the advantages and disadvantages of FAT and NTFS. You must also consider if users will need to dual-boot between Windows NT

Workstation and another operating system. Finally, your choice of file system might determine how much additional administrative work will be required to create and maintain shares on the machines.

By mastering the art of planning, you will enhance your job skills and value as a network professional, and you will be prepared to master the first objective of the Microsoft certification exam.

CHAPTER 2

Installation and Configuration

Objectives

Install Windows NT Workstation on an Intel platform in a given situation.

Set up a dual-boot system in a given situation.

Remove Windows NT Workstation in a given situation.

Install, configure, and remove hardware components for a given situation. Hardware components include:

- **Network adapter drivers**
- **SCSI device drivers**
- **Tape device drivers**
- **UPSs**
- **Multimedia devices**
- **Display drivers**
- **Keyboard drivers**
- **Mouse drivers**

continues

Installation is another key component in your mastery of Windows NT Workstation. After the planning is complete, but before you can manage and optimize a Windows NT Workstation, you must install and correctly perform the initial configuration. Installation, in Microsoft terminology, consists of installing and configuring the base operating system from the CD and optional boot disks or from a network server share point. After the operating system is installed and operational, you must maintain the installation by adding, removing, and configuring hardware components such as uninterruptable power supplies, SCSI and network adapters, input devices, and tape backup devices. This chapter is dedicated to examining the Windows NT installation process and the skills needed to maintain and enhance the initial installation.

OBJECTIVES (continued)

Use Control Panel applications to configure a Windows NT Workstation computer in a given situation.

Upgrade to Windows NT Workstation in a given situation.

Configure server-based installation for a wide-scale deployment in a given situation.

PRACTICE QUESTIONS

INSTALL WINDOWS NT WORKSTATION ON AN INTEL PLATFORM IN A GIVEN SITUATION

1. **Select the statement that accurately describes the use of switches for the Windows NT Setup application.**

   A. `/b` installs from the CD-ROM without creating the three boot disks; `/ox Setup` does not perform the check for required free space on the installation target volume; `udf` specifies the uniqueness database file, ID, and optional path for installation; `/s` specifies a path for the source files required for installation; and `/u` instructs Setup to perform an unattended installation.

   B. `/b` installs using the Typical setup option during the GUI phase of Setup; `/ox Setup` only creates the three boot disks and exits; `udf` specifies the uniqueness database file, ID, and optional path for installation; `/s` specifies a path for the source files required for installation; and `/u` instructs Setup to perform an unattended installation.

   C. `/b` installs from the CD-ROM without creating the three boot disks; `/ox Setup` only creates the three boot disks and exits; `udf` specifies the uniqueness database file, ID, and optional path for installation; `/s` specifies a path for the source files required for installation; and `/u` instructs Setup to perform an unattended installation.

   D. `/b` installs from the CD-ROM without creating the three boot disks; `/ox Setup` only creates the three boot disks and exits; `udf` specifies the uniqueness database file, ID, and optional path for installation; `/s` skips SCSI adapter detection during the Text Mode phase of Setup; and `/u` instructs Setup to perform an unattended installation.

   E. `/b` installs from the CD-ROM without creating the three boot disks; `/ox Setup` only creates the three boot disks and exits; `udf` specifies the uniqueness database file, ID, and optional path for installation; `/s` specifies a path for the source files required for installation; and `/i` instructs Setup to prompt for network setup information during the GUI phase of Setup.

2. **This question is based on the following scenario. Review the scenario first, followed by the objectives and the proposed solution. Then evaluate the proposed solution by choosing the best answer.**

Scenario:

The LMN Corporation has the following systems:

10 Intel Pentium 90 machines, 250MB hard disk, 16MB RAM, Windows 3.1 operating system, Windows NT-compatible network

interface card, IDE CD-ROM, and Windows NT-compatible video card/monitor.

15 Intel Pentium 166 machines, 1GB hard disk, 32MB RAM, Windows NT Workstation 3.51 operating system, Windows NT-compatible network interface card, IDE CD-ROM, and Windows NT-compatible video card/monitor.

50 Intel Pentium II 300Mhz machines, 4.2GB hard disk, 64MB RAM, Windows 95 operating system, Windows NT-compatible network interface card, IDE CD-ROM, and Windows NT-compatible video card/monitor.

Required Result:
Install Windows NT Workstation 4 on all computers.

Optional Results:
Minimize hardware upgrades.

Ensure the best performance for all workstations.

Proposed Solution:
Upgrade the hard disks in the 10 Pentium 90 machines to 1GB capacity. Add 16MB of memory to the 15 Intel Pentium 166 machines.

Evaluation of Proposed Solution:
The proposed solution achieves which of the following stated objectives:

A. Only the Required Result

B. The Required Result and both Optional Results

C. The Required Result and only one Optional Result

D. Both Optional Results

E. Neither the Required Result nor the Optional Result

3. Select all the operating systems that should use the winnt.exe setup application to initiate an upgrade to Windows NT Workstation 4.

A. OS/2

B. Windows NT Workstation 3.51

C. Windows 95

D. Windows 98

E. Windows 3.11

4. The tools provided by Microsoft in the \Support\HQTool directory on the Windows NT Workstation 4 CD enable you to complete which of the following tasks? Select all that apply.

A. Create a bootable floppy disk with the NTHQ.EXE program to help determine your hardware's compatibility with NT 4.0.

B. Query the hardware after installation to determine whether IRQ settings are conflicting.

C. Query the hardware before installation to determine whether IRQ settings are conflicting.

D. Install the latest drivers for outdated hardware.

E. Run the NT version of the MS-DOS FDISK utility to change the partition structure on your hard disk.

5. Which statement best describes the absolute minimum requirements to install Windows NT Workstation?

A. 110MB of free disk space (RISC) / 148MB of free disk space (Intel),

RISC processor or Intel 486 or better processor, 12MB of RAM, CD-ROM, 3.5-inch floppy drive, mouse, SVGA video adapter.

B. 110MB of free disk space (Intel) / 148MB of free disk space (RISC), RISC or Intel 486 or better processor, 12MB of RAM, CD-ROM, 3.5-inch floppy drive, mouse, VGA video adapter.

C. 110MB of free disk space (Intel) / 148MB of free disk space (RISC), RISC or Intel 386 or better processor, 16MB of RAM, 3.5-inch floppy drive, mouse, VGA video adapter.

D. 110MB of free disk space (Intel) / 148MB of free disk space (RISC), RISC or Intel 486 or better processor, 12MB RAM, 3.5-inch floppy drive, VGA video adapter.

E. 110MB of free disk space (Intel) / 148MB of free disk space (Intel), RISC or Intel 486 or better processor, 12MB of RAM, 3.5-inch floppy drive, VGA video adapter.

6. Windows NT Workstation can be installed on a disk with which of the following file systems? Choose all that apply.

A. FAT32

B. FAT

C. NTFS

D. HPFS

E. CDFS

7. You are installing Windows NT Workstation on your computer. Your CD-ROM drive works under Windows 95, but it is not detected by NTHQ. How can you install Windows NT Workstation from the DOS command prompt?

A. `winnt.exe /b /ox`

B. `winnt32.exe /b`

C. `winnt.exe /b`

D. `winnt.exe /ox`

E. `winnt32.exe /ox`

8. This question is based on the following scenario. Review the scenario first, followed by the objectives and the proposed solution. Then evaluate the proposed solution by choosing the best answer.

Scenario:

The administrative assistant for the CEO of the LMN Corporation needs to have Windows NT Workstation installed on her machine. The purchasing department ordered a Pentium II desktop PC appearing on the Windows NT HCL (Hardware Compatibility List). The ordered system arrives with Windows 98 installed. The MIS department has a Windows NT Workstation 4 CD, but no boot floppies.

Required Result:

Install Windows NT Workstation directly from the CD-ROM.

Optional Results:

Install Windows Messaging so the computer can connect to the local Exchange Server.

Create a set of startup disks for future installations.

Proposed Solution:
Start the installation of Windows NT Workstation from the CD-ROM using the /ox switch. After entering the GUI mode of Setup, select the Typical setup type.

Evaluation of Proposed Solution:
The proposed solution accomplishes which of the stated objectives?

A. Only the Required Result

B. The Required Result both Optional Results

C. The Required Result and only one Optional Result

D. Both Optional Results

E. Only one Optional Result

9. **Select each of the operating systems that should use the winnt32.exe setup application to initiate an upgrade to Windows NT Workstation 4.**

A. OS/2

B. Windows NT Workstation 3.51

C. Windows 95

D. Windows 98

E. Windows 3.11

ANSWER KEY

1. C
2. A
3. C-D-E
4. A
5. D
6. B-C
7. C
8. E
9. B

ANSWERS & EXPLANATIONS

INSTALL WINDOWS NT WORKSTATION ON AN INTEL PLATFORM IN A GIVEN SITUATION

1. Select the statement that accurately describes the use of switches for the Windows NT Setup application.

C. `/b` installs from the CD-ROM without creating the three boot disks; `/ox Setup` only creates the three boot disks and exits; `udf` specifies the uniqueness database file, ID, and optional path for installation; `/s` specifies a path for the source files required for installation; and `/u` instructs Setup to perform an unattended installation.

1. CORRECT ANSWER: C

Table 2.1 lists the switches used to modify the behavior of Windows NT Workstation Setup. It is important to note that winnt32.exe does not support all the switches available for winnt.exe.

TABLE 2.1 MODIFYING THE WINNT.EXE INSTALLATION PROCESS

Switch	*Effect*
`/b`	The system does not make the three Setup boot disks. Create a temporary folder named WIN_NT.~BT and copy to it the boot files that would normally be copied to the three floppy disks. Then when the user is prompted to restart the computer, the files in the temporary folder are used to boot the machine instead of the Setup boot disks.
`/c`	The system skips the check for available free space. **This switch is not supported by winnt32.exe.**
`/I:inf_file`	This enables you to specify the name of the Setup information file. (The default file name is Dosnet.inf.)
`/f`	The system does not verify files as they are copied. **This switch is not supported by winnt32.exe.**
`/l`	The system creates a log file called $WINNT.LOG that lists all errors that occur as files are being copied to the temporary directory. **This switch is not supported by winnt32.exe.**
`/ox`	The system creates the three Setup boot disks and then stops.
`/s:`*`server path`*	Enables you to specify the location of the installation source files.
`/u`	All or part of an installation proceeds unattended as explained in Chapter 1. When you use the `/u` switch, the `/b` option for floppyless installation is automatically invoked too, and the `/s` option for location of the source files must be used. The `/u` option can be followed with the name of an answer file to fully automate installation.
`/udf`	During an unattended installation, this enables you to specify settings unique to a specific computer by creating a uniqueness database file, as explained in Chapter 1.

TABLE 2.1 CONTINUED

Switch	*Effect*
/w	This *undocumented* flag enables the WINNT.EXE program to execute in Windows instead of requiring execution from an MS-DOS command prompt.
/x	The system does not create the three Setup boot disks. You must already have the three boot disks.

2. Proposed Solution:
Upgrade the hard disks in the 10 Pentium 90 machines to 1GB capacity. Add 16MB of memory to the 15 Intel Pentium 166 machines.

A. Only the Required Result

2. CORRECT ANSWER: A

Table 2.2 lists the minimum hardware requirements to run Windows NT Workstation 4.

TABLE 2.2 WINDOWS NT WORKSTATION 4 MINIMUM INSTALLATION REQUIREMENTS

Component	*Minimum Requirement*
CPU	32-bit Intel x86-based (80486/33 or higher) microprocessor or compatible (the 80386 microprocessor is no longer supported) Intel Pentium, Pentium Pro, or Pentium II microprocessor Digital Alpha AXP-based microprocessor
Memory	Intel x86-based computers: 12MB RAM RISC-based computers: 16MB RAM
Hard disk	Intel x86-based computers: 110MB RISC-based computers: 148MB
Display	VGA or better resolution
Other drives	Intel x86-based computers: high-density 3.5-inch floppy disk and a CD-ROM drive (unless you are planning to install Windows NT over a network)
Optional	Network adapter card and a mouse or other pointing device (such as a trackball)

The inventory of machines that LMN wants to upgrade meets or exceeds the minimum hardware requirements to run Windows NT Workstation 4. Therefore, the Required Result is met; all machines will be able to run Windows NT Workstation 4.

Windows NT Workstation performance on a Pentium 166MHz machine with 32MB of RAM will be acceptable, at least much more acceptable than that of a Pentium 90 with 16MB of RAM. A better decision on LMN's part would have been to add 16MB of memory to the Pentium 90 group of machines. Therefore, the second Optional Result is not attained. Adding the memory to the Pentium 90 group of machines would have also required the purchase of only 10 sets of memory as opposed to the 15 required by the Proposed Solution. Therefore, the first Optional Result was not achieved.

3. Select all the operating systems that should use the winnt.exe setup application to initiate an upgrade to Windows NT Workstation 4.

C. Windows 95

D. Windows 98

E. Windows 3.11

3. CORRECT ANSWER: C-D-E

The winnt.exe setup program is used for 16-bit operating systems such as Windows 95, Windows 98, MS-DOS, and Windows 3.x.

There is no upgrade from OS/2 to any version of Windows NT.

4. The tools provided by Microsoft in the \Support\HQTool directory on the Windows NT Workstation 4 CD enable you to complete which of the following tasks? Select all that apply.

A. Create a bootable floppy disk with the NTHQ.EXE program to help determine your hardware's compatibility with NT 4.0.

4. CORRECT ANSWER: A

The NT Hardware Qualifier program, or NTHQ, is used to determine the compatibility of a system's hardware with Windows NT. To determine if there is an IRQ conflict prior to installing Windows NT, it would be necessary to use your existing operating system. As an example, with Windows 95, you would use the System Control Panel application. To determine if there is an IRQ conflict after installation of Windows NT Workstation, it would be necessary to use the Windows NT Diagnostics program in the Administrative Tools group on the Start menu. Disk partition can be modified during the Text phase of Windows NT Workstation Setup or by using Disk Administrator after Windows NT is installed.

5. Which statement best describes the absolute minimum requirements to install Windows NT Workstation?

D. 110MB of free disk space (Intel) / 148MB of free disk space (RISC), RISC or Intel 486 or better processor, 12MB RAM, 3.5-inch floppy drive, VGA video adapter.

5. CORRECT ANSWER: D

Refer to Table 2.2 for a list of the minimum workstation requirements for installing Windows NT Workstation 4. Note that NT Workstation can be installed from a network share point that contains the source files; therefore, a local CD-ROM is not required for installation.

6. Windows NT Workstation can be installed on a disk with which of the following file systems? Choose all that apply.

B. FAT

C. NTFS

6. CORRECT ANSWER: B-C

FAT and NTFS are the only disk file systems that Windows NT Workstation can use for installation. Windows 95 OSR2 and Windows 98 are the only operating systems that currently support FAT32. Although NT does support the CDFS, it is a read-only file system. HPFS was supported in earlier versions of Windows NT Workstation, but support was dropped in version 4.0.

7. You are installing Windows NT Workstation on your computer. Your CD-ROM drive works under Windows 95, but is not detected by NTHQ. How can you install Windows NT Workstation?

C. `winnt.exe /b`

7. CORRECT ANSWER: C

Using the `/b` switch will cause Setup to copy the required source files to the local hard disk before beginning setup. During setup, the newly copied source files will be used by Setup. In this scenario, it is more than likely that your CD-ROM will be disabled when using Windows NT Workstation.

8. Proposed Solution:
Start the installation of Windows NT Workstation from the CD-ROM using the `/ox` switch. After entering the GUI mode of Setup, select the Typical setup type.

E. Only one Optional Result

8. CORRECT ANSWER: E

To install Windows NT Workstation from the CD-ROM without the boot floppies, the `/b` switch must be used to modify the default behavior of Windows NT Setup. The `/b` will copy all the distribution files from the CD-ROM to the local floppy disk. After Setup begins, it will look to the local disk instead of the floppies and CD-ROM for needed files. Therefore, the Required Result is not achieved by the Proposed Solution.

Choosing the Typical setup type during the GUI phase of Setup will install the following options: Accessibility Options, Accessories, Communications Programs, and Multimedia Options. Not installed are the Windows Messaging and Games programs. Therefore, the first Optional Result is not achieved with the Proposed Solution.

Using the `/ox` switch with Windows NT Setup will instruct Setup to create the three boot floppies and quit. Therefore, the second Optional Result is achieved with the Proposed Solution.

9. Select all the operating systems that should use the winnt32.exe setup application to initiate an upgrade to Windows NT Workstation 4.

B. Windows NT Workstation 3.51

9. CORRECT ANSWER: B

Only previous versions of Windows NT can use the winnt32.exe application to begin an upgrade to Windows NT Workstation 4.

FURTHER REVIEW

INSTALL WINDOWS NT WORKSTATION ON AN INTEL PLATFORM IN A GIVEN SITUATION

Before installing Microsoft Windows NT Workstation 4, you must ask yourself the following questions:

- Is your hardware on the Microsoft Windows NT 4.0 Hardware Compatibility List (HCL)?
- Does your target workstation meet the minimum requirements for processor, RAM, and hard disk space?
- Are you attempting to install Microsoft Windows NT Workstation 4 on a "clean" system? Or are you planning to upgrade a computer with an existing operating system?
- If you are upgrading a computer with an existing operating system, will the Microsoft Windows NT 4.0 operating system replace the other operating system? Or do you want to be able to use both operating systems and be able to switch between them by "dual booting?"
- Which type of installation do you want to perform: typical, portable, compact, or custom?
- Where are the installation files that you will use to install Microsoft Windows NT Workstation 4 located: on a local floppy disk or CD-ROM, or on a network distribution server?

This section highlights specific points that can help you to determine the answers to these questions.

Using NTHQ

One way to make sure that all your hardware is on the official Hardware Compatibility List (HCL) is to execute the Windows NT Hardware Qualifier Tool (NTHQ.EXE), which is available only for Intel x86-based computers or compatibles. Microsoft provides a batch file (Makedisk.bat) that actually creates a special MS-DOS bootable disk that contains NTHQ.EXE. Makedisk.bat is located in the \Support\HQTool folder on the Windows NT Workstation 4 installation CD.

NTHQ lists detected hardware devices in four categories: System, Motherboard, Video, and Others. The Others category is used for device types the tool cannot positively identify. For example, if the system has an old PCI adapter that does not support PCI version 2.0 or later, the tool might not be able to identify its device type.

By default, NTHQ will report the results graphically upon execution completion. As an option, NTHQ enables you to write the results found by NTHQ to a text file named NTHQ.TXT. You should then check the list of detected devices with the Windows NT 4.0 HCL to avoid unpleasant surprises during installation. The information in NTHQ.TXT is also very useful for avoiding IRQ conflicts when adding new hardware because, unlike Windows 95, Windows NT does not support Plug and Play. Note that IRQ, DMA, and I/O addresses for detected devices are included in the NTHQ.TXT file.

Minimum Requirements for Installation

You also have to make sure that your computer hardware meets the minimum requirements for the installation of Windows NT Workstation 4 (The minimum requirements are listed in Table 2.2 appearing in the "Answers & Explanations" section for question 2). If your hardware does not meet the minimum requirements, you need to make the necessary upgrades before you attempt to install Windows NT Workstation 4. If your computer has devices not listed in the HCL, you should check with the devices' manufacturers to see if device drivers that support Windows NT 4.0 are available. Unlike with Windows 95, you cannot use older 16-bit device drivers with Windows NT. If you cannot obtain the proper device drivers, you cannot use unsupported devices after you install Windows NT. Although it is not guaranteed, an unsupported device might work if it emulates another device that does have drivers for Windows NT 4.0. Then try to use the drivers for the emulated device (for example, standard VGA for video, Sound Blaster for audio, Novell NE2000-compatible for generic network adapter cards).

Microsoft Windows NT 4.0 actually requires slightly more hard disk space during the installation process to hold some temporary files than it requires after installation. If you don't have at least 119MB of free space in your partition, the Setup routine displays an error message and halts. The Setup routine also displays an error message and halts if you attempt to install Windows NT Workstation 4 to a Windows NT software-based volume set or stripe set (RAID 0). If you have a hardware-based volume set or stripe set, you might be able to install Windows NT Workstation 4 on it; ask your manufacturer.

Keep in mind that Table 2.2 lists the *minimum* requirements for installation of Windows NT Workstation 4. After you install your actual application software and data, you will probably find out that your hardware requirements are higher than these minimum values.

If you are upgrading a Windows 95-based computer to Windows NT Workstation 4, make sure that you do not have any compressed drives and that you are not using FAT32. FAT32 is the new optional partitioning format that is supported only by Windows 95 OEM Service Release 2 (which is also called Windows 95) and Windows 98. Windows NT cannot access Windows 95 compressed drives and FAT32 partitions.

Installation Options

During installation, you can make use of your knowledge from Chapter 1, "Planning," to decide whether you want to change the partitioning of your hard disk and/or convert hard disk partitions from FAT to NTFS.

Regardless of whether you install Microsoft Windows NT Workstation 4 locally via the three floppy disks and the CD or by means of a network connection to a network distribution server, you have four setup options: Typical, Portable, Compact, and Custom. The four setup options install varying components from several categories, as shown in Table 2.3.

TABLE 2.3 VARYING COMPONENTS IN FOUR SETUP OPTIONS. (AN X INDICATES THE COMPONENT IS INSTALLED WITH THE SETUP OPTION.)

	Typical	*Portable*	*Compact*	*Custom*
Accessibility options	X	X	None	All options
Accessories	X	X	None	All options
Communications programs	X	X	None	All options
Games			None	All options
Windows Messaging			None	All options
Multimedia	X	X	None	All options

Note that the Compact setup option is designed to conserve hard disk space and installs no optional components. The Portable setting should be used for installing Windows NT Workstation on laptop computers; it installs only the necessary components and leaves the others as optional to make the best use of limited disk space. The only way to install Windows Messaging or Games during installation is to choose Custom setup. You can change installation options after installation via the Add/Remove Programs application in Control Panel.

Installing Windows NT Workstation 4 on an Intel Computer with an Existing Operating System

If your computer already has an existing operating system with support for CD-ROM, you can install Windows NT Workstation 4 directly from the installation CD. All you have to do is execute WINNT.EXE, which is a 16-bit program compatible with MS-DOS, Windows 3.x, Windows 95, and Windows 98. WINNT.EXE is located in the \I386 folder on the Microsoft Windows NT 4.0 CD. It performs the following steps:

1. Creates the three Setup boot disks (requires three blank high-density formatted disks).
2. Creates the WIN_NT.~LS temporary folder and copies the contents of the \I386 folder to it.
3. Prompts the user to restart the computer from the first Setup boot disk.

You can also modify the installation process. Table 2.1, appearing in the "Answers & Explanations" section for question 1, lists the available switches for winnt.exe and their uses.

There is also a 32-bit version of the installation program called WINNT32.EXE that is used to upgrade earlier versions of Windows NT; it cannot be used to upgrade Windows 95 or Windows 98. WINNT32.EXE does not support the `/f`, `/c`, or `/l` options. See the section entitled "Upgrading to Windows NT Workstation 4" for more information.

PRACTICE QUESTIONS

SET UP A DUAL-BOOT SYSTEM IN A GIVEN SITUATION

1. **Select all of the operating systems Windows NT Workstation 4 can be set up with in a dual-boot situation, using Windows NT dual-boot manager.**

   A. Windows NT Workstation 3.51

   B. Windows 98

   C. Linux

   D. MS-DOS / Windows 3.x

   E. Windows NT Server 4.0

2. **Bill currently has a system with Windows 98 installed on a 6GB FAT32 formatted hard drive with a single partition. He is currently studying for Exam 70-73, Implementing and Supporting Microsoft Windows NT Workstation 4, and would like to configure his system to dual boot between Windows 98 and Windows NT Workstation 4. How should Bill proceed to install Windows NT Workstation on his system to enable the dual-boot feature of Windows NT Workstation 4?**

   A. Install Windows NT in a directory other than the Windows directory.

   B. Use the Windows 98 convert utility to change the format of the current disk to FAT, and then install Windows NT into a directory different than that of Windows 98.

   C. Bill cannot dual boot with his current configuration.

   D. Start Windows NT Setup as normal. During the Text Mode phase of Setup, reformat the existing partition with FAT.

   E. Reinstall Windows 98 as an upgrade to change the file system to FAT, and then install Windows NT into a directory other than the Windows 98 directory.

3. **Which of the following are valid reasons for setting up a dual-boot system between Windows NT Workstation 4 and Windows 3.x?**

   A. You want your users to make a gradual transition from their old operating system to Windows NT.

   B. You need to support multiple operating systems per user need, but you have only one computer available.

   C. You want to run 16-bit and 32-bit Windows applications.

   D. Your development team needs to compile and test software under two different Windows operating systems.

   E. You need increased security on your files.

4. **This question is based on the following scenario. Review the scenario first,**

followed by the objectives and the proposed solution. Then evaluate the proposed solution by choosing the best answer.

Scenario:
Dave purchased a new workstation that is listed on the Windows NT Workstation 4 Hardware Compatibility List (HCL). The machine has two 3.2GB hard disks installed. The workstation arrived with Windows 95 OSR2 installed on one disk, which is formatted with the FAT file system. The second disk is formatted with FAT32 but contains no data.

Required Result:
Configure the machine to dual boot between Windows 95 and Windows NT Workstation 4.

Optional Results:
Maximize file security.

Share data and applications (such as Office 97) between the two operating systems.

Proposed Solution:
Install Windows NT Workstation on the second hard disk. During the installation, format the partition with NTFS. Install Office 97 under Windows 95, and then create a shortcut to the required executable files for Office 97 (such as winword.exe, access.exe, and so on) under Windows NT Workstation. Use the FAT partition for all data storage.

Evaluation of Proposed Solution:
The proposed solution achieves which of the stated objectives:

A. Only the Required Result

B. The Required Result both Optional Results

C. The Required Result and only one Optional Result

D. Both Optional Results

E. Neither the Required Result nor the Optional Result

5. **You have a system running MS-DOS, and you want to be able to dual boot between Windows NT Workstation 4 and Windows 95. Which step must you take? (Choose only one.)**

   A. Install Windows NT Workstation before Windows 95.

   B. Install Windows 95 before Windows NT Workstation.

   C. Create two partitions for each operating system.

   D. Create two partitions for each file system, FAT and NTFS.

   E. Create a single FAT partition.

6. **You currently have a dual-boot system with Windows 98 and Windows NT Workstation 4 installed. The default operating system selection is Windows NT Workstation 4. You want to change your default operating system selection on the boot menu to Windows 98. How do you go about doing this?**

   A. Use the Registry Editor.

   B. Use the Network applet in Control Panel.

   C. Use the System applet in Control Panel.

   D. Edit the BOOTSECT.DOS file.

   E. Edit the boot.ini file directly.

7. **This question is based on the following scenario. Review the scenario first, followed by the objectives and the proposed solution. Then evaluate the proposed solution by choosing the best answer.**

Scenario:
You have a dual-boot system configured with Windows 3.11 and Windows NT Workstation 4. Your dual-boot functionality suddenly stops working. The Boot Loader menu does not appear, and the system boots directly into Windows 3.11.

Required Result:
Restore dual boot functionality.

Optional Results:
Maintain Windows 3.x settings.

Maintain Windows NT Workstation 4 installation.

Proposed Solution:
Reinstall a fresh copy of Windows NT Workstation 4.

Evaluation of Proposed Solution:
The proposed solution achieves which of the stated objectives:

A. Only the Required Result

B. The Required Result both Optional Results

C. The Required Result and only one Optional Result

D. Both Optional Results

E. Neither the Required Result nor the Optional Result

ANSWER KEY

1. A-B-D-E	4. C	6. C-E
2. C	5. B	7. C
3. A-B-C-D		

ANSWERS & EXPLANATIONS

SET UP A DUAL-BOOT SYSTEM IN A GIVEN SITUATION

1. **Select all of the operating systems Windows NT Workstation 4 can be set up with in a dual-boot situation, using Windows NT dual-boot manager.**

   A. Windows NT Workstation 3.51

   B. Windows 98

   D. MS-DOS / Windows 3.x

   E. Windows NT Server 4.0

1. CORRECT ANSWER: A-B-D-E

All of the Microsoft operating systems can be configured to dual boot with Windows NT Workstation using the Windows NT Boot Manager. Linux, a freeware version of UNIX, is the only operating system that cannot be dual booted with Windows NT Boot Manager.

2. **Bill currently has a system with Windows 98 installed on a 6GB FAT32 formatted hard drive with a single partition. He is currently studying for Exam 70-73, Implementing and Supporting Microsoft Windows NT Workstation 4, and would like to configure his system to dual boot between Windows 98 and Windows NT Workstation 4. How should Bill proceed to install Windows NT Workstation on his system to enable the dual-boot feature of Windows NT Workstation 4?**

   C. Bill cannot dual boot with his current configuration.

2. CORRECT ANSWER: C

Windows NT supports only CDFS, NTFS, and FAT file systems. Because there is no way to convert a FAT32 formatted disk to any other file system without reformatting the disk, Bill cannot dual boot his system in its existing configuration.

3. **Which of the following are valid reasons for setting up a dual-boot system between Windows NT Workstation 4 and Windows 3.x?**

   A. You want your users to make a gradual transition from their old operating system to Windows NT.

   B. You need to support multiple operating systems per user need, but you have only one computer available.

   C. You want to run 16-bit and 32-bit Windows applications.

3. CORRECT ANSWER: A-B-C-D

Dual booting Windows 3.x and Windows NT Workstation will provide all the benefits listed except increased file security. When dual booting Windows 3.1 and NT Workstation on the same partition, you must format that partition with FAT, as Windows 3.x cannot access NTFS formatted partitions. Although FAT enables you to assign share-level permissions for shared folders, it does not offer local file or folder security.

D. Your development team needs to compile and test software under two different Windows operating systems.

One additional point is that option C, running 16-bit and 32-bit applications applies to the inability of Windows 3.1 to provide support for 32-bit applications. If the system is booted with Windows NT, the user will be able to run both 16- and 32-bit applications.

4. Proposed Solution:
Install Windows on the second hard disk. During the installation, format the partition with NTFS. Install Office 97 under Windows 95, and then create a shortcut to the required executable files for Office 97 (such as winword.exe, access.exe, and so on) under Windows NT Workstation. Use the FAT partition for all data storage.

C. The Required Result and only one Optional Result

4. CORRECT ANSWER: C

Installing NTFS on a separate NTFS formatted partition allows the system to dual boot between operating systems. However, any data on the second disk (with the NTFS format) will not be accessible to Windows 95. Therefore, the Required Result is achieved with the Proposed Solution.

Applications cannot be shared under both Windows 95 and Windows NT on the same machine, regardless of the file systems used. However, the data can be shared if it is located on a FAT formatted partition. Therefore, the second Optional Result is not obtained.

Formatting the Windows NT partition maximizes file security for files residing on the NTFS partition. However, any files on the FAT formatted partition have only share-level permissions applied. In this scenario, Dave has achieved the highest level of file security he could with the given configuration. The first Optional Result has been achieved.

5. You have a system running MS-DOS, and you want to be able to dual boot between Windows NT Workstation 4 and Windows 95. Which step must you take? (Choose only one.)

B. Install Windows 95 before Windows NT Workstation.

5. CORRECT ANSWER: B

When you're configuring NT Workstation to dual boot, the operating system with which NT should dual boot must be installed first. When Windows NT is installed, the existing operating system will be detected. You are given the option to upgrade the existing operating system if it is MS-DOS or Windows 3.x. If the operating system is not upgraded, it will be added to the Boot Manager menu.

6. You currently have a dual-boot system with Windows 98 and Windows NT Workstation 4 installed. The default operating system selection is Windows NT Workstation 4. You want to change your default operating system selection on the boot menu to Windows 98. How do you go about doing this?

C. Use the System applet in Control Panel.

E. Edit the boot.ini file directly.

6. CORRECT ANSWER: C-E

To change the default operating system or the time delay to select an operating system, Microsoft recommends using the System applet in Control Panel. You could also edit the boot.ini file directly; however, one small mistake could prevent the system from booting. Microsoft ensured the boot.ini is a hidden read-only file for a good reason.

7. Proposed Solution:
Reinstall a fresh copy of Windows NT Workstation 4.

C. The Required Result and only one Optional Result

7. CORRECT ANSWER: C

By reinstalling the Windows NT Workstation 4 operating system, dual-boot functionality will be restored. Therefore, the Required Result is achieved.

Because reinstalling Windows NT Workstation does not affect the existing Windows 3.11 installation, the Windows 3.11 settings are not modified. The Proposed Solution accomplishes the first Optional Result.

Selecting the Install a Fresh Copy of Windows NT Workstation option during setup overwrites the settings of the current Windows NT Workstation installation. Therefore, the second Optional Result is not achieved with the Proposed Solution.

To maintain the Windows NT Workstation settings, you could have selected Repair an Existing Windows NT Installation, which would restore dual-boot functionality and maintain the existing installation's configuration and settings.

FURTHER REVIEW

SET UP A DUAL-BOOT SYSTEM IN A GIVEN SITUATION

Dual booting is a term for having more than one operating system on a single computer. A dual-boot system typically has a boot menu that appears whenever the computer is restarted. The boot menu then enables users to choose which of the available operating systems they would like to start. It is possible to install Windows NT Workstation 4 to operate as a dual-boot system. The other operating system can be any version of MS-DOS, Microsoft Windows, or even OS/2. Some operating systems, such as some versions of UNIX, can dual boot with Windows NT but might need to use their own boot loader. Also remember that other operating systems might use different file systems for their partitions.

Installing Windows NT as a second operating system is similar to installing it as the sole operating system. During installation, you choose a separate system directory from the existing operating system's directory, and Windows NT automatically configures the boot loader to display selections for Windows NT and the other operating system.

To change the default boot menu options, either edit the boot.ini file or change the default operating system selection on the Startup/Shutdown tab of the System applet in Control Panel. More information on the boot files can be found in the troubleshooting section.

A dual-boot system can easily be set up with Windows NT Workstation and Windows 95/98 if the limitations are thoroughly understood. In this type of dual-boot configuration, you must install all of your Windows applications twice—once for each operating system. No system or application settings are migrated or shared between the two operating systems. In addition, you should install Windows 95 first because it installs its own boot track and can effectively disable a Windows NT boot loader.

PRACTICE QUESTIONS

REMOVE WINDOWS NT WORKSTATION IN A GIVEN SITUATION

1. **This question is based on the following scenario. Review the scenario first, followed by the objectives and the proposed solution. Then evaluate the proposed solution by choosing the best answer.**

   Scenario:
   You have a Windows NT Workstation 4 with the C: drive formatted with FAT and the D: drive formatted NTFS.

   Required Result:
   Remove Windows NT Workstation 4 from the system.

   Optional Results:
   Maintain the existing data on the D: drive while changing the format from NTFS to FAT.

   Configure the machine for a Windows 98 installation.

   Proposed Solution:
   Use the Windows NT Workstation utility convert.exe to change the file system on the D: drive from NTFS to FAT. Delete the Windows NT folder on the C: drive. Delete all of the Windows NT boot files and page files.

   Evaluation of Proposed Solution:
   The proposed solution accomplishes which of the stated objectives?

   A. Only the Required Result

   B. The Required Result both Optional Results

   C. The Required Result and only one Optional Result

   D. Both Optional Results

   E. Neither the Required Result nor the Optional Result

2. **What should be your first consideration when completely removing a Windows NT Workstation 4 installation from a computer?**

   A. Removing any NTFS partitions

   B. Restoring the regular MS-DOS boot sequence by using sys.com

   C. Removing the system files

   D. Removing the pagefile(s)

   E. Removing the Windows NT boot files

3. **You are dual booting between Windows 95 and Windows NT, and you want to remove Windows NT but keep your Windows 95 installation intact. What steps do you take? (Choose all that apply.)**

   A. Use the Windows NT Setup boot disks to delete the Windows NT boot and system partitions.

   B. Use the Windows NT Setup boot disks to delete all NTFS partitions and reformat them as FAT.

C. Delete the Program Files directory.

D. Use a Windows 95 boot disk to copy the Windows 95 boot loader.

E. Reinstall Windows 95 using the Upgrade option to maintain all current program settings.

4. After removing Windows NT Workstation 4 from your computer with a FAT partition, you reboot and receive the following message: `BOOT: Couldn't find NTLDR. Please insert another disk.` What is wrong with your installation?

A. The BOOT.INI file has not been deleted.

B. The Windows NT system files were not deleted.

C. The Master Boot Record of your hard disk is corrupted.

D. You must use the emergency repair disk to finish removing your installation of Windows NT 4.0.

E. The Windows NT boot track was not removed from your computer.

5. You would like to completely remove Windows NT from your computer, which has FAT formatted system partitions and NTFS formatted partitions with extended logical drives on the data partitions. If you are not running any other operating system, you can forego manually deleting system files and other data by doing which of the following? Select all that apply.

A. Boot with an MS-DOS disk and use the FDISK.EXE utility to wipe each drive.

B. Boot with an MS-DOS disk and format each drive.

C. Boot with the Windows NT Setup disks, delete each partition, and reformat the partitions as FAT.

D. Install Windows 95 or MS-DOS over the current installation.

E. Use Disk Administrator to delete the NTFS extended partitions.

6. Which of the following are Windows NT 4.0 system files that should be deleted during removal of Windows NT 4.0 from your dual-boot computer? (Choose all that apply.)

A. BOOT.INI

B. BOOTSECT.DOS

C. AUTOEXEC.BAT

D. CONFIG.SYS

E. NTDETECT.COM

7. Your Windows NT system has logical drives in extended partitions, all of which are formatted with NTFS. You want to remove Windows NT 4.0 from your system and install a new copy of Windows 95, which must access all hard drives. The partition containing the Windows NT system files is formatted with FAT. What should you do first?

A. Use the MS-DOS FDISK.EXE utility to wipe the drives.

B. Reboot the machine and begin the Windows 95 installation as normal.

C. Reboot in MS-DOS and reformat the drives.

D. Delete the NTFS partitions with the Windows NT Disk Administrator utility.

E. Reboot in MS-DOS and use the `sys c:` command to transfer boot tracks.

8. This question is based on the following scenario. Review the scenario first, followed by the objectives and the proposed solution. Then evaluate the proposed solution by choosing the best answer.

Scenario:
You have Windows NT Workstation installed on a system that has a primary partition formatted with FAT and an extended partition with two logical drives formatted with FAT. There is no data that needs to be maintained.

Required Result:
Remove Windows NT Workstation 4 from the system.

Optional Results:
Prepare the system to install Windows 98 in the quickest possible manner.

Consolidate the two logical drives in the extended partition into one single logical drive.

Proposed Solution:
Use the Windows NT Disk Administrator to delete both logical drives in the extended partition. Using Disk Administrator, create a single logical drive and format the partition with the FAT file system. Reboot the system with the Windows NT Setup disks, delete the primary partition, and reformat the partition with the FAT file system. Install Windows 98 as normal.

Evaluation of Proposed Solution
The proposed solution accomplishes which of the stated objectives?

A. Only the Required Result

B. The Required Result both Optional Results

C. The Required Result and only one Optional Result

D. Both Optional Results

E. Neither the Required Result nor the Optional Result

ANSWER KEY

1. A	4. E	7. D
2. A	5. C	8. C
3. B-D	6. A-B-E	

ANSWERS & EXPLANATIONS

REMOVE WINDOWS NT WORKSTATION IN A GIVEN SITUATION

1. Proposed Solution:
Use the Windows NT Workstation utility convert.exe to change the file system on the D: drive from NTFS to FAT. Delete the Windows NT folder on the C: drive. Delete all of the Windows NT boot files and pagefiles.

A. Only the Required Result

1. CORRECT ANSWER: A

By removing the Windows NT system folder and all the Windows NT boot files, you have effectively removed Windows NT from the computer.

The Windows NT convert.exe utility can only convert partitions from FAT to NTFS. After they are formatted with NTFS, the only way to change the formatting of the partition is to reformat the partition with the Windows NT Disk Administrator utility. Copying the data to another hard disk or archiving to tape, reformatting the partition, and then restoring the data could preserve the existing data. Therefore, the first Optional Result is not obtained with the Proposed Solution.

For the Windows NT boot partition to be completely removed and made bootable for other operating systems, the Master Boot Record must be modified to boot MS-DOS. This can be accomplished with the SYS.COM MS-DOS utility. Because the system is not ready for Windows 98, the second Optional Result is not achieved with the Proposed Solution.

2. What should be your first consideration when completely removing a Windows NT Workstation 4 installation from a computer?

A. Removing any NTFS partitions

2. CORRECT ANSWER: A

Because NTFS formatted partitions cannot be accessed by any other operating systems, they must be removed with Windows NT before Windows NT is removed from the workstation.

3. You are dual booting between Windows 95 and Windows NT, and you want to remove Windows NT but keep your Windows 95 installation intact. What steps do you take? (Choose all that apply.)

B. Use the Windows NT Setup boot disks to delete all NTFS partitions and reformat them as FAT.

D. Use a Windows 95 boot disk to copy the Windows 95 boot loader.

3. CORRECT ANSWER: B-D

To make all disk partitions available to Windows 95 (the sole operating system after Windows NT Workstation is removed), you must format all partitions with FAT. Because NT is the only operating system that can access NTFS partitions, those partitions must be removed while Windows NT is still installed on the computer. If the partition containing the Windows NT system files is formatted with NTFS, the partition must be removed with the Windows NT Setup program.

Additionally, the NT Boot Loader program must be removed from the active partition. This is best accomplished with the MS-DOS SYS.COM utility.

4. After removing Windows NT Workstation 4 from your computer with a FAT partition, you reboot and receive the following message: `BOOT: Couldn't find NTLDR. Please insert another disk.` What is wrong with your installation?

E. The Windows NT boot track was not removed from your computer.

4. CORRECT ANSWER: E

This error message is a symptom of the problem that the Master Boot Record is still looking for the Windows NT boot files. Using the MS-DOS application SYS.COM resets the Master Boot Record of the disk to boot MS-DOS. You must boot from a DOS bootable floppy to accomplish this.

5. You would like to completely remove Windows NT from your computer, which has FAT formatted system partitions and NTFS formatted partitions with extended logical drives on the data partitions. If you are not running any other operating system, you can forego manually deleting system files and other data by doing which of the following? Select all that apply.

C. Boot with the Windows NT Setup disks, delete each partition, and reformat the partitions as FAT.

5. CORRECT ANSWER: C

If there is no data or other operating system on the disks, the easiest way to delete the Windows NT installation is to boot with the Windows NT Setup disks, delete the existing partitions, reformat them with FAT, and restart the machine.

6. Which of the following are Windows NT 4.0 system files that should be deleted during removal of Windows NT 4.0 from your dual-boot computer? (Choose all that apply.)

6. CORRECT ANSWER: A-B-E

The autoexec.bat and config.sys files are not specific to NT, and they might be required by the other operating system that is dual-booting with Windows NT. The NT-specific system files that should be deleted when removing a Windows NT

A. BOOT.INI
B. BOOTSECT.DOS
E. NTDETECT.COM

install are PAGEFILE.SYS (this might or might not be located on the same partition as the Windows NT system files, depending upon your virtual memory configuration), BOOT.INI, BOOTSECT.DOS, NTDETECT.COM, NTBOOTDD.SYS (which might or might not be present, based on your configuration), and NTLDR. See Chapter 7, "Troubleshooting," for more information on the boot files.

7. Your Windows NT system has logical drives in extended partitions, all of which are formatted with NTFS. You want to remove Windows NT 4.0 from your system and install a new copy of Windows 95, which must access all hard drives. The partition containing the Windows NT system files is formatted with FAT. What should you do first?

D. Delete the NTFS partitions with the Windows NT Disk Administrator utility.

7. CORRECT ANSWER: D

Before installing Windows 95, you must remove the NTFS formatted partitions to enable Windows 95 to access the disk area occupied by the existing NTFS partitions. The easiest way to accomplish this is by using the Windows NT Disk Administrator utility.

**8. Proposed Solution:
Use the Windows NT Disk Administrator to delete both logical drives in the extended partition. Using Disk Administrator, create a single logical drive and format the partition with the FAT file system. Reboot the system with the Windows NT Setup disks, delete the primary partition, and reformat the partition with the FAT file system. Install Windows 98 normally.**

C. The Required Result and only one Optional Result

8. CORRECT ANSWER: C

Deleting and re-creating the primary partition will surely remove any trace of Windows NT Workstation from the system. Therefore, the Required Result is met.

Using Disk Administrator to delete the two logical drives in the secondary partition and restructuring the partition with one single drive formatted with FAT will meet the requirements of the second Optional Result.

If the primary partition is already formatted with FAT, it is not necessary to delete, re-create, and reformat the partition with the Windows NT Setup disks. Windows 98 could have been installed without modification to the primary partition unless a different size or configuration was required. Although these steps will prepare the system for an installation of Windows 98, this is not the most efficient means of doing so. Therefore, the first Optional Result is not achieved.

FURTHER REVIEW

REMOVE WINDOWS NT WORKSTATION IN A GIVEN SITUATION

When you're removing NT Workstation from a system, it is first necessary to remove all NTFS formatted partitions by using either the Windows NT Setup program or the Disk Administrator utility. Because NT must be installed and functional, you obviously could not use the Disk Administrator program to remove a partition on which Windows NT is installed. After you have removed all the NTFS partitions, you need to start the computer with a Windows 95 or MS-DOS system disk that contains the sys.com file. Type the command **`sys c:`** to transfer the Windows 95 or MS-DOS system files to the boot track on drive C. You then need to remove all the remaining Windows NT Workstation files, as outlined here:

- All paging files (C:\Pagefile.sys)
- C:\BOOT.INI, C:\BOOTSECT.DOS, C:\NTDETECT.COM, C:\NTLDR, and C:\NTBOOTDD.SYS, which will only be present if a SCSI adapter is present without the BIOS enabled (all of these files have the hidden, system, read-only attributes set)
- The *winnt_root* folder
- The c:\Program files\Windows\Windows NT folder

If you fail to remove the Windows NT boot track from your computer, the following error message appears when you restart your computer:

```
BOOT: Couldn't find NTLDR.
Please insert another disk.
```

You can then install your choice of operating systems on your computer.

PRACTICE QUESTIONS

INSTALL, CONFIGURE, AND REMOVE HARDWARE COMPONENTS IN A GIVEN SITUATION

1. **This question is based on the following scenario. Review the scenario first, followed by the objectives and the proposed solution. Then evaluate the proposed solution by choosing the best answer.**

   Scenario:
   You have a workstation with Windows NT Workstation 4 installed with a token-ring network adapter. Your LAN engineering department is changing your local segment to Ethernet (utilizing TCP/IP), which requires the installation of a new adapter. After TCP/IP is installed, DHCP will be used to dynamically configure the TCP/IP parameters at boot time. The source files for Windows NT Workstation are located on a network file server.

   Required Result:
   Install the new adapter.

   Optional Results:
   Remove the drivers for the existing token-ring adapter.

   Set the configuration of your new network adapter to use DHCP.

   Proposed Solution:
   Shut down your workstation and install the new adapter. Reboot your machine and connect to the token-ring network as normal. Install the drivers for the new adapter by running the Add/Remove New Software application from Control Panel. During the installation, configure the network settings for the new adapter when prompted. After the drivers are installed, re-run the Add/Remove New Software application to remove the existing drivers for the token-ring card.

   Evaluation of Proposed Solution:
   The proposed solution accomplishes which of the following objectives:

   A. Only the Required Result

   B. The Required Result both Optional Results

   C. The Required Result and only one Optional Result

   D. Both Optional Results

   E. Neither the Required Result nor the Optional Result

2. **In the SCSI Adapters applet in Control Panel, you can perform which of the following actions? (Choose all that apply.)**

   A. View SCSI device information

   B. View IDE device information

   C. Add or remove SCSI drivers

   D. Format SCSI hard disks

   E. Install SCSI tape devices

3. **You have a UPS installed on your computer, but when you boot up in Windows NT, the UPS automatically shuts down. You suspect that the UPS may be interpreting Windows NT's serial port test**

messages. How can you determine whether this is the problem?

A. Disconnect your serial mouse or install a PS2 mouse.

B. Use the UPS applet in Control Panel to alter the configuration settings until the UPS is recognized.

C. Install the UPS on a different COM port.

D. Edit the BOOT.INI file and add the `/NoSerialMice` switch to the end of the boot entry you want to use.

E. Run the Windows NT Diagnostics program to identify IRQ conflicts.

4. **From within the UPS applet in Control Panel, you can configure the way Windows NT 4.0 works with your UPS in which of the following ways? (Choose all that apply.)**

   A. Specify a program to run upon shutdown.

   B. Specify the time to wait between a power failure and the initial warning message.

   C. Specify a user or computer to warn upon signaling the UPS.

   D. Specify whether the UPS Interface Voltages are positive or negative for the power failure signal.

   E. Specify which BackOffice applications should be shut down.

5. **The Multimedia applet in Control Panel enables you to set and view configurations on which of the following? (Choose all that apply.)**

   A. Audio adapter drivers

   B. Audio adapter IRQ and DMA settings

   C. Video resolution

   D. CD music

   E. DVD devices

6. **Which of the following can be configured using the Settings tab in the Display applet found in Control Panel? (Choose all that apply.)**

   A. Color Palette

   B. Desktop Area

   C. Screen Saver

   D. Windows wallpaper settings

   E. Monitor power save features

7. **You have Windows NT Workstation installed with display settings of 1024 x 768, a 72Hz refresh rate, and 65,536 colors. The monitor attached to the system stops working, and you replace the monitor with a spare monitor. When you boot the system, the screen is unreadable. What action should you take to change the display settings of the computer to make them compatible with the new monitor?**

   A. Reinstall Windows NT as an upgrade and use the default display adapter settings.

   B. Use the emergency repair disk.

   C. Reboot Windows NT and select the Windows NT Workstation Version 4.00 [VGA mode] option from the boot menu.

D. Do not use the system until a replacement monitor can be installed.

E. Boot from a DOS disk and run the VIDRST.EXE application from the \tools\NTHQ directory on the Windows NT Workstation CD-ROM.

8. You need to configure the keyboard to match the capabilities of a physically impaired user. What do you do?

A. Use the Keyboard Locale tab in the Keyboard applet to select an appropriate scheme for the user.

B. Use the General tab in the Keyboard applet.

C. Use the Speed tab in the Keyboard applet to change the response speed of the keyboard to suit the user.

D. Use the Accessibility Options applet in Control Panel to configure this.

E. Change the keyboard driver through the Devices applet in Control Panel.

9. Which of these options are configurable from the Mouse applet in Control Panel? (Choose all that apply.)

A. Buttons

B. Pointers

C. Dragging

D. General

E. Mouse types (PS/2 vs. serial)

10. You can make Windows NT Workstation 4 automatically detect tape backup devices using what tool?

A. The Registry Editor.

B. The Tape Devices applet in Control Panel.

C. The System applet in Control Panel.

D. Windows NT cannot be configured to detect tape devices.

E. The Devices applet in Control Panel.

11. You need to change the keyboard driver for your Windows NT 4.0 computer. Where do you do this?

A. The System applet in Control Panel.

B. You must reinstall or upgrade Windows NT to make this change.

C. The General tab in the Keyboard applet.

D. The Input Locale tab in the Keyboard applet.

E. The Drivers Control Panel applet.

ANSWER KEY

1. E	3. D	5. A-B-D
2. A-B-C	4. A-B-D	6. A-B

ANSWERS & EXPLANATIONS

INSTALL, CONFIGURE, AND REMOVE HARDWARE COMPONENTS IN A GIVEN SITUATION

1. Proposed Solution:
Shut down your workstation and install the new adapter. Reboot your machine and connect to the token-ring network as normal. Install the drivers for the new adapter by running the Add/Remove New Software application from Control Panel. During the installation, configure the network settings for the new adapter when prompted. After the drivers are installed, re-run the Add/Remove New Software application to remove the existing drivers for the token-ring card.

E. Neither the Required Result nor the Optional Result

1. CORRECT ANSWER: E

New adapters are installed using the Network Control Panel applet, not the Add/Remove Software applet. The Add/Remove applet is used to install new software applications and remove existing applications. Hardware devices and their drivers are usually installed through the various applets available in Control Panel. Therefore, the Required Result is not met with the Proposed Solution.

The Network Control Panel applet is also used to remove existing adapters. From the Adapters tab, select the desired adapter to remove and click the Remove button. The adapter will then be disabled, and the software drivers will not be loaded in subsequent boots. Therefore, the first Optional Result is not achieved with the Proposed Solution.

The Network applet in Control Panel is also used to configure network adapters. In this case, installation access and configuration for the TCP/IP protocol is accomplished through the Protocols tab of the Network applet.

2. In the SCSI Adapters applet in Control Panel, you can perform which of the following actions? (Choose all that apply.)

A. View SCSI device information

B. View IDE device information

C. Add or remove SCSI drivers

2. CORRECT ANSWER: A-B-C

The SCSI Adapter Control Panel applet enables you to access, configure, and add both SCSI and IDE devices within Windows NT Workstation.

After a disk is installed, whether it is SCSI or IDE, the disk is formatted through Disk Administrator.

The Tape Devices Control Panel applet is used to install SCSI tape devices.

3. You have a UPS installed on your computer, but when you boot up in Windows NT, the UPS automatically shuts down. You suspect that the UPS is interpreting Windows NT's serial port test messages. How can you determine whether this is the problem?

D. Edit the BOOT.INI file and add the `/NoSerialMice` switch to the end of the boot entry you want to use.

3. CORRECT ANSWER: D

The `/NoSerialMice` switch will stop NT from performing a search for serial mice on the specified COM port during boot up. These tests are interpreted by some UPSs as a signal to initiate a shutdown.

4. From within the UPS applet in Control Panel, you can configure the way Windows NT 4.0 works with your UPS in which of the following ways? (Choose all that apply.)

A. Specify a program to run upon shutdown.

B. Specify the time to wait between a power failure and the initial warning message.

D. Specify whether the UPS Interface Voltages are positive or negative for the power failure signal.

4. CORRECT ANSWER: A-B-D

The UPS Control Panel applet can be used to specify an application that should be run before shut down occurs and to specify how much time should pass between the power outage and the generation of a shutdown message. Additionally, the type of interface signal (positive or negative) used by the UPS for power failure, the option for using a low battery signal at least two minutes before shutdown, and options for initiating a remote UPS shutdown can be configured with the UPS applet.

Although the UPS applet does not specify which users should be notified of a power outage signal from the UPS or which BackOffice applications should be shut down, most UPSs include software that provides this functionality.

5. The Multimedia applet in Control Panel enables you to set and view configurations on which of the following? (Choose all that apply.)

A. Audio adapter drivers

B. Audio adapter IRQ and DMA settings

D. CD music

5. CORRECT ANSWER: A-B-D

The Multimedia Control Panel applet enables you to install and remove audio adapter device drivers, modifiy audio adapter hardware settings, and choose the drive letter to use, as well as enabling you to change the volume output settings of CD-ROM headphones.

6. Which of the following can be configured using the Settings tab in the Display applet found in Control Panel? (Choose all that apply.)

A. Color palette

B. Desktop area

6. CORRECT ANSWER: A-B

The Display applets Settings tab enables you to specify the color palette, desktop area, Refresh Frequency, and Font Size for the current display adapter. Additionally, you can list all compatible display settings for the current adapter, change the current adapter, and test new adapter settings from this tab.

The Windows wallpaper settings are controlled from the Background tab. The screen saver is set through the Screen Saver tab. Windows NT Workstation does not support the monitor power saving features.

7. You have Windows NT Workstation installed with display settings of 1024 x 768, a 72Hz refresh rate, and 65,536 colors. The monitor attached to the system stops working, and you replace the monitor with a spare monitor. When you boot the system, the screen is unreadable. What action should you take to change the display settings of the computer to make them compatible with the new monitor?

C. Reboot Windows NT and select the Windows NT Workstation Version 4.00 [VGA mode] option from the boot menu.

7. CORRECT ANSWER: C

The simplest way to fix any video problems with Windows NT is to reboot the system and select the VGA mode, which is supported by most monitors. After access to the system is achieved, the video driver can be configured appropriately.

8. You need to configure the keyboard to match the capabilities of a physically impaired user. What do you do?

D. Use the Accessibility Options applet in Control Panel to configure this.

8. CORRECT ANSWER: D

Windows NT Workstation can be configured for users with disabilities through the Accessibility Options applet in Control Panel. If it is not present (Windows NT can be installed without this option), it can be added through the Add/Remove Programs Control Panel applet.

9. Which of these options are configurable from the Mouse applet in Control Panel? (Choose all that apply.)

A. Buttons

B. Pointers

D. General

9. CORRECT ANSWER: A-B-D

The buttons, dragging operation, and general mouse properties are set up through the Mouse Control Panel applet.

The proper mouse driver is configured through the Devices applet. Specific mouse drivers might replace the Mouse applet in Control Panel to enable the selection of pointer types.

10. You can make Windows NT Workstation 4 automatically detect tape backup devices using what tool?

B. The Tape Devices applet in Control Panel.

10. CORRECT ANSWER: B

The Tape Devices applet in Control Panel is used to install, specify, and configure tape backup devices in Windows NT Workstation.

11. You need to change the keyboard driver for your Windows NT 4.0 computer. Where do you do this?

C. The General tab in the Keyboard applet.

11. CORRECT ANSWER: C

Keyboard drivers are managed through the General tab in the Keyboard Control Panel applet.

FURTHER REVIEW

INSTALL, CONFIGURE, AND REMOVE HARDWARE COMPONENTS IN A GIVEN SITUATION

Configurable hardware components in Windows NT Workstation include the following:

- Network adapter drivers
- SCSI device drivers
- Tape device drivers
- Uninterruptable power supplies
- Multimedia devices
- Display drivers
- Keyboard drivers
- Mouse drivers

All of these items are configured using the various applets available in Control Panel.

Network Adapter Drivers

You can configure network adapters by double-clicking the Network icon in the Control Panel and then selecting the Adapters tab.

Windows NT 4.0 allows for an unlimited number of network adapters, as discussed in Chapter 4, "Connectivity." You can also configure each network adapter separately. To configure a specific network adapter, select the Adapters tab of the dialog box, and then click the Properties button.

You also need to make sure that you have the proper device drivers for your network adapter.

Windows NT 4.0 is compatible with any device drivers that are compliant with Network Driver Interface Specification (NDIS) version 4.0 or version 3.0. However, Windows NT cannot use any 16-bit legacy device drivers or device drivers from Windows 95, which uses NDIS 3.1 drivers.

When modifying the settings of network adapters, be careful to select the proper settings. Windows NT does not support Plug and Play and has no way to determine whether the values that you select are correct.

SCSI Device Drivers

With Windows NT 4.0, installation and configuration of SCSI adapters is now accessed through the SCSI Adapters applet in Control Panel.

To view device properties, open the SCSI Adapters dialog box. Select the Devices tab, select the device, and then click the Properties button. You can then view information on the device properties, as well as the revision data on the devices drivers.

Although the dialog box is titled SCSI Adapters, this is also where you can view and modify information on your IDE adapters and devices. You must reboot Windows NT 4.0 after adding or deleting any SCSI or IDE adapters.

Tape Device Drivers

The user interface for viewing configuration information on tape devices in Windows NT 4.0 has also been moved to the Control Panel.

If you want to have Windows NT 4.0 automatically detect tape devices, click the Devices tab, and then click Detect. If you would rather view device properties, click Properties. You can also add and remove device drivers by using the Add and Remove buttons located on the Drivers tab. You do not have to restart Windows NT if you add or delete tape devices.

Uuninterruptable Power Supplies

An uninterruptible power supply (UPS) provides backup power in the event the local power source fails. Power for UPS units is typically provided by batteries that are continuously recharged and are rated to provide power for a specific (usually highly limited) period of time.

During a power failure, the UPS service of Windows NT communicates with the UPS unit until one of the following events occur:

- Local power is restored.
- The system is shut down by the UPS service or by an administrator.
- The UPS signals to Windows NT that its batteries are low.

During a power failure, the Windows NT Server service is paused (which prevents any new users from establishing sessions with the server). Any current users are warned to save their data and to close their open sessions. All users are notified when normal power is restored.

The UPS and the Windows NT system communicate via a standard RS-232 port. The cable is not, however, a standard cable. A special UPS cable *must* be used to ensure proper communications between the UPS system and your computer.

You must also be sure to test the UPS unit after it has been configured. On startup of Intel-based computers, ntdetect.com sends test messages to all serial ports to determine whether a serial mouse is attached. Some UPS units misinterpret these test messages and shut down. To prevent your UPS unit from doing so, add the `/NoSerialMice` switch to the appropriate line in the boot.ini file.

Multimedia Devices

The Multimedia applet in Control Panel is used to install, configure, and remove multimedia devices. Categories of multimedia devices that can be modified include audio, video, MIDI, and CD music. There is also a Devices tab, with which you can view information on all the multimedia devices and drivers installed on your system.

You must install drivers for sound cards after you have successfully installed Windows NT. You cannot configure them during an unattended installation.

Display Drivers

Use the Settings tab of the Display program in Control Panel to choose display options, including refresh frequency, font sizes, video resolution, and the number of colors.

The Settings tab also enables you to choose options for your display (see Table 2.4).

TABLE 2.4 OPTIONS FOR CONFIGURING DISPLAY SETTINGS

Option	*Description*
Color Palette	Lists color options for the display adapter.
Desktop Area	Configures screen area used by the display.
Display Type	Displays options about the display device driver and enables installation of new drivers.
Font Size	Enables selection of large or small display font sizes.
List All Modes	Gives the option to configure color and desktop area and to refresh frequency simultaneously.
Refresh Frequency	Configures the frequency of the screen refresh rate for high-resolution drivers only.
Test	Tests screen choices. (If you make changes and do not test them, you are prompted to test your choices when you try to apply them.)

Whenever you make changes to your display driver settings, you are prompted to test them before saving them. If you ignore the test option and save incompatible values, your screen might become unreadable. You can restore normal operations by restarting your computer and selecting the VGA option from the boot menu. The VGA option forces your video card into 16-color standard VGA. You can then try setting different values in the Display Properties dialog box.

Caution should be exercised when modifying display adapter settings. In extreme cases, it is possible to damage your display card or monitor by choosing incorrect settings.

Keyboard Drivers

The three tabs of the Keyboard aaplet in the Control Panel enable you to configure the following options:

- *Speed.* Enables you to control repeat character delay, character repeat rate, and cursor blink speed.
- *Input Locales.* Enables you to specify the proper international keyboard layout.
- *General.* Enables you to view or change the keyboard driver. You might want to change your keyboard driver if you need to support an international keyboard, or if your prefer a Dvorak-style keyboard to the standard QWERTY keyboard.

To configure a system to match the capabilities of a physically impaired user, you can specify keyboard options by using the Accessibility Options program in Control Panel.

Mouse Drivers

Use the Mouse program in Control Panel to change mouse options, including buttons, pointers, motion, and general. Table 2.5 details the various options that you can configure with the Mouse program.

TABLE 2.5 CONFIGURING MOUSE OPTIONS

Tab	*Available Options*
Buttons	Configure mouse for right-handed or left-handed operation and for double-click speed.
Pointers	Choose the pointer shapes to be associated with various system events.
Motion	Control pointer speed and specify if you want the mouse pointer to snap to the default button in dialog boxes.
General	View the current mouse driver, and change to a new mouse driver if desired.

All of the mouse options outlined in Table 2.5, with the exception of the mouse driver, can be configured individually for each user account and are saved in the user's profile.

PRACTICE QUESTIONS

USE CONTROL PANEL APPLICATIONS TO CONFIGURE A WINDOWS NT WORKSTATION COMPUTER IN A GIVEN SITUATION

1. **This question is based on the following scenario. Review the scenario first, followed by the objectives and the proposed solution. Then evaluate the proposed solution by choosing the best answer.**

   Scenario:
   Your supervisor has informed you the Accounting department has hired an individual who needs certain accessibility features of Windows NT enabled to perform his job.

   Required Result:
   Install the Windows NT Accessibility Options.

   Optional Results:
   Enable the computer to beep when the Caps Lock, Num Lock, and Scroll Lock keys are pressed.

   Enable the Windows NT operating system to generate visual clues when the system makes a sound.

   Proposed Solution:
   Use the Add/Remove Programs applet to install the Windows NT Accessibility Options. Use the General tab of the Keyboard applet and check the Enable Beep for Lock Keys check box. Use the Sounds tab in the Accessibility Options applet and check the Use SoundSentry if you want Windows to generate visual warnings when your system makes a sound check box.

   Evaluation of Proposed Solution:
   The proposed solution accomplishes which of the following objectives:

   A. Only the Required Result
   B. The Required Result both Optional Results
   C. The Required Result and only one Optional Result
   D. Both Optional Results
   E. Neither the Required Result nor the Optional Result

2. **Which of the following are examples of software that could be installed with the Add/Remove Programs applet in the Control Panel? (Choose all that apply.)**

   A. Multimedia drivers
   B. Modem drivers
   C. Games
   D. Display drivers
   E. Productivity programs (Office 97, for example)

3. **You want to uninstall Internet Explorer. Which Windows NT applet can you use to uninstall it?**

   A. System
   B. Internet
   C. Add/Remove Programs

D. Network

E. Telephony

4. **This question is based on the following scenario. Review the scenario first, followed by the objectives and the proposed solution. Then evaluate the proposed solution by choosing the best answer.**

Scenario:
Chris, a member of the Users group, needs to change the time/date on his Windows NT Workstation.

Required Result:
Change the Time Zone setting from (GMT -05:00) Eastern Time (US and Canada) to (GMT -07:00) Mountain Time (US and Canada).

Optional Result:
Reset the system time from 1:22AM to 11:22PM.

Reset the date from October 31 1998 to October 30 1998.

Proposed Solution:
Use the Time Zone tab in the Date/Time Control Panel applet to change the time zone setting to the correct value. Use the Date & Time tab to reset the time and date to the proper value.

Evaluation of Proposed Solution:
The proposed solution accomplishes which of the following objectives:

A. Only the Required Result

B. The Required Result both Optional Results

C. The Required Result and only one Optional Result

D. Both Optional Results

E. Neither the Required Result nor the Optional Result

5. **You want to install more components from the Accessories options. In the Windows NT Setup tab, the check box next to the Accessories tab is gray. What does this mean?**

A. You cannot install any components from this option.

B. You have already installed all of these components.

C. You have installed some, but not all of these components.

D. None of the components are installed.

E. These options are only available at the time of installation.

6. **You use the Windows NT Setup tab in Add/Remove Programs to install which of the following components?**

A. SCSI device drivers

B. A new network adapter

C. Windows wallpaper

D. Display adapters

E. Windows screen savers

7. **Which of the following components *cannot* be installed by using the Windows NT Setup tab in Add/Remove Programs?**

A. HyperTerminal

B. CD Player

C. Windows Messaging

D. ODBC database components

E. Notepad

8. Which choice best describes the best Control Panel applet and its associated tab to install the new screen saver you downloaded from the Internet?

A. Display

B. System

C. Add/Remove Programs

D. Screen Savers

E. Internet

9. Which choice best describes the options the ODBC Control Panel applet enables you to configure?

A. File DSNs

B. System DSNs

C. Installation of ODBC drivers

D. Database Management programs

E. ODBC call tracing options

10. Which statements best describe the use of the Console applet in Control Panel?

A. Configure NT Workstation actions in the event of a crash

B. Configure virtual memory settings

C. Configure Telnet session parameters

D. Configure the behavior of the window brought up with the MS-DOS Prompt selection on the Start menu

E. Configure the way MS-DOS windows appear in Windows NT Workstation

ANSWER KEY

1. C
2. C-E
3. C
4. E
5. C
6. C-E
7. D
8. C
9. A-B-E
10. D-E

ANSWERS & EXPLANATIONS

USE CONTROL PANEL APPLICATIONS TO CONFIGURE A WINDOWS NT WORKSTATION COMPUTER IN A GIVEN SITUATION

1. Proposed Solution:
Use the Add/Remove Programs applet to install the Windows NT Accessibility Options. Use the General tab of the Keyboard applet and check the Enable Beep for Lock Keys check box. Use the Sounds tab in the Accessibility Options applet and check the Use SoundSentry if you want Windows to generate visual warnings when your system makes a sound check box.

C. The Required Result and only one Optional Result

1. CORRECT ANSWER: C

If the Accessibility Options is not installed on a particular workstation, the Add/Remove programs applet (Windows NT Setup tab) will enable you to install the Accessibility Options. Therefore, the Proposed Solution accomplished the Required Result.

The SoundSentry feature that displays a video cue when the system generates a sound is enabled through the Accessibility Options applet. Therefore, the second Optional Result is achieved.

The Control Panel Keyboard applet enables you to set such keyboard parameters as repeat rate, repeat delay, keyboard driver, cursor blink rate, and input locale, but does not enable you to set the sounds associated with key presses. Again, this feature required in the scenario would be set through the Accessibility Options applet. Therefore, the first Optional Result is not achieved with the Proposed Solution.

2. Which of the following are examples of software that could be installed with the Add/Remove Programs applet in the Control Panel? (Choose all that apply.)

C. Games

E. Productivity programs (Office 97, for example)

2. CORRECT ANSWER: C-E

Multimedia drivers would be installed with the Multimedia applet, modem drivers would be installed with the Modems applet, and display drivers would be installed with the Display applet.

The Add/Remove Programs applet is typically used to install the software components available with Windows NT Setup and end user applications such as games and productivity applications.

3. You want to uninstall Internet Explorer. Which Windows NT applet can you use to uninstall it?

C. Add/Remove Programs

3. CORRECT ANSWER: C

Programs such as Internet Explorer are considered end user applications and are installed/removed using the Install/Remove Programs applet.

The Internet applet is used to configure browser-specific information such as connection types, security options, or navigation options.

4. Proposed Solution: Use the Time Zone tab in the Date/Time Control Panel applet to change the time zone setting to the correct value. Use the Date & Time tab to reset the time and date to the proper value.

E. Neither the Required Result nor the Optional Result

4. CORRECT ANSWER: E

By default, members of the Users group are not allowed to set the system time on NT Workstations. Had Chris been a member of the Power Users or Administrators group, or had his account been specifically granted the right to Change System Time, he could have accomplished the task using the Proposed Solution.

5. You want to install more components from the Accessories options. In the Windows NT Setup tab, the check box next to the Accessories tab is gray. What does this mean?

C. You have installed some, but not all of these components.

5. CORRECT ANSWER: C

When an option in the Windows NT Setup tab is grayed out, it indicates some of the optional components are already installed.

All components listed in this tab can be installed after NT Workstation setup. The absence of a check mark indicates that none of the optional components are installed. A check mark in a white box indicates all the optional components are installed.

6. You use the Windows NT Setup tab in Add/Remove Programs to install which of the following components?

C. Windows wallpaper

E. Windows screen savers

6. CORRECT ANSWER: C-E

The Windows NT Setup tab is used to install software components that were available at the time of Windows NT Setup.

SCSI device drivers are installed with the SCSI Devices applet, network adapters are installed with the Network applet, and display adapters are installed with the Display applet.

7. Which of the following components *cannot* be installed by using the Windows NT Setup tab in Add/Remove Programs?

D. ODBC database components

7. CORRECT ANSWER: D

ODBC database components are installed with the ODBC32 applet in Control Panel. All other components are installed with the Windows NT Setup tab in the Add/Remove Programs applet.

8. Which choice best describes the best Control Panel applet and its associated tab to install the new screen saver you downloaded from the Internet?

C. Add/Remove Programs

8. CORRECT ANSWER: C

Screen savers will have an installation component that can be run from the Install/Uninstall tab of the Add/Remove Programs applet. After the screen savers are installed, they can be selected using the Display applet in Control Panel.

9. Which choice best describes the options the ODBC Control Panel applet allows you to configure?

A. File DSNs

B. System DSNs

E. ODBC call tracing options

9. CORRECT ANSWER: A-B-E

The ODBC applet enables you to configure File, System, and User DSNs (Data Source Names), and ODBC call tracing options. Additionally, you can view what versions of which ODBC drivers are installed on the system.

Database Management Programs, such as Microsoft FoxPro and Access, are installed through the Add/Remove tab of the Add/Remove Programs applet. When a database program is installed, it will typically also install the appropriate ODBC drivers.

10. Which statements best describe the use of the Console applet in Control Panel?

D. Configure the behavior of the window brought up with the MS-DOS Prompt selection on the Start menu

E. Configure the way MS-DOS windows appear in Windows NT Workstation

10. CORRECT ANSWER: D-E

The MS-DOS Console Control Panel applet is used to alter the screen color, window style, font size and family, cursor size, and command buffer history for all application-generated, MS-DOS windows, including the system console window accessed through the MD-DOS Prompt entry on the Start menu.

FURTHER REVIEW

USE CONTROL PANEL APPLICATIONS TO CONFIGURE A WINDOWS NT WORKSTATION COMPUTER IN A GIVEN SITUATION

Not all Control Panel applets are used to install, configure, and manage hardware devices. Many of the Control Panel applets are used to alter the actions or performance of Windows NT Workstation itself.

Accessibility Options

The Accessibility Options applet enables you to configure the Windows NT Workstation for use by individuals with vision, hearing, or movement challenges. With this applet, you can make modifications such as making the keyboard easier to use, graphically represent system sounds, and transferring mouse functionality to the keyboard.

Add/Remove Programs

This applet enables you to install or remove applications such as games and Windows components available during setup. It also enables you to install applications from CD-ROM or floppy disk utilizing a setup.exe or install.exe installation program. In programs installed in this manner, Add/Remove Programs records the installation steps and enables you to remove the applications with the Uninstall Wizard.

MS-DOS Console

The MS-DOS Console applet enables you to modify the way a DOS window appears within NT Workstations. You can set the screen color, window style, font size and family, cursor size, and command buffer history.

Devices

The Devices applet displays all device drivers detected and installed by Windows NT that are currently running. You can also modify the startup parameters as well as start and stop device drivers from this applet.

Fonts

The Fonts applet shows the currently installed fonts for the Workstation as well as enabling you to add new or remove existing fonts.

Internet

The Internet applet will only appear in Control Panel if Internet Explorer is installed on the workstation. It enables you to set and modify connection information as well as modify the behavior of Internet Explorer.

ODBC

The ODBC applet enables you to manage and configure the ODBC components for the workstation. ODBC, or Open DataBase Connectivity, is a system-level data access method developed by Microsoft. From the applet, you can enable tracing for application calls to the ODBC drivers as well as view installed drivers and their versions. Also, the applet enables you to create, delete, and modify System, File, and User DSNs. DSNs, or Data Source Names, contain ODBC connectivity information, such as the location of a specific database and the driver that should be used to connect to the database.

PC Card (PCMCIA)

The PC Card applet displays the presence of PCMCIA services on your computer and which PCMCIA cards are installed, as well as their resource usage.

Ports

The Ports applet enables you to modify and delete parameters for the available COM ports on the workstation.

Printers

This applet is a replacement for the Printer Manager available in earlier versions of Windows NT. Printers displays icons for each printer currently installed. This enables you to completely manage and configure individual printers. Additionally, you can add or remove printers from the Printers applet.

Server

Server displays the statistics of the server-based activities of the workstation; this includes the number of users connected, shared resources in use, and replication settings.

Sounds

The Sounds applet enables you to assign custom .wav files to system events.

System

The System applet displays a properties sheet through which you can set the default operating system at boot time, set recovery options for Stop errors, manage user profiles, manage hardware profiles, manage environment variables, configure virtual memory settings, and modify application performance.

Services

This applet displays a listing of all services installed on the system and their current statuses. Services are Windows NT system functions or applications that are loaded as part of the Windows NT Executive component. From this applet, you can set the start up parameters of services, assign services to specific hardware profiles, and start and stop specific services.

PRACTICE QUESTIONS

UPGRADE TO WINDOWS NT WORKSTATION 4 IN A GIVEN SITUATION

1. **To upgrade from a previous installation of Windows NT, which program should you use to begin the upgrade?**

   A. WINNT.EXE

   B. WINNT32.EXE

   C. UPGRADE.EXE

   D. SETUP.EXE

2. **Which of the following are preserved in an upgrade from Windows NT 3.x to Windows NT Workstation 4? (Choose all that apply.)**

   A. User settings

   B. Application settings

   C. Windows NT 3.x interface

   D. Security settings

   E. All of the above

3. **You want to upgrade an existing installation of Windows NT 3.x to Windows NT 4.0, yet still maintain all of your Windows NT 3.x application settings and configuration. What must you do?**

   A. Install Windows NT 4.0 in a separate directory and manually migrate applications and settings.

   B. Install Windows NT 4.0 in a separate directory and choose the Upgrade option.

   C. Nothing. Windows NT will automatically detect and update a Windows NT 3.x installation without prompting you for any other information.

   D. Install Windows NT 4.0 in the same directory as Windows NT 3.x and choose the Upgrade option.

   E. None of the above.

4. **Which operating systems can be directly upgraded to Windows NT Workstation 4? (Choose all that apply.)**

   A. Windows NT 3.51 Workstation

   B. Windows 95

   C. Windows NT 3.51 Server

   D. Windows NT 4.0 Server

   E. Windows 98

5. **You have a Windows 95 machine in a networked environment with user profiles enabled. You want to completely replace Windows 95 with Windows NT. Considering that Windows 95 cannot be directly upgraded to Windows NT, which of the following options must be completed to install Windows NT Workstation on this system? Select all that apply.**

A. You must install Windows NT Workstation 4 in a separate directory.

B. You must convert the file system to NTFS.

C. You must migrate user profiles to Windows NT.

D. You must reinstall all 32-bit applications under Windows NT.

E. You must remove Windows 95 from the workstation.

6. Why can't you directly upgrade a system from Windows 95 to Windows NT Workstation 4? (Choose two.)

A. Windows NT requires the NTFS file system and cannot be upgraded over Windows 95's FAT file system.

B. There are differences in Registry structure.

C. Windows 95 supports FAT32, and Windows NT cannot access FAT32 volumes.

D. There are differences in hardware device support.

E. Windows 95 is not a true 32-bit operating system.

7. You have upgraded a Windows 3.x installation to Windows NT Workstation 4. None of the user settings were migrated. Select the best option for forcing the upgrade to occur.

A. Reinstall Windows NT Workstation using the Upgrade Existing Installation option during setup.

B. Reinstall Windows NT Workstation using the Repair Existing Installation option during setup.

C. Windows 3.x cannot be upgraded to Windows NT Workstation 4.

D. Remove the Registry key \HKEY_CURRENT_USER\Windows Migration Status.

E. Add the Registry key \HKEY_CURRENT_USER\Windows Migration Status.

8. When Windows NT Workstation is installed as an upgrade to Windows 3.1, what settings are maintained? Select all that apply.

A. Desktop wallpaper and color schemes

B. Security information

C. Network information such as network protocol, printer mappings, and so on

D. Program groups

E. Non-system files

ANSWER KEY

1. B
2. A-B-D
3. D
4. A
5. D
6. B-D
7. D
8. A-C-D-E

ANSWERS & EXPLANATIONS

UPGRADE TO WINDOWS NT WORKSTATION 4 IN A GIVEN SITUATION

1. To upgrade from a previous installation of Windows NT, which program should you use to begin the upgrade?

B. WINNT32.EXE

1. CORRECT ANSWER: B

WINNT.EXE and WINNT32.EXE are the two versions of the Windows NT Setup application. When upgrading all previous versions of Windows NT Workstation, you should start the upgrade with the WINNT.EXE program.

2. Which of the following are preserved in an upgrade from Windows NT 3.x to Windows NT Workstation 4? (Choose all that apply.)

A. User settings

B. Application settings

D. Security settings

2. CORRECT ANSWER: A-B-D

When Windows NT 3.x is upgraded to Windows NT Workstation, user-specific settings, security settings on files, folders, and shares, and application settings are maintained after Windows NT Workstation 4 is installed.

3. You want to upgrade an existing installation of Windows NT 3.x to Windows NT 4.0, yet still maintain all of your Windows NT 3.x application settings and configuration. What must you do?

D. Install Windows NT 4.0 in the same directory as Windows NT 3.x and choose the Upgrade option.

3. CORRECT ANSWER: D

To upgrade an existing installation of Windows NT Workstation to version 4.0, you must install NT Workstation 4 into the same directory where the earlier version is installed. When the previous installation is detected, Setup will ask you if an upgrade should be completed or if a fresh copy should be installed. Installing a fresh copy will overwrite the existing installation, and information from the previous version will not be migrated.

Installing to a separate directory will set up a dual-boot configuration between Windows NT Workstation 4 and the previous version of Workstation.

4. Which operating systems can be directly upgraded to Windows NT Workstation 4? (Choose all that apply.)

A. Windows NT 3.51 Workstation

4. CORRECT ANSWER: A

Windows NT Workstation can be installed with the upgrade option for Windows 3.x and earlier versions of NT Workstation.

Although both Windows NT and Windows 95/Windows 98 are Registry based, their respective Registries differ enough that a direct upgrade is not possible. To upgrade any Windows 95/Windows 98 system to Windows NT Workstation, you must install a fresh copy of Workstation, reinstall all existing applications, and re-create all user information.

5. You have a Windows 95 machine in a networked environment with user profiles enabled. You want to completely replace Windows 95 with Windows NT. Considering that Windows 95 cannot be directly upgraded to Windows NT, which of the following options must be completed to install Windows NT Workstation on this system? Select all that apply.

D. You must reinstall all 32-bit applications under Windows NT.

5. CORRECT ANSWER: D

To upgrade a Windows 95 installation to Windows NT Workstation 4, you must reinstall all the applications.

Neither the selected file system nor the directory chosen to install Windows NT Workstation has any consequence on the upgradability of Windows 95 to Windows NT Workstation.

Windows 95 user profiles are not compatible with Windows NT Workstation 4.

Installing Windows NT to a directory other than that in which Windows 95 is installed results in a dual-boot system. Installing Workstation into the same directory as Windows 95 results in the removal of the Windows 95 operating system.

6. Why can't you directly upgrade a system from Windows 95 to Windows NT Workstation 4? (Choose two.)

B. There are differences in Registry structure.

D. There are differences in hardware device support.

6. CORRECT ANSWER: B-D

Although both Windows 95 and Windows NT are Registry-based operating systems, the Registry structure differs enough to make an upgrade impossible.

Windows 95 provides a greater range of hardware support than does Windows NT Workstation. Consequently, upgrade attempts might fail due to lack of hardware support for crucial system devices.

7. You have upgraded a Windows 3.x installation to Windows NT Workstation 4. None of the user settings were migrated. Select the best option for forcing the upgrade to occur.

D. Remove the Registry key \HKEY_CURRENT_USER\Windows Migration Status.

7. CORRECT ANSWER: D

In the event that user settings are not migrated after a Windows NT Workstation 4 upgrade from Windows 3.x, removing the \HKEY_CURRENT_USER\Windows Migration Status Registry key will usually result in the migration occurring normally during the next boot.

8. When Windows NT Workstation is installed as an upgrade to Windows 3.1, what settings are maintained? Select all that apply.

A. Desktop wallpaper and color schemes

C. Network information such as network protocol, printer mappings, and so on

D. Program groups

E. Non-system files

8. CORRECT ANSWER: A-C-D-E

When Windows 3.x is upgraded to Windows NT Workstation, all user and application information is maintained. Windows 3.x does not have any security settings to be upgraded.

FURTHER REVIEW

UPGRADE TO WINDOWS NT WORKSTATION 4 IN A GIVEN SITUATION

If you are upgrading an earlier version of Microsoft Windows NT Workstation to Microsoft Windows NT Workstation 4, you need to use the 32-bit version of the installation program—WINNT32.EXE. WINNT32.EXE was explained earlier in this chapter, in the section entitled "Installing Windows NT Workstation 4 on an Intel Computer." Installations of any version of Windows NT Server cannot be upgraded to Windows NT Workstation 4, and you must install into a new folder and reinstall all of your Windows applications.

If Windows NT Workstation 3.x is upgraded to Windows NT Workstation 4, all the existing Registry entries are preserved, including the following:

- User and group settings
- Preferences for applications
- Network settings
- Desktop environment

To upgrade Windows NT Workstation 3.x to Windows NT Workstation 4, install to the same folder as the existing installation and answer Yes to the upgrade question that you are asked during the installation process. Then follow the instructions.

In the event that the migration does not take place during setup, you can force the migration to take place by deleting the HKEY_CURRENT_USER\Windows Migration Status key from the Registry. When you restart Windows, the migration should proceed.

Because of differences in hardware device support and differences in the internal structure of the Registry, there is no upgrade path from Microsoft Windows 95 to Microsoft Windows NT 4.0. You need to perform a new installation of Windows NT to a new folder and then reinstall all your Windows applications. No system or application settings are shared or migrated. After you install Microsoft Windows NT Workstation 4 and your applications, you should delete the Windows 95 directory. Additionally, if you are configuring a dual-boot system with Windows 95 and Windows NT, you need to install all applications under both operating systems.

Table 2.6 lists the available upgrade paths to Windows NT Workstation 4 from various Microsoft operating systems.

TABLE 2.6 THE AVAILABLE UPGRADES TO WINDOWS NT WORKSTATION FROM VARIOUS MICROSOFT OPERATING SYSTEMS

Operating System	*Upgrade*	*Settings Migrated*
Windows 3.1	Yes	Yes
Windows 95	No	No
Windows 98	No	No
Windows NT 3.1	Yes	Yes
NT Workstation 3.5	Yes	Yes
NT Workstation 3.51	Yes	Yes

PRACTICE QUESTIONS

CONFIGURE SERVER-BASED INSTALLATION FOR WIDE-SCALE DEPLOYMENT IN A GIVEN SITUATION

1. **Which of the following statements describes the best method for concurrently installing Windows NT Workstation 4 on a large number of computers?**

   A. Install from the CD-ROM and Setup boot disks.

   B. Install from the CD-ROM using the `/b` switch to avoid using Setup boot disks.

   C. Use an answer file and uniqueness database file to install from a network distribution server that contains a share point to the installation files on the local CD-ROM.

   D. Use an answer file and uniqueness database file to install from a networked workstation that contains a share point to the installation files on the local hard disk.

   E. Use a uniqueness database file to install from a network distribution server that contains a share point to the installation files on the local hard disk.

2. **Which of the following best enables you to greatly increase the speed of the file transfer portion of your network Windows NT installations?**

   A. Using multiple `/s` switches and multiple servers containing the Windows NT installation files

   B. Choosing the `/f` switch for installation without file verification

   C. Using the fastest server on your network for the share point of the Windows NT installation files

   D. Choosing the `/b` switch for installation without Setup disks

   E. Copying the source files from the CD-ROM to a shared directory on a server hard disk

3. **This question is based on the following scenario. Review the scenario first, followed by the objectives and the proposed solution. Then evaluate the proposed solution by choosing the best answer.**

   Scenario:
   You need to install Windows NT 4.0 on all machines in a 100-workstation network. The network is a single domain with two Windows NT 3.51 servers.

   Required Result:
   Upgrade all workstations to Windows NT 4.0.

   Optional Results:
   Complete the upgrade in the shortest possible time.

   Automate the installation.

Proposed Solution:
Share the CD-ROM in one of the servers. Place the Windows NT Workstation CD in the CD-ROM drive. Develop the answer files and a uniqueness database file for the installation. Use the `/b`, `/s`, `/f`, `/u`, and `/udf` switches when starting setup.

Evaluation of Proposed Solution:
The proposed solution accomplishes which of the following objectives:

A. Only the Required Result

B. The Required Result both Optional Results

C. The Required Result and only one Optional Result

D. Both Optional Results

E. Neither the Required Result nor the Optional Result

4. **The command winnt32 `/b /s:\\SVR1\NTWS /s:\\SVR2\NTWS` accomplishes what?**

A. It installs Windows NT on the computers SVR1 and SVR2 in each computer's specified NTWS directory.

B. It performs a diskless installation, creating the setup information on SVR1 and SVR2.

C. It installs Windows NT without Setup boot disks, copying installation files from both SVR1 and SVR2.

D. It copies Setup files from the local computer to \\SVR1\NTWS and \\SVR2\NTWS.

E. It copies the files needed for the Windows NT Setup disks to the directory \NTWS on the servers named SVR1 and SVR2.

5. **Which of the following statements best describes a network distribution server for installing Windows NT Workstation in a network environment?**

A. A Windows NT server with a shared CD-ROM drive in which the Windows NT Workstation CD-ROM is inserted

B. A Windows NT or Novell NetWare Server with a network share created for the CD-ROM containing the Windows NT Workstation CD

C. A Windows NT or Novell NetWare Server with a network share pointing to the server's hard disk containing a copy of the required NT Workstation installation files for the specific target platform (for example, Alpha, RISC, or Intel)

D. A Windows NT Server with a network share created on the hard disk containing a copy of the required NT Workstation installation files for the specific target platform (for example, Alpha, RISC, or Intel)

E. A Windows NT or Novell NetWare Server with a network share pointing to the server's hard disk containing a copy of the required NT Workstation installation files for the specific target platform (for example, Alpha, RISC, or Intel) and any additional OEM supplied files

6. **What is the best method for installing Windows NT Workstation on a large number of workstations within an enterprise environment?**

   A. Install from the CD-ROM and Setup boot disks

   B. Install from the CD-ROM using the `/b` switch to avoid using Setup boot disks

   C. Install using the `/s` switch pointing to multiple network distribution servers containing share points to the servers' local disks containing copies of the source files from the CD-ROM

   D. Use an answer file and UDB file that point to the local CD-ROM

   E. Install using the `/s` switch pointing to multiple network distribution servers that contain share points to the servers' CD-ROM drives

7. **To copy the Windows NT installation files necessary for creating a network share for remote installation, what option must be set in Windows NT or Windows 95 Explorer?**

   A. Hide Files of Specified Types

   B. Show All Files

   C. The Shared-As radio button must be selected and a share name must be specified for the CD-ROM installation directory

   D. All of the above

   E. None of the above

ANSWER KEY

1. D	4. C	6. C
2. A	5. E	7. B
3. C		

ANSWERS & EXPLANATIONS

CONFIGURE SERVER-BASED INSTALLATION FOR WIDE-SCALE DEPLOYMENT IN A GIVEN SITUATION

1. Which of the following statements describes the best method for concurrently installing Windows NT Workstation 4 on a large number of computers?

D. Use an answer file and uniqueness database file to install from a networked workstation that contains a share point to the installation files on the local hard disk.

1. CORRECT ANSWER: D

The most efficient means of installing Windows NT Workstation from the options listed is to use a share point to a network server hard disk that contains the source files required for the platform types on which Windows NT Workstation will be installed. Because disk access times are significantly less than CD-ROM access times for network servers, you will receive much better response time if the distribution files are placed on the server hard disk.

Using the /s switch to start the installation on the workstation will allow the Windows NT Workstation Setup program to draw the source files needed from multiple servers. Using answer files and uniqueness database files, as discussed in Chapter 1, "Planning," you can completely automate the setup, resulting in an even quicker installation time. The ideal way to install Windows NT Workstation would be to also combine pulling the source files from distribution servers with answer files and UDB files to automate the setup.

2. Which of the following best enables you to greatly increase the speed of the file transfer portion of your network Windows NT installations?

A. Using multiple /s switches and multiple servers containing the Windows NT installation files

2. CORRECT ANSWER: A

Using the /s switch enables Windows NT Workstation Setup to draw the source files from multiple servers, thereby eliminating the bottleneck imposed from performing concurrent installations and attempting to access the files from a single server.

3. Proposed Solution:
Share the CD-ROM in one of the servers. Place the Windows NT Workstation CD in the CD-ROM drive. Develop the answer files and a uniqueness database file for the installation. Use the `/b`, `/s`, `/f`, `/u`, and `/udf` switches when starting setup.

C. The Required Result and only one Optional Result

3. CORRECT ANSWER: C

The method described in the Proposed Solution upgrades all the existing machines on the network to Windows NT Workstation 4. Therefore, the Required Result is achieved with the Proposed Solution. Creating the required answer files and uniqueness database files automates the installation, thereby accomplishing the second Optional Result.

When performing an upgrade, it is helpful to provide multiple network share points containing the source files to reduce the time required in copying the source files during the installation. The scenario indicated there were two NT Servers available, but the Proposed Solution used only one server to supply the Windows NT Workstation source files. Because both servers are not used, the installation time is significantly increased. Additionally, the first Optional Result is not achieved because the source files were shared from the CD-ROM. It would have been more efficient if the source files were first copied to the servers' hard disks because disk access time is quicker than CD-ROM access time. The first Optional Result was not accomplished with the Proposed Solution.

As an additional note, it is not necessary to explicitly include the `/b` and `/f` switches when using the `/u` switch. When the `/u` switch is used, Windows NT Setup automatically starts the installation with the `/b` and `/f` switches.

4. The command `winnt32 /b /s:\\SVR1\NTWS /s:\\SVR2\NTWS` accomplishes what?

C. It installs Windows NT without Setup boot disks, copying installation files from both SVR1 and SVR2.

4. CORRECT ANSWER: C

The `/b` switch instructs the Windows NT Setup program to not create or use the boot disks during the installation, but rather to copy the required files to the local hard disk.

The multiple `/s` switches provide the Setup program with two network share points from which to draw the required source files. In this example, both SVR1 and SVR2 have a share point named NTWS that contains the source files for Windows NT Workstation.

5. Which of the following statements best describes a network distribution server for installing Windows NT Workstation in a network environment?

E. A Windows NT or Novell NetWare Server with a network share pointing to the server's hard disk containing a copy of the required NT Workstation installation files for the specific target platform (for example, Alpha, RISC, or Intel) and any additional OEM supplied files

5. CORRECT ANSWER: E

Windows NT Setup can draw files from any network share point, regardless of the operating system on that server, as long as the proper protocols for communicating with the server are loaded on the target workstation. Better performance will be realized during the file copy phase of Windows NT Setup if the source files are located on the server's hard disk as opposed to the server's CD-ROM.

6. What is the best method for installing Windows NT Workstation on a large number of workstations within an enterprise environment?

C. Install using the `/s` switch pointing to multiple network distribution servers containing share points to the servers' local disks containing copies of the source files from the CD-ROM

6. CORRECT ANSWER: C

Best performance will be realized if the files are pulled from multiple network servers with the source files located on the server's hard disk as opposed to the server's CD-ROM.

7. To copy the Windows NT installation files necessary for creating a network share for remote installation, what option must be set in Windows NT or Windows 95 Explorer?

B. Show All Files

7. CORRECT ANSWER: B

Because the Windows NT Workstation source files contain .DLL, .VXD, and .SYS files not shown in Windows Explorer by default, Windows Explorer display options must be modified to Show All Files.

FURTHER REVIEW

CONFIGURE SERVER-BASED INSTALLATION FOR WIDE-SCALE DEPLOYMENT IN A GIVEN SITUATION

The quickest way to install Windows NT Workstation 4 on a large number of computers is to use a network distribution server as the source of the installation files (especially when you need to install Windows NT Workstation 4 on computers that have network connectivity but don't have CD-ROM drives).

This is the basic procedure for setting up a network distribution server:

1. Use the Windows NT Explorer, the Windows 95 Explorer, or the MS-DOS `XCOPY` command to copy the I386 folder from the Windows NT Workstation 4 CD to a folder on the network server. Make sure that you copy all the subfolders, too.
2. Share the folder on the network server with the appropriate permissions so those authorized users can access the files. (Alternatively, you could share the I386 folder on the Windows NT Workstation 4 CD, but your installations will be performed much more slowly. Therefore, that method should be used only if you must conserve hard disk space on your network server.)

Keep in mind that if you use Windows NT Explorer or Windows 95 Explorer to copy the files, the default options must be changed to allow for hidden files and system files with extensions such as .dll, .sys, and .vxd to be displayed and copied. Choose the View, Options command. Then, in the dialog box that appears, select Show All Files from the Hidden Files list.

If you are using WINNT32.EXE to upgrade an existing copy of Windows NT, you can use more than one network server to significantly speed up the rate at which the installation files are downloaded to your client computers. If you set up two network servers called SERVER1 and SERVER2 with installation shares called NTW, for example, the proper command line option to use both servers during the installation process is:

```
WINNT32 /B /S:\\SERVER1\NTW
➥/S:\\SERVER2\NTW
```

CHAPTER SUMMARY

After planning is complete, the next logical steps are installation and the initial configuration of Windows NT Workstation. Installation starts with making key decisions regarding how the operating system will be installed and if Windows NT Workstation will co-exist with other operating systems on the same machine. Also, you need to determine what, if any, upgrade paths exist and how the upgrade will be performed.

After the base operating system is installed, you must possess the skills to configure that workstation. The configuration topics discussed in this chapter will be used time and again throughout the lifecycle of the workstation.

Mastering the fundamentals of installation and configuration is an important part of working with Windows NT Workstation and nearly 15 percent of the certification exam.

At this point, this study guide has presented the key elements you need to address in planning and configuring a Windows NT Workstation, both in the real world and for successfully completing the certification exam. The next concept you need to understand and master is the management of resources (which includes users, files and folders, and printers).

CHAPTER 3

Managing Resources

After planning for and installing Windows NT Workstation, it is important to be able to manage resources on the workstation. The term *resource* is used to represent components of the operating system with which users interact, such as disks, files and folders, printers, or the user accounts themselves. Many of the decisions you made during the planning for and the installation of Windows NT Workstation (see Chapter 1, "Planning") will dictate how you manage the resources on a particular machine.

After completing this chapter, you should be able to successfully answer the questions presented by Microsoft on the certification exam about managing resources. Microsoft defines the exam objectives for managing resources as listed in the following section.

OBJECTIVES

Create and manage local user accounts and local group accounts to meet given requirements.

Set up and modify user profiles.

Set up shared folders and permissions.

Set up permissions on NTFS partitions, folders, and files.

Install and configure printers in a given environment.

PRACTICE QUESTIONS

CREATE AND MANAGE LOCAL USER ACCOUNTS AND LOCAL GROUP ACCOUNTS TO MEET GIVEN REQUIREMENTS

1. **This question is based on the following scenario. Review the scenario first, followed by the objectives and the proposed solution. Then evaluate the proposed solution by choosing the best answer.**

   Scenario:
   You have just finished installing Windows NT Workstation and have not created any new user accounts. The Administrator account and Guest account have not been modified in any way since the installation.

   Required Result:
   Tighten security on the workstation as much as possible.

   Optional Results:
   Minimize the chances of unauthorized users accessing the system through the Administrator account.

   Eliminate access to the workstation through the Guest account.

   Proposed Solution:
   Delete the default Guest account created during the setup of Windows NT Workstation. Rename the Administrator account WS@ADMINX:5 and set the password to a random string of characters. Through User Manager, access the Account Policy window. Enable an account lockout policy and set the password options in accordance with your company's security policy.

   Evaluation of Proposed Solution:
   Which of the following objectives does the proposed solution accomplish?

   A. Only the Required Result

   B. The Required Result and both Optional Results

   C. The Required Result and only one Optional Result

   D. Only one Optional Result

   E. Neither the Required Result nor the Optional Result

2. **This question is based on the following scenario. Review the scenario first, followed by the objectives and the proposed solution. Then evaluate the proposed solution by choosing the best answer.**

   Scenario:
   You are the network administrator at a small company. The network architecture consists of two mainframe computers, 15 UNIX servers, and approximately 150 NT Workstations in three offices located throughout the city. Each office's workstations are members of a local workgroup. Files are shared from the NT Workstations, and backups are done locally every night from a machine with a SCSI tape backup device installed. To provide support, you have identified three power users—one in each location—to provide limited technical support for that office. You have decided to

ask Ralph to provide technical support for one of the offices. His department consists of 20 NT Workstations.

Required Result:
Provide Ralph with the minimum system access required to accomplish the required tasks.

Optional Results:
Enable Ralph to create and manage local shares for his workgroup and perform backups for the shared folders.

Enable Ralph to change the system time/date on the local workstations in his workgroup.

Proposed Solution:
Place Ralph in the Power Users group.

Evaluation of Proposed Solution:
Which of the following objectives does the proposed solution accomplish?

A. Only the Required Result

B. The Required Result and both Optional Results

C. The Required Result and only one Optional Result

D. Only one of the Optional Results

E. Neither the Required Result nor the Optional Result

3. Which statement best describes the default built-in Windows NT Workstation local groups?

A. Administrators, Power Users, Guests, Replicator, Print Operator

B. Administrators, Users, Power Users, Guests, Replicator, Backup Operator

C. Administrators, Power Users, Guests, Replicator, Account Operator

D. Administrators, Power Users, Guests, Replicator, Users, Print Operator

E. Administrators, Power Users, Guests, Replicator, Users, Account Operator

4. Alice is taking a leave of absence for six months. What should you do with her account?

A. Delete it and then re-create it when she returns.

B. Rename the account so that no one else can use it.

C. Disable the account while she is gone.

D. Leave the account alone.

E. Set up an account lockout policy.

5. You have a default installation of Windows NT Workstation. You have not changed any of the audit or account policies. You suspect that someone is trying to hack into an account in the Administrators local group. What can you do to confirm this suspicion? (Select the best two options.)

A. Enable auditing on logon attempt failures.

B. Disable the Administrator account.

C. Delete the Administrator account.

D. Implement a lockout policy.

E. Rename the Administrator account.

6. When creating a new user account, what information must be supplied? (Select all that apply.)

A. Password

B. Maximum password length

C. User name

D. Description

E. Profile directory for the user

7. **Which of the following are functional tasks that by default can be completed by an account with membership in the Administrators group?**

   A. Create network shares

   B. Delete default Guest account

   C. Change workstation time

   D. Add users to the Users group

   E. Log on as a service

8. **Which of the following are functional tasks that by default can be completed by members of the Power Users group?**

   A. Create printer shares

   B. Delete user accounts in the Administrators group

   C. Take ownership of any file

   D. Change workstation time

   E. Add new accounts to the Power Users group

9. **Which of the following are true statements about local groups on Windows NT Workstation? (Select all that apply.)**

   A. Local groups can contain global groups.

   B. Local groups can be deleted and renamed.

   C. Local groups can contain users and resources.

   D. Local group SIDs are maintained in the Workstation SAM.

   E. Local groups can contain other local groups.

10. **Phil, a member of the Users group, complains that he cannot change the time on his Windows NT Workstation. What should you do to enable Phil to change the time but limit his ability, while maintaining the maximum amount of security possible on the workstation?**

    A. Tell him to reboot his machine. After his machine restarts, it will automatically resynchronize with other members in the workgroup.

    B. Add Phil to the Administrators group of the workstation.

    C. Remotely edit the Registry on his machine and set the time from your workstation.

    D. Use the User Manager program to assign Phil's account the right to change system time.

    E. Add Phil to the Power Users group on the workstation.

11. **What is the minimum/maximum password length imposed with a default installation of Windows NT?**

    A. 8 / 14 characters

    B. 0 / 8 characters

    C. 0 / 14 characters

D. 6 / 12 characters

E. 0 / 15 characters

12. **How do you set the Minimum Password Age property for user accounts?**

    A. In User Manager, select Account from the Policies menu.

    B. In User Manager, select Passwords from the User menu.

    C. In User Manager, select Rights from the Policy menu.

    D. In User Manager, select Permissions from the User menu.

    E. Double-click the user account in User Manager and click the Profiles button.

13. **You want to change the name of the local Administrators group to Admins. How should you proceed?**

    A. Delete the Administrators group and create a new group named "Admins."

    B. You cannot rename Windows NT's built-in groups.

    C. Double-click the group in User Manager and select New Name.

    D. Select the desired group, and then select Rename from the User menu.

    E. None of the above.

14. **This question is based on the following scenario. Review the scenario first, followed by the objectives and the proposed solution. Then evaluate the proposed solution by choosing the best answer.**

Scenario:
You create a local group named Web Managers. A week later, you decide you need to change the name to Web Masters.

Required Result:
Change the name of the Web Managers local group to Web Masters.

Optional Results:
Maintain the account membership in the renamed group.

Ensure the renamed group has the same permissions to access resources on the workstation.

Proposed Solution:
Create a new local group named Web Masters. Double-click on the new group in User Manager, click the Add... button and select the Web Managers group from the list.

Evaluation of Proposed Solution:
Which of the following objectives does the proposed solution accomplish?

A. Only the Required Result

B. The Required Result and both Optional Results

C. The Required Result and only one Optional Result

D. Both Optional Results

E. Neither the Required Result nor the Optional Result

15. **James needs to access your workstation remotely through a dial-up connection. When he connects, he is unable to log on. What is wrong?**

    A. He is probably using the wrong networking protocol. Have him change his protocol to TCP/IP and try again.

B. You need to enable dial-in permission through the User Manager.

C. Windows NT Workstation cannot support dial-in clients.

D. You must add his account to the Remote Users group built into Windows NT Workstation 4.

E. He is probably not using the correct password, or the Caps Lock might be enabled on his workstation.

16. Which statement best describes the functionality encompassed by User Manager?

A. Assign user profiles; assign user home directories; create, rename, disable, and delete user accounts; create, disable, and delete local groups

B. Create user profiles; assign user home directories; create, rename, disable, and delete user accounts; create local groups

C. Assign user profiles; assign user home directories; create, rename, disable, and delete user accounts; create, rename, and delete local groups

D. Create user profiles; assign user home directories; create, rename, disable, and delete user accounts; create, rename, and delete local groups

E. Assign user profiles; create and assign user home directories; create, rename, disable, and delete user accounts; create and delete local groups

17. Which of the following are true statements about accounts installed during a Windows NT Workstation installation? (Select all that apply.)

A. The Administrator account is enabled and can be renamed. The Guest account is enabled and can be renamed.

B. The Administrator account is enabled and can be renamed. The Guest account is disabled and cannot be renamed.

C. The Administrator account is enabled and can be renamed. The Guest account is disabled and can be renamed.

D. The Guest account is disabled and can be deleted. The Administrator account is enabled and can be deleted.

E. The Guest account is disabled and cannot be renamed. The Administrator account is enabled and can be renamed.

18. This question is based on the following scenario. Review the scenario first, followed by the objectives and the proposed solution. Then evaluate the proposed solution by choosing the best answer.

Scenario:

You have a Windows NT Workstation. No accounts or local groups have been created or modified. Jim needs a user account with the ability to create and manage shares and manage the audit policy of the workstation.

Required Result:
Enable Jim to create and manage shares.

Optional Results:
Enable Jim to manage the audit policy for the workstation.

Minimize Jim's access to operating system functions other than those required by the scenario.

Proposed Solution:
Place Jim's account in the Administrators built-in Windows NT Workstation local group.

Evaluation of Proposed Solution:
Which of the following objectives does the proposed solution accomplish?

A. Only the Required Result

B. The Required Result and both Optional Results

C. The Required Result and only one Optional Result

D. Both Optional Results

E. Neither the Required Result nor the Optional Result

19. Which of the following are true statements about local and global groups? (Select all that apply.)

A. Local groups and global groups can exist on a Windows NT domain controller.

B. Local and global groups can exist on a Windows NT Workstation.

C. Global groups, but not local groups, can exist on a Windows NT domain controller.

D. Local groups, but not global groups, can exist on a Windows NT Workstation.

E. Local groups can contain other local groups, but not global groups.

20. This question is based on the following scenario. Review the scenario first, followed by the objectives and the proposed solution. Then evaluate the proposed solution by choosing the best answer.

Scenario:
You have a Windows NT Workstation installation with no new user or local groups created. The sole disk partition is formatted with NTFS. You have to create a large number of user accounts that will require identical access permissions on the workstation.

Required Result:
Create the user accounts, ensuring each account is a member of the "Web Masters" local group and has a default password of "webworks."

Optional Results:
Create a home directory for each user.

Minimize the time required to create the accounts.

Proposed Solution:
Create a new local group with User Manager named "Web Masters." Assign the "Web Masters" group the proper permissions to the required resources.

Create a new user account named "template" with a password of "webworks" and add the account to the "Web Masters" group.

Copy the "template" account, completing the user name, description, and full name fields with the required information.

Click on the Groups button and add the new account to the "Web Masters" group.

Click OK to confirm the profile information and click OK again to create the new user account.

Repeat the previous three steps for all the required accounts.

Evaluation of Proposed Solution:
Which of the following objectives does the proposed solution accomplish?

A. Only the Required Result

B. The Required Result and both Optional Results

C. The Required Result and only one Optional Result

D. Only one Optional Result

E. Neither the Required Result nor the Optional Result

ANSWER KEY

1. E	6. C	11. C	16. E
2. D	7. A-C-D	12. A	17. C
3. B	8. A-D-E	13. B	18. C
4. C	9. A-D	14. E	19. A-D
5. A-D	10. D	15. B	20. D

ANSWERS & EXPLANATIONS

CREATE AND MANAGE LOCAL USER ACCOUNTS AND LOCAL GROUP ACCOUNTS TO MEET GIVEN REQUIREMENTS

1. **Proposed Solution:**
   Delete the default Guest account created during the setup of Windows NT Workstation. Rename the Administrator account to WS@ADMINX:5 and set the password to a random string of characters. Through User Manager, access the Account Policy window. Enable an account lockout policy and set the password options in accordance with your company's security policy.

   E. Neither the Required Result nor the Optional Result

1. CORRECT ANSWER: E

The best security possible for the workstation would be to ensure the Guest account is disabled (which it is by default) and change the Administrator account name and password from the default installation values. While the proposed solution attempts to achieve these measures, those measures will fail for numerous reasons.

The default Guest account cannot be deleted. Therefore, the Proposed Solution does not accomplish the first Optional Result. Although the Guest account cannot be deleted, it is disabled by default after Windows NT Workstation is installed. Access to the workstation cannot be gained through an account that is disabled; therefore, the first Optional Result is achieved by default, not by using the Proposed Solution.

User account names cannot contain any of the following characters:

“ / \ [ ] : ; | = , + * ? < >

Because the proposed name for renaming the Administrator account contains the @ symbol, it is an invalid Windows NT user name. Therefore, the first Optional Result is not achieved by the Proposed Solution.

Although enabling a lockout policy and setting the password options will help tighten security, the system is still vulnerable through the default named Administrator account. Therefore, the Required Result of tightening security as much as possible on the workstation was not achieved.

2. Proposed Solution:
Place Ralph in the Power Users group.

D. Only one of the Optional Results

2. CORRECT ANSWER: D

The primary determining factor for assigning Ralph's user account is the need to create and manage shares. Only two built-in groups have this right—Administrators and Power Users. Additionally, the problem cannot be solved by assigning rights to a local group or user, because the right to create and manage network shares is not assignable, it is only a built-in account right.

However, both the "Backup and Restore Files" right and the "Change System Time" right are assignable to any account. By default, the "Change System Time" right is assigned to Power Users and Administrators local groups. Therefore, including Ralph in the Power Users group will enable him to change the time, thereby accomplishing the second Optional Result.

By default, the "Backup Files and Directories" and "Restore Files and Directories" rights are assigned to the Administrators group and Backup Operators group only. To accomplish the first Optional Result, these rights would have had to have been assigned to the Power Users group or Ralph's account. Therefore, the first Optional Result is not accomplished by the Proposed Solution.

Because Ralph was not assigned the rights required to perform file/folder backup and file/folder restores, the selection of group memberships for Ralph in the Proposed Solution does not accomplish the Required Result.

Had the "Backup Files and Directories" and "Restore Files and Directories" rights been assigned to Ralph's account, the Required Result and both Optional Results would have been achieved.

3. Which statement best describes the default built-in Windows NT Workstation local groups?

B. Administrators, Users, Power Users, Guests, Replicator, Backup Operator

3. CORRECT ANSWER: B

Table 3.1 lists the Windows NT Workstation default built-in groups and their abilities.

TABLE 3.1 DEFAULT RIGHTS AND PRIVILEGES OF BUILT-IN GROUPS

Administrators	This group has complete administrative control over the computer. Members of this group can create users and assign them to any group, create and manage network shares, and gain access to any file or resource on the local machine.
Power Users	Similar to Administrators, but they cannot fully administer the computer. Can create accounts in any group but Administrators.
Users	Default group for all new user accounts. This group has enough rights and privileges to productively operate the machine on a daily basis.
Guests	This group has the least access to resources of all groups. The default Guest account is disabled during installation.
Backup Operators	Members of this group have enough access to all files and folders to enable data backups and restoration.
Replicator	When directory replication is configured, this group identifies the Windows NT service account used to perform replication.

The Print Operator and Account Operator are default built-in groups installed with Windows NT Server.

4. Alice is taking a leave of absence for six months. What should you do with her account?

C. Disable the account while she is gone.

4. CORRECT ANSWER: C

When a user will be gone temporarily, it is wise to disable the account to eliminate the possibility of unauthorized access through the inactive account. When the user returns, it is a simple matter of re-enabling the account.

When a user account is created in Windows NT, it is given a unique identification called a security identifier (SID). This SID is designed to be unique in all of space and time.

It is not usually a good idea to delete a user account. When you delete an account, you delete the SID, and the deleted account can never be retrieved. And after deleting an account, creating a new account with the same name will not restore the rights, privileges, or local group memberships associated with the original account.

Because the SID is eliminated when an account is deleted, it is generally better to disable an account using the User Manager than to delete the account. If you are certain that another user will not require the same permissions, rights, and local group associations of the account, you can delete the account.

5. You have a default installation of Windows NT Workstation. You have not changed any of the audit or account policies. You suspect that someone is trying to hack into an account in the Administrators local group. What can you do to confirm this suspicion? (Select the best two options.)

A. Enable auditing on logon attempt failures.

D. Implement a lockout policy.

5. CORRECT ANSWER: A-D

To determine if a suspected attack is taking place, you should begin auditing failed logon attempts. A high number of failed logon attempts with one account could be an indication that someone is trying to use a password-cracking program to gain access to the system.

To thwart these types of attacks, a lockout policy should be created and enforced. This will lock an account out for a specified or indefinite (until the administrator re-enables the account) amount of time. During the lockout period, even if the correct password is supplied, access will be denied. It is important to also understand that the default Administrator account created during the Windows NT installation is not subject to lockout, even when that account is renamed.

6. When creating a new user account, what information must be supplied? (Select all that apply.)

C. User name

6. CORRECT ANSWER: C

The only required information when creating a new user is a valid Windows NT user name. All of the other user attributes specified in the question are optional.

7. Which of the following are functional tasks that by default can be completed by an account with membership in the Administrators group?

A. Create network shares

C. Change workstation time

D. Add users to the Users group

7. CORRECT ANSWER: A-C-D

By default, members of the Administrators group can create network shares, change workstation time, and add users to the Users group. Of these three rights, only the right to change workstation time can also be assigned to other local groups or individual accounts and taken away from the Administrators group.

8. Which of the following are functional tasks that by default can be completed by members of the Power Users group?

A. Create printer shares

D. Change workstation time

E. Add new accounts to the Power Users group

8. CORRECT ANSWER: A-D-E

By default, members of the Power Users local group have the ability to create printer shares, change workstation time, and add new accounts to the Power Users group. Of these three rights, only change workstation time can also be assigned to other local groups or individual accounts and taken away from the Administrators group.

9. Which of the following are true statements about local groups? (Select all that apply.)

A. Local groups can contain global groups.

D. Local group SIDs are maintained in the Workstation SAM.

9. CORRECT ANSWER: A-D

Local group SIDs (Security Account Identifiers) are maintained in the Workstation SAM (Security Access Manager) database. Global groups and local groups on a domain controller have their SIDs stored in the domain SAM. See the section titled "Understanding Windows NT Security" in the "Setup Shared Folders and Permissions" section for further information on how storing SIDs locally affects the sharing of resources and security in Windows NT Workstation.

Local groups can only contain global groups defined on a Windows NT domain controller and user accounts. Local groups cannot contain other local groups or resources such as printers or shared folders.

10. Phil, a member of the Users group, complains that he cannot change the time on his Windows NT Workstation. What should you do to enable Phil to change the time but limit his ability, while maintaining the maximum amount of security possible on the workstation?

D. Use the User Manager program to assign Phil's account the right to change system time.

10. CORRECT ANSWER: D

The most secure way to enable Phil to change the time on his workstation would be to assign the right "Change Workstation Time" to Phil's account.

Phil could be added to the Administrators or Power Users local group; however, this would be a security risk, as Phil would then have the ability to perform administrative tasks on the workstation that he might not be qualified or trusted to do.

11. What is the minimum/maximum password length imposed with a default installation of Windows NT?

C. 0 / 14 characters

11. CORRECT ANSWER: C

By default, Windows NT does not require a minimum password length for account passwords. This option can be changed through the Policy, Account menu in User Manager.

The resulting dialog box enables you to specify a minimum password length of up to 14 characters, which is the maximum length of a Windows NT password. If this option is enabled, the length is set to 6 characters by default. This is a global setting, affecting all users with accounts on the workstation. None of the options available from the Account Policy window can be set on a per-user basis.

12. How do you set the Minimum Password Age property for user accounts?

A. In User Manager, select Account from the Policies menu.

12. CORRECT ANSWER: A

The minimum password age property is not set by default. Selecting Account from the Policies menu in User Manager allows you to set this property.

13. You want to change the name of the local Administrators group to Admins. How should you proceed?

B. You cannot rename Windows NT's built-in groups.

13. CORRECT ANSWER: B

Built-in Windows NT Workstation groups cannot be deleted or renamed.

14. Proposed Solution: Create a new local group named Web Masters. Double-click on the new group in User Manager, click the Add... button and select the Web Managers group from the list.

E. Neither the Required Result nor the Optional Result

14. CORRECT ANSWER: E

Local groups cannot contain other local groups. Local groups can only contain users and global groups. Global groups are created on Windows NT domain controllers. (See the "Further Review" section later in this chapter for additional information on global groups.)

To rename a local group, another local must be created with the desired name. You must then manually assign the permissions to resources the initial local group had. All the members of the original local group must be added as members of the new renamed local group. Finally, the old group can be deleted.

15. James needs to access your workstation remotely through a dial-up connection. When he connects, he is unable to log on. What is wrong?

B. You need to enable dial-in permission through the User Manager.

15. CORRECT ANSWER: B

A user account must have dial-in permission enabled before attempting a dial-up connection to a Windows NT Workstation. By default, user accounts are not granted dial-in permission.

In addition to enabling dial-in permission, you must ensure the user is using the same networking protocols that the dial-in server has configured.

Although the major reason for user login failure is typing an incorrect password or inadvertently setting the caps lock function of the keyboard, the first area to look when a dial-in user cannot access the dial-up server is account permissions.

16. Which statement best describes the functionality encompassed by User Manager?

E. Assign user profiles; create and assign user home directories; create, rename, disable, and delete user accounts; create and delete local groups

16. CORRECT ANSWER: E

User Manager is used to create and assign user home directories and assign user profiles (through the Profile button in the Account Properties tab); to create, rename, disable, and delete user accounts; and to create and delete local groups.

User profiles are created and managed with the System Control Panel applet.

Local groups cannot be disabled or renamed.

17. Which of the following are true statements about accounts installed during a Windows NT Workstation installation? (Select all that apply.)

C. The Administrator account is enabled and can be renamed. The Guest account is disabled and can be renamed.

17. CORRECT ANSWER: C

The Administrator account can be renamed and is enabled by default. The account cannot be deleted or disabled. The Guest account is disabled and can be renamed by default, but not deleted.

18. Proposed Solution: Place Jim's account in the Administrators built-in Windows NT Workstation local group.

C. The Required Result and only one Optional Result

18. CORRECT ANSWER: C

By placing Jim in the local Administrators group, you enable him to manage the audit policy and create and manage network shares. Therefore the Proposed Solution achieves the Required Result and the first Optional Result.

However, placing Jim in the Administrators group also enables him to create other administrative accounts, which could open a security hole on the workstation. Additionally, Jim now has the ability to start and stop services, format hard disks, and completely administer the workstation. One mistake, from lack of knowledge or other reasons, could cause the system to become unstable or crash. Jim could have been added to the Power Users group with the right to "Manage auditing and security log" and still meet the requirements set forth in the scenario. Therefore, the Proposed Solution does not meet the second Optional Result.

19. Which of the following are true statements about local and global groups? (Select all that apply.)

A. Local groups and global groups can exist on a Windows NT domain controller.

D. Local groups, but not global groups, can exist on a Windows NT Workstation.

19. CORRECT ANSWER: A-D

Both local and global groups can be defined on a Windows NT domain controller. However, local groups defined on a domain controller are available on all domain controllers. Only local groups can be defined and exist on a Windows NT Workstation; however, those local groups can contain global groups defined on a domain controller. Local groups can never contain other local groups.

20. Proposed Solution:

- **Create a new local group with User Manager named "Web Masters." Assign the "Web Masters" group the proper permissions to the required resources.**
- **Create a new user account named "template" with a password of "webworks" and add the account to the "Web Masters" group.**
- **Copy the "template" account, completing the user name, description, and full name fields with the required information.**
- **Click on the Groups button and add the new account to the "Web Masters" group.**
- **Click OK to confirm the profile information and click OK again to create the new user account.**
- **Repeat the previous three steps for all the required accounts.**

D. Only one Optional Result

20. CORRECT ANSWER: D

If you specify the home directory for the template user with the %USERNAME% environment variable, every account created with the template account will have a home directory created in the location specified in the profile section of the account. The %USERNAME% variable will create a home directory in the location specified, substituting the account name supplied for the %USERNAME% variable. This variable can also be used to specify the directory in which profiles should be stored. Therefore, the Proposed Solution realizes the first Optional Result.

Placing the template account in the "Web Masters" local group could have saved a great deal of time. When a template account is copied, all group memberships and rights assigned to the account are also copied. Therefore, the Proposed Solution does not accomplish the second Optional Result.

When a template account is copied, the Password and Confirm Password fields are not copied. Because the required password of "webworks" was not specified and confirmed for each account, the Proposed Solution does not completely accomplish the Required Result.

FURTHER REVIEW

CREATE AND MANAGE LOCAL USER ACCOUNTS AND LOCAL GROUP ACCOUNTS TO MEET GIVEN REQUIREMENTS

Every user who uses Windows NT Workstation must have a username and password to gain access to the workstation. Windows NT stores this information in a user account. Other items, such as a description of the user, the user's home directory and profile path, and password options are also stored with the account. User and group accounts are stored on the local machine in the Security Accounts Manager database, also known as the SAM database.

In addition to user accounts, Windows NT Workstation provides local groups to ease administrative burdens. By placing individual user accounts that require similar access to resources into local groups, the administrator can apply the required permissions and rights to the local group. All members of that local group automatically inherit those rights and privileges.

Accounts and groups are created and managed through the Windows NT Workstation utility called User Manager. You can launch User Manager from the Administrative Tools (Common) program group or by executing the musrmgr.exe from the Run dialog box.

Creating User Accounts

To create user accounts, you must be logged on with an account that has the appropriate rights to create the account and assign it to the desired local group. The only two built-in Windows NT groups that can create user accounts are the Administrators group and the Power Users group. Only a member of the Administrators group can create and add other accounts to the Administrators group; members of the Power Users group can assign accounts to any group except Administrators.

When you create a new user, Windows NT requires you to complete only the Username field. All other information is optional, but it is recommended that you fill it in.

The Full Name and Description fields are used for informational purposes. If you choose to preassign passwords to users when creating their accounts, you specify those passwords in the Password field as well as the Confirm Password field. The password in Windows NT can be up to 14 characters long. If you have specified an account policy that requires a minimum password length, you must enter a password that is at least that long when creating the user account. (Account policies are covered later in this chapter.)

Assigning Local Group Memberships

You can assign membership in any local group by clicking the Groups button from the New User screen. The Group Memberships window appears.

To add a user to a group, select the appropriate group from the Not Member Of box and click the Add button. This user will become a member of that group and will automatically inherit all the rights and permissions assigned to that group. To remove a user from a group, select the group from which you want to remove the user in the Member Of list and click Remove.

It is important to note that group membership changes will not take effect until the user logs out and logs back on to the workstation. As an example, if you add a user to a group to grant access to a file, those permissions will not take effect until the user logs off and logs back on.

Configuring a User Environment Profile

You can access the User Environment Profile settings by clicking the Profile button from the New User window. There are three items you can configure from the User Profile Environment window within User Manager:

- *User Profile Path.* This setting is used to specify a path for a user profile to be available centrally on a server or to assign a mandatory user profile for this user. To use a roaming or mandatory user profile, you must create a share on a server and then specify the path to that share in the user's profile, where the path follows the syntax of the standard Universal Naming Convention, or UNC, which follows:

  `\\servername\sharename\profilename`

- *Logon Script Name.* This setting is used to specify a logon script to be used (if desired). If a logon script is specified, it will be launched when the user logs on to the Windows NT Workstation. Logon scripts can have the extension .cmd, .bat, or .exe.
- *Home Directory.* To specify a home directory for a user's personal use, specify it here. You can configure two types of home directories: local or remote. A remote home directory will always be available to the user, regardless of where he or she logs on. If you choose to use a remote home directory, you must select a drive letter and specify the path to that remote share in a UNC format such as this:

  `\\servername\sharename\JillB`

  A local home directory will always be local to the machine from which the user logs on. Therefore, if users use multiple machines, they might not always be able to access information stored in their home directories on other machines. If you choose to use local home directories, specify the full path in this setting like this:

  `C:\users\JillB`

Granting Dial-In Permission

The final set of parameters you can set for an individual user account is dial-in permissions. By default, Windows NT does not grant the right to dial in to the network remotely. These are the call-back options for dial-in access:

- *No Call Back.* This setting disables call-back for a particular user account. If this is set, the user initiates the phone call with the RAS server, and the user is responsible for the phone charges.

- *Set by Caller.* This enables the remote user to specify the number the server can use to call the user back. This is typically used so that the server is responsible for the phone charges instead of the user.
- *Preset To.* When set, this specifies a number at which the server can call the user back when the user initiates a dial-in session. This tends to be used for security so that a user is called back at a predefined number only.

Modifying User Accounts

Modifying a user account is very similar to creating a new user. To modify an existing account, select the account from the top pane of the User Manager window and select Properties from the User menu, or simply double-click the user account. This brings up the User Properties window.

The only difference between this window and the window you saw when creating a new user is that all user information for this account already appears in the fields. You can set any of the values as you did when creating a new user, except the username. In addition, the Groups, Profile, and Dial-In buttons perform the same tasks as they do when you're creating a new user. The user name can be changed by selecting the account and using the Rename… command from the User menu.

When a user account is created in Windows NT, it is given a unique identification called a security identifier (SID). This SID is designed to be unique in all of space and time. Because the SID is not related to the account name, renaming the user account does not make a difference to Windows NT. When an account is renamed, all the rights, permissions, and group associations for that account remain and are transferred to the new user name.

Setting Account Policies

Account policies are global: They affect all accounts equally, regardless of local group membership. Some account policies, such as Maximum Password Age, can be overridden by your selection of password options (such as Password Never Expires, which you learned about earlier). Account policies address such issues as these: How often do you want users to have to change their passwords? What do you want to happen if a user makes multiple bad logon attempts? How many passwords do you want "remembered?" You configure the Account Policy within User Manager by choosing Account from the Policies menu.

The following is a list of the password restrictions available:

- *Maximum Password Age.* This option enables you to specify how long a user's password is valid. The default is that passwords expire in 42 days. Note that this policy will be overridden if you select Password Never Expires for a user account.
- *Minimum Password Age.* This specifies how long a user must keep a particular password before the password can be changed. Setting this option to a reasonable amount of time will prevent users from reusing passwords, thereby increasing your security.
- *Minimum Password Length.* By default, Windows NT allows blank passwords. You can set a minimum password length of up to

14 characters, which is the maximum password length allowed under Windows NT.

- *Password Uniqueness.* If you want to force users to use different passwords each time they change their passwords, you can set a value for password uniqueness. If you set the password uniqueness value to remember two passwords, when a user is prompted to change her password, she cannot use the same password again until she changes the password for the third time.

The following is a list of the account lockout options:

- *Lockout After Bad Logon Attempts.* Setting a value for this option prevents the account from being used after the specified number of unsuccessful login attempts. After an account is locked out, only an administrator can restore the account if there is no lockout duration specified. When this option is enabled, Windows NT sets this option to five by default.
- *Reset Counter After.* This value specifies when to reset the counter for bad logon attempts. The default value is 30 minutes. That means if Account Lockout is set to five and a user tries to log on unsuccessfully four times and then tries again in 45 minutes, the counter will have been reset, and the account will not be locked out.
- *Lockout Duration.* This value specifies how long the account should remain locked out if the lockout counter is exceeded. It is generally more secure to set Lockout Duration to Forever so that the administrator must unlock the account. That way the administrator is warned of the activity on that account.
- *User Must Log On in Order to Change Password.* This setting requires a user to log on successfully before changing the password. If a user's password expires, the user cannot log on until the administrator changes the password for the user.

Account Rights

Account rights are set from the User Rights Policy window. You access the User Rights Policy window by selecting User Rights from the Policies menu.

Select the appropriate right from the drop-down list, and then select the individual user account or group to which this right should be applied.

Template Accounts

You can create a template account for any other groups of user accounts that require the same description, groups, home directories, logon scripts, user profile paths, or dial-in access.

In addition, you can also assign home and profile directories based on the Username field. In the User Environment Profiles window's fields, you can use the %USERNAME% variable to facilitate the creation of the home and profile directories. When the new account is created from the template, User Manager automatically substitutes the user name you entered for the %USERNAME% variable. After the Template account has been created, you can use that account to create the user accounts for the sales representatives, for example.

Creating Group Accounts

To create a local group account on Windows NT Workstation, select the New Local Group command from the User menu. Fill in the Group Name text box and the Description text box. Then click the Add button to select local user accounts to populate the group. When all desired members have been added, click the OK button to create the group. The lower pane of the User Manager window will be updated to reflect the change.

Alternatively, you can Ctrl+click to select all the desired users, and then select New Local Group from the User menu to add any number of users to a new group immediately.

Renaming Local Group Accounts

You cannot rename a local group account. If you decide that you want to change the name of a group, you must create a new group with the new name. You then give the new group the appropriate rights to resources and add the desired users to the new group.

Deleting Local Group Accounts

If you choose to delete a group account, that group will be gone forever. In the same way that an individual user account is given a SID when it is created, so is a group account. If you delete the group accidentally, you must re-create the group and reassign all the permissions for the group. After it is re-created, the new group will have a different unique SID.

Deleting a group does not delete the individual user accounts within the group, just the group itself. You cannot delete any of the six built-in Windows NT Workstation local groups.

PRACTICE QUESTIONS

SET UP AND MODIFY USER PROFILES

1. **Which of the following statements about a mandatory user profile are true? (Select all that apply.)**

    A. Users with mandatory profiles can edit their desktops while logged on.

    B. A mandatory profile must be stored on the server.

    C. User changes to a mandatory profile are saved when the user exits.

    D. If a user's mandatory profile is not available at the time of log on, the user cannot log on.

    E. User changes to a mandatory profile are discarded when the user logs off.

2. **This question is based on the following scenario. Review the scenario first, followed by the objectives and the proposed solution. Then evaluate the proposed solution by choosing the best answer.**

    Scenario:
    You are the LAN administrator with 10 Windows NT Workstations on a local LAN with roaming mandatory profiles enabled. The profiles are stored in subfolders corresponding to the users' user names within a local directory on your workstation that is shared for all users to access. One of your users calls and requests some changes to the work environment.

    Required Result:
    Make the user changes in the most efficient manner.

    Optional Results:
    Add a shortcut within Network Neighborhood to the folder "logfiles" on the server named "WWW."

    Add a shortcut to "WinZip" on the user's desktop.

    Proposed Solution:
    Change the extension from .man to .dat on the NTUser file in the user's profile directory. Instruct the user how to make the changes. You tell her to create a shortcut to the "logfiles" folder and copy the shortcut to the NetHood folder. You also show her how to create the shortcut on the desktop. You ask her to notify you when the changes are complete. When the changes are complete, change the extension back to .man on the NTUser.dat file in the user's profile directory.

    Evaluation of Proposed Solution:
    Which of the following objectives does the proposed solution accomplish?

    A. Only the Required Result

    B. The Required Result and both Optional Results

    C. The Required Result and only one Optional Result

    D. Both Optional Results

    E. Neither the Required Result nor the Optional Result

3. **What utility should you use to assign a roaming profile for a user? (Select all that apply.)**

A. User Manager

B. System applet in Control Panel

C. Account Manager

D. Server Manager

E. Disk Manager

4. **This question is based on the following scenario. Review the scenario first, followed by the objectives and the proposed solution. Then evaluate the proposed solution by choosing the best answer.**

Scenario:
You have 20 Windows NT Workstations on a local area network. All workstations are members of the local domain. There are two Windows NT Servers; one is a primary domain controller, and the other is a member server. You currently have roaming profiles enabled for all accounts.

Required Result:
Eliminate the ability for users to change the desktop appearance to enforce a consistent look and feel to every desktop.

Optional Results:
Add a shortcut for the users to access a folder on the new file server.

Add a shortcut for the users to access a new network printer.

Proposed Solution:
Create a temporary user account and set up the desired standardized work environment.

Select the new account through the User Profiles tab in the System applet in Control Panel and choose Copy To.

In the Copy Profile To box, enter the UNC to the location where the mandatory profile will be maintained.

Select Change from the Choose User dialog box, and then select all the users or groups that will be assigned this profile.

Choose OK and Exit.

In User Manager, modify the profile path for each account to point to the new mandatory profile path.

Create a shortcut to the folder on the new file server. Place this shortcut into the NetHood subfolder in the newly created mandatory profile folder.

Create a shortcut for the new network printer and place the shortcut into the NetHood subfolder in the newly created mandatory profile folder.

Evaluation of Proposed Solution:
Which of the following objectives does the proposed solution accomplish?

A. Only the Required Result

B. The Required Result and both Optional Results

C. The Required Result and only one Optional Result

D. Only one Optional Result

E. Neither the Required Result nor the Optional Result

5. **As an administrator, you browse into C:\Winnt\system32\profiles\LutherS\ to find the network shortcuts mapped for the user LutherS, but you cannot find the NetHood folder. What is wrong?**

A. By default, the NetHood folder is hidden.

B. The NetHood folder does not exist if the user does not have any shortcuts mapped.

C. The NetHood folder is located in the Desktop folder.

D. The NetHood folder is located in the Personal folder.

E. The NetHood folder is workstation-specific and resides in the All Users profile folder.

6. You create a default installation of Windows NT in the C:\WINNT folder. What is the complete path to the Recent folder on the Start menu for a user with the user name of RobertP? (RobertP has been assigned a local profile.)

A. C:\Winnt\System32\Profiles\RobertP\Desktop\Recent

B. C:\Winnt\System32\Profiles\RobertP\Recent

C. C:\Winnt\System\Profiles\RobertP\Recent

D. C:\Winnt\System32\Profiles\RobertP\Applications\Recent

E. C:\Winnt\Profiles\RobertP\Recent

7. When a user first logs on to a Windows NT Workstation, what folders are copied to the user's profile directory?

A. Default User

B. All Users

C. Default Profiles

D. Common User Profiles

E. Administrator

8. You need to add a shortcut for Microsoft Word to all users' desktops. Which of the following tasks do you need to complete in order to ensure that all users who log on to the workstation can access the shortcut? (Select all that apply.)

A. Log in with an account in the Administrators group.

B. Add the shortcut to the Default User folder in the Profiles folder.

C. Add the shortcut to the All Users folder in the Profiles folder.

D. Copy the shortcut to the Desktop folder of every user who maintains a local profile on the workstation.

E. Add a shortcut to the Common folder.

9. This question is based on the following scenario. Review the scenario first, followed by the objectives and the proposed solution. Then evaluate the proposed solution by choosing the best answer.

Scenario:

You have 20 Windows NT Workstations on a local area network. All workstations are members of the local domain. There are two Windows NT Servers; one is a primary domain controller, and the other is a member server.

Required Result:

Enable users to customize their desktops and save the settings.

Optional Results:

Ensure the profile is available from anywhere on the network.

Ensure every user has icons for Microsoft Word 97 and Microsoft Excel 97 on the Start menu.

Proposed Solution:
Create a "Profiles" directory on one of the NT Servers in the domain. Change the profile path (using User Manager) to point to the new profiles directory. Append the user name to the end of each path. Add shortcuts (pointing to a valid executable) for Microsoft Word and Microsoft Excel to the Default Users folder on *each* workstation.

Evaluation of Proposed Solution:
Which of the following objectives does the proposed solution accomplish?

A. Only the Required Result

B. The Required Result and both Optional Results

C. The Required Result and only one Optional Result

D. Both Optional Results

E. Neither the Required Result nor the Optional Result

10. Which of the following statements about a roaming profile are true?

A. Roaming profiles are stored only on the local workstation.

B. Users cannot change roaming profiles.

C. The roaming profile is compared to the locally stored profile for the user when the user logs on. If the locally stored profile is newer, it will be used.

D. Both the roaming profile and the locally cached profile are updated when a user logs off.

E. Roaming profiles must be stored on a domain controller.

ANSWER KEY

1. A-E
2. D
3. B
4. D
5. A
6. E
7. A-B
8. A-C
9. C
10. D

ANSWERS & EXPLANATIONS

SET UP AND MODIFY USER PROFILES

1. Which of the following statements about a mandatory user profile are true? (Select all that apply.)

A. Users with mandatory profiles can edit their desktops while logged on.

E. User changes to a mandatory profile are discarded when the user logs off.

1. CORRECT ANSWER: A-E

Mandatory profiles do not prevent the user from editing his desktop while logged on; however, any changes made to the desktop configuration are discarded when the user logs off. If a mandatory profile is server-based, the user will not be able to log on if the server is unavailable. Users with local mandatory profiles will be logged on regardless of server status.

2. Proposed Solution:
Change the extension from .man to .dat on the NTUser file in the user's profile directory. Instruct the user how to make the changes. You tell her to create a shortcut to the "logfiles" folder and copy the shortcut to the NetHood folder. You also show her how to create the shortcut on the desktop. You ask her to notify you when the changes are complete. When the changes are complete, change the extension back to .man on the NTUser.dat file in the user's profile directory.

D. Both Optional Results

2. CORRECT ANSWER: D

Enabling the user to change the profile is not the most efficient way to handle this request. It would be simpler to make the edits on your workstation without going through the instructions with the user. It is amazing that, as the network administrator, you have enough time to walk the user through the required steps. Therefore, the Proposed Solution does not accomplish the Required Result.

The steps the user was walked through are correct to achieve both Optional Results.

3. What utility should you use to assign a roaming profile for a user? (Select all that apply.)

B. System applet in Control Panel

3. CORRECT ANSWER: B

The locations of user profiles are specified through User Manager. The type of profile, however, is managed through the Profile tab in the System Control Panel applet.

4. **Proposed Solution:**
   - **Create a temporary user account and set up the desired standardized work environment.**
   - **Select the new account through the User Profiles tab in the System applet in Control Panel and choose Copy To.**
   - **In the Copy Profile To box, enter the UNC to the location where the mandatory profile will be maintained.**
   - **Select Change from the Choose User dialog box, and then select all the users or groups that will be assigned this profile.**
   - **Choose OK and Exit.**
   - **In User Manager, modify the profile path for each account to point to the new mandatory profile path.**
   - **Create a shortcut to the folder on the new file server. Place this shortcut into the NetHood subfolder in the newly created mandatory profile folder.**
   - **Create a shortcut for the new network printer and place the shortcut into the NetHood subfolder in the newly created mandatory profile folder.**

   D. Only one Optional Result

4. CORRECT ANSWER: D

To "flag" a profile as mandatory to Windows NT, the NTUser.dat file residing in the user's profile directory must be renamed NTUser.man. The Proposed Solution never includes this step; therefore, the profiles will not be mandatory. The Required Result is not met.

Printer shortcuts must be placed in the hidden folder "PrintHood" in the user's profile directory. The Proposed Solution does not accomplish the second Optional Result.

The "NetHood" folder contains user-specific network shortcuts that appear in Network Neighborhood. The Proposed Solution does place the shortcut in the "NetHood" folder, accomplishing the first Optional Result.

5. **As an administrator, you browse into C:\Winnt\system32\profiles\LutherS\ to find the network shortcuts mapped for the user LutherS, but you cannot find the NetHood folder. What is wrong?**

   A. By default, the NetHood folder is hidden.

5. CORRECT ANSWER: A

By default, the NetHood, PrintHood, Recent, and Templates folders are hidden in Windows Explorer. The Explorer option View All Files must be enabled for these folders to appear in Explorer.

6. You create a default installation of Windows NT in the C:\WINNT folder. What is the complete path to the "Recent" folder on the Start menu for a user with the user name of RobertP? (RobertP has been assigned a local profile.)

E. C:\Winnt\Profiles\RobertP\Recent

6. CORRECT ANSWER: E

The Recent folder appears in the top level folder of the user's profile and is hidden by default.

7. When a user first logs on to a Windows NT Workstation, what folders are copied to the user's profile directory?

A. Default User

B. All Users

7. CORRECT ANSWER: A-B

When a user logs on to a Windows NT Workstation for the first time without a predefined profile assigned through User Manager, a profile is created from a combination of the Default User and All Users folders in the C:\Winnt\Profiles folder.

8. You need to add a shortcut for Microsoft Word to all users' desktops. Which of the following tasks do you need to complete in order to ensure that all users who log on to the workstation can access the shortcut? (Select all that apply.)

A. Log in with an account in the Administrators group.

C. Add the shortcut to the All Users folder in the Profiles folder.

8. CORRECT ANSWER: A-C

Only members of the Administrators group can add contents to the All Users profile folder. The shortcut could be added to every profile on the workstation, but the contents of the All Users folder are included in the profile of every user that logs on to the workstation, regardless of the type of profile—local or roaming.

9. Proposed Solution:
Create a "Profiles" directory on one of the NT Servers in the domain. Change the profile path (using User Manager) to point to the new profiles directory. Append the user name to the end of each path. Add shortcuts (pointing to a valid executable) for Microsoft Word and Microsoft Excel to the Default Users folder on each workstation.

C. The Required Result and only one Optional Result

9. CORRECT ANSWER: C

By default, Windows NT profiles are not mandatory. By not changing the default extension of the NTUser file in the user's profile directory from .dat to .man, the profiles will remain non-mandatory. Therefore, the Proposed Solution accomplished the Required Result.

Changing the user's profile path to that of a network share through User Manager will ensure the profile becomes a roaming profile. Therefore, the first Optional Result is accomplished with the Proposed Solution.

For the two icons to appear on the users' desktops, they should be placed in the All Users folder, not the Default User folder. The second Optional Result is not achieved.

10. Which of the following statements about a roaming profile are true?

D. Both the roaming profile and the locally cached profile are updated when a user logs off.

10. CORRECT ANSWER: D

When a roaming profile is enabled, a copy is stored on the server as well as the local workstation. In the event that the server containing the user's profile is not available at the next logon, Windows NT will automatically use the cached information until the server containing the profile is available.

In the event that the local profile is newer than that on the server, the user will be prompted to choose which profile should be used.

Roaming profiles must be stored in a directory that is accessible from across the network. This location does not have to reside on a server; it may be located on a workstation with the proper shares.

FURTHER REVIEW

SET UP AND MODIFY USER PROFILES

User profiles are automatically created when a user logs on to a computer running Windows NT. A user profile maintains the settings that contribute to a user's working environment. This includes such settings as wallpaper, desktop shortcuts, and network connections. The user's profile contains all user-definable settings for the user's environment.

User profiles in Windows NT are completely different from and incompatible with user profiles in Windows 95 or Windows NT 3.51. On Windows NT Workstation, a user profile is automatically created for every user who logs on to the workstation. Windows 95, on the other hand, enables you to select whether to use user profiles. If you have users that will use both Windows 95 and Windows NT 4, you need to maintain multiple profiles for those users.

User profiles are primarily used for convenience, but they can be used by an administrator to establish control over the user's environment. (For more information, see the section entitled "Mandatory User Profiles.") A user profile can be stored either locally on the user's Windows NT Workstation or centrally on a server so it's accessible from any location in the network. If user profiles are stored on the server and set as roaming user profiles, they can be accessed from any machine on the network running Windows NT 4.

User Profile Settings

A user profile stores information associated with a user's work environment. Table 3.2 identifies these items.

TABLE 3.2 ITEMS INCLUDED IN A USER'S PROFILE

Item	*Description*
Accessories	Any user-specific settings that affect the user's environment, such as Calculator, Clock, Notepad, and Paint.
Control Panel	Any user-defined settings defined within the Control Panel, such as mouse pointers, modem dialing properties, and mail and fax properties.
Printers	Any printer connections made within Windows NT Workstation to network printers.
Start menu	Any personal program groups and their properties, such as the working directory.
Taskbar	Any taskbar settings, such as Always on Top or Auto Hide.
Windows NT Explorer	Any user-specific settings for Windows NT Explorer, such as whether to view the toolbar, whether to show large icons, and how to arrange icons.

User Profile Directory Structure

Below the user's directory within the C:\Winnt\Profiles folder (the default location for user profiles) is a structure of settings relating to the user's profile. Table 3.3 describes that structure.

TABLE 3.3 FOLDERS WITHIN A USER'S PROFILE DIRECTORY

Folder	*Description*
Application Data	Application-specific data. The contents of this folder are determined by application vendors.
Desktop	Desktop items, such as shortcuts, folders, documents, or files.
Favorites	A list of favorite locations, such as Internet URLs for different Web sites.
NetHood	Shortcuts to Network Neighborhood items.
Personal	Shortcuts to program items.
PrintHood	Shortcuts to printers.
Recent	Shortcuts to recently used items.
SendTo	Shortcuts to items in the SendTo context menu. You can add items to this folder, such as Notepad or a printer.
Start menu	Shortcuts to the program items found in the Start menu.
Templates	Shortcuts to any template items.

By default, the NetHood, PrintHood, Recent, and Templates folders are not visible in NT Explorer.

All Users

The All Users public folder is used for Start menu shortcuts that apply to all users of a local workstation. These settings are not added to the user's profile, but they are used along with it to define the user's working environment. The common program groups—common to all users who log on to the Windows NT Workstation—are stored under the All Users directory. Only members of the Administrators group can add items to the All Users folder for common access.

Default User

The Default User folder contains the settings that new users inherit the first time they log on to the workstation. If no pre-configured profile exists for a user when he logs on, he inherits the settings from the Default User folder. Those settings are copied into the user's new profile directory. Any changes that the user makes while logged on are saved into his user profile, which means the Default User folder remains unchanged.

User Profile Types

Setting user profiles can help you to configure a user's environment. User profiles enable you to restrict users and enable users to retain their own settings when they move from one machine to another throughout your network. There are three types of user profiles: mandatory, local, and roaming.

Mandatory User Profiles

Use mandatory user profiles when you need a higher level of control than that of the standard user profile environment. Although the user can change items associated with the profile while logged on (such as screen colors or desktop icons), these changes are not saved when the user logs off. Mandatory user profiles are configured through the Control Panel's System icon. To make a profile mandatory, the file extension on the NTUser.dat file within the user's profile folder must be changed to .man.

Local User Profiles

The term *local user profile* refers to a user's profile that is created and stored on the Windows NT Workstation machine that she is logging on to. Local user profiles are the default in Windows NT Workstation, and one is created the first time that a user logs on to a Windows NT Workstation.

Local profiles are most effective if a user uses only one machine and never needs the settings while sitting at another Windows NT Workstation.

Roaming User Profiles

If you have users who will "roam" from one Windows NT Workstation computer to another in your environment, default local user profiles do not enable the users to maintain a consistent work environment on each machine. However, the administrator can configure a roaming user profile to enable the user to retain consistent settings regardless of which machine the user logs on to. Roaming profiles work with Windows NT 4 only. When the user makes a change to a roaming personal profile, that change is saved on the server where the profile is stored.

If the user is logged on to two machines simultaneously, the settings that were used in the *last* session from which she logged off will be the settings retained for the user's profile. If the administrator decides to create a roaming mandatory profile, the user cannot change it. A roaming mandatory profile can be used for multiple users. If a change needs to be made to the profile, the administrator has to make the change only once, and it affects all users who have that mandatory profile.

PRACTICE QUESTIONS

SET UP SHARED FOLDERS AND PERMISSIONS

1. **This question is based on the following scenario. Review the scenario first, followed by the objectives and the proposed solution. Then evaluate the proposed solution by choosing the best answer.**

   Scenario:
   You have a Windows NT Workstation with an NTFS partition. You have six users that need access to a shared folder named "Inetpub" that is shared as "InetPub" on the workstation named "WWW." The default share permissions for the folder have not been altered.

   Required Result:
   Share the "Inetpub" from Windows NT Explorer.

   Optional Results:
   Deny access to all users except the specific six, and limit their access in such a way that they cannot delete files from the folder through the share.

   Set access for the administrator account, Hstanton, to Full Control through the share.

   Proposed Solution:
   Right-click on the folder from Windows NT Explorer and select the Sharing command.

   Click on the Permissions button and change the default access permission of Everyone Full Control to Everyone No Access.

   Add the six required user accounts with Read permissions.

   Add the Hstanton account to the permission list with Full Control access.

   Evaluation of Proposed Solution:
   Which of the following objectives does the proposed solution accomplish?

   A. Only the Required Result

   B. The Required Result and both Optional Results

   C. The Required Result and only one Optional Result

   D. Only one of the Optional Results

   E. Neither the Required Result nor the Optional Results

2. **You have a shared folder with the following permissions:**

Account	*Shared Folder Permissions*	*NTFS Permissions*
AlexA	**(none specified)**	**(none specified)**
Sales	**Read**	**Change**
Users	**(none specified)**	**Read**

   If AlexA is a member of the Sales group and the Users group, what are AlexA's effective permissions when accessing this resource from across the network?

   A. No Access

   B. Change

   C. Read

   D. Full Control

   E. This cannot be determined from the given information

3. **This question is based on the following scenario. Review the scenario first, followed by the objectives and the proposed solution. Then evaluate the proposed solution by choosing the best answer.**

Scenario:
You have a Windows NT Workstation with an NTFS partition. You have eight users that need access to a shared folder named "Temp" that is shared as "TempFolder" on the workstation name "DEV2." The default share permissions for the folder have not been altered.

Required Result:
Share the "Temp" resource in the most efficient manner possible.

Optional Results:
Deny access to all users except the specific eight, and limit their access in such a way that they cannot delete files from the folder through the share.

Set access for the administrator account, Hstanton, to Full Control through the share.

Proposed Solution:
Right-click on the folder from Windows NT Explorer and select the Sharing command.

Click on the Permissions button to change the default access permissions on the folder. Remove the Everyone group.

Add the eight required user accounts with Read permissions.

Add the Hstanton account to the permission list with Full Control access.

Evaluation of Proposed Solution:
Which of the following objectives does the proposed solution accomplish?

A. Only the Required Result

B. The Required Result and both Optional Results

C. The Required Result and only one Optional Result

D. Only the Optional Results

E. Neither the Required Result nor the Optional Result

4. **Where does Windows NT maintain the Access Control List defining access to a specified resource?**

A. In the SAM database

B. With the user's access token

C. With the resource

D. In the HKEY_LOCAL_MACHINE/Hardware Registry key

E. With the user account after it is successfully authenticated

5. **You have assigned the following NTFS permissions on a folder:**

Account	*Permissions*
KathyS	**Full Control**
Sales	**(none specified)**
Users	**Read**

If KathyS is a member of the Sales and the Users groups, what are KathyS's effective permissions?

A. Full Control

B. Change

C. Read

D. No Access

E. This cannot be determined from the given information

6. **All resource access requests must pass through which of the following resources?**

   A. Access Control List

   B. Windows NT Security Manager

   C. SAM Data Manager

   D. Security Reference Monitor

   E. Workstation service

7. **This question is based on the following scenario. Review the scenario first, followed by the objectives and the proposed solution. Then evaluate the proposed solution by choosing the best answer.**

   Scenario:
   You have a Windows NT Workstation with ten user accounts. All user accounts are in the WebMaster group.

   Required Result:
   Provide the members of the "WebMaster" group Change access through a network share to a folder named "InetPub."

   Optional Results:
   Ensure that the account "Lstanton," a member of the "WebMaster" group, has only Read access to the folder through the share.

   Provide the user account "Hstanton," a member of the "WebMaster" group, with Full Control permissions.

   Proposed Solution:
   Right-click on the "InetPub" folder, select Sharing, and click on the Permissions button. Remove the Everyone group from the permissions list. Select the "WebMaster" group and add the group to the access list with Change permission. Select the "Lstanton" account and add the account to the access list with Read access. Select the "Hstanton" account from the list and add the account with Full Control permissions.

   Evaluation of Proposed Solution:
   Which of the following objectives does the proposed solution accomplish?

   A. Only the Required Result

   B. The Required Result and both Optional Results

   C. The Required Result and only one Optional Result

   D. Only one of the Optional Results

   E. Neither the Required Result nor the Optional Result

8. **To stop sharing a resource, you must do what? (Select all that apply.)**

   A. Log on with an account in the Administrators group.

   B. Choose Sharing from the resource's context menu.

   C. Delete and re-create the resource.

   D. Click the Not Shared radio button on the Sharing tab of the resource's properties sheet.

   E. From the Services Control Panel applet, stop the Workstation service.

9. **When does a user receive an access token? (Select all that apply.)**

   A. When a user receives permission to access a resource

   B. When a user successfully logs on

   C. When a user requests access to a resource

D. When a user account is created

E. When a resource is shared

10. **This question is based on the following scenario. Review the scenario first, followed by the objectives and the proposed solution. Then evaluate the proposed solution by choosing the best answer.**

Scenario:
You have a Windows NT Workstation with a FAT formatted partition. There is a local group on the workstation named "brewmasters." Three accounts named Louie, Frank, and George are all members of the "brewmasters" group.

Required Result:
Share a directory named "Plots" with Read access for everyone in the "brewmasters" group.

Optional Results:
Provide Louie with Read and Write permissions to the "Plots" folder.

Deny access to all other users that are not members of the "brewmasters" group.

Proposed Solution:
Right-click on the folder from Windows NT Explorer and select the Sharing command. Click on the Permissions button and remove the Everyone group from the permission list. Add the "brewmasters" group with the Change permission. Add the user accounts Frank and George with Read access in the permissions list.

Evaluation of Proposed Solution:
Which of the following objectives does the proposed solution accomplish?

A. Only the Required Result

B. The Required Result and both Optional Results

C. The Required Result and only one Optional Result

D. Only both Optional Results

E. Neither the Required Result nor the Optional Result

ANSWER KEY

1. E
2. C
3. D
4. C
5. A
6. D
7. C
8. B-D
9. B
10. D

ANSWERS & EXPLANATIONS

SET UP SHARED FOLDERS AND PERMISSIONS

1. Proposed Solution:

- **Right-click on the folder from Windows NT Explorer and select the Sharing command.**
- **Click on the Permissions button and change the default access permission of Everyone Full Control to Everyone No Access.**
- **Add the six required user accounts with Read permissions.**
- **Add the "Hstanton" account to the permission list with Full Control access.**

E. Neither the Required Result nor the Optional Results

1. CORRECT ANSWER: E

The Everyone group contains just that, every NT user. Additionally, the No Access permission overrides every other permission. Therefore, setting the share permission on the folder to Everyone No Access will effectively prevent all users from accessing the folder through the share. Therefore, the Proposed Solution does not accomplish any of the objectives.

Removing the Everyone group from the ACL for the folder would result in members of that group not having access; in effect, no listing in the ACL prevents members of all groups not explicitly listed from gaining access. If you then add the six users and the administrator account, only those seven accounts would have access to the resource.

It also would have been more efficient to create a new local group, add the six users to that group, and then add the new group to the ACL for the resource. This is a good example of how using local groups can ease administrative burdens.

2. You have a shared folder with the following permissions:

Account	***Shared Folder Permissions***	***NTFS Permissions***
AlexA	**(none specified)**	**(none specified)**
Sales	**Read**	**Change**
Users	**(none specified)**	**Read**

If AlexA is a member of the Sales group and the Users group, what are AlexA's effective permissions when accessing this resource from across the network?

C. Read

2. CORRECT ANSWER: C

Not listing a group on an ACL for a resource excludes members of the group from gaining access. Specifically adding the AlexA account to the ACL for the resource will grant that account access at the level specified. When you combine group and user access to an ACL for a resource, the resulting permission is the sum of the least restrictive permissions. The only exception is No Access, which overrides all other permissions.

3. Proposed Solution:

- **Right-click on the folder from Windows NT Explorer and select the Sharing command.**
- **Click on the Permissions button to change the default access permissions on the folder. Remove the Everyone group.**
- **Add the eight required user accounts with Read permissions.**
- **Add the Hstanton account to the permission list with Full Control access.**

D. Only the Optional Results

3. CORRECT ANSWER: D

Removing the Everyone group from the default ACL for the resource excludes all members of the Everyone group from gaining access to the resource. Explicitly adding the eight users with Read access would enable those users to access the resource without the ability to delete or add files. The Read permission also grants those users execute permissions on the resource. Therefore, the first Optional Result is achieved with the Proposed Solution.

Explicitly adding the Hstanton account will also give the account the permissions required by the scenario. Therefore, the second Optional Result is accomplished with the Proposed Solution.

It would have been more efficient to create a new local group and add the eight users to that group. The new group could have then been given the required rights on the resource that would have been inherited by the accounts maintaining membership in the local group. Therefore, the Proposed Solution does not achieve the Required Result.

4. Where does Windows NT maintain the Access Control List defining access to a specified resource?

C. With the resource

4. CORRECT ANSWER: C

The ACL for a resource is maintained with the resource itself.

5. You have assigned the following NTFS permissions on a folder:

Account	***Permissions***
KathyS	**Full Control**
Sales	**(none specified)**
Users	**Read**

If KathyS is a member of the Sales and the Users groups, what are KathyS's effective permissions?

A. Full Control

5. CORRECT ANSWER: A

The net access to a resource is determined by the least restrictive sum of user and group permissions. The only exception is No Access, which overrides all other permissions. In this case, the sum of the permissions would be None Specified + Read + Full Control, resulting in a net permission of Full Control.

6. All resource access requests must pass through which of the following resources?

D. Security Reference Monitor

6. CORRECT ANSWER: D

All resource requests are passed through the Security Reference Monitor before a user is given access to a resource. The SRM compares the ACL and the SID of the account requesting access to determine the level of access that should be granted.

7. Proposed Solution:
Right-click on the "InetPub" folder, select Sharing, and click on the Permissions button. Remove the Everyone group from the permissions list. Select the "WebMaster" group and add the group to the access list with Change permission. Select the "Lstanton" account and add the account to the access list with Read access. Select the "Hstanton" account from the list and add the account with Full Control permissions.

C. The Required Result and only one Optional Result

7. CORRECT ANSWER: C

Assigning the WebMaster group to the ACL for the shared resource with Change permission will give the members of this group the permissions to the resource required by the scenario. It is important to ensure the Everyone group is removed from the ACL for the resource; otherwise, everyone, including the WebMaster group members, would have Full Control permissions on the resource. Therefore, the Required Result was met with the Proposed Solution.

Explicitly adding the Lstanton account will not set the permissions to this account to Read. Since the permissions are the least restrictive sum of the assigned group and individual account permissions, the net result for the Lstanton account will be Change. This is due to the fact that the Lstanton account is a member of the WebMaster group, which is assigned Change permission on the resource. The Proposed Solution does not accomplish the first Optional Result.

Explicitly adding the Hstanton account with the Full Control permission will result in that account having a combined permission (between the individual account and the group that account is a member of) of Full Control, thereby accomplishing the second Optional Result.

8. To stop sharing a resource, you must do what? (Select all that apply.)

B. Choose Sharing from the resource's context menu.

D. Click the Not Shared radio button on the Sharing tab of the resource's properties sheet.

8. CORRECT ANSWER: B-D

To stop sharing a resource, you must right-click the resource in Windows Explorer, select Sharing from the resulting context menu, and click the Not Shared radio button.

You can stop sharing all resources by stopping the Server service through the Services applet of Control Panel. This will also immediately terminate current connections to shared resources on the workstation.

9. When does a user receive an access token? (Select all that apply.)

B. When a user successfully logs on

9. CORRECT ANSWER: B

The user receives an access token when she successfully logs on to the workstation (or domain). This is important because of the fact that if you add a user to a group, the permissions for resources associated with that group will not be inherited by the user's account until the user receives an access token at the next logon.

10. Proposed Solution:
Right-click on the folder from Windows NT Explorer and select the Sharing command. Click on the Permissions button and remove the Everyone group from the permission list. Add the "brewmasters" group with the Change permission. Add the user accounts Frank and George with Read access in the permissions list.

D. Only both Optional Results

10. CORRECT ANSWER: D

If you remove the Everyone group from the resource ACL and add the "brewmasters" group to the ACL, users not in the "brewmasters" group will not have access to the folder, thereby accomplishing the second Optional Result.

Because Louie is a member of the "brewmasters" group and the "brewmasters" group was given Change permissions, Louie will have read/write access to the folder "Plots." The Proposed Solution accomplishes the first Optional Result.

Explicitly adding Frank and George to the ACL for the resource with explicit Read access will not limit their access to reading. Because they are also members of the "brewmasters" group and that group has Change access, their net permissions will be Change. When considering group and individual account permissions, remember that the Security Reference Monitor determines net permissions as the least restrictive sum of the permissions. The Proposed Solution does not accomplish the Required Result.

FURTHER REVIEW

SET UP SHARED FOLDERS AND PERMISSIONS

To allow remote access to your resources, you must make them available on the network to users on other computers. Windows NT enables you to selectively choose folders to which you want to allow access, also known as *sharing*, and which you want to keep private to that workstation. Before you delve into folder sharing and permissions, you need to understand how Windows NT Workstation implements security.

Understanding Windows NT Security

When discussing Windows NT security, it is important to understand the difference between a user right and a user permission. User rights define *what* a user is allowed to do, such as changing the time on the local workstation. User permissions define *where* a user can use his assigned rights.

Windows NT allows administrators to define two types of permissions: share level and resource level. Share-level permissions are exercised through network connections, such as connecting to a shared folder. Resource-level permissions are exercised on the resource itself, such as copying a file from one local folder to another.

When a user authenticates to Windows NT, the user is given an access token. This token remains with the user until the user logs off the system. Along with other information, the access token contains the user's SID. When a user logs on to a local workstation that is not participating in a Windows NT domain, that access token contains a SID that is valid only for the local machine.

When a user attempts to access a resource, the Security Reference Monitor compares the information in the access token with the information contained in the ACL for the resource to which the user requested access. This ACL contains only SIDs in the local SAM database. Therefore, to access resources on another workstation that's not participating in a domain, the user must also have a SID in the remote workstation's SAM database.

Windows NT will automatically attempt to log the user on to the remote machine when a user is accessing resources on a remote machine. Instead of sending the user's SID, which would be useless on the remote machine, Windows NT passes the user name and password in an attempt to create a new access token on the remote machine.

When the user requests access to a remote resource, the Security Reference Monitor on the remote machine compares the user's SID with the SIDs in the remote resource's ACL to determine the level of access to grant to the user.

It is important to understand that a user's access token is not dynamic. It cannot change during a given session. Even if an administrator adds a user to the ACL during that user's session, the user will not have access to the resource until he gains another access token by logging off and logging back on to the workstation.

Creating Shared Folders

Only Administrators and Power Users group members have the ability to create network shares. Additionally, this is a "built-in" right; that is, it cannot be assigned to other users or groups with User Manager.

Sharing can only be done at the folder level, not at the individual file level. All subfolders inherit the share access level of the parent directory. Care should be taken when planning directory structures to ensure that users and groups do not inadvertently gain access to folders you want to keep local to the workstation. Remember to consider the type of client that will be accessing a share. Windows 3.x and DOS clients can only access shares that conform to the 8.3 naming convention.

Establishing Shared Folder Permissions

Windows NT provides four levels of access that you can give to users or groups that will connect to the shared folder. These permissions include:

- *No Access.* If a user or group is given the No Access permission to a shared folder, that user or group cannot even open the shared folder—although users will see the shared folder on the network. The No Access permission overrides all other permissions that a user or group might have to the folder.
- *Read.* Read permission allows the user or group to view files and subfolders within the shared folder. It also allows the user or group to execute programs that might be located within the shared folder.
- *Change.* Change permission allows the user or group to add files or subfolders to the shared folder, as well as to append or delete information from existing files and subfolders. The Change permission also encompasses everything included within the Read permission.
- *Full Control.* If a user or group is given the Full Control permission, that user or group has the ability to change the file permissions, to take ownership of files, and to perform all options allowed by the Change permission. This is the default permission applied by Windows NT when the share is created.

Sharing a Folder Locally

When you share a folder locally, you are logged on to the workstation that holds the folder you would like to share. To access that folder, right-click the folder and choose the Sharing option. This brings up the properties of the folder, with the focus on the Sharing tab. All options associated with sharing this folder are accessible from this tab. Each element of this dialog box is discussed here:

- *Shared.* Click this option button to enable users to share this resource across the network.
- *Not Shared.* Click this option button to stop sharing a resource.
- *Share Name.* Enter a name users will see when browsing the resources on this machine. Note that if you will have DOS or Windows 3.x clients, you must use the 8.3 naming convention.
- *Comment.* This is a text comment that will appear next to the share when users browse available resources on this machine.

- *User Limit.* This option enables you to limit the number of inbound connections. It is important to remember that Windows NT Workstation has a built-in limit of 10 inbound networking connections.
- *Permissions.* This button enables you to set individual user and group permissions for access to this share. Remember that all subfolders will inherit this permission. (See the next section for the options available for setting share permissions.)

Setting Permissions on a Shared Folder

You set permissions on shares by right-clicking the folder and choosing Sharing from the context menu that appears. Click the Permissions button to activate the dialog box. Note that the default permissions on a shared folder are Everyone: Full Control. These default share permissions should be changed if there is a need for security, because the group Everyone includes just that—everyone from your workstation (or your domain if this workstation is part of a Windows NT domain).

To change the default permissions, click the Add button. By default, just groups are shown. To grant access to a specific user account, click the Show Users button and select the appropriate user or group. Then from the Type of Access field, select the access you want to assign to that user or group. After you have granted permissions to the user or group to make the share more secure, you should remove the permission for Everyone: Full Control.

Managing Shared Folders

After you create your shared folders, you will likely need to manage them at a later point. Managing folders includes creating a new share from an existing share, stopping sharing for a folder, modifying permissions on a shared folder, and modifying the share name after a folder has been shared.

Creating a New Share

The steps for creating a new share are slightly different from those for creating the shared directory from the beginning. It's important that you understand the differences because of the real-life need for implementation and for the exam. When you configure a new share for an existing shared directory, a button labeled New Share appears.

To create a new share from an existing shared directory, complete the following steps:

1. Right-click the existing shared folder and choose the Sharing option.
2. Click the New Share button. (Notice that you cannot change the existing share name through this dialog box.)
3. Enter the new share name and any comments, and then set the permissions for this new shared directory.
4. Click OK to close the New Share dialog box. Then click OK to close the folder's Properties dialog box and create the new share.

Stopping Sharing

To stop sharing a directory on Windows NT Workstation, complete the following steps:

1. Right-click the directory that you would like to stop sharing and choose Sharing from the context menu that appears.

2. Click the Not Shared option button.
3. Click OK. This stops sharing the directory.

One way to prevent any access to your Windows NT Workstation is to stop the Server service through Control Panel, Services. Although this also stops the Computer Browser service, it is the most effective way of preventing access to your workstation.

Modifying Permissions on a Shared Directory

Having set up your shared directories, you might need to change the directory permissions at a later time. To modify the permissions of a shared directory after it has been shared, complete the following steps:

1. Right-click the shared directory and choose Sharing from the context menu that appears.
2. On the Sharing tab, click the Permissions button.
3. Add or remove groups as needed from the list of users and groups with permissions.

Modifying Share Names

Another aspect of managing shared resources is changing the name of a shared resource after it has been shared. To change the name of a share, you must actually get rid of the first share (stop sharing it), and then create a new share with the new name. The order in which you do this is not critical: You can create a new share (as described in "Creating a New Share," earlier in this chapter), or you can stop sharing the resource (as described in "Stopping Sharing," earlier in this chapter) and then re-create the share (as described in "Sharing a Folder," earlier in this chapter). You cannot modify a share name without re-creating the share.

Implementation of Shared Folder Permissions

When you're setting up permissions on shared folders, it is important that you understand how those permissions will apply or be implemented in your environment. Before you set up shared folder permissions, you need to know how user and group permissions will interact, as well as how the No Access permission can override any other permission set for that user or group.

You can grant shared folder permissions to both users and groups. Because of this, you might have a situation in which a user is given permission to a shared resource, and a group that the user is a member of is given different permissions. Another possible scenario is one in which a user is a member of more than one group that have been given access to the resource. In those cases, you need to understand how user and group permissions interact in shared folder permissions.

When working with the combined permissions of users and groups assigned to a share, Windows NT combines all the associated permissions and applies the least restrictive one. If any user or any group that a user belongs to is assigned the No Access permission to the share, that user will not have access to the share, regardless of any other permissions. If access is not specified for a particular group or user, this permission has no effect on the net permissions.

PRACTICE QUESTIONS

SET PERMISSIONS ON NTFS PARTITIONS, FOLDERS, AND FILES

1. **What are the default permissions that you can apply to files located on an NTFS formatted partition? (Select all that apply.)**

   A. Read

   B. Delete

   C. Accept Ownership

   D. No Access

   E. Execute

2. **This question is based on the following scenario. Review the scenario first, followed by the objectives and the proposed solution. Then evaluate the proposed solution by choosing the best answer.**

   Scenario:
   You have a Windows NT Workstation with an NTFS partition. You have six users that need access to a local folder named "Apps." The default permissions for the folder have not been altered.

   Required Result:
   Manage the permissions for the "Apps" folder in the most efficient manner possible.

   Optional Results:
   Deny access to all users except the specific six, and limit their access in such a way that they cannot delete files from the folder.

   Set access for the administrator account, JamesK, to Full Control.

   Proposed Solution:
   Create a new local group on the Windows NT Workstation with User Manager, and name the group Managers.

   Right-click on the folder from Windows NT Explorer and select Security from the Property menu.

   Click on the Permissions button and remove the Everyone group from the ACL.

   Add the Managers group with Read permissions.

   Add the JamesK account to the permission list with Full Control access.

   Evaluation of Proposed Solution:
   Which of the following objectives does the proposed solution accomplish?

   A. Only the Required Result

   B. The Required Result and both Optional Results

   C. The Required Result and only one Optional Result

   D. Only one of the Optional Results

   E. Neither the Required Result nor the Optional Results

3. **Cindy, a member of the Sales group, copies a file with Users: Full Control, Managers: No Access, and Sales: Change NTFS permissions to a folder on the same partition that has the permissions**

Everyone: Full Control. After the copy, what permissions will the file have?

A. Users: Full Control; Everyone: Full Control; Sales: Change; Managers: No Access

B. Users: Full Control; Managers: No Access; Sales: Change

C. Everyone: Full Control; Managers: No Access

D. Everyone: Full Control

E. This cannot be determined from the given information

4. **You have a folder on an NTFS partition with the following permissions:**

Account	*NTFS Folder Permissions*	*NTFS Permissions*
HeidiS	**Full Control**	**(none specified)**
Sales	**List**	**(none specified)**

You also have a file in the folder with the following NTFS permissions:

Account	*NTFS Permissions*
HeidiS	**Read**
Sales	**Change**

If HeidiS is a member of the Sales group, what are HeidiS's effective permissions when accessing the file?

A. Full Control

B. Change

C. List

D. Read

E. This cannot be determined from the given information

5. **This question is based on the following scenario. Review the scenario first, followed by the objectives and the proposed solution. Then evaluate the proposed solution by choosing the best answer.**

Scenario:
You have a Windows NT Workstation with ten user accounts. All user accounts are in the "Accounting" group.

Required Result:
Provide only the members of the "Sales" group Change access to a folder named "Clients."

Optional Results:
Ensure the account "BobQ," a member of the "Sales" group, has only local Read access to the "Clients" folder.

Provide the user account "PaulM," a member of the "Sales" group, with Full Control permissions.

Proposed Solution:
Right-click on the "Clients" folder, select Sharing, and click on the Permissions button. Remove the Everyone group from the permissions list. Select the "Sales" group and add the group to the access list with Change permission. Select the "BobQ" account and add the account to the access list with Read access. Select the "PaulM" account from the list and add the account with Full Control permissions.

Evaluation of Proposed Solution:
Which of the following objectives does the proposed solution accomplish?

A. Only the Required Result

B. The Required Result and both Optional Results

C. The Required Result and only one Optional Result

D. Only one of the Optional Results

E. Neither the Required Result nor the Optional Result

6. Cindy, a member of the Sales group, moves a file with Users: Full Control, Sales: Change, and Administrators: No Access NTFS permissions to a folder on the same partition that has the permissions Everyone: Full Control. After the move, what permissions will the file have?

A. Everyone: Full Control

B. Users: Full Control; Sales: Change; Administrators: No Access

C. Everyone: Full Control; Administrators: No Access

D. Everyone: No Access

E. This cannot be determined from the given information

7. This question is based on the following scenario. Review the scenario first, followed by the objectives and the proposed solution. Then evaluate the proposed solution by choosing the best answer.

Scenario:

You have a Windows NT Workstation with an NTFS formatted partition. There is a local group on the workstation named "developers." Three accounts named JBanks, Lmilhouse, and DSams are all members of the "developers" local group.

Required Result:

Set permissions on a directory named "Plans" with Read access for everyone in the "developers" group.

Optional Results:

Provide JBanks with Read and Write permissions to the "Plans" folder.

Deny access to all other users.

Proposed Solution:

Right-click on the folder from Windows NT Explorer and select the Sharing command. Click on the Permissions button and remove the Everyone group from the permission list. Add the "developers" group with the List permission. Add the user JBanks with Change access in the permissions list.

Evaluation of Proposed Solution:

Which of the following objectives does the proposed solution accomplish?

A. Only the Required Result

B. The Required Result and both Optional Results

C. The Required Result and only one Optional Result

D. Only one of the Optional Results

E. Neither the Required Result nor the Optional Result

8. Matt, a member of the Users group, moves a file from a folder on one NTFS partition to a folder in a different NTFS partition. The original folder had the permissions Everyone: Full Control. The new folder has the permissions Users: Full Control, Power Users: No Access. What are the permissions on the new file after the move?

A. Everyone: Full Control

B. Everyone: Full Control; Power Users: No Access; Users: Full Control

C. Everyone: No Access

D. Users: Full Control; Power Users: No Access

E. The new permission cannot be determined based on the amount of information supplied

9. By default, which of the following local groups are allowed to take ownership on a file that is created with the default permissions? (Select the best answer.)

A. Everyone

B. Administrators

C. Power Users

D. Backup Operators

E. Replicator

10. When viewing the directory permissions for the Docs directory, you see that the Sales group is assigned the permissions: Special Access (RWX). What could members of the Sales group do with files and subfolders contained in the Docs directory? (Select all that apply.)

A. Read

B. Execute

C. Change file permissions

D. Take ownership

E. Create a new folder

11. This question is based on the following scenario. Review the scenario first, followed by the objectives and the proposed solution. Then evaluate the proposed solution by choosing the best answer.

Scenario:

You have a Windows NT Workstation with an NTFS formatted partition. John has an account named JAdams on the machine.

Required Result:

Provide John with Read access to all the files in a folder named "confidential."

Optional Results:

Ensure John does not have access to a file named salaries.XLS in the "confidential" folder.

Provide John with Read/Write access to a file named security.doc in the "confidential" folder.

Proposed Solution:

Right-click on the "confidential" folder, select Properties, and click on the Permissions tab.

Select the JAdams account from the list and set Read access for the account. Remove the Everyone group from the permissions list. Ensure the Replace Permissions on Existing Files box is checked.

Right-click on the salaries.xls file in Windows NT Explorer and select Properties. Click on the Security tab and click the Permissions button.

Add JAdams with No Access to the list.

Right-click on the security.doc file in Windows NT Explorer and select Properties. Click on the Security tab and click the Permissions button.

Add JAdams with Change permissions to the list.

Evaluation of Proposed Solution:
Which of the following objectives does the proposed solution accomplish?

A. Only the Required Result

B. The Required Result and both Optional Results

C. The Required Result and only one Optional Result

D. Only one of the Optional Results

E. Neither the Required Result nor the Optional Results

ANSWER KEY

1. A-D
2. B
3. D
4. B
5. C
6. B
7. B
8. D
9. A
10. A-B
11. B

ANSWERS & EXPLANATIONS

SET PERMISSIONS ON NTFS PARTITIONS, FOLDERS, AND FILES

1. What are the default permissions that you can apply to files located on an NTFS formatted partition? (Select all that apply.)

A. Read

D. No Access

1. CORRECT ANSWER: A-D

By default, you can apply Read, Change, No Access, Full Control, and Special Access to files on an NTFS partition. Within the Special Access permission, you can apply the following individual permissions to a file: Read, Write, Execute, Delete, Change Permissions, and Take Ownership.

Table 3.4 defines what individual permissions are contained within each of the aggregate permissions: Read, Change, No Access, and Full Control. Table 3.5 defines what each individual permission will enable a user to do when the permission is assigned.

TABLE 3.4 STANDARD NTFS FILE PERMISSIONS

Standard File Permission	*Individual NTFS Permissions*
No Access	(None)
Read	(RX)
Change	(RWXD)
Full Control	(All Permissions)

TABLE 3.5 STANDARD NTFS PERMISSIONS

Permission	*Folder*	*File*
Read (R)	Display the folder and subfolders, attributes, and permissions	Display the file and its attributes and permissions

Permission	*Folder*	*File*
Write (W)	Add files or folders, change attributes for the folder, and display permissions	Change file attributes and add or append data to the file
Execute (X)	Make changes to subfolders, display permissions, and display attributes	Run a file if it is an executable and display attributes and permissions
Delete (D)	Remove the folder	Remove the file
Change Permission (P)	Modify folder permissions	Modify file permissions
Take Ownership (O)	Take ownership of the folder	Take ownership of a file

2. Proposed Solution:

- **Create a new local group on the Windows NT Workstation with User Manager, and name the group Managers.**
- **Right-click on the folder from Windows NT Explorer and select Security from the Property menu.**
- **Click on the Permissions button and remove the Everyone group from the ACL.**
- **Add the Managers group with Read permissions.**
- **Add the JamesK account to the permission list with Full Control access.**

B. The Required Result and both Optional Results

2. CORRECT ANSWER: B

By using groups to manage the permissions, you are using the most efficient means to manage permissions for any resource, thereby achieving the Required Result.

By removing the Everyone group from the ACL, you eliminate access to the resource for all users except for those individual and group accounts explicitly listed on the ACL. Additionally, the group in which all six accounts have membership was granted Read permission, thereby eliminating the possibility of any user deleting any files within the folder. The Proposed Solution achieves the first Optional Result.

Explicitly adding the JamesK account with Full Control permissions achieves the second Optional Result.

3. Cindy, a member of the Sales group, copies a file with Users: Full Control, Managers: No Access, and Sales: Change NTFS permissions to a folder on the same partition that has the permissions Everyone: Full Control. After the copy, what permissions will the file have?

D. Everyone: Full Control

3. CORRECT ANSWER: D

When a file is copied, the file is physically relocated to the new directory, and that file assumes the permissions of the new folder.

4. You have a folder on an NTFS partition with the following permissions:

Account	*NTFS Folder Permissions*	*NTFS Permissions*
HeidiS	Full Control	(none specified)
Sales	List	(none specified)

You also have a file in the folder with the following NTFS permissions:

Account	*NTFS Permissions*
HeidiS	Read
Sales	Change

If HeidiS is member of the Sales group, what are HeidiS's effective permissions when accessing the file?

B. Change

4. CORRECT ANSWER: B

Regardless of folder permissions, except the case of No Access, a file's permission will always supercede folder permissions. However, when comparing group and individual account permissions on files and folders, the least restrictive permission will apply, except in the case of No Access, which overrides all other permissions.

5. Proposed Solution:
Right-click on the "Clients" folder, select Sharing, and click on the Permissions button. Remove the Everyone group from the permissions list. Select the "Sales" group and add the group to the access list with Change permission. Select the "BobQ" account and add the account to the access list with Read access. Select the "PaulM" account from the list and add the account with Full Control permissions.

C. The Required Result and only one Optional Result

5. CORRECT ANSWER: C

By adding the "Sales" group to the ACL of the resource with Change permissions and removing the Everyone group completely, you ensure that the "Sales" group is the only group with Change access to the folder. Therefore, the Proposed Solution accomplishes the Required Result.

Explicitly adding the "BobQ" account with Read permissions does not have the desired result. Because "BobQ" is a member of the "Sales" group, and the net access to the resource is determined by the least restrictive sum of the group and individual account permissions, the "BobQ" account will have Change access due to the membership in the "Sales" group. The Proposed Solution does not accomplish the first Optional Result. For the solution to work, "BobQ" must be removed from the "Sales" group.

Explicitly adding the "PaulM" account will have the effect of giving that account Full Control permission, which accomplishes the second Optional Result.

6. Cindy, a member of the Sales group, moves a file with Users: Full Control, Sales: Change, and Administrators: No Access NTFS permissions to a folder on the same partition that has the permissions Everyone: Full Control. After the move, what permissions will the file have?

B. Users: Full Control; Sales: Change; Administrators: No Access

6. CORRECT ANSWER: B

When a file is moved on the same partition, only a pointer to the file is actually changed. Therefore, the file maintains its original permissions. If a file is copied or moved between partitions, the file is actually relocated, and it assumes the permissions of the new folder.

7. Proposed Solution:
Right-click on the folder from Windows NT Explorer and select the Sharing command. Click on the Permissions button and remove the Everyone group from the permission list. Add the "developers" group with the List permission. Add the user JBanks with Change access in the permissions list.

B. The Required Result and both Optional Results

7. CORRECT ANSWER: B

Applying the List permission to the "developers" group enables all members of the group to read or view the contents of the folder. Therefore, the Required Result is met.

If you remove the Everyone group, all users not in the "developers" group are denied access to the folder, accomplishing the second Optional Result.

Explicitly adding the JBanks account with Change permissions gives that account Read and Write access to the directory, achieving the first Optional Result.

8. Matt, a member of the Users group, moves a file from a folder on one NTFS partition to a folder in a different NTFS partition. The original folder had the permissions Everyone: Full Control. The new folder has the permissions Users: Full Control, Power Users: No Access. What are the permissions on the new file after the move?

D. Users: Full Control; Power Users: No Access

8. CORRECT ANSWER: D

Moving a file between partitions has the same effect as copying the file; therefore, the file will assume the permissions of the new folder. A file retains its original permissions only when it is moved between folders *on the same partition.*

9. By default, which of the following local groups are allowed to take ownership on a file that is created with the default permissions? (Select the best answer.)

A. Everyone

9. CORRECT ANSWER: A

Part of the Full Control permission is the ability to take ownership. Therefore, because the default permission is Everyone: Full Control, Everyone is allowed to take ownership by default.

10. When viewing the directory permissions for the Docs directory, you see that the Sales group is assigned the permissions: Special Access (RWX). What could members of the Sales group do with files and subfolders contained in the Docs directory? (Select all that apply.)

A. Read

B. Execute

10. CORRECT ANSWER: A-B

In the Special Permissions list, R is Read permission, W is Write permission and X is Execute permission. Table 3.5 lists the actions allowed by each of these permissions.

11. Proposed Solution:

- **Right-click on the "confidential" folder, select Properties, and click on the Permissions tab.**
- **Select the JAdams account from the list and set Read access for the account. Remove the Everyone group from the permissions list. Ensure the Replace Permissions on Existing Files box is checked.**
- **Right-click on the salaries.xls file in Windows NT Explorer and select Properties. Click on the Security tab and click the Permissions button.**
- **Add JAdams with No Access to the list.**
- **Right-click on the security.doc file in Windows NT Explorer and select Properties. Click on the Security tab and click the Permissions button.**
- **Add JAdams with Change permissions to the list.**

B. The Required Result and both Optional Results

11. CORRECT ANSWER: B

Removing the Everyone group from the folder ACL and adding the JAdams account will ensure only the JAdams account has Read permissions for the folder. If the "Replace Permissions on Existing Files" box was not checked, the files within the folder would have the permission Everyone: Full Control. Because the JAdams account is a member of the Everyone group, and file permissions override folder permissions, JAdams has full control of all the files. Therefore, the Proposed Solution meets the Required Result.

Explicitly setting the permissions on both the salaries.xls and security.doc files ensures the proper access for the JAdams account, thereby accomplishing the first and second Optional Results.

FURTHER REVIEW

SET PERMISSIONS ON NTFS PARTITIONS, FOLDERS, AND FILES

One of the benefits of using NTFS over FAT as a file system on a Windows NT Workstation is the added security that NTFS enables you to take advantage of under Windows NT. NTFS permissions enable you to get beyond the security limitations of shared folder permissions (that they are effective only when accessing the directory from across the network) and implement local security on both the folder and the file level. Shared permissions can be assigned only at the folder level. NTFS permissions can also apply to a user who is accessing a shared network resource or a local resource.

As an administrator, you must be careful and remember that by default, Windows NT allows Full Permission to the Everyone local group.

NTFS Folder Permissions

NTFS folder permissions are also combined into a standard set of permissions. Table 3.6 shows the NTFS folder permissions. In a list of NTFS folder permissions, each permission is typically followed by two sets of parentheses. The first set represents the standard permissions on the folder itself. The second set represents the permissions inherited by any file created within that folder.

TABLE 3.6 STANDARD NTFS FOLDER PERMISSIONS

Standard Folder Permission	*Individual NTFS Permissions*
No Access	(None)(None)
Read	(RX)(RX)
Change	(RWXD)(RWXD)
Add	(WX)(Not Specified)
Add & Read	(RWX)(RX)
List	(RX)(Not Specified)
Full Control	(All)(All)

Setting NTFS Permissions

When a partition is created, the default NTFS permission is Everyone: Full Control. NTFS permissions can enhance shared folder permissions that you might have already implemented on your Windows NT Workstation. You set NTFS permissions through the Security tab of a file or folder's properties sheet.

Assigning NTFS Permissions

To assign NTFS permissions, you must be a part of a group that has been given that right, or your user account must be given that right. By default, the group Everyone is assigned Full Control when an NTFS partition is created. If that default permission is left, part of the Full Control permission includes the right to Change Permissions (P).

Suppose that the default Everyone: Full Control is changed. To assign NTFS permissions, you must be in one of the following situations:

- The file/folder creator.
- Have Full Control (ALL) or Change Permissions (P) for NTFS permission.
- Given special access to Take Ownership (O). With the ability to Take Ownership, a user can give himself the right to Change Permissions (P). (For a description of the Take Ownership permission, see the section entitled "Taking Ownership of Files or Folders," later in this chapter.)

Using Special Access Permissions

The Special Access permission is a combination of the individual NTFS permissions and is not one of the standard NTFS permissions. Typically, the standard permissions are what you will assign to files or folders; however, it is possible that you might want to implement a customized version of the individual NTFS permissions. If you need to assign individual permissions, you can assign Special Access permissions. The Special Access permissions are the same for both files and folders—they just list the individual NTFS permissions.

Special directory access can be used when you have a situation that requires customizing the NTFS permissions assigned to a resource.

Taking Ownership of Files or Folders with NTFS

Taking ownership of files or folders is one of the NTFS permissions that can be assigned through special directory or file permissions. The user who creates a file or a folder is the owner of that file or folder. As the owner, that individual has Full Control to that file or folder. To take ownership, you have to have been given that right through the NTFS permissions. If a user removes everyone but himself from the list of permissions on the resource, only an administrator can take ownership of the files. An administrator can always take ownership, even if he has been given No Access permission to the file or folder.

You cannot actually give ownership to another user or group; you can give only the *permission* to take ownership. Because of this, if an administrator takes ownership of a user's files, that administrator remains the owner. This prevents any user or administrator from altering or creating files or folders and then making it look like those files or folders belong to another user.

To give someone the right to take ownership, you must grant that person Full Control, Take Ownership special permission, or Change Permission special permission.

Using the No Access Permission for NTFS Permissions

The No Access permission overrides all other permissions. As in shared folder permissions, in NTFS permissions, the No Access permission is unique in that it can override all other permissions granted for a user or group if it exists in the list of permissions for that user or group.

File Delete Child with NTFS Permissions

File Delete Child refers to a specific scenario relating to NTFS permissions under Windows

NT. If a user has been given the NTFS No Access permission to a particular file but has Full Control of the directory that contains the file, the user can actually delete the file even though he doesn't even have the ability to read it. This is true only if the user actually tries to delete the file, not if he attempts to move it to the Recycle Bin.

This situation is called File Delete Child. It is a part of Windows NT that meets the POSIX-compliance requirements. To get around this problem and prevent users from being able to delete a file to which they should not have access, follow these steps:

1. Access the properties sheet for the directory that contains the file.
2. Instead of selecting Full Control as the directory permission, select Custom.
3. When the list of Custom Options appears, put a check in each check box. This is the same as Full Control, except that it bypasses the File Delete Child problem.
4. Make sure the file permissions are still set to No Access for that user.

Combining Shared Folder and NTFS Permissions

When combining shared folder permissions with NTFS permissions, it is important that you understand how NTFS file and folder permissions interact with the applied shared permissions. When different permissions exist for the file or folder level and the folder share, Windows NT applies the most restrictive permission.

For example, JohnA is a member of the Security group. The Security group is assigned Read permission to the folder share and Change control to the folder. When accessing the folder through the share, JohnA's net permission will be Read. However, if JohnA accesses the folder locally (if he's logged on to the workstation where the folder resides), his permission will be Change.

Understanding the interaction between shared folder permissions and NTFS permissions is critical to you understanding how to manage the security of resources in your Windows NT environment, and it is a critical part of successfully completing the exam. Remember these key points when determining a user's net access permissions to files or folders:

- When user and group permissions for shared folders are combined, the effective permission is the cumulative permission.
- When user and group permissions for NTFS security are combined, the effective permission is the cumulative permission.
- When shared folder permissions and NTFS permissions are combined, the most restrictive permission is always the effective permission.
- With NTFS permissions, file permissions override folder permissions.
- Using NTFS permissions is the only way to provide local security.
- Shared folder permissions present the only way to provide security on a FAT partition and are effective only when the folder is accessed from across the network.

PRACTICE QUESTIONS

INSTALL AND CONFIGURE PRINTERS IN A GIVEN ENVIRONMENT

1. **This question is based on the following scenario. Review the scenario first, followed by the objectives and the proposed solution. Then evaluate the proposed solution by choosing the best answer.**

Scenario:
You have a Windows NT Workstation 4 set up with a print device attached locally. During normal business hours, users have called complaining the print jobs take too long to print due to the volume of print jobs sent to the printer. Some users complain of wasting paper with the banner pages that print out with each print job. The sales managers have been complaining that the engineering group prints large files that monopolize the printer.

Required Result:
Accelerate the processing of print jobs.

Optional Results:
Eliminate the paper wasted by printing banners.

Ensure print jobs from the members of the Managers local group receive the highest priority on the printer.

Proposed Solution:
Install a printer and give only members of the Managers local group access to the printer. Set the priority to 99.

Create another printer for the Everyone group and set the priority to 50.

Add more RAM and an additional hard disk to the workstation that is acting as the printer server. Change the spooler directory setting to a location on the new hard disk.

From the General tab of the printer's properties page, click the Separator Page button and clear the selection.

Evaluation of Proposed Solution:
Which of the following objectives does the proposed solution accomplish?

A. Only the Required Result

B. The Required Result and both Optional Results

C. Both Optional Results

D. Only one of the Optional Results

E. Neither the Required Result nor the Optional Results

2. **You want to print to a printer managed by a Windows NT Server 4. What should you do?**

A. Use Print Manager to connect to the printer.

B. Use Print Manager to create a printer.

C. Use the Add Printer Wizard to create a new printer using the My Computer option.

D. Use the Add Printer Wizard to create a new printer using the Network Printer Server option.

E. Use the Network Neighborhood to connect an existing printer on the system to the network print server.

3. **Which of the following statements best describes the functions of the following printing components in Windows NT: the print processor, print monitor, and print spooler? Select only one.**

   A. The print processor renders the print job for the specific printer; the print monitor tracks print job status; the print spooler sends print jobs to the appropriate ports and assigns priorities to print jobs.

   B. The print processor transfers the print job to the spooler directory; the print spooler assigns priorities to print jobs and assigns print jobs to appropriate ports.

   C. The print processor monitors the status of the print device and monitors print device status; the print spooler assigns priorities to print jobs.

   D. The print processor manages the print job flow; the print monitor releases the port when printing is complete; and the print spooler assigns print jobs to appropriate ports and connects to the spooler on remote print servers.

   E. The print processor assigns priorities to the incoming print jobs; the print monitor releases the port when printing is complete; and the print spooler assigns print jobs to appropriate ports and connects to the spooler on remote print servers.

4. **This question is based on the following scenario. Review the scenario first, followed by the objectives and the proposed solution. Then evaluate the proposed solution by choosing the best answer.**

Scenario:
You have a system with Windows NT Workstation. You need to install a laser printer on the local workstation and share it for your local workgroup.

Required Result:
Install the laser printer on the local machine.

Optional Results:
Share the printer for the workgroup to use.

Ensure members of the "developers" group can pause and stop the printing of documents and delete print jobs created by other users.

Change the default location of the print spool directory to reside on the second partition of the primary disk, which is the D:\ drive.

Proposed Solution:
Attach the printer to the parallel port of the workstation. Install the appropriate print device on the workstation. Begin the installation of the printer by double-clicking the Add Printer icon in the Printers folder. Select the Network Print Server option.

When the installation is complete, add the "developers" group to the printer's ACL with the Manage Documents permission by right-clicking on the printer and selecting the Sharing... option from the context menu. From the Printers folder, right-click on the printer, select Properties, and select the Advanced tab from the Server properties window. Change the default spool directory to "D:\ ."

Evaluation of Proposed Solution:
Which of the following objectives does the proposed solution accomplish?

A. Only the Required Result

B. The Required Result and the Optional Results

C. The Required Result and only one Optional Result

D. Both Optional Results

E. Neither the Required Result nor the Optional Results

5. Where can you select an alternative print processor for a printer?

A. From the General tab of the printer's properties sheet

B. From the Ports tab of the printer's properties sheet

C. From the Device Options tab of the printer's properties sheet

D. From the Sharing tab of the printer's properties sheet

E. From the Security tab of the printer's properties sheet

6. This question is based on the following scenario. Review the scenario first, followed by the objectives and the proposed solution. Then evaluate the proposed solution by choosing the best answer.

Scenario:
You have a Windows NT Workstation 4 set up with a Lexmark print device attached locally. You look at the print queue for the print device and find jammed print jobs in the queue. While you are there, Bill, who usually uses the workstation, asks you why there is a lot of hard disk activity only when he prints large documents and then tells you that at times his job never prints. You would like to share the printer for two other users sitting near the printer.

Required Result:
Clear the jammed print jobs to resume normal printing operations.

Optional Results:
Share the printer to provide access for the other two users.

Address the excessive hard disk activity problem reported by Bill.

Proposed Solution:
Delete and reinstall the printer to clear the jammed print queue. Add an additional 64MB of RAM to the machine to provide better print performance. Right-click on the printer in the Printers folder after it is reinstalled. From the Properties menu for the printer, click the Sharing tab and enable sharing. Click the Permissions button and add Bill's account and the other two user accounts that need access to the ACL.

Evaluation of Proposed Solution:
Which of the following objectives does the proposed solution accomplish?

A. Only the Required Result

B. The Required Result and both Optional Results

C. The Required Result and only one Optional Result

D. Only one of the Optional Results

E. Neither the Required Result nor the Optional Results

7. Jane calls to ask you why she was not prompted to load the Windows 3.1 printer drivers for a new printer she is creating on her Windows NT 4 Workstation. What should you tell her?

A. That particular printer probably does not support downloading the files to Windows 3.1 clients.

B. She needs to download a patch from the Microsoft Web site.

C. She must install the printer as a network print server in order to specify the drivers.

D. Windows NT 4 will not support downloading drivers to Windows 3.1 clients.

E. Windows 3.1 cannot connect to network printers shared by Windows NT Workstation.

8. Which of the following are valid methods of stopping the Spooler service on an NT Workstation not connected to a network? (Select all that apply.)

A. Use Server Manager

B. Use Service Manager (Control Panel)

C. Use Print Manager

D. Log off the workstation and log back on

E. Shut down and restart the workstation

9. This question is based on the following scenario. Review the scenario first, followed by the objectives and the proposed solution. Then evaluate the proposed solution by choosing the best answer.

Scenario:
You have a Windows NT Workstation 4 set up with a print device attached locally. During normal business hours, the human resources department prints small print jobs to the printer. During the evening, the accounting department would like to use the printer for larger print jobs. Two local groups also exist on the workstation, Accounting and HR.

Required Result:
Create a printer that both departments can access.

Optional Results:
Ensure the accounting department has access only during non-business hours.

Configure the printer in such a way that any jobs sent by the human resources department always have a higher priority than those jobs sent by the accounting department.

Proposed Solution:
Install and share a printer, giving only members of the HR local group access to the printer. Ensure the Available time is set to Always.

Create and share another printer, giving only members of the Accounting local group access. Set the Available time from 8:00PM to 7:00AM.

Set the priority on the printer defined for the Accounting group to 80.

Set the priority on the printer assigned to the HR group to 1.

Evaluation of Proposed Solution:
Which of the following objectives does the proposed solution accomplish?

A. Only the Required Result

B. The Required Result and both Optional Results

C. The Required Result and only one Optional Result

D. Only one of the Optional Results

E. Neither the Required Result nor the Optional Results

10. What will happen to a jammed print job when the Spooler service is stopped?

A. The print job will be restarted when the spooler is restarted.

B. The print job will be deleted.

C. The print job will resume.

D. The print job will be rescheduled.

E. The print job will be placed on hold.

ANSWER KEY

1. C
2. D
3. A
4. D
5. A
6. D
7. D
8. B-E
9. C
10. B

ANSWERS & EXPLANATIONS

INSTALL AND CONFIGURE PRINTERS IN A GIVEN ENVIRONMENT

1. Proposed Solution:

- **Install a printer and give only members of the Managers local group access to the printer. Set the priority to 99.**
- **Create another printer for the Everyone group and set the priority to 50.**
- **Add more RAM and an additional hard disk to the workstation that is acting as the printer server. Change the spooler directory setting to a location on the new hard disk.**
- **From the General tab of the printer's properties page, click the Separator Page button and clear the selection.**

C. Both Optional Results

1. CORRECT ANSWER: C

Although adding more RAM to a Windows NT Workstation is the best way to increase speed on an anemic system, the bottleneck in printing is more than likely due to the output device itself. In this instance, adding more RAM will not significantly speed up print processing. Although adding another hard disk to the machine and relocating the spooler directory will create more room for spooled documents, thereby allowing the print server to process more print jobs, it will not affect printing speed. Therefore, the Proposed Solution does not accomplish the Required Result.

Removing the banner page through the General tab on the printer's properties page will eliminate the printing of banner pages; therefore, the first Optional Result is accomplished.

Creating a second printer for the Managers group and assigning a higher priority to the new printer than to that of the Everyone group will ensure the print jobs submitted by members of the Managers local group will take precedence. It is important to note that priorities must be assigned within the range of 1 (lowest) to 99 (highest). Therefore, the second Optional Result is achieved. Creating multiple printers for a single print device and assigning differing priorities to each printer while restricting access to certain local groups is the only way to prioritize print jobs.

The best solution to accomplish the Required Result would have been to create a printer pool. A printer pool is the association of a single printer with multiple print devices. This enables one set of drivers to control more than one print device, which is effective for printers that serve a large number of print jobs. As print jobs are received, they are automatically routed to free printers to balance the load among the print devices and speed up print job completion. You must ensure that all the print devices associated with the printer pool driver are compatible so the users don't get garbled output.

2. You want to print to a printer managed by a Windows NT Server 4. What should you do?

D. Use the Add Printer Wizard to create a new printer using the Network Printer Server option.

2. CORRECT ANSWER: D

All printer installation under Windows NT Workstation 4 is done through the Add Printer Wizard. The Print Manager application was used with earlier versions of NT Workstation, but it does not exist in the current version.

3. Which of the following statements best describes the functions of the following printing components in Windows NT: the print processor, print monitor, and print spooler? Select only one.

A. The print processor renders the print job for the specific printer; the print monitor tracks print job status; the print spooler sends print jobs to the appropriate ports and assigns priorities to print jobs.

3. CORRECT ANSWER: A

The print processor is responsible for rendering the print job for the specific printer.

The print monitor tracks print job status, monitors print device status (such as paper outages and low toner conditions), and releases the port when printing is complete.

The print spooler sends print jobs to the appropriate ports, assigns priorities to print jobs, assigns print jobs to appropriate ports, and connects to the spooler on remote print servers when sending print jobs to a network print server.

4. Proposed Solution:
Attach the printer to the parallel port of the workstation. Install the appropriate print device on the workstation. Begin the installation of the printer by double-clicking the Add Printer icon in the Printers folder. Select the Network Print Server option.

When the installation is complete, add the "developers" group to the printer's ACL with the Manage Documents permission by right-clicking on the printer and selecting the Sharing... option from the context menu. From the Printers folder, right-click on the printer, select Properties, and select the Advanced tab from the Server properties window. Change the default spool directory to "D:\."

D. Both Optional Results

4. CORRECT ANSWER: D

In Windows NT, "print device" refers to the device that creates the marks on the paper, and "printer" the software that controls the print device. To install the laser printer, the Proposed Solution should be to attach the print device to the workstation's parallel port and install the appropriate printer (software) component.

Additionally, when installing a printer with the Add Printer Wizard, you have two options. The My Computer option should be used when the printer will be attached to and managed by the workstation, even if the workstation will be a network print server. Use the Network Print Server option to connect to a printer already defined on another NT system.

Because of the two reasons above, the Proposed Solution does not achieve the Required Result.

Printers are shared by selecting the Sharing... option from the context menu, or by first selecting Properties from the context menu and then selecting the Sharing tab. Assigning the "Manage Documents" permission will enable members of that group to start, stop, and delete print jobs. Table 3.7 lists the other permissions applicable to printer shares.

TABLE 3.7 CAPABILITIES GRANTED WITH PRINTER PERMISSIONS

Capability	*Full Control*	*Manage Documents*	*Print*	*No Access*
Print documents	X	X	X	
Pause, resume, restart, and cancel the user's own documents	X	X	X	
Connect to a printer	X	X	X	
Control job settings for all documents	X	X		
Pause, restart, and delete all documents	X	X		
Share a printer	X			
Change printer properties	X			
Delete printers	X			
Change printer permissions	X			

Therefore, the Proposed Solution accomplishes the first Optional Result.

The spooler directory is the area of the hard disk where the print spooler stores jobs destined for the printer. If sufficient disk space is not available (minimally about 5MB free, more for complex print jobs), you must free up some disk space. If that is not possible, you must move the spool directory to another location. You can do this by going into the Server properties sheet in the Printers folder.

To change the spool directory's location, complete the following steps:

1. Open the Printers folder by opening the Start menu, choosing Settings, and choosing Printers.

2. From the File menu, choose Server Properties.
3. On the Advanced tab, type in the new location for the spool directory.

   The Proposed Solution accomplishes the second Optional Result.

5. Where can you select an alternative print processor for a printer?

A. From the General tab of the printer's properties sheet

5. CORRECT ANSWER: A

An alternative print processor can be selected by clicking the Print Processor… button on the General tab of the printer's properties sheet.

6. Proposed Solution:
Delete and reinstall the printer to clear the jammed print queue. Add an additional 64MB of RAM to the machine to provide better print performance. Right-click on the printer in the Printers folder after it is reinstalled. From the Properties menu for the printer, click the Sharing tab and enable sharing. Click the Permissions button and add Bill's account and the other two user accounts that need access to the ACL.

D. Only one of the Optional Results

6. CORRECT ANSWER: D

Deleting the printer to clear a jammed print job is not necessary. Stopping and restarting the Spooler service through the Services applet in the Control Panel will clear a jammed queue. When the Spooler service is stopped and restarted in this manner, only the jammed print job will be lost. All other spooled print jobs will print normally once the Spooler service is restarted. Therefore, the Proposed Solution does not achieve the Required Result.

Adding memory is a good start when trying to improve system performance with Windows NT Workstation; however, the hard disk thrashing during the spooling of print jobs is an indication of insufficient disk space available for the spool directory. When jobs are spooled, they are never spooled to memory, only to disk. Therefore, adding RAM will not address the spooling problem. To fix the spooling problem, disk space should be cleaned up and made available, or the spool directory should be redirected to another disk volume with more available space. Therefore, the Proposed Solution does not accomplish the second Optional Result.

A printer can be shared after installation by selecting the Sharing tab, clicking the Permissions… button, and configuring the Access Control List accordingly. The first Optional Result is accomplished with the Proposed Solution.

7. Jane calls to ask you why she was not prompted to load the Windows 3.1 printer drivers for a new printer she is creating on her Windows NT 4 Workstation. What should you tell her?

D. Windows NT 4 will not support downloading drivers to Windows 3.1 clients.

7. CORRECT ANSWER: D

Windows NT Workstation and Server 4 acting as print servers will only dynamically download and update print drivers for Windows 95, Windows 98, and Windows NT clients.

8. Which of the following are valid methods of stopping the Spooler service on an NT Workstation not connected to a network? (Select all that apply.)

B. Use Service Manager (Control Panel)

E. Shut down and restart the workstation

8. CORRECT ANSWER: B-E

Rebooting the workstation or stopping and starting the Spooler service through the Services applet in Control Panel will stop the print spooler services. Using the Services applet will allow other print jobs already spooled to finish printing, whereas rebooting the workstation will delete all spooled print jobs.

If a workstation is participating in a Windows network, the Spooler service could be stopped by using Server Manager from one of the NT Server computers on the network.

9. Proposed Solution:

- **Install and share a printer, giving only members of the HR local group access to the printer. Ensure the Available time is set to Always.**
- **Create and share another printer, giving only members of the Accounting local group access. Set the Available time from 8:00PM to 7:00AM.**
- **Set the priority on the printer defined for the Accounting group to 80.**
- **Set the priority on the printer assigned to the HR group to 1.**

C. The Required Result and only one Optional Result

9. CORRECT ANSWER: C

By creating two printers and setting the availability times appropriately, you will ensure that the HR group will be able to access the printer at any time of the day and the Accounting group members will be able to access the printer only between the hours of 8:00PM to 7:00AM. Therefore, the first Optional Result is achieved by the Proposed Solution. Because both printers are shared, both groups will have access to the printer; therefore, the Required Result is accomplished.

Assigning differing priorities to two printers defined for the same print device is the only way to prioritize print jobs for select groups; however, the Proposed Solution has reversed the priorities. Print prioritizes must be assigned on a scale from 1 (lowest) to 99 (highest). To accomplish the second Optional Result, the priority on the HR group's printer should be a larger value than that assigned to the Accounting group's printer. The second Optional Result is not accomplished by the Proposed Solution.

10. What will happen to a jammed print job when the Spooler service is stopped?

B. The print job will be deleted.

10. CORRECT ANSWER: B

When the Spooler service is stopped and restarted, the current print job will be deleted. Any other spooled jobs will be completed.

FURTHER REVIEW

INSTALL AND CONFIGURE PRINTERS IN A GIVEN ENVIRONMENT

One of the key elements of successfully completing the Windows NT Workstation exam is a solid understanding of both local and network printing and printer management in a Windows NT environment.

Installing a Printer

As with any hardware device, you must ensure that the device is listed on the most recent version of the Windows NT Hardware Compatibility List (HCL) prior to installing the device. If the print device is not listed on the HCL, consult the manufacturer to ensure that a Windows NT 4 driver is available. To install a printer, you must also be logged on with an account that has the right to install or create a printer. The groups in Windows NT Workstation that have that right are:

- Administrators
- Power Users

To install a printer in Windows NT 4, use the Add Printer Wizard. Print Manager is no longer used in Windows NT; the Add Printer Wizard took its place. Be careful of exam questions that refer to configuring or adding printers by using Print Manager.

When you install a printer, you have the option of either installing the printer to My Computer (locally) or installing to a network print server.

Notice that when you install a printer using the Network Print Server option, you never have to specify the printer driver as you do when you install a printer using the My Computer option. That is because the driver is automatically downloaded to your workstation from the print server when you select the Network Print Server option.

Managing Printer Properties

Managing printer properties involves the following actions:

- Configuring printer drivers and general properties
- Managing ports
- Scheduling print jobs
- Sharing printers
- Managing printer security
- Managing device options

Understanding the ins and outs of printer management is essential to being able to administer printing effectively and to successfully completing the Microsoft exam.

Configuring Printer Drivers and General Properties

The printer drivers and general properties are accessed through the General tab on the Printer properties sheet.

From this tab, you can specify a new device driver for this printer. The three command buttons on the bottom of the General tab enable you to specify whether you want a separator page, if you want to specify an alternate print processor, and if you want to generate a test page.

Separator pages, also known as banner pages, supply information such as the name of the user who sent the print job and the time that the print job was sent. Additionally, these separator pages can switch the mode of the printer, such as forcing an HP device to enter PCL mode or switch to PostScript mode. Besides the three default pages, administrators may define additional separator pages for specific functions.

The Print Process command button enables you to specify an alternate print processor for the print device. As an example, WINPRINT offers five default print-job types that specify such parameters as form feed generation after completing the print job.

Managing Ports

The Ports tab displays which ports have associated printers and print devices and enables you to change those port associations. For example, if COM1 experiences a hardware failure, you could switch the defined device to COM2 instead of creating a new printer.

Additionally, this tab enables you to specify additional ports, configure existing ports, and delete ports. You might need to add additional ports, such as a port for network print devices. In the Configure Ports area, you can change the baud rate of COM ports or the transmission retry value for LPT ports. Finally, you can use Delete Port to remove any unneeded ports.

Also from this tab, you can enable bidirectional support for printers so that the printer can return a status update, such as a paper jam, to the selected port.

Scheduling Print Jobs

To manage the scheduling of print jobs, select the Scheduling tab from the Printer properties sheet. The first option on this tab enables you to specify the times when this printer will be available to service print jobs. By specifying two printers for one print device and staggering their availability times, you can manage the order in which documents are printed and alleviate congestion. By having users send large or low-priority print jobs to the printer that's available only during non-business hours, you can effectively ensure the print device will be available for small or high-priority jobs during business hours.

In addition, you can define printer priorities. This option is most effective when two or more printers are associated with a single print device (which is the exact inverse of printer pooling). By setting different priorities for each printer, you can manage the priorities of documents sent to the print device through the different printers. Print priorities do not affect documents that have begun printing.

Lastly, this tab enables you to manage spooler settings on a per-printer basis. You can configure spool settings to make the printing process more efficient. The spool settings that can be set include the following:

- *Spool Print Documents So Program Finishes Printing Faster.* If you choose this option, the documents will spool. This option has two choices within it:

Start Printing After Last Page Is Spooled. Documents will not print until they are completely spooled.

Start Printing Immediately. Documents will print before they have spooled completely, which speeds up printing.

- *Print Directly to the Printer.* This prevents the document from spooling. Although this option speeds up printing, it is not an option for a shared printer, which has to support multiple incoming documents simultaneously.
- *Hold Mismatched Documents.* This prevents incorrect documents from printing. Incorrect documents are those that do not match the configuration of the printer.
- *Print Spooled Documents Faster.* Spooled documents will print ahead of partially spooled documents, even if they have a lower priority. This speeds up printing.
- *Keep Documents After They Have Been Printed.* Documents remain in the spooler after they have been printed.

Using the spool settings to fit your environment can greatly increase the efficiency of your printing.

Sharing Printers

You can designate a printer as shared when you create it, or you can designate an existing printer as shared by using the options on the Sharing tab of the printer's properties sheet. You can do this only if your account has sufficient rights to share the printer.

The Sharing tab enables you to provide a share name and select all the appropriate operating system drivers that should be loaded. Remember that with any share, long share names are supported only under Windows NT and Windows 95.

After you have selected those alternative operating systems from the list, you receive a prompt for the location of the drivers for each operating system. This is so the drivers for each operating system that you have selected can be downloaded when the client tries to print to your printer.

Managing Printer Security

The Security tab from the printer's properties sheet enables you to set permissions for the printer. The four types of printer permissions are:

- Full Control
- Manage Documents
- Print
- No Access

By default, all users are given the Print permission; the creator owner is given Manage Documents permission; and administrators are given Full Control.

Managing Device Options

The final tab of the printer's properties sheet is Device Options. This tab enables you to set specific device options such as color, resolution, and paper tray selection. The options available here will be specific to the print device and should be covered in the particular print device's documentation.

Troubleshooting the Spooler Service

The Spooler service is what controls the print spooling process under Windows NT. If your users cannot print to a printer, or if there are documents in the print queue that will not print and cannot be deleted (even by the administrator), you might need to stop and restart the Spooler service.

While the Spooler service is stopped, no one can print to the shared printer. Stopping and restarting the Spooler service clears only the jammed print job from the queue. Then it allows the other print jobs to continue printing.

CHAPTER SUMMARY

Windows NT resource management is a key element of maintaining an NT Workstation, as well as successfully passing the Microsoft Certification Exam. Managing resources is a broad topic, which Microsoft defines as the ability to perform the following tasks:

- Create and manage local user accounts and local group accounts to meet given requirements.
- Set up and modify user profiles.
- Set up shared folders and permissions.
- Set up permissions on NTFS partitions, folders, and files.
- Install and configure printers in a given environment.

A key part of resource management is managing user and group accounts, as well as understanding how to effectively use local groups to manage the access to shared network resources such as printers and folders. Inherent in this understanding is the ability to determine the net permissions to resources given the interaction of individual user, group, share, and folder/file permissions on both NTFS and FAT formatted volumes.

CHAPTER 4

Connectivity

OBJECTIVES

Add and configure the network components of Windows NT Workstation.

Use various methods to access network resources.

Implement Windows NT Workstation as a client in a NetWare environment.

Use various configurations to install Windows NT as a TCP/IP client.

Configure and install Dial-Up Networking in a given situation.

Configure Microsoft Peer Web Services in a given situation.

After completing this chapter, you should be able to successfully answer the questions presented by Microsoft on the certification exam about connectivity within the Windows NT Workstation environment. Connectivity is a very important part of configuring and managing an NT Workstation. Although Windows NT can be a powerful and productive operating system on a standalone workstation, connecting Windows NT Workstation to a network drastically increases the amount and scope of work that can be done with the workstation.

Microsoft has gone to great lengths to ensure Windows NT Workstation is a good community member, by providing connectivity to the predominant network architectures and network operating systems found in enterprise computing today. You can also be certain that Microsoft will go to great lengths to test your knowledge on configuring and maintaining Windows NT in a network environment.

PRACTICE QUESTIONS

ADD AND CONFIGURE THE NETWORK COMPONENTS OF WINDOWS NT WORKSTATION

1. **Which of the following Control Panel applets enables you to view the Network Properties dialog box? Select all that apply.**

   A. System

   B. Services

   C. Network

   D. Device Manager

   E. Ports

2. **This question is based on the following scenario. Review the scenario first, followed by the objectives and the proposed solution. Then evaluate the proposed solution by choosing the best answer.**

   Scenario:
   You have a Windows NT Workstation computer that is connected to a local area network. There is an NT-compatible adapter installed on the machine with the proper drivers loaded. You want to configure the workstation to share files with another machine located on a different segment of the network.

   Required Result:
   Select the proper network protocol.

   Optional Results:
   Correctly configure the selected protocol.

   Successfully configure your network installation to access files on the remote workstation as well as allowing the remote machine to access files on the local workstation.

   Proposed Solution:
   Install the NetBEUI network protocol on both machines. Disable the Server service on both workstations. There are no user-configurable parameters with the NetBEUI protocol.

   Evaluation of Proposed Solution:
   The proposed solution accomplishes which of the following objectives?

   A. The Required Result only

   B. The Required Result and both Optional Results

   C. The Required Result and one Optional Result

   D. Only one Optional Result

   E. Neither the Required Result nor any Optional Results

3. **Which Windows NT built-in local groups are allowed to make network configuration changes?**

   A. Users

   B. Administrators

   C. Guest

   D. Backup Operators

   E. Power Users

4. **What are the maximum lengths for a computer name and a domain name in Windows NT networking?**

   A. computer name, 15 characters; domain name, 15 characters

   B. computer name, 8 characters; domain name, 15 characters

   C. computer name, 15 characters; domain name, 8 characters

   D. computer name, 14 characters; domain name, 15 characters

   E. computer name, 15 characters; domain name, 22 characters

5. **This question is based on the following scenario. Review the scenario first, followed by the objectives and the proposed solution. Then evaluate the proposed solution by choosing the best answer.**

Scenario:
You have a Windows NT Workstation that needs to participate on the local area network. You turn off the machine, install an NE2000-compatible adapter, and connect the computer to the network. You ask Alex how you can complete the following tasks.

Required Result:
Assign the computer a NetBIOS name.

Optional Results:
Enter the computer into the domain WWSE.NET.

Configure the NetBEUI protocol for network connectivity.

Proposed Solution:
Alex instructs you to do the following:

From Control Panel, start the Network applet.

Click the Adapters tab and click the Add button. Select the NE2000-compatible adapter and supply the correct I/O and IRQ values for the adapter.

Click the Protocols tab and click the Add button. Select the NetBEUI protocol. After the protocol is installed, click the Properties button and enter the network number specified by the LAN administrator.

Click the Identification tab and click the Change button. Enter the appropriate value supplied by your LAN administrator for the NetBIOS name and enter WWSE.NET for the domain name.

Evaluation of Proposed Solution:
The proposed solution accomplishes which of the following objectives?

   A. The Required Result only

   B. The Required Result and both Optional Results

   C. The Required Result and one Optional Result

   D. Only one Optional Result

   E. Neither the Required Result nor any Optional Results

6. **What is the maximum length allowed for a workgroup name?**

   A. 8 characters

   B. 9 characters

   C. 15 characters

   D. 255 characters

   E. 10 characters

7. **This question is based on the following scenario. Review the scenario first, followed by the objectives and the proposed solution. Then evaluate the proposed solution by choosing the best answer.**

Scenario:
You have a Windows NT Workstation computer that is connected to a network running *only* NetWare IPX/SPX. You have two adapters installed in the computer, a 3Com and an NE2000 clone. When examining the computer, you find that the IPX/SPX and TCP/IP services are installed on the computer and bound to one adapter (TCP/IP has the lowest binding to the adapter), and NetBEUI is installed and bound to the second adapter. You have noticed the computer is sluggish when copying network files.

Required Result:
Restore workstation performance.

Optional Results:
Remove all unnecessary protocols.

Optimize the binding order of the network protocols.

Proposed Solution:
From the Network applet in Control Panel, click on the Adapters tab and remove the adapter that has NetBEUI bound to it. Click on the Protocols tab and remove the NetBEUI protocol. Shut down the workstation and physically remove the adapter that you just removed through the Network applet. Reboot the machine and ensure network connectivity on the IPX/SPX network is enabled.

Evaluation of Proposed Solution:
The proposed solution accomplishes which of the following objectives?

A. The Required Result only

B. The Required Result and both Optional Results

C. The Required Result and one Optional Result

D. Only one Optional Result

E. Neither the Required Result nor any Optional Results

8. **Which tab in the Network Properties sheet is used to view and modify the transport protocols for your computer?**

A. System

B. Connectivity

C. Protocols

D. Services

E. Routing

9. **This question is based on the following scenario. Review the scenario first, followed by the objectives and the proposed solution. Then evaluate the proposed solution by choosing the best answer.**

Scenario:
You have a Windows NT Workstation computer that is connected to a local area network. There is an NT-compatible adapter physically installed on the machine. You want to configure the workstation to share files with three other machines on the same segment of the local area network. You ask your friend Josh for some advice.

Required Result:
Select a Microsoft networking model.

Optional Results:
Install the correct drivers for the network interface card.

Select the proper networking protocol.

Proposed Solution:
Josh suggests that you install the NetBEUI protocol, choose the Microsoft Domain networking model, and install the network drivers for the interface card through the Devices applet in Control Panel.

Evaluation of Proposed Solution:
The proposed solution accomplishes which of the following objectives?

A. The Required Result only

B. The Required Result and both Optional Results

C. The Required Result and one Optional Result

D. Only one Optional Result

E. Neither the Required Result nor any Optional Results

10. Which of the following protocols are included with Windows NT Workstation?

A. NetBEUI

B. TCP/IP

C. AppleShare

D. IPX/SPX-compatible

E. IBM SNA

11. Which protocol is installed by default in Windows NT Workstation 4?

A. NetBEUI

B. TCP/IP

C. AppleShare

D. IPX/SPX-compatible

E. DEC LAT

12. To join a domain, you must have network connectivity to which of the following?

A. A member server

B. A backup domain controller

C. The primary domain controller

D. Another workstation

E. All domain controllers

ANSWER KEY

1. C	5. C	9. D
2. D	6. C	10. A-B-D
3. B	7. E	11. B
4. A	8. C	12. C

ANSWERS & EXPLANATIONS

ADD AND CONFIGURE THE NETWORK COMPONENTS OF WINDOWS NT WORKSTATION

1. Which of the following Control Panel applets enables you to view the Network Properties dialog box? Select all that apply.

C. Network

1. CORRECT ANSWER: C

The Network Control Panel applet enables you to access the property pages of the network installation for the workstation. From these property pages, you can add, remove, and configure the available network-related services; change the machine identification information; add, configure, and remove network protocols and adapters; and change the protocol and service binding orders.

2. Proposed Solution:
Install the NetBEUI network protocol on both machines. Disable the Server service on both workstations. There are no user configurable parameters with the NetBEUI protocol.

D. Only one Optional Result

2. CORRECT ANSWER: D

Selecting the NetBEUI protocol does not allow your machine to communicate and collaborate with machines on different segments because the NetBEUI protocol is not routable. NetBEUI is a broadcast-based network protocol, meaning that when a NetBEUI-configured computer wants to talk to another machine, the address of a target machine is broadcast on to the network. Routers, which are used to link segments together, will not propagate the NetBIOS broadcasts used by NetBEUI for name resolution in an effort to reduce excessive network noise. Therefore, NetBEUI traffic cannot transcend segments. The Required Result is not achieved with the Proposed Solution.

NetBEUI is a Microsoft proprietary network protocol designed for ease of use in small, single-segment networks. In striving to make the protocol easy to use, Microsoft designed the protocol as self-configuring, that is, there are no user-configurable parameters. Therefore, the Proposed Solution does accomplish the first Optional Result.

There are two network services within Windows NT (on both Workstation and Server) that must be configured to enable resource sharing and access to shared resources. They are the Server service and the Workstation service. The Server service allows the workstation to make local resources available to the network via sharing. The Workstation service allows the local machine to connect to remotely shared resources via the network. The naming of these services has no relationship to the role of the computer (workstation or server) in the network environment. Therefore, the Proposed Solution does not accomplish the second Optional Result.

3. Which Windows NT built-in local groups are allowed to make network configuration changes?

B. Administrators

3. CORRECT ANSWER: B

Only members of the Administrators group are allowed to make network component configuration changes. Note, however, that both Administrators and Power Users are allowed to create and manage network shares.

4. What are the maximum lengths for a computer name and a domain name in Windows NT networking?

A. computer name, 15 characters; domain name, 15 characters

4. CORRECT ANSWER: A

Within the Microsoft networking model, both machine names and domain names can be up to 15 characters in length. Unlike user passwords, the computer name and domain name are *not* case sensitive.

5. Proposed Solution:
Alex instructs you to do the following:

- **From Control Panel, start the Network applet.**
- **Click the Adapters tab and click the Add button. Select the NE2000-compatible adapter and supply the correct I/O and IRQ values for the adapter.**
- **Click the Protocols tab and click the Add button. Select the NetBEUI protocol. After the protocol is installed, click the Properties button and enter the network number specified by the LAN administrator.**

5. CORRECT ANSWER: C

Both the NetBIOS name and the domain name for the workstation are configured through the Identification tab in the Network Properties for the workstation. The Change button must be clicked prior to editing these values. The Proposed Solution accomplishes the Required Result and the first Optional Result.

- **Click the Identification tab and click the Change button. Enter the appropriate value supplied by your LAN administrator for the NetBIOS name and enter WWSE.NET for the domain name.**

C. The Required Result and one Optional Result

NetBEUI is a self-configuring protocol. There are no user-configurable protocols. The Proposed Solution does not accomplish the second Optional Result.

6. What is the maximum length allowed for a workgroup name?

C. 15 characters

6. CORRECT ANSWER: C

As with the machine and domain names, workgroup names can be no more than 15 characters in length.

7. Proposed Solution:
From the Network applet in Control Panel, click on the Adapters tab and remove the adapter that has NetBEUI bound to it. Click on the Protocols tab and remove the NetBEUI protocol. Shut down the workstation and physically remove the adapter that you just removed through the Network applet. Reboot the machine and ensure network connectivity on the IPX/SPX network is enabled.

E. Neither the Required Result nor any Optional Results

7. CORRECT ANSWER: E

Although removing the unneeded adapter was a step in the right direction, you did not go far enough. Because the workstation is connected to an IPX/SPX-only network, TCP/IP is also not needed for network connectivity. Therefore, the first Optional Result was not accomplished.

Additionally, because TCP/IP is still installed, it still maintains the lowest binding (that is, closest to the adapter) to the remaining adapter. The most used (or default) protocol should enjoy the tightest binding to the network adapter for best performance. Because the default protocol for this network is IPX/SPX, the second Optional Result is not achieved.

Optimizing the binding order and maximizing network performance goes hand in hand. Because the default protocol is not bound closest to the adapter, the Required Result is not accomplished. Note, however, that performance should increase with the removal of the unnecessary device (that is, the second adapter) and the NetBEUI protocol.

8. Which tab in the Network Properties sheet is used to view and modify the transport protocols for your computer?

C. Protocols

8. CORRECT ANSWER: C

The intuitively named Protocols tab in the Network Properties page is used to configure the network transport protocols for Windows NT Workstation (and Server).

See the "Further Review" section for a complete discussion on the availability and function of all the tabs within Network Properties.

9. **Proposed Solution:**

   Josh suggests that you install the NetBEUI protocol, choose the Microsoft Domain networking model, and install the network drivers for the interface card through the Devices applet in Control Panel.

   D. Only one Optional Result

9. CORRECT ANSWER: D

For a small, single-segment network, NetBEUI is an appropriate choice due to the ease of configuration and maintenance. Note, however, that it is not the best choice if the network grows beyond 10 or so machines, or if it becomes segmented, because NetBEUI is a chatty protocol that is not routable. The Proposed Solution accomplishes the second Optional Result.

The Microsoft Domain networking model would not be appropriate in this situation. Establishing a domain requires, at a minimum, an NT Server acting as a primary domain controller. In a scenario where fewer than ten machines will be connected via the network and no NT Servers are present, Microsoft's Workgroup network model should suffice. The Required Result is not met with the Proposed Solution.

Network interface card drivers, protocols, network services, and network protocol binding orders are controlled through the Network applet in Control Panel. Therefore, the Proposed Solution does not meet the first Optional Result.

10. **Which of the following protocols are included with Windows NT Workstation?**

    A. NetBEUI

    B. TCP/IP

    D. IPX/SPX-compatible

10. CORRECT ANSWER: A-B-D

Windows NT Workstation includes the NetBEUI, TCP/IP, and IPX/SPX-compatible protocols on the distribution media. Windows NT is an open architecture system, which means that protocols from other manufactures that are ODI and NDIS 3.0 compatible can, in fact, be installed.

NetBEUI is a Microsoft proprietary protocol that is designed to be easy to install and maintain. It is a broadcast-intensive protocol that is best suited for smaller networks. It is non-routable; however, individual segments can be connected by a bridge.

TCP/IP has become the de-facto standard networking protocol for Enterprise networks and disparate network connectivity. Started in the late 1960s as a Department of Defense project, TCP/IP has gained wide acceptance in the industry thanks to the explosive growth of the Internet. TCP/IP is fully routable but is the most difficult protocol to set up.

The NWLink IPX/SPX-compatible transport is Microsoft's reverse-engineered implementation of Novell's IPX/SPX protocol used with the NetWare network operating system. NWLink is fully routable and is the fastest protocol available for Windows NT.

11. Which protocol is installed by default in Windows NT Workstation 4?

B. TCP/IP

11. CORRECT ANSWER: B

By default, the TCP/IP protocol is automatically selected during the installation of the networking components within Windows NT Workstation setup.

12. To join a domain, you must have network connectivity to which of the following?

C. The primary domain controller

12. CORRECT ANSWER: C

All machine and user accounts are maintained on the primary domain controller in the SAM (Security Access Manager) database. Copies of this database are maintained by the backup domain controllers; however, updates to the SAM database can only be made through the master copy. Therefore, the workstation must be able to establish network connectivity with the primary domain controller in order to join the domain.

FURTHER REVIEW

ADD AND CONFIGURE THE NETWORK COMPONENTS OF WINDOWS NT WORKSTATION

You can configure all of your network components when you install Windows NT Workstation 4. If you want to examine how your network components are configured or make changes to your network configuration, double-click the Network program in Control Panel to view the Network Properties dialog box. You must be an administrator to make changes to the network settings on your computer.

Identification Options

Use the Identification tab in the Network properties sheet to view your computer name and your workgroup or domain name. Click the Change button to change your computer name (maximum length for a computer name is 15 characters) or to join a workgroup or domain (maximum length for a workgroup or domain name is 15 characters).

The Windows NT security system requires that all Windows NT computers in a domain have accounts. Only domain administrators and other users that have been granted the user right of Add Workstations to Domain by a domain administrator can create computer accounts in a Windows NT domain.

If you are a domain administrator, you can give any user or group the user right of Add Workstations to Domain. First, open User Manager for Domains. From the Policies menu, choose User Rights. Then make sure that you check the Show Advanced User Rights box.

How you change your domain name on the Identification tab depends on whether or not you already have an account:

- If a domain administrator has already created a computer account for your computer, type the domain name into the Domain box and click OK.
- To create your own computer account in the domain, you must specify the user name and password of a domain administrator or of an account that has been granted the user right of Add Workstations to Domain by a domain administrator. If you use a username with legitimate rights, you can type the domain name into the Domain box and click OK.
- If you are changing the machine name, the old computer account should be deleted from the domain.

Regardless of which method you use to join a domain, you should see a status message welcoming you to your new domain. You must then restart your computer to complete the process of joining the new domain.

Services Options

Use the Services tab in the Network properties sheet to view and modify the network services for your computer. You might want to add some of the following network services to a Windows NT workstation:

- *Client Services for NetWare (CSNW).* Enables you to access files and/or printers on a NetWare server.
- *Microsoft Peer Web Services.* Installs an intranet Web server on your computer.
- *Microsoft TCP/IP Printing.* Configures your computer to act as a print server to which TCP/IP-based clients, such as UNIX systems, can submit print jobs.
- *Remote Access Server.* Enables your computer to connect via telephone lines or the Internet to remote networks.
- *SNMP Service.* Enables your computer to transmit status information via TCP/IP to network management stations.

Protocols Options

Use the Protocols tab in the Network properties sheet to view and modify the transport protocols for your computer. Windows NT Workstation 4 allows an unlimited number of network transport protocols.

You can also add third-party transport protocols that are ODI and NDIS 3.0 compliant. (Third-party components are those not developed by Microsoft.)

Adapters Options

You can use the Adapters tab in the Network properties sheet to add, remove, view properties of, or update your network adapter drivers. Windows NT Workstation 4 allows an unlimited number of network adapters.

Bindings Options

Network bindings are the connections between network services, transport protocols, and adapter card drivers. You can use the Bindings tab in the Network properties sheet to view, enable, disable, and change the order of the bindings on your computer. The current default protocol for each network service appears at the top of each section in the display.

PRACTICE QUESTIONS

USE VARIOUS METHODS TO ACCESS NETWORK RESOURCES

1. **This question is based on the following scenario. Review the scenario first, followed by the objectives and the proposed solution. Then evaluate the proposed solution by choosing the best answer.**

Scenario:
You have a Windows NT Workstation with connectivity to a LAN. Your supervisor has asked you to connect through the network to various resources located on other workstations and servers. The created connections should be persistent, meaning they should be available when the computer is shut down and rebooted.

Required Result:
Connect to the share MyDocuments$ located on the server named WWW.

Optional Results:
Connect to a network printer named LaserJet5 on the workstation DEV1.

Connect to a network share named Ernest on a workstation named DEV2.

Proposed Solution:
From Network Neighborhood, double-click the computer icon for DEV2. Right-click on the share Ernest and select Map Network Drive from the resulting context menu. Select the preferred drive, ensure Reconnect at Logon is checked, and click OK.

From Network Neighborhood, double-click the computer icon for WWW. Right-click on the share MyDocuments$ and select Map Network Drive from the resulting context menu. Select the preferred drive, ensure Reconnect at Logon is checked, and click OK.

From My Computer, double-click on the Printers icon and install a network printer, specifying both the appropriate drivers for the LaserJet 5 and the proper network path when prompted. Ensure the configuration is correct by printing a test page.

Evaluation of Proposed Solution:
The proposed solution accomplishes which of the following objectives?

A. The Required Result only

B. The Required Result and both Optional Results

C. The Required Result and one Optional Result

D. Only both Optional Results

E. Neither the Required Result nor any Optional Results

2. **To how many characters is a UNC limited (including the filename)?**

A. 8 characters

B. 10 characters

C. 15 characters

D. 256 characters

E. 255 characters

3. **Which of the following is the correct format for the UNC path?**

   A. `\\computername\sharename [\optional path]`

   B. `\\sharename\computername [\optional path]`

   C. `\\sharename [\optional path]`

   D. `\\computername [\optional path]`

   E. `//computername/sharename [/optional path]`

4. **To make a share "invisible," which of the following characters must be added to the name?**

   A. #

   B. $

   C. ;

   D. :

   E. %

5. **This question is based on the following scenario. Review the scenario first, followed by the objectives and the proposed solution. Then evaluate the proposed solution by choosing the best answer.**

Scenario:
You have a folder on a Windows NT Workstation named 10AUGUST1998 Network Monitor Files that you need to share on the network.

Required Result:
Make the share name available to only specified users.

Optional Results:
Ensure Windows 98 machines can utilize the share.

Ensure Windows 3.11 machines can utilize the share.

Proposed Solution:
Create a share named netmon1$.

Evaluation of Proposed Solution:
The proposed solution accomplishes which of the following objectives?

   A. The Required Result only

   B. The Required Result and both Optional Results

   C. The Required Result and one Optional Result

   D. Only one Optional Result

   E. Neither the Required Result nor any Optional Results

6. **Where within the share name must the $ character be placed to create a hidden share?**

   A. At the beginning

   B. Anywhere within the name

   C. At the end of the name

   D. Within quotation marks anywhere within the name

   E. Within double quotation marks anywhere within the name

7. **This question is based on the following scenario. Review the scenario first, followed by the objectives and the proposed solution. Then evaluate the proposed solution by choosing the best answer.**

   Scenario:
   You need to utilize an application located within a hidden share created as secret$ on the workstation named Apps1.

   Required Result:
   Provide users the ability to access and run the application by double-clicking the icon for the application in Windows NT Explorer.

   Optional Results:
   Map a network drive to the application.

   Ensure the mapped drive will be available next time you log on to the workstation.

   Proposed Solution:
   From the MS-DOS console, execute the `net` command with the following syntax:

   ```
   net use h:\ \\apps1\secret$
   ```

   (For purposes of this scenario, assume the H:\ drive is available.)

   Create a shortcut to the newly mapped H:\ drive and place the shortcut on the desktop.

   Evaluation of Proposed Solution:
   The proposed solution accomplishes which of the following objectives?

   A. The Required Result only

   B. The Required Result and both Optional Results

   C. The Required Result and one Optional Result

   D. Only one Optional Result

   E. Neither the Required Result nor any Optional Results

8. **UNC names are supported by what percent of Windows NT Workstation functions?**

   A. 50%

   B. 75%

   C. 78%

   D. 100%

   E. None of the Windows NT Workstation network functions support the UNC standard

9. **UNC names can be used to access which of the following network devices?**

   A. Windows NT servers

   B. Routers

   C. Gateways

   D. NetWare servers

   E. Windows 3.11 clients

10. **Which of the following is the correct UNC path for a file named HSTANTON.DAT in a directory named PROFILES in a share named USERDATA on a server named WWW?**

A. `\\WWW\USERDATA\PROFILES\`
`➥HSTANTON.DAT`

B. `\\ HSTANTON.DAT\PROFILES\`
`➥USERDATA\WWW`

C. `\\USERDATA\WWW\PROFILES\`
`➥HSTANTON.DAT`

D. `//HSTANTON.DAT/PROFILES/`
`➥USERDATA/WWW`

E. `\\WWW\USERDATA-PROFILES\`
`➥HSTANTON.DAT`

ANSWER KEY

1. D
2. E
3. A
4. B
5. B
6. C
7. C
8. D
9. A-D-E
10. A

ANSWERS & EXPLANATIONS

USE VARIOUS METHODS TO ACCESS NETWORK RESOURCES

1. Proposed Solution:
From Network Neighborhood, double-click the computer icon for DEV2. Right-click on the share Ernest and select Map Network Drive from the resulting context menu. Select the preferred drive, ensure Reconnect at Logon is checked, and click OK.

From Network Neighborhood, double-click the computer icon for WWW. Right-click on the share MyDocuments$ and select Map Network Drive from the resulting context menu. Select the preferred drive, ensure Reconnect at Logon is checked, and click OK.

From My Computer, double-click on the Printers icon and install a network printer, specifying both the appropriate drivers for the LaserJet 5 and the proper network path when prompted. Ensure the configuration is correct by printing a test page.

D. Only both Optional Results

1. CORRECT ANSWER: D

Non-hidden shares (those without a $ character appended to the end) will appear in Network Neighborhood to users browsing the specified machine. While in Network Neighborhood, you can right-click on any share to map a network drive to the specified share. The Proposed Solution accomplishes the second Optional Result.

Printers are not mapped through Network Neighborhood, but rather through the Add New Printers application that is accessible through the Printers folder. To connect to a network printer, a new printer must be installed on the workstation using the Network Printer option. The Proposed Solution accomplishes the first Optional Result.

Hidden shares (those shares with the $ character appended to the share name) will not appear in Network Neighborhood to users browsing a network server. Because the Proposed Solution indicated the hidden share was mapped through Network Neighborhood, the Required Result has not been accomplished with the Proposed Solution.

However, hidden shares may be mapped to a local drive using the `net` command with the following syntax:

```
net use <device> <share name> [/Persistent:YES]
```

where

- *device* is the local drive, such as M:.
- *share name* is the UNC path to the share, such as \\www\test. A UNC, which stands for Universal Naming Convention, is a way to uniquely identify shares on a network. The format is the server name, followed by the share name and an optional path:

  ```
  \\servername\sharename\optional path
  ```

2. To how many characters is a UNC limited (including the filename)?

E. 255 characters

2. CORRECT ANSWER: E

A UNC with a filename cannot exceed 255 characters.

3. Which of the following is the correct format for the UNC path?

A. *computername**sharename* [*optional path*]

3. CORRECT ANSWER: A

The UNC follows the format

```
\\computername\sharename[\optional path]
```

It is important that you not confuse the direction of the slashes; the forward slash is used with UNIX-style directories and Internet URLs.

4. To make a share "invisible," which of the following characters must be added to the name?

B. $

4. CORRECT ANSWER: B

The $ character appended to the end of a share name will make that share name invisible to users browsing the shares through Network Neighborhood. You can still connect directly to the share via the Run command or from the command prompt by typing the explicit UNC for the share.

5. Proposed Solution: Create a share named netmon1$.

B. The Required Result and both Optional Results

5. CORRECT ANSWER: B

Appending the $ character to any share name will make the share invisible to users browsing shares on that particular machine. The share will be accessible to those individuals who know the complete UNC and enter the UNC through the Run dialog box (from the Start menu) or the command prompt. The Proposed Solution accomplishes the Required Result.

Windows 98 clients can access any share name, regardless of length, assuming the complete path (the UNC and filename) is within the limit of 255 characters. The Proposed Solution accomplishes the first Optional Result.

Windows 3.11 and earlier network clients, including MS-DOS clients, can access only share names that conform to the 8.3 DOS naming convention. Because the share is fewer than eight characters in length, the second Optional Result is achieved.

6. Where within the share name must the $ character be placed to create a hidden share?

C. At the end of the name

6. CORRECT ANSWER: C

A share will only be hidden if the designated share hiding character (the $) is appended to the end of the share name.

7. Proposed Solution:
From the MS-DOS console, execute the `net` command with the following syntax:

```
net use h:\ \\apps1\secret$
```

(For purposes of this scenario, assume the H:\ drive is available.)

Create a shortcut to the newly mapped H:\ drive and place the shortcut on the desktop.

C. The Required Result and one Optional Result

7. CORRECT ANSWER: C

Because a hidden share will not appear to users browsing with Network Neighborhood, a drive can be mapped to a hidden network share by using the `net` command with the `use` parameter. The Proposed Solution therefore accomplishes the first Optional Result.

Without the `/PERSISTENT:YES` switch with the `net use` command, the drive will not be permanently stored and remapped when the user logs off and back on to the workstation. The Proposed Solution does not accomplish the second Optional Result.

By mapping the network drive and creating a shortcut to that drive on the desktop, you enable users to double-click the shortcut and see the contents of the mapped share in a Windows NT Explorer window. In this respect, a mapped drive is like any other drive available through Windows NT Explorer: Users can double-click on applications to launch them. The Proposed Solution accomplishes the Required Result. Note that it is not necessary to create the shortcut to satisfy the Required Result; it is done as a matter of convenience for the user.

8. UNC names are supported by what percent of Windows NT Workstation functions?

D. 100%

8. CORRECT ANSWER: D

All Windows NT Workstation network functions will accept the UNC name as a valid argument.

9. UNC names can be used to access which of the following network devices?

A. Windows NT servers

D. NetWare servers

E. Windows 3.11 clients

9. CORRECT ANSWER: A-D-E

UNCs can be used to access all devices that have NetBIOS names assigned, which are typically NetWare servers and computers running a networked Microsoft operating system (Windows 3.11, Windows 95, Windows 98, or Windows

NT). Routers and gateways are typically referred to only by IP address.

10. Which of the following is the correct UNC path for a file named HSTANTON.DAT in a directory named PROFILES in a share named USERDATA on a server named WWW?

A. `\\WWW\USERDATA\PROFILES\`
`➥HSTANTON.DAT`

10. CORRECT ANSWER: A

Files with a UNC path are specified with the following syntax:

`\\`*`SERVERNAME`*`\`*`SHARE`*`\[`*`PATH`*`]\`*`FILENAME`*

FURTHER REVIEW

USE VARIOUS METHODS TO ACCESS NETWORK RESOURCES

Windows NT Workstation 4 offers several methods of working with network resources, and each of those methods offers different ways of determining what network resources are available to you and the different types of connections you can make to those network resources.

Universal Naming Convention

The *Universal Naming Convention* (UNC) is a standardized way of specifying a share name on a specific computer. Share names can refer to folders or to printers. The UNC path takes the form of `\\computer_name\share_name`.

It is important to note that connections made via UNC paths take place immediately and do not require the use of a drive letter. It is also important to note that if a dollar sign is placed at the end of a share name, the share becomes "hidden" and does not show up in listings, but it can still be accessed by using the UNC name.

Many 16-bit applications do not work with UNC paths. If you need to use a 16-bit application that doesn't work with UNC paths, you must either map a drive letter to the shared folder or connect a port to the network printer.

Network Neighborhood

When you view lists of computers in Network Neighborhood, you are actually viewing a graphical representation of what is called a browse list. The browse list is actually maintained by a computer that has been designated as a browse master. All computers on the network (that have an active Server service) periodically announce their presence to the browse master to keep the browse list current.

Note that a Windows 95 computer in a workgroup that has the same name as a Windows NT domain will be listed with the Windows NT computers in the browse list if it has file or printer sharing enabled.

Net View Command

You can access the current browse list from the command prompt by typing **`NET VIEW`**. The current browse list is displayed on your screen. A sample browse list looks like this:

```
C:\>net view
Server Name      Remark

-------------------------
\\TEST1
\\TEST2
\\TESTPDC
The command completed successfully.
```

Net Use Command

In addition to using the `net use` command for accessing folder shares (as discussed above) you can also use the `net use` command to connect clients to network printers. For instance, if you wanted to connect port LPT1: to a network printer named HP5 on a server named SERVER1, you could use the following command:

```
net use LPT1: \\SERVER1\HP5
```

To disconnect the network resources for these two, use the following two commands:

```
net use X: /d
net use LPT1: /d
```

PRACTICE QUESTIONS

IMPLEMENT WINDOWS NT WORKSTATION AS A CLIENT IN A NETWARE ENVIRONMENT

1. **Which three components listed enable a Windows NT Workstation 4 computer to access files and printers on a NetWare server?**

   A. Client Services for NetWare

   B. Gateway Services for NetWare

   C. NWLink IPX/SPX Compatible Transport

   D. File and Print Services for NetWare

   E. Microsoft Client32 for NetWare

2. **To access files or printers on a NetWare server, which of the following must you install in addition to NWLink?**

   A. Gateway Services for NetWare

   B. Microsoft Client Services for NetWare Networks

   C. Microsoft File and Print Services for NetWare

   D. IPX/SPX

   E. Novell's NetWare redirector

3. **This question is based on the following scenario. Review the scenario first, followed by the objectives and the proposed solution. Then evaluate the proposed solution by choosing the best answer.**

Scenario:
You have an NT Workstation that needs to connect to a network that is running only the IPX/SPX protocol with NetWare 4.11. Currently, there is an NE2000-compatible adapter installed, and the NetBEUI protocol is bound to the adapter. There are no other network protocols installed on the workstation.

Required Result:
Configure the computer to connect to the NetWare file servers on the network.

Optional Results:
Set the default tree to LIMNET.

Optimize the networking performance of the workstation.

Proposed Solution:
From the Network applet, select the Protocols tab and choose NWLink IPX/SPX Compatible Transport. After the protocol is installed, reboot the workstation. Logon normally. Using the Network applet in Control Panel, set the default tree and context to the desired values.

Evaluation of Proposed Solution:
The proposed solution accomplishes which of the following objectives?

   A. The Required Result only

   B. The Required Result and both Optional Results

   C. The Required Result and one Optional Result

D. Only one Optional Result

E. Neither the Required Result nor any Optional Results

4. **A Windows NT Workstation computer can access NetWare servers via a Windows NT server as long as the Windows NT server is running which of the following?**

A. Gateway Services for NetWare

B. Microsoft Client Services for NetWare Networks

C. Microsoft File and Print Services for NetWare

D. IPX/SPX

E. NWLink IPX/SPX Compatible Transport

5. **Which of the following is the protocol used to negotiate and determine the largest possible frame size that can be used to communicate with NetWare servers?**

A. IPX

B. SPX

C. NCP

D. LIP

E. LAT

6. **Which of the following is the standard Novell protocol for file and print sharing?**

A. IPX

B. SPX

C. NCP

D. LIP

E. IP

7. **This question is based on the following scenario. Review the scenario first, followed by the objectives and the proposed solution. Then evaluate the proposed solution by choosing the best answer.**

Scenario:
You have an NT Workstation that will participate on a NetWare network. There are servers configured with both 3.11 and 3.12 versions of Novell's NetWare network operating system. Also installed are an NT-compatible adapter and the appropriate drivers. No network protocols are installed.

Required Result:
Configure the NT Workstation to attach to the NetWare 3.12 servers.

Optional Results:
Optimize network performance.

Configure the workstation to attach to the NetWare 3.11 servers.

Proposed Solution:
Install Client Services for NetWare through the Services tab in the Network Control Panel applet.

Evaluation of Proposed Solution:
The proposed solution accomplishes which of the following objectives?

A. The Required Result only

B. The Required Result and both Optional Results

C. The Required Result and one Optional Result

D. Only one Optional Result

E. Neither the Required Result nor any Optional Results

8. CSNW is installed from which Control Panel applet?

A. Network

B. System

C. Services

D. User Manager for Domains

E. Devices

ANSWER KEY

1. A-B-C
2. B
3. E
4. A-B-E
5. D
6. C
7. C
8. A

ANSWERS & EXPLANATIONS

IMPLEMENT WINDOWS NT WORKSTATION AS A CLIENT IN A NETWARE ENVIRONMENT

1. Which three components listed enable a Windows NT Workstation 4 computer to access files and printers on a NetWare server?

A. Client Services for NetWare

B. Gateway Services for NetWare

C. NWLink IPX/SPX Compatible Transport

1. CORRECT ANSWER: A-B-C

Client Services for NetWare, also known as CSNW, is a network service that will enable a workstation to act as a Novell NetWare client on a Novell NetWare network. By default, when installed, CSNW also installs the NWLink IPX/SPX Compatible Transport.

NWLink IPX/SPX Compatible Transport is the network protocol used, in conjunction with CSNW, by Windows NT to enable the workstation to act as a NetWare client.

Gateway Services for NetWare, also known as GSNW, is an NT Server component that enables the NT Server on which it is installed to act as a gateway for clients to access the NetWare network. The important aspect of GSNW is that it does not require the clients connecting to the server to have any NetWare components installed to access the resources. Because all requests for NetWare resources have to pass through the network interface on the server, GSNW is an appropriate solution only for a short time, such as in the case of a migration or when only a small number of clients have low usage requirements. Although GSNW is not a Workstation component, you must be aware of GSNW and its uses for the certification exam.

File and Print Services for NetWare, or FPNW, is an NT Server component add-on. In other words, it is not included with the NT Server product that enables Novell clients to attach and use Microsoft resources such as folder shares and printers.

Microsoft Client 32 for NetWare is the Windows 95/98 NDS client.

2. In order to access files or printers on a NetWare server, which of the following must you install in addition to NWLink?

B. Microsoft Client Services for NetWare Networks

2. CORRECT ANSWER: B

NWLink, or more appropriately NWLink IPX/SPX Compatible Transport, is only a network protocol. The Client Services for NetWare must also be installed for a user to be authenticated to the NetWare environment and access resources.

3. Proposed Solution:
From the Network applet, select the Protocols tab and choose NWLink IPX/SPX Compatible Transport. After the protocol is installed, reboot the workstation. Logon normally. Using the Network applet in Control Panel, set the default tree and context to the desired values.

E. Neither the Required Result nor any Optional Results

3. CORRECT ANSWER: E

To connect with file shares and printers on a NetWare network, Client Services for NetWare (CSNW) must be installed. Installing only NWLink IPX/SPX Compatible Transport enables the workstation to communicate on a NetWare network but not access resources. When CSNW is installed, NWLink IPX/SPX Compatible Transport is automatically installed. The Proposed Solution does not accomplish the Required Result.

The tree and context for authenticating to a NetWare network are not set through the Network Control Panel applet, but rather through the CSNW applet in Control Panel. The CSNW applet will not appear in Control Panel until the CSNW service is installed through the Services tab in the Network Control Panel applet. Installing only the protocol will not allow you to log on to the NetWare network (in this case, because NetWare 4.11 is running, users will not be able to authenticate to the NetWare Directory Services). The Proposed Solution does not accomplish the first Optional Result.

When configuring the workstation to connect to a NetWare-only network (that is, a network running only IPX/SPX), it is not necessary to have the NetBEUI protocol installed. When the CSNW is installed, the NetBEUI protocol should be removed. In this scenario, not only is an extra protocol installed and running, but it is also bound closest to the adapter, thereby creating an even greater performance degradation. The Proposed Solution does not accomplish the second Optional Result.

4. A Windows NT Workstation computer can access NetWare servers via a Windows NT server as long as the Windows NT server is running which of the following?

A. Gateway Services for NetWare

B. Microsoft Client Services for NetWare Networks

E. NWLink IPX/SPX Compatible Transport

4. CORRECT ANSWER: A-B-E

For a Windows NT Workstation to access NetWare resources through an NT Server, the server must be running a protocol (NWLink), a network client (Microsoft Client Services for NetWare Networks), and a gateway (Gateway Services for NetWare). It is only necessary to install GSNW and NWLink, however, as installing GSNW automatically installs CSNW.

5. Which of the following is the protocol used to negotiate and determine the largest possible frame size that can be used to communicate with NetWare servers?

D. LIP

5. CORRECT ANSWER: D

The LIP, or Large Internet Protocol, is the protocol used to negotiate the largest possible frame type when establishing communications with a NetWare server.

6. Which of the following is the standard Novell protocol for file and print sharing?

C. NCP

6. CORRECT ANSWER: C

NCP, or NetWare Control Protocol, is Novell's standard protocol for file and print sharing.

7. Proposed Solution:

Install Client Services for NetWare through the Services tab in the Network Control Panel applet.

C. The Required Result and one Optional Result

7. CORRECT ANSWER: C

Installing the Client Services for NetWare (CSNW) service will enable the client computer to communicate with an access resource for NetWare servers. Additionally, CSNW will automatically detect the frame type used by the network topology. For NetWare versions 3.12 and later, the frame type utilized by default is 802.2. For NetWare versions 3.11 and earlier, the frame type by default is 802.3. Therefore, there will be multiple frame types present on the network. When Windows NT's CSNW detects multiple frame types, it defaults to the 802.2. Therefore, the proposed solution will accomplish the Required Result because the Required Result requires use of the 802.2 frame type.

Because the frame type is 802.2 and the NetWare 3.11 servers use the 802.3 frame type by default, the Proposed Solution does not accomplish the second Optional Result.

To choose which frame type Windows NT Workstation CSNW will use, select the NWLink IPX/SPX Compatible Transport properties from the Protocols tab in the Network Control Panel applet. In this case, switching frame types would not meet the requirement, because if you switch frame types, the workstation will be able to communicate with the NetWare 3.11 servers and not the 3.12 servers. The solution is to edit the following Registry key:

```
HKEY_LOCAL_MACHINE\System\CurrentControlSet\Services
➥\Nwlinklpx\NetConfig\Network adapter card1
```

By default, this key is set to 0xff to indicate the frame should be auto-detected. Allowable values for the key are:

0	Ethernet
1	Ethernet 802.3
2	Ethernet 802.2
3	Ethernet SNAP
4	ArcNet

For the exam, you will not need to know the particular values for the Registry key or the Registry key itself. You only need to know that the Registry must be modified to use multiple frame types on a NetWare network.

Because the NWLink IPX/SPX Compatible Transport is the only protocol installed on the workstation, the network performance of the workstation will be maximized. The Proposed Solution accomplishes the first Optional Result.

8. CSNW is installed from which Control Panel applet?

A. Network

8. CORRECT ANSWER: A

The Network applet in Control Panel is used to configure all network services, protocols, and adapters.

FURTHER REVIEW

IMPLEMENT WINDOWS NT WORKSTATION AS A CLIENT IN A NETWARE ENVIRONMENT

Windows NT Workstation can run NetWare connectivity services and access NetWare networks quite easily. To enable a Windows NT Workstation 4 computer to access and share resources on a NetWare server, you might have to install additional software besides the NWLink protocol on the Windows NT Workstation 4 computers. What type of access you are trying to establish determines whether you need to install the additional software. NWLink can establish client/server connections but does not provide access to files and printers on NetWare servers.

If you want to be able to access files or printers on a NetWare server, you must install the Microsoft Client Services for NetWare (CSNW), which is included with Windows NT Workstation 4. CSNW enables Windows NT Workstation 4 to access files and printers at NetWare servers running NetWare 2.15 or later (including NetWare 4.x servers running NDS). CSNW installs an additional network redirector.

Windows NT Workstation 4 computers that have NWLink and CSNW installed gain the following benefits:

- A new network redirector compatible with NetWare Control Protocol (NCP). NCP is the standard Novell protocol for file and print sharing.
- Freedom to use long filenames (when the NetWare server is configured to support long filenames).
- Large Internet Protocol (LIP) to automatically negotiate and determine the largest possible frame size to communicate with NetWare servers.

A Windows NT Workstation 4 computer can access files and printers on a NetWare server without adding CSNW by connecting through a Windows NT Server configured with Gateway Services for NetWare (GSNW).

Installing CSNW

CSNW is installed the same way as any other network service, through the Network program in the Control Panel. After you install CSNW, you will notice a new CSNW program listed in the Control Panel.

Configuring CSNW

After you install CSNW on your computer, users that log on receive a prompt to enter the details of their NetWare accounts. Users can enter a preferred server for NetWare 2.15 or above or 3.x, or they can enter their default trees and context for NDS (the default in NetWare 4.x), or they can specify <None> if they do not have NetWare accounts. Every time the same user logs on to that computer, that user automatically connects to the specified NetWare account in addition to the Windows NT account.

Each user is asked to enter the NetWare account information only once. The only way to change a user's recorded NetWare account information is to double-click the CSNW program in Control Panel and make the change there. You can also use the CSNW program in Control Panel to modify your print options for NetWare printers (to add form feeds or print banners, for example).

Even though Windows NT Workstation 4 attempts to automatically connect you to your NetWare system, there is no direct link between the two account databases. If you change either network password, the other password does not automatically change to match your new network password. If you press Ctrl+Alt+Delete and choose Change Password, you have the option of selecting NetWare or Compatible Network in the Domain field. From there you can change the NetWare password. (On NetWare servers running in bindery mode, you can also use the NetWare Setpass utility.)

Connecting to NetWare Resources

After you install NWLink and CSNW, you access the NetWare servers in your network using the same methods you use to connect to any other Windows NT server. You can connect to files and printers on the NetWare servers without any special procedures:

- *Browsing.* After you install NWLink and CSNW, double-click Network Neighborhood, and then double-click Entire Network. You can choose to browse either the Microsoft Windows Network or the NetWare or Compatible Network.
- *Map command.* After you install NWLink and CSNW, right-click Network Neighborhood and choose Map Network Drive from the shortcut menu. You can then assign any drive letter to any shared directory on a NetWare server.
- *Other commands.* The Capture, Login, Logout, and Attach commands, all from NetWare, can cause problems if run from a Windows NT Workstation. However, their functionality is available from other utilities supplied with Workstation. So you should avoid these four utilities to prevent execution failures.

PRACTICE QUESTIONS

USE VARIOUS CONFIGURATIONS TO INSTALL WINDOWS NT WORKSTATION AS A TCP/IP CLIENT

1. **Which of the following is the default protocol for Windows NT Workstation 4?**

   A. IPX/SPX

   B. NCP

   C. TCP/IP

   D. NetBEUI

   E. LAT

2. **Which of the following is defined as a value used to determine whether a host is on the same network or a different network?**

   A. Default gateway

   B. Subnet mask

   C. IP address

   D. DNS server address

   E. WINS server address

3. **This question is based on the following scenario. Review the scenario first, followed by the objectives and the proposed solution. Then evaluate the proposed solution by choosing the best answer.**

Scenario:
You have a Windows NT Workstation with a network adapter card installed and the appropriate drivers loaded. The TCP/IP protocol is installed, but not yet configured.

Required Result:
Configure the adapter to use the DHCP protocol for dynamic configuration of TCP/IP.

Optional Results:
Configure the machine to use a WINS server with an IP address of 209.94.22.226.

Configure the TCP/IP properties to use the DNS server at the IP address 209.94.22.228 as the primary DNS server and to use the DNS server at the IP address 209.94.22.229 as the secondary DNS server.

Proposed Solution:
From Control Panel, double-click the Network applet. Select the Protocols tab, click on TCP/IP, and click the Properties button.

Click the DNS tab. Click the Add button and enter **209.94.22.229**. Click Add. Click the Add button again, enter **209.94.22.228**, and click Add again.

Click the WINS Address tab and enter **209.94.22.226** for the primary WINS server.

Click OK on the TCP/IP properties page and return to the Network Properties page. Click the Services tab and add the DHCP service to enable DHCP client configuration for this machine.

Evaluation of Proposed Solution:
The proposed solution accomplishes which of the following objectives?

A. The Required Result only

B. The Required Result and both Optional Results

C. The Required Result and one Optional Result

D. Only one Optional Result

E. Neither the Required Result nor any Optional Results

4. **Which of the following is the optional setting that identifies the router for the local TCP/IP network segment?**

   A. Default gateway

   B. Subnet mask

   C. IP address

   D. DNS server address

   E. WINS address

5. **Which of the following is defined as a unique, logical 32-bit address used to identify a TCP/IP host?**

   A. Default gateway

   B. Subnet mask

   C. IP address

   D. DNS server address

   E. WINS address

6. **Name resolution is commonly performed by which of the following?**

   A. Default gateway

   B. Subnet mask

   C. IP address

   D. DNS server

   E. NetBIOS name

7. **Which of the following commands displays your computer's IP address?**

   A. IPCONFIG

   B. DHCP

   C. IPX

   D. NETCONFIG

   E. WINIPCFG

8. **How many WINS servers must you specify in order to configure Windows NT Workstation as a TCP/IP client for Internet connectivity?**

   A. None

   B. One

   C. Two

   D. Four

   E. None of the above

9. **Which two of the following are used for name resolution processes?**

   A. DHCP

   B. WINS

   C. IPCONFIG

   D. DNS

   E. RIP

10. **This question is based on the following scenario. Review the scenario first, followed by the objectives and the proposed solution. Then evaluate the proposed solution by choosing the best answer.**

Scenario:

You have a Windows NT Workstation that has an NE2000-compatible NIC installed with the appropriate drivers. TCP/IP is installed and configured to use DHCP.

Required Result:
Configure the machine to not use DHCP, but to use a static IP address instead.

Optional Results:
Add the IP address 209.94.9.250 to the TCP/IP configuration.

Configure the machine for an additional IP address of 209.94.9.251.

Proposed Solution:
From Control Panel, double-click the Network applet. Select the Protocols tab, click on TCP/IP, and click the Properties button.

Click the Services tab and remove the DHCP service from the workstation.

Click the Protocols tab and open the properties for the existing TCP/IP protocol. On the IP Address tab, add the address 209.94.9.250. Click OK to return to the Protocol tab of the Network property page.

Click the Add button and add another instance of the TCP/IP protocol. Open the properties for the newly installed TCP/IP protocol. On the IP Address tab, add the address 209.94.9.251. Click OK to return to the Protocol tab of the Network property page.

Evaluation of Proposed Solution:
The proposed solution accomplishes which of the following objectives?

A. The Required Result only

B. The Required Result and both Optional Results

C. The Required Result and one Optional Result

D. Only one Optional Result

E. Neither the Required Result nor any Optional Results

11. Of the following, which addresses are valid TCP/IP addresses?

A. 192.200.14.7

B. 1.1.1.200

C. 34.56.76.256

D. 127.120.200.14

E. 255.255.255.255

12. IP addresses given to clients from a DHCP server are said to be which of the following?

A. Issued

B. In use

C. Leased

D. Reserved

E. Masked

13. Host name lookup files provided for Windows NT Workstation by Microsoft include which of the following?

A. Services

B. Networks

C. HOSTS

D. LMHOSTS

E. LMHOSTS.SAM

14. This question is based on the following scenario. Review the scenario first, followed by the objectives and the proposed solution. Then evaluate the proposed solution by choosing the best answer.

Scenario:

You have an NT Workstation with a 3Com adapter installed and properly configured. The TCP/IP protocol is the only protocol bound to the adapter. The TCP/IP configuration is using DHCP to receive an IP address, subnet mask, default gateway, and DNS server information. The network the Workstation is connected to has Internet connectivity. You try to reach `www.microsoft.com` but receive a timeout error.

Required Result:

Ensure the TCP/IP protocol is properly installed on the workstation.

Optional Results:

Ensure the TCP/IP configuration received from the DHCP server is correct.

Ensure network connectivity with the gateway is functional.

Proposed Solution:

Use the `PING` command to test the connection to 127.0.0.1. Contact the LAN administrator and request the address of the DHCP server and the default gateway. From the Console windows, use the PING utility to test connectivity to both of these addresses.

Evaluation of Proposed Solution:

The proposed solution accomplishes which of the following objectives?

A. The Required Result only

B. The Required Result and both Optional Results

C. The Required Result and one Optional Result

D. Only one Optional Result

E. Neither the Required Result nor any Optional Results

ANSWER KEY

1. C
2. B
3. D
4. A
5. C
6. C
7. A
8. A
9. B-D
10. E
11. A-B
12. C
13. C-D-E
14. C

ANSWERS & EXPLANATIONS

USE VARIOUS CONFIGURATIONS TO INSTALL WINDOWS NT WORKSTATION AS A TCP/IP CLIENT

1. Which of the following is the default protocol for Windows NT Workstation 4?

C. TCP/IP

1. CORRECT ANSWER: C

If network components are installed, TCP/IP is the default networking protocol installed with Windows NT Workstation.

The NetBEUI and NWLink IPX/SPX Compatible Transport (abbreviated as IPX/SPX in setup) protocols are also choices from Windows NT Setup. Other protocols can be added after the Workstation is set up and initially configured.

2. Which of the following is defined as a value used to determine whether a host is on the same network or a different network?

B. Subnet mask

2. CORRECT ANSWER: B

The subnet mask is used to divide large IP address spaces (such as a Class A, Class B, or Class C network) into smaller, more manageable networks or subnets. A subnet mask consists of four octets. If the bit in an octet is a 1, that portion of the IP address is considered a network address. If the bit is a 0, that bit of the address is considered part of the host address.

3. Proposed Solution:
From Control Panel, double-click the Network applet. Select the Protocols tab, click on TCP/IP, and click the Properties button.

Click the DNS tab. Click the Add button and enter 209.94.22.229. Click Add. Click the Add button again and enter 209.94.22.228. Click Add again.

Click the WINS Address tab and enter 209.94.22.226 for the primary WINS server.

Click OK on the TCP/IP properties page and return to the Network Properties page. Click the Services tab and add the DHCP service to enable DHCP client configuration for this machine.

D. Only one Optional Result

3. CORRECT ANSWER: D

There are two components to DHCP: the server and the client. The server must be installed and configured on a Windows NT Server. When used on the service, the DHCP service is in fact loaded through the Services tab of the Network Control Panel applet. To configure the client to utilize DHCP, you enable it through the TCP/IP IP Address tab, which is accessed through the TCP/IP protocol properties found in the Protocols tab of the Network applet. The Proposed Solution does not accomplish the Required Result.

WINS server addresses are added through the WINS tab in the TCP/IP protocol properties. The Proposed Solution accomplishes the first Optional Result.

DNS server addresses are configured through the DNS tab of the TCP/IP protocol properties. The order the addresses are inserted is Primary first, followed by Secondary, Tertiary, and so on. After the addresses are entered, you can rearrange their order by using the arrows to the right of the DNS server address listing. The Proposed Solution does not accomplish the second Optional Result.

4. Which of the following is the optional setting that identifies the router for the local TCP/IP network segment?

A. Default gateway

4. CORRECT ANSWER: A

The router is the address to which a workstation will pass traffic if the address is determined to not be located on the local segment. TCP/IP terms this address the default gateway.

As with all network devices on a TCP/IP network, the address of the router, or default gateway, consists of four octets, resulting in a 32-bit address.

5. Which of the following is defined as a unique, logical 32-bit address used to identify a TCP/IP host?

C. IP address

5. CORRECT ANSWER: C

The IP address of a machine is its unique 32-bit address expressed as four octets.

6. Name resolution is commonly performed by which of the following?

C. IP address

6. CORRECT ANSWER: C

A people-friendly name such as `www.wwse.net` is easier to remember than the IP address of a machine, such as 209.94.9.243. The Domain Name Service, or DNS, is a distributed database system that provides name to address resolution to network clients.

7. Which of the following commands displays your computer's IP address?

A. IPCONFIG

7. CORRECT ANSWER: A

IPCONFIG is a Windows NT Console utility that will display TCP/IP configuration information. Used alone, the IPCONFIG utility will display the IP address, subnet mask, and default gateway. Extended information, such as the DNS server and WINS server addresses can be displayed using the `/all` switch with the IPCONFIG utility.

This command should not be confused with WINIPCFG, which is the Windows 95/98 counterpart.

8. How many WINS servers must you specify to configure Windows NT Workstation as a TCP/IP client for Internet connectivity?

A. None

8. CORRECT ANSWER: A

WINS, or Windows Internet Naming Service, is a Microsoft proprietary name resolution solution that provides NetBIOS (computer name) to IP address resolution for Microsoft clients. For Internet connectivity, DNS is used to resolve host names to IP addresses.

WINS is required on a routed Microsoft network because Microsoft's implementation of TCP/IP encapsulates NetBIOS. The TCP/IP used in Internet connectivity is a pure IP solution developed for use with UNIX. Therefore, Internet host names and name resolution knows nothing of WINS.

Additionally, most current DNS implementations are static. A machine is assigned an IP address, the address is placed in the DNS database, and the same address is always returned for a given name.

WINS is a dynamic name resolution database, developed for use with DHCP. DHCP, or Dynamic Host Configuration Protocol, is an IP management solution. With DHCP, machines are not assigned a static address, but rather they have an IP address assigned at boot up by a DHCP server from a scope of defined addresses. This simplifies address management because each machine's IP address does not have to be individually tracked. When a machine receives a DHCP address, it then registers its NetBIOS name, also known as the computer name, and its assigned address with the WINS server. When a particular name is to be resolved, the WINS server checks its database to determine the current correct address for the machine.

9. Which two of the following are used for name resolution processes?

B. WINS

D. DNS

9. CORRECT ANSWER: B-D

DNS is used for name resolution in a pure IP environment such as the Internet, and WINS is used for name resolution in a NetBIOS encapsulation within TCP/IP environment such as Microsoft's TCP/IP implementation. Said another way, DNS resolves host and Fully Qualified Domain Names (FQNs); WINS resolves NetBIOS computer names.

10. Proposed Solution:
From Control Panel, double-click the Network applet. Select the Protocols tab, click on TCP/IP, and click the Properties button.

Click the Services tab and remove the DHCP service from the workstation.

Click the Protocols tab and open the properties for the existing TCP/IP protocol. On the IP Address tab, add the address 209.94.9.250. Click OK to return to the Protocol tab of the Network property page.

Click the Add button and add another instance of the TCP/IP protocol. Open the properties for the newly installed TCP/IP protocol. On the IP Address tab, add the address 209.94.9.251. Click OK to return to the Protocol tab of the Network property page.

E. Neither the Required Result nor any Optional Results

10. CORRECT ANSWER: E

There is no Services tab for the TCP/IP properties. The radio button on the IP Address tab should be set to use a static address rather than a DHCP address. The Proposed Solution does not accomplish the Required Result.

Adding only an IP address in the IP Address tab of the TCP/IP properties will not configure the machine to use a static IP address. At least the IP address and subnet mask must be specified. The Proposed Solution does not accomplish the first Optional Result.

Adding a second instance of the TCP/IP protocol is not the proper way to add an additional IP address to a Windows NT Workstation. Clicking the Advanced button from the IP Address tab of the TCP/IP properties will enable you to add an additional IP to the TCP/IP instance bound to the installed adapter. Additionally, clicking the Security button will enable you to specify which TCP, UDP, and IP ports will be accepted by the machine, installing a firewall of sorts on the local machine. The Proposed Solution does not accomplish the second Optional Result.

Windows NT will enable you to specify up to five TCP/IP addresses with the default installation. Editing the Registry can increase the number of addresses that can be bound to a single adapter.

11. Of the following, which addresses are valid TCP/IP addresses?

A. 192.200.14.7
B. 1.1.1.200

11. CORRECT ANSWER: A-B

An IP address is a 32-bit number expressed as four octets. Each octet has 8 bits, for a numeric range of 0–255. Certain addresses, such as 255.255.255.255, are reserved for special purposes such as network broadcasts and cannot be used as a normal address. Additionally, 127 in the first octet is a reserved address.

12. IP addresses given to clients from a DHCP server are said to be which of the following?

C. Leased

12. CORRECT ANSWER: C

When a DHCP server distributes an address, also known as doling out an address, the address is temporarily assigned, or leased, to the client workstation.

13. Host name lookup files provided for Windows NT Workstation by Microsoft include which of the following?

C. HOSTS

D. LMHOSTS

E. LMHOSTS.SAM

13. CORRECT ANSWER: C-D-E

In addition to checking a DNS server or a WINS server for address resolution, Windows NT Workstation also has the built-in capability to determine an address from a given name by looking in a local file. For NetBIOS name resolution, this file is named LMHOSTS and is located in the C:\WINNT\SYSTEM32\Drivers\etc folder. Setup installs a sample file, named LMHOSTS.SAM, as a template for creating an LMHOST file. For host name resolution (such as with connectivity to the Internet or UNIX networks), Windows NT Workstation uses the HOSTS file, also located in the C:\WINNT\SYSTEM32\Drivers\etc folder. The HOSTS file was originally used with TCP/IP (UNIX systems also denote the file as HOSTS), but it was replaced by DNS as the size of the Internet grew to a point where it was not feasible to keep accurate files of all available Internet addresses on every machine with Internet connectivity.

14. Proposed Solution:
Use the `PING` command to test the connection to 127.0.0.1. Contact the LAN administrator and request the address of the DHCP server and the default gateway. From the Console windows, use the PING utility to test connectivity to both of these addresses.

C. The Required Result and one Optional Result

14. CORRECT ANSWER: C

Pinging the loopback adapter (IP address 127.0.0.1) will test the installation of TCP/IP on the workstation. The Proposed Solution accomplishes the Required Result. Additionally, pinging the assigned IP address will test the functionality of the network adapter.

The loopback adapter is a virtual adapter than can be configured to test and work with the TCP/IP protocol only on the local workstation. Any requests sent to the adapter are looped back to the machine, hence the name loopback adapter. On Windows NT Workstation, the adapter can be installed by selecting MS Loopback Adapter from the list of network adapters. The address of the loopback adapter is always 127.0.0.1.

Only checking the address of the DHCP server does nothing to verify that the information doled out by the DHCP server is accurate. The Proposed Solution does not accomplish the first Optional Result. To check the IP configuration of the machine, you must run the `IPCONFIG /ALL` command from the Windows NT Command Console. This would have also negated the need to contact the LAN administrator for the information.

Using the `PING` command to contact the gateway determines if the gateway is available and reachable. The Proposed Solution accomplishes the second Optional Result.

FURTHER REVIEW

USE VARIOUS CONFIGURATIONS TO INSTALL WINDOWS NT WORKSTATION AS A TCP/IP CLIENT

TCP/IP, the default protocol for Windows NT Workstation 4, is a suite of protocols originally designed for the Internet and, as such, is ideally suited for WANs. TCP/IP is supported by most common operating systems and is required for connectivity to the Internet.

TCP/IP Terminology

When you manually configure a computer as a TCP/IP host, you must enter the appropriate settings required for connectivity with your network. The most common network settings include the following:

- *IP address.* A logical 32-bit address used to identify a TCP/IP host. Each network adapter configured for TCP/IP must have a unique IP address. IP networks are divided into classes that determine the number of available networks of that class and the number of hosts for that class by the numeric value of the first octet, as shown in Table 4.1.

TABLE 4.1 THE FIRST OCTET OF THE IP ADDRESS DETERMINES THE CLASS OF THE IP NETWORK

First Octet Range	*IP Network Class*
1-126	Class A
128-191	Class B
192-223	Class C
224-247	Reserved
247-256	Undefined

- *Subnet mask.* A subnet is a division of a larger network environment that's typically connected with routers. Whenever a TCP/IP host tries to communicate with another TCP/IP host, the subnet mask is used to determine whether the other TCP/IP host is on the same network or a different network. If the other TCP/IP host is on a different network, the message must be sent via a router that connects to the other network. A typical subnet mask for a Class C address is 255.255.255.0. All computers on a particular subnet must have identical subnet masks.
- *Default gateway (router).* This optional setting is the address of the router for this subnet that controls communications with all other subnets. If this address is not specified, this TCP/IP host can communicate only with other TCP/IP hosts on its subnet.
- *Name resolution.* This is the process of translating user-friendly computer names to IP addresses. If the specified settings for the TCP/IP protocol are incorrect, you experience problems that keep your computer from establishing communications with other TCP/IP hosts in your network. In extreme cases, communications on your entire subnet can be disrupted.

You can specify all the settings for the TCP/IP protocol manually, or you can have them configured automatically through a network service called Dynamic Host Configuration Protocol (DHCP).

Understanding DHCP

One way to avoid the possible problems of administrative overhead and incorrect settings for the TCP/IP protocol (which occur during manual configurations) is to set up your network so that all your clients receive their TCP/IP configuration information automatically through DHCP. DHCP automatically centralizes and manages the allocation of the TCP/IP settings required for proper network functionality for computers that have been configured as DHCP clients.

One major advantage of using DHCP is that most of your network settings have to be configured only once—at the DHCP server. Also, the TCP/IP settings configured by the DHCP server are only *leased* to the client and must be periodically renewed. This lease and renewal sequence gives a network administrator the opportunity to change client TCP/IP settings if necessary.

Using DHCP

To configure a computer as a DHCP client, all you do is select Obtain an IP Address from a DHCP Server in the TCP/IP properties sheet.

Manually Configuring TCP/IP

To manually configure your TCP/IP settings, you must enter all the required values into the TCP/IP properties sheet. The three required items you must supply are:

- IP address
- Subnet mask
- Default gateway

You must define the default gateway if you will need to communicate with other computers not attached to your local subnet.

PRACTICE QUESTIONS

CONFIGURE AND INSTALL DIAL-UP NETWORKING IN A GIVEN SITUATION

1. **Which of the following is an extension to PPP that enables clients to connect to remote servers over the Internet?**

   A. SLIP

   B. POP

   C. CHAP

   D. PPP+

   E. PPTP

2. **Windows NT Workstation 4 supports which two line protocols?**

   A. SLIP

   B. PPP

   C. PPTP

   D. TCP/IP

   E. PAP

3. **This question is based on the following scenario. Review the scenario first, followed by the objectives and the proposed solution. Then evaluate the proposed solution by choosing the best answer.**

   Scenario:
   You have a Windows NT Workstation with an ISDN adapter installed and properly configured. You want to enable a RAS server for remote access connectivity. You ask your friend Dave for advice.

   Required Result:
   Configure a Remote Access Service (RAS) server.

   Optional Results:
   Maximize network security.

   Minimize client configuration requirements.

   Proposed Solution:
   Configure a Windows NT Workstation RAS server with a SLIP connection.

   Evaluation of Proposed Solution:
   The proposed solution accomplishes which of the following objectives?

   A. The Required Result only

   B. The Required Result and both Optional Results

   C. The Required Result and one Optional Result

   D. Only one Optional Result

   E. Neither the Required Result nor any Optional Results

4. **Of the following, select all protocols that PPP supports.**

   A. TCP/IP

   B. NetBEUI

   C. IPX/SPX

   D. AppleTalk

   E. LAT

5. **How many RAS sessions can Windows NT Workstation serve at one time?**
   A. 2
   B. 3
   C. 5
   D. 255
   E. 1

6. **RAS can be configured in which three of the following ways?**
   A. Dial Out Only
   B. Receive Calls Only
   C. Dial Out and Receive Calls
   D. Manual
   E. Automatic

7. **This question is based on the following scenario. Review the scenario first, followed by the objectives and the proposed solution. Then evaluate the proposed solution by choosing the best answer.**

Scenario:
You have a Windows NT Workstation that needs to connect to a Microsoft Windows Domain network model over a dial-up connection. The Workstation has two ISDN dial-up adapters installed and correctly configured. The RAS server is connected to four ISDN modems that support only a single-channel (64KB) ISDN connection.

Required Result:
Establish dial-up connectivity for the workstation's user.

Optional Results:
Maximize security for the dial-up connection.

Enable two-channel ISDN connectivity (that is, both 64KB channels).

Proposed Solution:
Create a Phonebook entry for the server and select Dial Using Multiple Lines. In the configuration windows, select both ISDN modems installed on the workstation. Through User Manager, ensure the user's account has been granted dial-in permission. Configure the security settings on the NT RAS server to enable dial-back security. Enable the Multilink protocol on the server.

Evaluation of Proposed Solution:
The proposed solution accomplishes which of the following objectives?

   A. The Required Result only
   B. The Required Result and both Optional Results
   C. The Required Result and one Optional Result
   D. Only one Optional Result
   E. Neither the Required Result nor any Optional Results

8. **Which local groups have the ability to create Phonebook entries for the Windows NT Dial-Up Networking client? Select all the correct answers.**
   A. Backup Operators
   B. Power Users
   C. Users
   D. Guests
   E. None of the above

9. This question is based on the following scenario. Review the scenario first, followed by the objectives and the proposed solution. Then evaluate the proposed solution by choosing the best answer.

Scenario:
You have a Windows NT Workstation configured as a RAS server. A Windows 98 client trying to connect to your machine through Dial-Up Networking can establish a connection, but the connection drops after a few seconds.

Required Result:
Correctly configure the encryption settings for the RAS server.

Optional Results:
Enable logging on the RAS server.

Minimize client configuration requirements.

Proposed Solution:
Click the Properties setting for the Remote Access Service from the Services tab of the Network Control Panel applet. From the Security tab, ensure the Accept Only Microsoft Encrypted Authentication radio button is selected. From the Network tab of the properties sheet for the RAS Server service, assign a pool of IP addresses that can be used for RAS clients. From the Server tab, enable logging to assist in identifying any additional connectivity problems.

Evaluation of Proposed Solution:
The proposed solution accomplishes which of the following objectives?

A. The Required Result only

B. The Required Result and both Optional Results

C. The Required Result and one Optional Result

D. Only one Optional Result

E. Neither the Required Result nor any Optional Results

10. This question is based on the following scenario. Review the scenario first, followed by the objectives and the proposed solution. Then evaluate the proposed solution by choosing the best answer.

Scenario:
An end user calls you asking for assistance in setting up a Phonebook entry for her Internet service provider.

Required Result:
Create a new Phonebook entry.

Optional Results:
Configure the Phonebook entry's connection properties to dial 9 first to get an outside line.

Configure the Phonebook entry to use a phone calling card number for long distance calls.

Proposed Solution:
Right-click on the desktop. From the context menu, select New and then choose Create a New Phonebook Entry. From Control Panel, double-click on the Modems applet. Click Dialing Properties for the Device. In the How I Dial from This Location area in the resulting window, enter 9 in the To Access an Outside Line, First Dial: text box, and check the Dial Using Calling Card check box. Click the Change button if necessary to enter additional information about the calling card. Click OK and then Close to save the changes.

Evaluation of Proposed Solution:
The proposed solution accomplishes which of the following objectives?

A. The Required Result only

B. The Required Result and both Optional Results

C. The Required Result and one Optional Result

D. Only both Optional Results

E. Neither the Required Result nor any Optional Results

ANSWER KEY

1. E
2. A-B
3. E
4. A-B-C
5. E
6. A-B-C
7. C
8. A-B-C-D
9. E
10. D

ANSWERS & EXPLANATIONS

CONFIGURE AND INSTALL DIAL-UP NETWORKING IN A GIVEN SITUATION

1. Which of the following is an extension to PPP that enables clients to connect to remote servers over the Internet?

E. PPTP

1. CORRECT ANSWER: E

Point-to-Point Tunneling Protocol, or PPTP, is the extension to the PPP protocol that enables secure connections to servers over the Internet. PPTP derives its name from its ability to "tunnel" through the Internet to connect to RAS servers running the PPTP protocol, without sacrificing security. PPTP is Microsoft's enabling technology for VPNs, or Virtual Private Networks, which let users connect to servers and remote networks as if they were using a leased line and at the cost of Internet access.

2. Windows NT Workstation 4 supports which two line protocols?

A. SLIP

B. PPP

2. CORRECT ANSWER: A-B

Windows NT supports both the PPP (Point-to-Point Protocol) and SLIP (Serial Line Internet Protocol) in the client role, but only PPP in the server role. SLIP is an older technology that supports limited security. Although NT does provide support for TCP/IP, it does not provide facilities for using DHCP. In addition to supporting increased security, TCP/IP, and DHCP, PPP also supports the use of other network protocols such as IPX/SPX and NetBEUI.

3. Proposed Solution: Configure a Windows NT Workstation RAS server with a SLIP connection.

E. Neither the Required Result nor any Optional Results

3. CORRECT ANSWER: E

Unfortunately, your friend's advice on how to configure a Windows NT Workstation RAS server was not very good. A Windows NT Workstation RAS server can be configured to use only the PPP protocol. However, Windows NT Workstation Dial-Up Networking (DUN) can be used as a SLIP or PPP client. The Proposed Solution does not accomplish the Required Result.

The SLIP protocol provides security as robust as that of PPP. The Proposed Solution does not accomplish the first Optional Result.

SLIP does support automatic client configuration utilities such as DHCP. The Proposed Solution does not accomplish the second Optional Result.

4. Of the following, select all protocols that PPP supports.

A. TCP/IP

B. NetBEUI

C. IPX/SPX

4. CORRECT ANSWER: A-B-C

PPP is a robust protocol in that it will support TCP/IP, IPX/SPX, and the NetBEUI protocols.

5. How many RAS sessions can Windows NT Workstation serve at one time?

E. 1

5. CORRECT ANSWER: E

When serving in a RAS server role, Windows NT Workstation can support only a single connection. If your requirements are greater, you should consider using Windows NT Server as the RAS server instead. Windows NT Server RAS services can support up to 256 concurrent connections.

6. RAS can be configured in which three of the following ways?

A. Dial Out Only

B. Receive Calls Only

C. Dial Out and Receive Calls

6. CORRECT ANSWER: A-B-C

A RAS server can be configured to support inbound calls, outbound calls, or a combination of both. This setting is accessed through the Server tab in the Remote Access Services properties from the Services tab in the Network Control Panel applet.

7. Proposed Solution:
Create a Phonebook entry for the server and select Dial Using Multiple Lines. In the configuration windows, select both ISDN modems installed on the workstation. Through User Manager, ensure the user's account has been granted dial-in permission. Configure the security settings on the NT RAS server to enable dial-back security. Enable the Multilink protocol on the server.

C. The Required Result and one Optional Result

7. CORRECT ANSWER: C

Creating a Phonebook entry for the user on the workstation will enable the user to create a dial-up connection successfully. If the server is running the Multilink protocol, selecting the Dial Using Multiple Lines option will enable the client to establish a dial-up connection using both channels of the ISDN line for a data transfer rate of 128Kbps. The Proposed Solution does accomplish the Required Result.

Using dial-back security will further increase the security of the dial-up connection over using no type of call-back authentication. The proposed solution accomplishes the first Optional Result.

There are two types of call-back security that can be implemented. The first will call the workstation initiating the call at a number specified when the server is configured. This will ensure the connection is being established from a known origin. If a malicious user determined the dial-in number and a user's ID and password, that user would still not be able to gain access to the network unless the user were physically located at the number specified in the call-back option.

The second type of call-back security enables the user to specify the number that the server should call. Obviously this is not as secure as the first method of call-back, but it can be useful for reversing long distance charges to the server's dialing location rather than the user's dialing location. Although call-back security settings are only available when using NT Server as the RAS server, you must understand the concepts and options for the Workstation certification exam.

When using call-back security, the server can be configured to call back only one number. Because the workstation is connected to two separate ISDN channels and, therefore, two separate phone numbers, the Multilink protocol cannot be used when call back security is enabled. The Proposed Solution does not accomplish the second Optional Result.

8. Which local groups have the ability to create Phonebook entries for the Windows NT Dial-Up Networking client? Select all the correct answers.

A. Backup Operators

B. Power Users

C. Users

D. Guests

8. CORRECT ANSWER: A-B-C-D

Phonebook entries are stored with the user's profile. Any user can create a Phonebook entry. If mandatory profiles are enabled (see Chapter 3, "Managing Resources," for more information about user profiles), the new Phonebook entry will not be saved when the user logs off the workstation.

9. Proposed Solution:
Click the Properties setting for the Remote Access Service from the Services tab of the Network Control Panel applet. From the Security tab, ensure the Accept Only Microsoft Encrypted Authentication radio button is selected. From the Network tab of the properties sheet for the RAS Server service, assign a pool of IP addresses that can be used for RAS clients. From the Server tab, enable logging to assist in identifying any additional connectivity problems.

E. Neither the Required Result nor any Optional Results

9. CORRECT ANSWER: E

The encryption methods available with RAS server are:

- *Accept Any Authentication Method Including Clear Text.* Use this setting when you don't care about security.
- *Accept Only Encrypted Authentication.* RAS supports several industry-standard encrypted authentication procedures (such as RSA, DES, and Shiva) to support connections to non-Microsoft remote networks.
- *Accept Only Microsoft Encrypted Authentication.* If you select this option, you can also choose to have your entire session with the remote network encrypted, not just your logon. This setting is available only if you are connecting to a Windows NT RAS server.

When dealing with various types of clients, it is best, although not necessarily the most secure method, to utilize the first option: Accept Any Authentication Method Including Clear Text. This is especially useful during troubleshooting.

The method used for setting the security options given in the Proposed Solution is not correct. Unlike most of the other network configuration tasks, the RAS service is not managed through tabbed property sheets. When the RAS service property is clicked, a dialog box appears, listing the RAS ports available on the machine. Highlighting a particular device and clicking the Configure button will enable you to set the option of whether the port should only dial out, only accept incoming calls, or use a combination of both. Clicking the Network button enables you to set the authentication method, as well as the type of network protocols that will be supported when dialing and accepting calls on the port. The Proposed Solution does not meet the Required Result.

When TCP/IP is enabled as a protocol, you can configure how addresses will be assigned to the client—either via DHCP or through a pool assigned to the RAS server. Again, the Proposed Solution specifies the use of a property page tab, which is not how the RAS service is configured. The Proposed Solution does not accomplish the first Optional Result.

Logging is configured through the Modems applet in Control Panel, not through the RAS Service properties. To enable logging, you select the desired device in the Modems applet and click Properties. On the Connection tab, click the Advanced button. In the Advanced Connection Settings dialog box, check the Record a Log File check box. The Proposed Solution does not accomplish the second Optional Result.

10. Proposed Solution:
Right-click on the desktop. From the context menu, select New and then choose Create a New Phonebook Entry. From Control Panel, double-click on the Modems applet. Click Dialing Properties for the Device. In the How I Dial from This Location area in the resulting window, enter 9 in the To Access an Outside Line, First Dial: text box and check the Dial Using Calling Card check box. Click the Change button if necessary to enter additional information about the calling card. Click OK and then Close to save the changes.

D. Only both Optional Results

10. CORRECT ANSWER: D

New Phonebook entries are created through Dial-Up Networking, not the New option in the desktop context menu. From My Computer, you double-click the Dial-Up Networking application and click the New button to create a new Phonebook entry. The Proposed Solution does not accomplish the Required Result.

Modem dialing information (such as the number to dial for accessing an outside line) and credit card information are parameters configured for the dialing location, not the Phonebook entry. The Phonebook entry does enable you to specify what dialing location to use for the connection, but the parameters are set through the Modems applet in Control Panel. The Proposed Solution accomplishes both the first and second Optional Results.

FURTHER REVIEW

CONFIGURE AND INSTALL DIAL-UP NETWORKING IN A GIVEN SITUATION

Remote Access Service (RAS) and Dial-Up Networking (DUN) enable you to extend your network to unlimited locations. RAS servers and DUN clients enable remote clients to make connections to your LAN either via ordinary telephone lines or through higher-speed technologies, such as ISDN or X.25. The incoming connections can also be made via industry-standard Point-to-Point Protocol (PPP) or the newer Point-to-Point Tunneling Protocol (PPTP) that makes use of the Internet. DUN also supports the use of Serial Line Internet Protocol (SLIP) to initiate dial-up connections with SLIP servers.

The Point-to-Point Tunneling Protocol (PPTP) is an extension of PPP that enables clients to connect to remote servers over the Internet. PPTP was designed to provide secure VPN access to networks, especially via the Internet.

Whether using PPP or PPTP, after a client establishes a connection to a RAS server, the client is registered into the local network and can take advantage of the same network services and data that any client could if the client were actually physically connected to the local network.

Line Protocols

The network transport protocols (NetBEUI, NWLink, and TCP/IP) were designed for the characteristics of LANs and are not suitable for use in phone-based connections. For the network transport protocols to function properly in phone-based connections, they must be encapsulated in a line protocol. Windows NT Workstation 4 supports two line protocols: SLIP and PPP.

Serial Line Internet Protocol (SLIP)

SLIP is an industry-standard line protocol supporting TCP/IP connections made over serial lines. Unfortunately, SLIP has several limitations, as outlined here:

- SLIP supports TCP/IP only; it does not support IPX or NetBEUI.
- SLIP does not support DHCP.
- SLIP transmits authentication passwords as clear text; it does not support encryption.
- SLIP usually requires a scripting system for the logon process.
- SLIP does not support packet window size negotiation; the window size must be set as part of the connection configuration.

Windows NT Workstation 4 supports SLIP client functionality only; it cannot act as a SLIP server.

Point-to-Point Protocol (PPP)

The limitations of SLIP prompted the development of a newer industry-standard protocol: Point-to-Point Protocol (PPP). Some of the advantages of using PPP include the following:

- PPP supports TCP/IP, IPX, NetBEUI, and others.

- PPP supports DHCP or static addresses.
- PPP supports encryption for authentication.
- PPP doesn't require a scripting system for the logon process.

New to Windows NT Workstation 4 is support for *PPP Multilink*, which enables you to combine multiple physical links into one logical connection. A client with two ordinary phone lines and two 28.8Kbps modems, for example, could establish a PPP Multilink session with a RAS server and maintain an effective throughput of up to 57.6Kbps. The two modems do not have to be the same type or speed; however, both the RAS server and the DUN client must have PPP Multilink enabled.

Point-to-Point Tunneling Protocol

New to Windows NT Workstation 4 is an extension to PPP called Point-to-Point Tunneling Protocol (PPTP). PPTP enables a DUN client to establish a communications session with a RAS server over the Internet. PPTP supports multi-protocol virtual private networks (VPNs), so remote users can gain secure encrypted access to their corporate networks over the Internet. Because PPTP encapsulates TCP/IP, NWLink, and NetBEUI, it makes it possible for the Internet to be used as a backbone for NWLink and NetBEUI.

To use PPTP, establish a connection from the DUN client to the Internet, and then establish a connection to the RAS server over the Internet.

Installing the Dial-Up Networking Client

You can install DUN when you install Windows NT Workstation 4.0 or later. If you select Remote Access to the Network during setup, both RAS and DUN are installed. However, either or both services can be installed separately after installation of Windows NT Workstation 4.0.

To install DUN after installation of Windows NT Workstation 4.0, double-click the Dial-Up Networking icon in My Computer, click Install to start the Installation Wizard, and then follow the wizard's instructions. Windows NT Workstation 4.0 is limited to one RAS session at a time—either dial-out or receive. If you need to support more than one simultaneous RAS session, you should purchase Windows NT Server 4.0.

Multilink, although using multiple modems (and therefore, multiple dial-out sessions) is still considered a single RAS session for purposes of Windows NT Workstation RAS support.

Configuring the Dial-Up Networking (DUN) Client

The first step in configuring the Dial-Up Networking (DUN) client is to install the DUN software and a modem. The entire installation process is automated and is invoked when you double-click the Dial-Up Networking program in My Computer. When you click Yes to start the Modem Installer, the Install New Modem Wizard appears.

The wizard gives you three options: You can allow the Install New Modem Wizard to automatically detect your modem; you can select your modem from a list; or you can supply a manufacturer's installation disk. The next step in the installation process is to add the modem as a RAS device. After you add the modem, you must configure it.

After you configure your modem, you must specify how RAS uses the phone line. You have the following options:

- Dial Out Only (the default setting for Microsoft Windows NT Workstation 4.0)
- Receive Calls Only
- Dial Out and Receive Calls

You can also select which of the network transport protocols (TCP/IP, IPX, or NetBEUI) you want to use after you have made a connection to the remote network.

Follow these steps to change your RAS configuration after you finish the installation process:

1. Double-click the Network applet in Control Panel.
2. Click the Services tab.
3. Double-click the Remote Access Service in the list.
4. In the Remote Access Setup dialog box, make the following selections:

   Click Configure to configure port usage.

   Click Network to select dial-out protocols.

You must restart your computer after you change your RAS configuration.

Authentication

Security is a major consideration in the design of DUN. You can choose from several security settings, including the following:

- *Accept Any Authentication Method Including Clear Text.* Use this setting when security is not an issue.
- *Accept Only Encrypted Authentication.* RAS supports several industry-standard encrypted authentication procedures (such as RSA, DES, and Shiva) to support connections to non-Microsoft remote networks.
- *Accept Only Microsoft Encrypted Authentication.* If you select this option, you can also choose to have your entire session with the remote network encrypted, not just your logon. This setting is available only if you are connecting to a Windows NT RAS server.

The authentication and encryption settings are set individually for each Phonebook entry (see the following section). The security method only defines how user information, such as the account name and password, are communicated with the server. Regardless of the method chosen, the user must have a valid username and password on the remote machine.

Creating a Phonebook Entry

Each user on a computer has a unique Phonebook stored as part of his or her user profile. Each user can customize his or her own Phonebook by adding entries for numbers he or she might want to call.

Configuring a Location

When you double-click the Telephony applet in Control Panel, the Dialing Properties dialog box appears. You can enter calling card information by clicking the Dial Using Calling Card check box and then clicking the Change button.

PRACTICE QUESTIONS

CONFIGURE MICROSOFT PEER WEB SERVICES IN A GIVEN SITUATION

1. **Which of the following is a hierarchical indexing system that identifies files in directories and is included with PWS?**

   A. HTTP

   B. ISAPI

   C. Gopher

   D. FTP

   E. WWW Service

2. **Which of the following is the service used to transfer files between TCP/IP hosts?**

   A. HTTP

   B. ISAPI

   C. Gopher

   D. FTP

   E. Telnet

3. **Which Internet services does PWS support?**

   A. HTTP

   B. WAIS

   C. Gopher

   D. FTP

   E. Telnet

4. **Which of the following programs is used to create interactive Web-based applications?**

   A. HTTP

   B. ISAPI

   C. Gopher

   D. FTP

   E. FrontPage Server Extensions

5. **This question is based on the following scenario. Review the scenario first, followed by the objectives and the proposed solution. Then evaluate the proposed solution by choosing the best answer.**

Scenario:
You have a workstation with a default installation of Windows NT. An NE2000-compatible network adapter has been installed with the appropriate drivers. There are no network protocols loaded on the machine.

Required Result:
Install Peer Web Services.

Optional Results:
Disable the Gopher service.

Configure the FTP server root directory to be C:\FTPROOT.

Proposed Solution:
From the Services tab of the Network Control Panel applet, click Add and select the Microsoft Peer Web Server. During the installation, specify the default directory of the FTP service to be C:\FTPROOT instead of the

default C:\Inetpub\ftproot. After Peer Web Services is installed, launch the Services applet from Control Panel. Disable the Gopher service.

Evaluation of Proposed Solution:
The proposed solution accomplishes which of the following objectives?

A. The Required Result only

B. The Required Result and both Optional Results

C. The Required Result and one Optional Result

D. Only both Optional Results

E. Neither the Required Result nor any Optional Results

6. Which network components need to be installed before installing Peer Web Services?

A. A network interface card

B. TCP/IP

C. NetBEUI

D. Microsoft FrontPage

E. SNMP service

7. How many concurrent inbound HTTP or FTP connections does the Microsoft NT Workstation 4 license enable you to maintain with Peer Web Services?

A. 1

B. 2

C. 10

D. 50

E. Unlimited

ANSWER KEY

1. C
2. D
3. A-C-D
4. B
5. D
6. B
7. C

ANSWERS & EXPLANATIONS

CONFIGURE MICROSOFT PEER WEB SERVICES IN A GIVEN SITUATION

1. Which of the following is a hierarchical indexing system that identifies files in directories and is included with PWS?

C. Gopher

1. CORRECT ANSWER: C

Gopher is the component included with Peer Web Services that will index files and directories within the specified content directory for Peer Web Services (by default C:\Inetpub).

2. Which of the following is the service used to transfer files between TCP/IP hosts?

D. FTP

2. CORRECT ANSWER: D

FTP, or File Transfer Protocol, is the service included with Peer Web Services that will utilize TCP/IP to transfer files between hosts. When TCP/IP is installed on Windows 95, Windows 98, or Windows NT, an FTP client is automatically installed. Installing Peer Web Services also installs an FTP server for Windows NT Workstation 4.

3. Which Internet services does PWS support?

A. HTTP

C. Gopher

D. FTP

3. CORRECT ANSWER: A-C-D

Peer Web Services includes an HTTP server, the WWW service, a File Transfer Protocol server, the FTP service, an indexing server, and the Gopher service.

4. Which of the following programs is used to create interactive Web-based applications?

B. ISAPI

4. CORRECT ANSWER: B

ISAPI, or Internet Server API, is the application programming interface for the WWW service. With ISAPI, you can use C++ to create DLLs that can interact with the Web service for such activities as logging, redirection, and database queries. Subsequent releases of Peer Web Services (version 2.0, 3.0, and NT Option Pack 4) also include support for Active Server Pages. ASP is an ISAPI application that supports Web application development using the VBScript or JScript scripting language.

5. Proposed Solution:
From the Services tab of the Network Control Panel applet, click Add and select the Microsoft Peer Web Server. During the installation, specify the default directory of the FTP service to be C:\FTPROOT instead of the default C:\Inetpub\ftproot. After Peer Web Services is installed, launch the Services applet from Control Panel. Disable the Gopher service.

D. Only both Optional Results

5. CORRECT ANSWER: D

In order to install Peer Web Services, TCP/IP must be installed. You can actually install the MS-Loopback Adapter and bind TCP/IP to it instead of installing a physical network interface card, in order to use Peer Web Services. Without a physical adapter card installed, however, your webs will not be accessible to other machines. The Proposed Solution does not accomplish the Required Result.

Setup of the Peer Web Services enables you to specify the default or *home* directories for each of the services installed with Peer Web Services. By default, an Inetpub directory is created on the C:\ drive, and subfolders are created for each of the services. Additionally, you may elect to not install all three services with the installation application. The Proposed Solution accomplishes the first Optional Result.

The FTP, WWW, and Gopher services are managed like any other NT services; that is, they are managed through the Services applet in Control Panel. The Proposed Solution accomplishes the second Optional Result.

6. Which network components need to be installed before installing Peer Web Services?

B. TCP/IP

6. CORRECT ANSWER: B

TCP/IP must be installed on the workstation before Peer Web Services can be installed. A network adapter card does not have to be installed; the MS-Loopback adapter can be used instead.

7. How many concurrent inbound HTTP or FTP connections does the Microsoft NT Workstation 4 license enable you to maintain with Peer Web Services?

C. 10

7. CORRECT ANSWER: C

The Workstation license allows 10 concurrent inbound connections to Peer Web Services. If you need to support an unlimited number of connections, you should use the IIS product included with NT Server 4.

FURTHER REVIEW

CONFIGURE MICROSOFT PEER WEB SERVICES IN A GIVEN SITUATION

Peer Web Services (PWS) gives users the ability to publish information on private intranets. PWS includes capabilities for hypertext documents, interactive Web applications, and client/server applications, and it is optimized for use as a small-scale Web server.

Installing Peer Web Services

Before you start the installation of Peer Web Services (PWS), make sure you remove all other Internet services (Gopher, FTP, and so on) that are already installed. Also make sure that you have properly configured your computer to function as a TCP/IP host.

Configuring Peer Web Services

When you install PWS, a new program group containing the PWS utilities is added to your desktop. The Internet Service Manager enables management of multiple Web servers from any location on your network. Some of the capabilities of the Internet Service Manager include the following:

- Find and list all PWS and IIS servers on your network.
- Connect to servers and view their installed services.
- Start, stop, or pause any service.
- Configure service properties.

You can also choose to install a version of the Internet Service Manager accessible via HTML that enables you to manage your PWS server with any standard Web browser. However, it does not include the properties sheet, which means you cannot remotely start, stop, or pause services.

CHAPTER SUMMARY

Connectivity is a crucial part of any Windows NT Workstation installation. Although a Windows NT Workstation can function very capably as a stand-alone workstation, the operating system was designed to interact with various network topologies using the prevalent network protocols in use today, namely TCP/IP and Novell's IPX/SPX.

There are many scenarios in which you will be expected to implement NT Workstation as a network client. Microsoft has placed heavy focus on three areas: Windows NT Domain networks, integration into Novell NetWare networks, and Internet connectivity, often through a dial-up connection. Mastering the concepts needed to enable Windows NT Workstation to communicate and access resources in these environments will place you on the road to mastering the Connectivity objective on the certification exam.

CHAPTER 5

Running Applications

Although the Running Applications objective for the Implementing and Supporting Microsoft Windows NT Workstation Certification Exam has only two sub-objectives, it is nonetheless important. Your Windows NT Workstation might be configured and attached to the network, either locally or through Dial-Up Networking, but it would not be a very useful system without the ability to run applications.

An extremely important part of this objective is configuring 16-bit legacy applications to run and share data, whether that sharing is made possible through shared memory or through Microsoft defined schema such as OLE. It is so important that you can be certain you will see questions about running 16-bit applications on your exam.

OBJECTIVES

Start applications on the Intel and RISC platforms in various operating system environments.

Start applications at various priorities.

PRACTICE QUESTIONS

START APPLICATIONS ON THE INTEL AND RISC PLATFORMS IN VARIOUS OPERATING SYSTEM ENVIRONMENTS

1. **This is a scenario question. First you must review the scenario, then review the required and optional results. Following that is a solution. You must pick the best evaluation of that solution.**

   Scenario:
   You have five Win16 applications (applications designed for use on Windows 3.x) that execute on your Windows NT Workstation at startup. Three of those applications are part of a suite and share information through common memory. One of the three applications has experienced execution problems in the past that result in it abnormally terminating and corrupting other applications on your system.

   Required Result:
   Run the applications without one corrupt application crashing all other applications.

   Optional Results:
   Launch all programs on startup.

   Ensure the suite of applications is able to share memory.

   Proposed Solution:
   Start the problem application first.

   Run each of the other applications in its own memory space, by using the command `start /separate` *<application name>*.

   Evaluation of Proposed Solution:
   This implementation achieves the following objectives:

   A. The Required Result only

   B. The Required Result and both Optional Results

   C. The Required Result and one Optional Result

   D. Only one Optional Result

   E. Neither the Required Result nor any Optional Results

2. **Which of the following are valid switches for the `start` command?**

   A. `/base`

   B. `/separate`

   C. `/high`

   D. `/kernel`

   E. `/fast`

3. **Which of the following statements best describes limitations of MS-DOS applications running on Windows NT?**

   A. They cannot share memory space.

   B. They cannot be preemptively multitasked.

   C. They cannot be started with any priority other than NORMAL.

   D. They cannot be selectively terminated using Task Manager.

   E. They use RAM more efficiently.

4. **This is a scenario question. First you must review the scenario, then review the required and optional results. Following that is a solution. You must pick the best evaluation of that solution.**

Scenario:
Bill has three Win16 applications that are executed on his Windows NT Workstation at startup. Two of the applications are part of a suite that share data through common memory; the other is a stand-alone application. One of the two applications in the suite has experienced execution problems in the past that result in it abnormally terminating and corrupting other applications on his system.

Required Result:
Ensure a crash of one of the applications in the collaborative suite does not affect the stand-alone application.

Optional Results:
Launch all applications at boot up.

Ensure the two applications are able to collaborate.

Proposed Solution:
You instruct Bill to do the following:

Launch the lone application first in the default NTVDM, using the `start/separate` switch in the shortcut to the application.

Launch the two collaborative apps in the same memory space.

Include shortcuts for each of the applications in the Startup folder on the Start menu.

Evaluation of Proposed Solution:
This implementation achieves the following objectives:

A. The Required Result only

B. The Required Result and both Optional Results

C. The Required Result and only one Optional Result

D. Only one Optional Result

E. Neither the Required Result nor any Optional Results

5. **POSIX support in Windows NT includes which of the following features?**

A. Additional time stamp

B. Hard links

C. Binary compatibility

D. Case-sensitive naming

E. Symbolic links

6. **This is a scenario question. First you must review the scenario, then review the required and optional results. Following that is a solution. You must pick the best evaluation of that solution.**

Scenario:
You have three Win16 applications that are executed on your Windows NT Workstation at startup. Two of the applications are part of a suite that shares data through common memory; the other is a stand-alone application. One of the two applications in the suite has experienced execution problems in the past that result in it abnormally terminating and corrupting other applications on your system.

Required Result:
Ensure a crash of one of the applications in the collaborative suite does not affect the stand-alone application.

Optional Results:
Launch all applications at start up.

Ensure the two applications are able to collaborate.

Proposed Solution:
Launch the two applications in the collaborative suite first in the default NTVDM. Next, launch the lone application in its own NTVDM by checking the Run in Separate Memory Space box on the Memory tab in the application's PIF.

Associate the applications with PIFs placed in the Startup group on the Start menu.

Evaluation of Proposed Solution:
Which of the following results does this solution achieve?

A. The Required Result only

B. The Required Result and both Optional Results

C. The Required Result and only one Optional Result

D. Only one Optional Result

E. Neither the Required Result nor any Optional Results

7. Which statement best describes how 16-bit Windows applications are run by default on a Windows NT Workstation computer?

A. 16-bit Windows applications are run as a single thread in a single NTVDM with a shared address space.

B. 16-bit Windows applications are run as a single thread in a single NTVDM with separate address spaces.

C. 16-bit Windows applications are run as separate threads in a single NTVDM with a shared address space.

D. 16-bit Windows applications are run as separate threads in a single NTVDM with separate address spaces.

E. 16-bit Windows applications are run as separate threads in separate NTVDMs with separate address spaces.

8. Select all the advantages of running Win16 applications in their own separate memory spaces.

A. OLE runs more efficiently.

B. Preemptive multitasking.

C. Non-preemptive multitasking.

D. Reliability: One Win16 application crashing does not affect other Win16 applications.

E. Support for multiple processors.

9. Which command executes a bound OS/2 application in an NTVDM on an Intel-based Windows NT system?

A. `start /ntvdm os2app.exe`

B. `start /separate os2app.exe`

C. `Forcedos`

D. `Forcecmd`

E. `Forcerun`

10. This is a scenario question. First you must review the scenario, then review the required and optional results. Following that is a solution. You must pick the best evaluation of that solution.

Scenario:
You have a Windows NT Workstation that has started showing a decrease in performance. You typically run the Office 97 productivity suite and two legacy DOS applications, one for accounts payable and the other for invoicing. You have spoken with various co-workers who have suggested you remove unneeded application subsystems from your computer and configure all your MS-DOS applications to run in the same NTVDM to restore performance.

Required Result:
Configure all your DOS applications to run within the same NTVDM.

Optional Result:
Remove the POSIX subsystem from your computer.

Remove the OS/2 subsystem from your computer.

Proposed Solution:
Modify the shortcut for the two MS-DOS applications (i.e., the PIF files) by selecting the Memory tab and checking the Run in Default NTVDM box.

Use the NT Resource Kit C2 security tool to disable and remove the POSIX subsystem.

Delete the OS2.exe and OS2ss.exe files from your Windows NT directory to disable the OS/2 subsystem.

Evaluation of Proposed Solution:
Which of the following results does this solution achieve?

A. The Required Result only

B. The Required Result and both Optional Results

C. The Required Result and only one Optional Result

D. Only one Optional Result

E. Neither the Required Result nor any Optional Results

11. What is an Instruction Execution Unit?

A. A Windows NT kernel thread

B. The smallest unit of application execution on an Intel processor platform

C. The smallest unit of application execution on a RISC processor platform

D. A register on the Pentium Pro processor

E. An Intel 80486 emulator for the RISC environment

12. Select all of the locations where the OS/2 subsystem configuration is stored in a Windows NT Workstation installation.

A. CONFIG.SYS

B. OS2.SYS

C. AUTOEXEC.BAT

D. STARTUP.CMD

E. CONFIG.OS2

ANSWER KEY

1. A
2. B-C
3. A
4. E
5. A-B-D
6. B
7. C
8. B-D-E
9. C
10. D
11. E
12. A-D

ANSWERS & EXPLANATIONS

START APPLICATIONS ON THE INTEL AND RISC PLATFORMS IN VARIOUS OPERATING SYSTEM ENVIRONMENTS

1. **Proposed Solution: Start the problem application first.**

   Run each of the other applications in its own memory space, by using the command `start/separate <application name>`.

   A. The Required Result only

1. CORRECT ANSWER: A

If you start the applications manually with the `start` command, they are not automatically started at boot time. Therefore, the first Optional Result is not achieved.

By default, Windows NT runs all Win16 applications in the WOW (Windows On Windows) subsystem. This allows Windows NT to emulate the cooperative multi-tasking model found in Windows 3.1, for which these applications are designed. The draw back to cooperative multitasking is that one program crash will more than likely cause the other applications running in the WOW subsystem to hang. You can start each WOW in a separate memory space by using the `start /separate` command to start the application. With each application running in its own memory space, a crash in one application will not affect the memory space or the execution of the applications in the other memory spaces. By running each application in its own private memory space, you isolate the effects of one application crashing. The Required Result is achieved.

Win16 applications commonly use two methods to share data: common memory and OLE/DDE (Object Linking and Embedding / Dynamic Data Exchange). From the scenario, it is known that this suite of applications uses the former, memory-sharing model for data exchange. When Win16 applications are running in separate memory spaces, they cannot share data through common memory. Therefore, the second Optional Result is not achieved. It is important to note, however, that OLE and DDE will function correctly with Win16 applications when they are run in separate memory spaces.

2. Which of the following are valid switches for the `start` command?

B. `/separate`

C. `/high`

2. CORRECT ANSWER: B-C

The `/separate` switch is used to start Win16 applications in their own separate memory spaces; by default, they are started in the same memory space. The `/high` switch is used to start an application with a base priority of 13 rather than the default priority of 8.

3. Which of the following statements best describes limitations of MS-DOS applications running on Windows NT?

A. They cannot share memory space.

3. CORRECT ANSWER: A

MS-DOS applications are run in separate NTVDMs. Because of this, they cannot share memory spaces. They can be pre-emptively multitasked, started with different priorities, and terminated selectively using Task Manager.

4. Proposed Solution:
You instruct Bill to do the following:

Launch the lone application first in the default NTVDM, using the `start /separate` switch in the shortcut to the application.

Launch the two collaborative apps in the same memory space.

Include shortcuts for each of the applications in the Startup folder on the Start menu.

E. Neither the Required Result nor any Optional Results

4. CORRECT ANSWER: E

Running the lone application in its own memory space is the correct way to prevent a crash in one of the applications included in the suite from affecting the stand-alone application; however, the start up order is incorrect.

When you start the first NTVDM running WOW, all applications to be included in the same NTVDM must be included in the *first* NTVDM. Subsequent NTVDMs can only contain a single application. Therefore, the Proposed Solution would not be able to be implemented on a Windows NT Workstation, which means the Required Result is not met. If the suite of two applications was started first, the solution would indeed accomplish the Required Result.

For the applications to launch at boot up, they would need to have their shortcuts included in the Startup folder on the Start menu. The first Optional Result is not achieved.

Running the two collaborative applications in the same memory space would enable data sharing through common memory; however, they would both need to be running in the first NTVDM. The second Optional Result is not achieved.

5. POSIX support in Windows NT includes which of the following features?

A. Additional time stamp

B. Hard links

D. Case-sensitive naming

5. CORRECT ANSWER: A-B-D

With the NTFS file system, Windows NT provides hard links, or the capability to store the same data in two files with different names. Changing the data in one also changes the data of the other. Case-sensitive naming is also supported for POSIX applications, which means that Data.txt and DATA.txt are two different files. Finally, POSIX support provides for not only a last-modified time stamp, but also a last-accessed time stamp.

6. Proposed Solution:
Launch the two applications in the collaborative suite first in the default NTVDM. Next, launch the lone application in its own NTVDM by checking the Run in Separate Memory Space box on the Memory tab in the application's PIF.

Associate the applications with PIFs placed in the Startup group on the Start menu.

B. The Required Result and both Optional Results

6. CORRECT ANSWER: B

Running the two applications in their own memory spaces in the first NTVDM will allow the two applications in the suite to share data through common memory. Therefore, the second Optional Result is achieved.

Launching the stand-alone application in an NTVDM with a separate memory space ensures the application is not affected by any crashes in the applications running in the default NTVDM. The Required Result is achieved.

Including the PIFs in the Startup folder on the Start menu ensures the applications will be launched at boot up. A PIF, or Program Information File, is a shortcut for DOS and Win16 applications. See the section titled "Further Review" for additional information on configuring PIF files. The first Optional Result is achieved.

7. Which statement best describes how 16-bit Windows applications are run by default on a Windows NT Workstation computer?

C. 16-bit Windows applications are run as separate threads in a single NTVDM with a shared address space.

7. CORRECT ANSWER: C

16-bit Windows applications run as separate, cooperatively multitasked threads in the Win16 NTVDM or WOW. All 16-bit Windows applications running in the WOW share a common address space. The Win16 NTVDM can be preemptively multitasked with other processes running on Windows NT; however, the threads within the Win16 NTVDM (16-bit application programs) cannot be preemptively multitasked, only cooperatively multitasked, which emulates the environment in which they were designed to run.

8. Select all the advantages of running Win16 applications in their own separate memory spaces.

B. Preemptive multitasking.

D. Reliability: One Win16 application crashing does not affect other Win16 applications.

E. Support for multiple processors.

8. CORRECT ANSWER: B-D-E

Running Win16 applications in their own separate memory spaces enables them to participate in preemptive multitasking, because each Win16 application has a separate thread of execution. Running the application in a separate memory space also prevents the crash of one Win16 application from affecting other Win16 applications. Finally, with each Win16 application having a separate thread of execution, they could now take advantage of multiple processors in the system because Windows NT could now schedule each thread independently.

9. Which command executes a bound OS/2 application in an NTVDM on an Intel-based Windows NT system?

C. `Forcedos`

9. CORRECT ANSWER: C

The `Forcedos` command must be used to run bound applications in MS-DOS mode on Intel-based Windows NT systems.

10. Proposed Solution:
Modify the shortcut for the two MS-DOS applications (i.e., the PIF files) by selecting the Memory tab and checking the Run in Default NTVDM box.

Use the NT Resource Kit C2 security tool to disable and remove the POSIX subsystem.

Delete the OS2.exe and OS2ss.exe files from your Windows NT directory to disable the OS/2 subsystem.

D. Only one Optional Result

10. CORRECT ANSWER: D

DOS is not a multitasking environment by default. Because of this, the Windows NT Workstation emulation of the DOS environment, the NTVDM, does not allow multiple DOS applications to run in the same NTVDM. DOS applications will always run in separate NTVDMs. Therefore, the Required Result is not accomplished.

The POSIX subsystem should be removed using the C2 Configuration Tool, found in the Windows NT Resource Kit. To disable the POSIX subsystem, follow these steps:

1. Start the C2 Configuration Tool (open the Start menu and choose Programs, Resource Kit 4.0, Configuration, C2 Configuration).
2. In the list of Security Features, double-click the POSIX Subsystem entry.
3. Click the OK button to disable the POSIX subsystem.
4. Click the OK button to confirm that you do want to permanently remove support for the POSIX subsystem.

The icon to the left of the POSIX subsystem now appears as a red closed lock, indicating full C2 Orange Book compliance.

The Proposed Solution accomplishes the first Optional Result.

The OS/2 subsystem should also be removed using the C2 Configuration Tool. Although the OS2.exe and OS2ss.exe files are removed, they should be removed using the C2 Configuration Tool, which will also complete the required system settings changes. The Proposed Solution does not accomplish the second Optional Result.

11. What is an Instruction Execution Unit?

E. An Intel 80486 emulator for the RISC environment

11. CORRECT ANSWER: E

On RISC systems, the Instruction Execution Unit (IEU) emulates an Intel 80486 microprocessor. On x86 computers, the IEU acts as a trap handler. Any instructions that cause hardware traps have their control transferred to the code in Windows NT that handles them.

12. Select all of the locations where the OS/2 subsystem configuration is stored in a Windows NT Workstation installation.

A. CONFIG.SYS

D. STARTUP.CMD

12. CORRECT ANSWER: A-D

OS/2 subsystem configuration information is stored in the CONFIG.SYS and STARTUP.CMD files located in the root directory. It is important to remember that the CONFIG.SYS file *must* be edited with an OS/2 text editor; specific information is written into the header, marking the file as a configuration file.

Additional OS/2 subsystem configuration information is stored in the following Registry keys:

- Hkey_Local_Machine\System\CurrentControlSet\Control\Session Manager\Subsystems
- Hkey_local_machine\Software\Microsoft\OS/2 Subsystem for NT

FURTHER REVIEW

START APPLICATIONS ON THE INTEL AND RISC PLATFORMS IN VARIOUS OPERATING SYSTEM ENVIRONMENTS

Windows NT is designed to run applications originally designed to run under other operating systems. Windows NT can support running applications designed for the following operating systems:

- Windows 95
- MS-DOS
- Windows 3.x
- OS/2
- POSIX

Windows NT accomplishes this by using the subsystems discussed in the following sections.

Win32 Subsystem Support

The Win32 subsystem (also known as the Client/Server subsystem) supports all 32-bit Windows applications and the rest of the environment subsystems. Some of the primary features of Win32 applications include the following:

- Reliability (due to each application having its own 4GB address space)
- Support of multithreaded applications
- Capability to take advantage of multiprocessor systems
- Capability to take advantage of preemptive multitasking

Each Windows 32-bit application runs in its own 4GB virtual address space. However, the upper 2GB of that memory space is reserved for use by privileged code, that is code running under the Windows NT Executive process. The lower 2GB of memory is accessible by unprivileged code, or that code running in the Windows NT user mode—the application. This design prevents one 32-bit application from overwriting the memory space of another 32-bit application. In other words, the failure of one 32-bit application does not affect other running 32-bit applications.

MS-DOS Application Support

Windows NT supports any MS-DOS applications that do not attempt to directly access hardware. The Windows NT architecture does not allow any user-mode processes to directly access the system hardware.

MS-DOS applications run in a special Win32 application known as a Windows NT virtual DOS machine (NTVDM). The NTVDM creates a pseudo MS-DOS environment in which the application is capable of running. Each NTVDM has a single thread of execution and its own address space. This enables preemptive multitasking between MS-DOS applications and protection from other MS-DOS application failures. An NTVDM is comprised of the following components:

- *NTVDM.EXE.* Provides the MS-DOS emulation and manages the NTVDM.
- *NTIO.SYS.* The NTVDM equivalent of IO.SYS in MS-DOS.
- *NTDOS.SYS.* The NTVDM equivalent of the MS-DOS kernel.
- *Instruction Execution Unit (IEU).* On RISC systems, this emulates an Intel 80486 microprocessor. On x86 computers, the IEU acts as a trap handler. Any instructions that cause hardware traps have their control transferred to the code in Windows NT that handles them.

Because applications cannot directly access the hardware in the Windows NT architectural model, the NTVDM's virtual device drivers intercept any attempt by an application to access the hardware. The NTVDM provides virtual device drivers for the mouse, keyboard, parallel ports, and COM ports.

If there isn't a virtual device driver for a particular hardware device, any application trying to access that hardware device directly cannot run in an NTVDM. Many MS-DOS applications do not execute in Windows NT for this reason.

Windows NT virtual DOS machines are configured through the various property tabs exposed by right-clicking on the DOS executable. Two of the most crucial, the Program tab and the Memory tab, are discussed more in depth in the following section.

Configuring the Program Properties of an MS-DOS application

In the Properties dialog box for a DOS application, you can configure default locations for where the program is located on the hard disk. By accessing the Program tab, you can also specify the directory in which the program will execute. Table 5.1 shows the settings you can configure in the Program Properties dialog box.

TABLE 5.1 PROGRAM PROPERTY SETTINGS FOR AN MS-DOS APPLICATION

Setting	*Description*
Cmd Line	The full path to the MS-DOS application's executable file.
Working	Default directory to which you want to save an application's data files.
Batch File	The name of a batch file that runs each time the application is run. (This is functional only in the Windows 95 operating system.)
Shortcut Key	Used to set a shortcut key combination for launching the application. To remove a shortcut key combination, use the Backspace key.
Run	Determines the windows state in which the program starts. Choices include normal window, minimized, or maximized.
Close on Exit	When selected, automatically closes the MS-DOS window in which the MS-DOS application runs.
Windows NT	Enables the application to specify tailored Autoexec and Config files that are processed every time the application is run.
Change Icon	Enables the user to change the icon displayed for the shortcut.

Each MS-DOS application shortcut can point to a different Autoexec and Config file. By default, these are Autoexec.nt and Config.nt, which are located in the %Systemroot%\System32 directory. These configuration files must follow MS-DOS 5.0 conventions. This does not include multiple configurations.

Configuring the Memory Properties of an MS-DOS Application

Running MS-DOS applications under Windows NT does ease one area of configuration. MS-DOS applications use one of two methods for providing additional memory beyond conventional memory:

- Expanded memory
- Extended memory

On an MS-DOS machine, these settings are typically controlled through the config.sys file. For the altered settings to take effect, the machine has to be rebooted. In Windows NT, these parameters have been moved to the Memory tab of the DOS application's property sheet.

Win16 Application Support

Windows NT supports Windows 16-bit applications by using Win16 on Win32 (WOW). Note that the WOW environment runs within a Windows NT virtual DOS machine. This is just like Windows 3.x, which ran over MS-DOS. Table 5.2 describes the WOW components.

TABLE 5.2 WOW COMPONENTS

Component	*Description*
Wowexec.exe	The Wowexec provides the Windows 3.1 emulation for the NTVDM.
WOW32.dll	The supporting dynamic link library for the Wowexec.
Win16 application	The Windows 16-bit application that is being executed. This application must not use any Windows 16-bit VxDs. Windows NT might not provide support for Win16 applications.
Krnl386.exe	This is a modified version of the Windows 3.x kernel. It translates calls meant for the Windows 3.x kernel to Win32 calls. Basic operating system functions are handled by Krnl386.exe.
User.exe	The User.exe is a modified version of the Windows 3.x User.exe files. It handles all user interface API calls and translates them to Win32 calls.
Gdi.exe	The Gdi.exe captures API calls related to graphics and printing. These calls are translated to Win32 calls.

A PIF, or Program Information File, is associated with Win16 applications. In addition to the MS-DOS settings described above, the PIF for a Win16 application has the ability to configure the application to run in its own memory space.

OS/2 Application Support

Windows NT has limited support for OS/2 applications. This list outlines the essentials of the OS/2 support Windows NT provides by default:

- OS/2 1.x-character-based applications are supported only on the Intel platform running the OS/2 subsystem.
- If the OS/2 application makes any calls to the Presentation Manager, by default they are not supported in the OS/2 subsystem.
- OS/2 applications can be executed on RISC-based Windows NT systems if the OS/2 applications are *bound* applications. Bound applications are those that have been written to execute in either OS/2 or MS-DOS. Because there is no OS/2 subsystem for RISC-based systems, these bound
  applications execute only in an NTVDM.

  You can force a bound application to execute in an NTVDM on an Intel-based Windows NT system by using the `Forcedos` command. By default though, bound applications always choose to run in the OS/2 subsystem because they execute faster in their native environment.

- Windows NT no longer provides support for the HPFS file system.

POSIX Application Support

POSIX (Portable Operating System Interface based on UNIX) support is provided in Windows NT because of a U.S. government requirement for government computing contracts. Because it includes support for POSIX applications, Windows NT can be considered for government quotes. The implementation of POSIX in Windows NT enables the portability of common applications from a UNIX system to Windows NT running the POSIX subsystem.

Windows NT provides POSIX support through the POSIX subsystem. POSIX defines a C language source-code-level application programming interface (API) to an operating system environment. To have full POSIX compliance, the NTFS file system must be implemented on the computer that will be executing POSIX applications. This provides the user with the following POSIX-compliance features:

- *Case-sensitive file naming.* NTFS preserves case for both directories and filenames.
- *Hard links.* POSIX applications can store the same data in two differently named files.
- *An additional time stamp on files.* This tracks the last time the file was accessed. The default on FAT volumes is to track when the file was last modified.

Modifying Support for the POSIX Subsystem

For full POSIX compliance, one of the Windows NT user rights must be modified. By default, the user right Bypass Traverse Checking is granted to the special group Everyone. This right enables a user to change directories through a directory tree even if the user has no permission for those directories. This user right must be disabled for all accounts that will be using POSIX applications.

To disable the Bypass Traverse Checking right, follow these steps:

1. Start the User Manager. To perform this process, you must be logged on as a member of the Administrators local group.
2. Create a global group that contains all users who will *not* be running POSIX applications. It is imperative that no POSIX users be members of this global group.
3. From the Policies menu, choose User Rights.
4. Ensure that the Show Advanced User Rights check box is selected.
5. Select the User Right Bypass Traverse Checking.
6. Click Remove to remove the Everyone group.
7. Click the Add button and select the new global group of non-POSIX users that you created in step 2. Then click the OK button to add this group.
8. Click the OK button to complete this user rights change.

Application Support on RISC and Intel Platforms

Although you can run Windows NT on both the Intel and RISC platforms, you face compatibility issues when considering applications to support. Applications are either *source-compatible* or *binary-compatible.* Source-compatible applications must be recompiled for each hardware platform on which they are going to be executed. Binary-compatible applications can be run on any Windows NT platform without being recompiled. Table 5.3 outlines application compatibility on the Windows NT platforms.

Typically, the exam tests your knowledge of the terms *source compatible* and *binary compatible.* Be sure to know the difference between the two and how each type of application is supported on each platform.

Although products such as Digital's FX!32 exist, the exam still considers Win32-based applications to be source-compatible across platforms, not binary-compatible.

TABLE 5.3. APPLICATION COMPATIBILITY ACROSS WINDOWS NT PLATFORMS

Platform	*MS-DOS*	*Win16*	*Win32*	*OS/2*	*POSIX*
Intel	Binary	Binary	Source	Binary	Source
Alpha	Binary	Binary	Source*	Binary**	Source
Mips	Binary	Binary	Source	Binary**	Source
PowerPC	Binary	Binary	Source	Binary**	Source

* Third-party utilities such as Digital FX!32 enable Win32-based Intel programs to execute on Digital Alpha AXP microprocessors. Although these utilities interpret the code on-the-fly, they end up performing faster on the Alpha due to the increased speed of the processor.

** Only bound applications can be run on the three RISC hardware platforms. They will run in an NTVDM because the OS/2 subsystem is not provided in RISC-based versions of Windows NT.

Building Distributed Applications Across Platforms with DCOM

Distributed application development is based on creating applications made up of multiple components that can be spread across multiple platforms. The Distributed Component Object Model (DCOM) integrates the following capabilities to make the rapid development of distributed applications possible:

- DCOM supports communications between components over connection-oriented and connectionless network transports including TCP/IP, UDP/IP, IPX/SPX, AppleTalk, HTTP, and Remote Procedure Calls (RPCs). These objects can communicate over public networks such as the Internet.
- DCOM is an open technology capable of running on multiple implementations of UNIX-based systems, including Solaris.
- DCOM can lead to lower integration costs because DCOM is based on a common set of interfaces for software programs. This will lead to a lesser requirement for customization when implementing components from outside vendors.

- DCOM supports remote activation. A client can start an application just by calling a component on another computer.
- DCOM is capable of implementing Internet certificate-based security or Windows NT-based Challenge/Response security. This ensures the best of both worlds for security. Security is supported for the launch of objects, access to objects, and context. Security can also be based on whether the application is launched locally or remotely.

In a pure Windows NT environment, RPCs can be used to enable communication and interoperability between various DCOM objects. RPCs make it possible for an application to execute procedures and call objects on other remote computers.

These steps outline the flow of communication for a DCOM application when a client makes a call to a DCOM object located on another server:

1. A client initiates a remote procedure call.
2. The RPC client stub packages the call for transport across the network. The RPC runtime library on the client transmits the package to the indicated server, which it finds by using a name resolution method (this might include NetBIOS Name Server or Domain Name Service methods).
3. The RPC runtime library on the server receives the package and forwards it to its own RPC stub, which converts the package into the same RPC that was sent from the client.
4. The remote procedure call is carried out at the security level specified in the Server object.
5. The RPC server stub packages the results of the procedure call, and the server's RPC runtime library transmits this package back to the calling client application.
6. The RPC runtime library on the client receives the package and forwards it to the client's RPC stub, which unpacks the data for the client application to use.

You need to know the basic configuration of DCOM objects. This includes where the application resides; who can access, launch, or modify a DCOM object; and whose security context is used to run the DCOM object. All of these settings can be managed through the DCOM configuration manager, accessed by running dcomcnfg.exe from the command line or by using the Run command on the Start menu.

PRACTICE QUESTIONS

START APPLICATIONS AT VARIOUS PRIORITIES

1. **The 16-bit Windows application you are using on your Windows NT workstation is running extremely slowly due to other applications occupying the CPU on your system. What is the best way to run your application so it will be more responsive?**

   A. Run the application in its own memory space.

   B. Run the application with HIGH priority.

   C. Run the application with REALTIME priority.

   D. Run the application in its own NTVDM.

   E. Run the application with LOW priority.

2. **What is the default value when an application is started with NORMAL priority?**

   A. 3

   B. 8

   C. 24

   D. 13

   E. 1

3. **You want to start a 16-bit Windows application named measure.exe from the command line. The application needs to run minimized and in its own memory space with HIGH priority. What is the proper syntax to accomplish this?**

   A. `net start measure.exe /min/ separate`

   B. `net start /min /separate measure.exe`

   C. `start measure.exe /min /separate`

   D. `start /min /separate /high measure.exe`

   E. `start measure.exe /high /net / min /separate`

4. **What is the applet in Control Panel that enables you to boost the performance of foreground applications?**

   A. Network

   B. System

   C. Devices

   D. Add/Remove Programs

   E. Services

5. **Which groups have the capability to run applications at the Realtime base priority?**

   A. Server Operators

   B. Administrators

   C. Account Operators

   D. Replicator

   E. Power Users

6. **This is a scenario question. First you must review the scenario, then review the required and optional results. Following that is a solution. You must pick the best evaluation of that solution.**

Scenario:
John has a Windows NT Workstation with 32MB of RAM. He would like to do some performance bench-marking on the system. You have a monitoring application that requires 24MB of RAM to execute. The application must also run at REALTIME priority to provide accurate results. Two other applications that will provide a simulated load on the system need to be executed at the same time the monitoring program is run. John asks you how he can accomplish the following tasks.

Required Result:
Run the monitoring application at the REALTIME priority.

Optional Results:
Run one application for stress, testing the system at a lower than normal priority.

Stop one of the load simulation applications mid-way through the test to measure the effect on the system.

Proposed Solution:
You provide John with the following advice:

Log on as a Power User.

Start the monitoring application with the command `start /realtime monitor.exe` (assume the monitoring application executable file is monitor.exe).

Start the stressing application (stress.exe) with the command `start /low stress.exe.`

Use the Applications tab on the Task Manager (press Ctrl+Alt+Del and select Task Manager to invoke it) to terminate the desired application.

Evaluation of Proposed Solution:
Which results does the proposed solution produce?

A. The Required Result only

B. The Required Result and both Optional Results

C. The Required Result and one Optional Result

D. Both Optional Results

E. Neither the Required Result nor any Optional Results

7. **Without changing the priority of an application, what can you do to make it run more quickly? Choose all that apply.**

A. Terminate other applications.

B. Bring that application to the foreground.

C. Maximize the application window.

D. Assign more CPU resources to the application through Task Manager.

E. Minimize all other application windows.

ANSWER KEY

1. B
2. B
3. D
4. B
5. B
6. D
7. A-B-E

ANSWERS & EXPLANATIONS

START APPLICATIONS AT VARIOUS PRIORITIES

1. The 16-bit Windows application you are using on your Windows NT workstation is running extremely slowly due to other applications occupying the CPU on your system. What is the best way to run your application so it will be more responsive?

B. Run the application with HIGH priority.

1. CORRECT ANSWER: B

Applications can be started at the following priority levels: LOW, NORMAL, HIGH, and REALTIME. Although starting an application in REALTIME mode would make it more responsive than one started with HIGH priority, this is not recommended because applications using REALTIME mode can interfere with the Windows NT operating system. Only users with administrative rights can start programs in REALTIME mode. To start an application using a separate memory space, it must be started in its own NTVDM. Starting an application in its own NTVDM has no effect on the responsiveness of the application. To start a 16-bit Windows application with a priority other than NORMAL, you must run it in its own NTVDM; otherwise, the priority of the Win16 NTVDM will need to be changed in Task Manager. This is because all applications running within a single NTVDM will run at the same priority level.

2. What is the default value when an application is started with NORMAL priority?

B. 8

2. CORRECT ANSWER: B

8 is the NORMAL priority. REALTIME priority is 24. HIGH priority is 13. LOW priority is 4.

3. You want to start a 16-bit Windows application named measure.exe from the command line. The application needs to run minimized and in its own memory space with HIGH priority. What is the proper syntax to accomplish this?

D. `start /min /separate /high measure.exe`

3. CORRECT ANSWER: D

The proper syntax for running an application from the command line is:

```
START [Start parameters] ApplicationName
➥[Application parameters]
```

In the above example, measure.exe can be started from the command line by typing:

```
START /min /separate measure.exe
```

Applications can be started with varying priorities (`/low`, `/normal`, `/high`, `/realtime`), started minimized (`/min`) or maximized (`/max`), or started in separate NTVDMs (`/separate`). Other options are available as well. The `net start` command is used to start Windows NT networking resources.

4. What is the applet in Control Panel that enables you to boost the performance of foreground applications?

B. System

4. CORRECT ANSWER: B

The System applet is where you would boost foreground applications' performance. The Network applet controls network settings. Services and Devices start, stop, and disable services and devices.

5. Which groups have the capability to run applications at the REALTIME base priority?

B. Administrators

5. CORRECT ANSWER: B

Because switching application priorities can have serious consequences on the operating system and overall stability of the workstation, Windows NT limits the right to run applications at the REALTIME priority to the Administrators local group.

6. Proposed Solution:
You provide John with the following advice:

- **Log on as a Power User.**
- **Start the monitoring application with the command `start /realtime monitor.exe` (assume the monitoring application executable file is monitor.exe).**
- **Start the stressing application (stress.exe) with the command `start /low stress.exe`.**
- **Use the Applications Tab on the Task Manager (press Ctrl+Alt+Del and select Task Manager to invoke it) to terminate the desired application.**

D. Both Optional Results

6. CORRECT ANSWER: D

The proposed solution fails to accomplish the Required Result for two reasons. First, only members of the Administrators group have the right to start applications at the REALTIME priority.

Additionally, applications run at the REALTIME priority will not be swapped to the paging file. Therefore, the system must have enough physical memory for Windows NT Workstation, which requires 12MB, and the application, which in this case is 24MB. To run the monitoring application at a REALTIME priority, the system would need to have a minimum of 36MB of RAM.

Applications are started at various priorities by using the `start /<priority>` switch from the command line. The *<priority>* can be LOW (base priority=4), NORMAL (base priority=8), HIGH (base priority=13), or REALTIME (base priority=24). The Proposed Solution accomplishes the first Optional Result.

Within the Windows NT environment, the Applications tab in Windows NT Task Manager can be used to terminate applications. Pressing Ctrl+Alt+Del and clicking on the Task Manager button launches Task Manager. Additionally, the KILL.EXE utility included in the Resource Kit can be used to terminate applications.

7. Without changing the priority of an application, what can you do to make it run more quickly? Choose all that apply.

A. Terminate other applications.

B. Bring that application to the foreground.

E. Minimize all other application windows.

7. CORRECT ANSWER: A-B-E

Obviously, terminating other applications will free system resources, possibly reducing swapping requirements, thereby increasing the speed and responsiveness of the application in question.

Bringing the application to the foreground automatically boosts the priority of the application from seven to nine, increasing application performance.

Minimizing all other windows also frees system resources, although not as much as terminating the applications would. With additional system resources available, the application's performance improves.

There is no way to assign CPU resources; this is done automatically by the Windows NT kernel.

Maximizing the application will have no effect on application performance.

FURTHER REVIEW

START APPLICATIONS AT VARIOUS PRIORITIES

Under preemptive multitasking, Windows NT determines which application should get access to the processor for execution by using priority levels. Each application starts at a base priority level of eight. The system dynamically adjusts the priority level to give all applications access to the processor. The process or thread with the highest priority base at any one time has access to the processor. Some of the factors that cause Windows NT to adjust the priority of a thread or process include the following:

- Windows NT boosts the base priority of whichever process is running in the foreground. This ensures that the response time is maximized for the currently used application.
- Windows NT randomly boosts the priority for lower-priority threads. This has two major benefits. The first benefit is that low-priority threads that would normally not be able to run can do so after their priority base is raised. The second benefit is that if a lower-priority process has access to a resource that is to be shared with a higher-priority process, the higher-priority process could end up monopolizing the resource. The boost in the lower-priority thread's base priority frees up the resource sooner.
- Anytime a thread has been in a voluntary wait state, Windows NT boosts its priority. The size of the boost depends on how long the resource has been in a wait state.

Priority levels zero through 15 are used by dynamic applications. Anything running at a dynamic level can be written to the Windows NT pagefile. By default, this includes user applications and operating system functions that are not imperative to the performance of the operating system. Priority levels 16 through 31 are reserved for real-time applications that cannot be written to the Windows NT pagefile. This includes all Executive Services and the Windows NT kernel.

Starting Applications at Different Levels

The user can change the default priority level from Normal by using the command prompt to start an application, or he can adjust the priority level after the application has started by using the Task Manager. Table 5.4 shows the four priority levels the user can set.

TABLE 5.4 BASE PRIORITY LEVELS UNDER WINDOWS NT

Priority Level	*Base Priority*	*Command Line*
Low	4	`start /low executable.exe`
Normal	8	`start /normal executable.exe`
High	13	`start /high executable.exe`
Realtime	24	`start /realtime executable.exe`

When an application is running, you can use the Task Manager to change the base priority. To change the priority of a running application, follow these steps:

1. Right-click the taskbar and select Task Manager from the shortcut menu.
2. Click the Processes tab to view all running processes.
3. If the Base Priority column is not visible, add it to the view by choosing Select Columns from the View menu. In the resulting dialog box, ensure that Base Priority is selected.
4. Right-click the process in the Process list.
5. Click Set Priority, and then click the desired priority at which you want the process to run.

Changing the Default Priority Boost for Foreground Applications

On some Windows NT computers, you might want to improve the responsiveness of background applications. By default, the foreground application is given a priority boost of two levels. This changes the base priority for foreground applications to 10 from the default of 8 in the case of Normal priority applications. If you want to change the priority level, use the Performance tab in the System Control Panel applet.

CHAPTER SUMMARY

Windows NT was designed as an operating system with the ability to run applications from a variety of other operating systems (such as OS/2, Windows 3.1, MS-DOS, and POSIX-compliant applications). Understanding how to configure the various emulation environments for these applications within Windows NT is an important part of your mastery of the Windows NT Workstation operating system.

Along with configuring the environments that execute other operating system applications, you must also understand and be able to configure the way applications interact with one another and the operating system by setting the priorities of the applications. Although NT offers 32 distinct priorities, there are four common priorities: Low, Normal, High, and Realtime. Understanding how to set the various priorities of applications is paramount in maintaining a well-tuned, stable, and effiecient multitasking system. Additionally, you will be expected to demonstrate your knowledge of these concepts to successfully complete the certification exam.

CHAPTER 6

Monitoring and Optimization

Monitoring and Optimization is an important part of managing, using, and administering installations of Windows NT Workstation 4. After the system is configured and connected to the network, it is important to ensure the system is performing optimally. As more and more applications are loaded and the workstation is expected to perform additional tasks, the system must be tuned to handle the additional load efficiently. Additionally, if system performance suddenly becomes sluggish, the concepts and tools discussed in this chapter will enable you to diagnose the problem and take the proper steps to correct the situation to restore performance.

OBJECTIVES

Monitor system performance using various tools.

Identify and resolve a given performance problem.

Optimize system performance in various areas.

PRACTICE QUESTIONS

MONITOR SYSTEM PERFORMANCE USING VARIOUS TOOLS

1. **From the following list, select all tools that can provide information about CPU utilization:**

   A. Performance Monitor

   B. WinMSD

   C. Resource Meter

   D. CPU Manager

   E. Task Manager

2. **This is a scenario question. First you must review the scenario, then review the required and optional results. Following that is a solution. You must pick the best evaluation of that solution.**

   Scenario:
   You have an installation of NT Workstation 4 that is currently configured in a Windows NT Domain environment. Your supervisor has asked you to add a database application from a third-party vendor.

   Required Result:
   Measure the immediate impact on the system processor to identify if an additional processor will be required.

   Optional Results:
   Save the information for later analysis.

   Create a graph with Microsoft Excel to present to your supervisor.

   Proposed Solution:
   Install the application and monitor the following Performance Monitor counters: % Processor Time, % User Time, and % Interrupt Time. Use the Chart view to add the counters.

   Save the data from Performance Monitor to a file using the Save Chart Setting from the File menu in Performance Monitor.

   Evaluation of Proposed Solution:
   The proposed solution accomplishes which of the following objectives?

   A. The Required Result only

   B. The Required Result and both Optional Results

   C. The Required Result and only one Optional Result

   D. Only one Optional Result

   E. Neither the Required Result nor any Optional Results

3. **You want to print a detailed summary of the current state of your system, including drivers, system services, and IRQ settings. Which tool do you use?**

   A. Task Manager

   B. WinMSD

   C. Performance Monitor

   D. The System applet in Control Panel

   E. Resource Meter

4. **This is a scenario question. First you must review the scenario, then review the required and optional results. Following**

that is a solution. You must pick the best evaluation of that solution.

Scenario:
A user with a Windows NT Workstation connected to a Microsoft Domain networking environment calls you to report that system response has become sluggish. She would like to increase the performance as well as install a new sound card.

Required Result:
Determine if additional memory is required in the system.

Optional Results:
Determine if IRQ 7 is available for use by the new sound card.

Determine the processor utilization in the workstation over a period of time.

Proposed Solution:
Use Performance Monitor to create a log over a period of three hours to monitor the memory utilization of the system. Log the Page Faults counter, Pages Input/sec counter, and Page Reads/sec counter in the Memory object.

Utilize WinMSD to determine what interrupts are in use by the system. In particular, check for the availability of IRQ 7.

Instruct the user to launch the Task Manager. Ask her to record the processor utilization reported by Task Manager every hour during business hours for three days.

Evaluation of Proposed Solution:
The proposed solution accomplishes which of the following objectives?

A. The Required Result only

B. The Required Result and both Optional Results

C. The Required Result and only one Optional Result

D. Only one Optional Result

E. Neither the Required Result nor any Optional Results

5. **You are looking at the Processes tab of Task Manager, but certain information regarding memory usage is not listed. How can you display more information in this window? (Choose all that apply.)**

   A. Use the Performance Monitor's memory counters.

   B. Open two Task Manager windows.

   C. Use the View menu's Select Columns command.

   D. Change the size of the window using the mouse.

   E. Select the viewable columns through the Properties command on the File menu.

6. **Select the statement that best describes the relationship between counters, instances, and objects within Performance Monitor.**

   A. Objects are categories that contain specific counters for all instances.

   B. An object is a unit of each instance. A counter is used only to determine the number of events occurring on a system.

   C. Performance Monitor uses counters only.

   D. All objects are divided into counters. Each counter can be monitored for a particular instance of a component instance.

E. Performance Monitor uses objects only.

7. **This is a scenario question. First you must review the scenario, then review the required and optional results. Following that is a solution. You must pick the best evaluation of that solution.**

Scenario:
A user contacts you and indicates his data files are corrupting more and more frequently. He thinks the disk controller or hard disk may be going bad. The Windows NT installation has not been modified from its default, except for the addition of Office 97 and FrontPage 98.

Required Result:
Determine if the user's disk controller or hard disk is malfunctioning.

Optional Results:
Analyze disk performance of the machine in question.

Determine the performance of the network subsystem in the workstation.

Proposed Solution:
Set up a Performance Monitor alert of disk bytes written to disk.

Evaluation of Proposed Solution:
The Proposed Solution accomplishes which of the following objectives?

A. The Required Result only

B. The Required Result and both Optional Results

C. The Required Result and only one Optional Result

D. Only one Optional Result

E. Neither the Required Result nor any Optional Results

8. **You want to know the BIOS version and date for your computer. Which tool can you use to find out this information?**

A. System applet in Control Panel

B. WinMSD

C. The `net computer` command at the command prompt

D. Performance Monitor

E. Devices applet in Control Panel

9. **When you're using Performance Monitor to set alerts on specific counter values, at what frequency can alerts be reported? (Choose all that apply.)**

A. At user-defined intervals, such as every time a counter exceeds the threshold defined to cause the alert

B. Each time the counter exceeds the threshold defined to cause the alert

C. When the counter falls back below the value set to trigger the alert

D. The first time the counter exceeds the set value

E. Only every 15 minutes

10. **This is a scenario question. First you must review the scenario, then review the required and optional results. Following that is a solution. You must pick the best evaluation of that solution.**

Scenario:
You have a Windows NT Workstation with a network adapter and the appropriate drivers installed. TCP/IP is bound to the adapter. The network performance of the workstation has been noticeably slow lately.

Required Result:
Determine the amount of network traffic destined for the network adapter installed in the workstation.

Optional Results:
Determine the number of connections sustained and rejected by the adapter.

Determine the number of bytes sent and received per second.

Proposed Solution:
Install Network Monitor to determine the amount of packets being received by the network adapter.

Using Performance Monitor, monitor the Bytes Received/sec and Bytes Sent/sec for the TCP object.

Using Performance Monitor, monitor the Connections Active for the TCP object.

Evaluation of Proposed Solution:
The proposed solution accomplishes which of the following objectives?

A. The Required Result only

B. The Required Result and both Optional Results

C. The Required Result and only one Optional Result

D. Only one Optional Result

E. Neither the Required Result nor any Optional Results

11. You are using the Task Manager to monitor your CPU usage, but you want the chart to be updated more frequently. What can you do?

A. You must use the Performance Monitor's Processor object to tailor CPU monitoring in this way.

B. Close all other applications while the Task Manager is running.

C. Change the Update Speed parameter in Task Manager.

D. Run Task Manager using the `/high` switch.

E. Run Task Manager using the `/realtime` switch.

12. Which two services must be running on your Windows NT 4 machine for Performance Monitor alerts to work properly?

A. Messenger service

B SNMP service

C. Replication service

D. Server service

E. Alerter service

13. You want to monitor the resources being used by remote users on your Windows NT 4 Workstation, and you want the option of disconnecting them from a resource. Which tool do you use?

A. User Manager

B. Task Manager

C. The My Computer icon

D. Server applet (Control Panel)

E. System applet (Control Panel)

14. You want to be able to easily start Performance Monitor and begin monitoring a pre-established group of objects and their counters. Which is the best method of doing this? (Choose one.)

A. Leave Performance Monitor running in the background at all times.

B. Decide on the configuration you want, and then stick with it. Performance Monitor automatically restores the last settings used.

C. You must reconfigure Performance Monitor with each use.

D. Create a log file with the desired settings and load the file when Performance Monitor is launched.

E. Create a Settings file with all the settings, counters, and information you need to begin monitoring.

15. This is a scenario question. First you must review the scenario, then review the required and optional results. Following that is a solution. You must pick the best evaluation of that solution.

Scenario:
You have a Windows NT Workstation configured in a Windows NT Domain networking model.

Required Result:
View all shares available from the workstation.

Optional Results:
Determine the number of users connected to each share.

Determine the number of bytes sent and received by the Workstation.

Proposed Solution:
Open Network Neighborhood and browse the local machine to determine what shares are available for the workstation.

Using Performance Monitor, monitor the Active Connections counter for the TCP object.

Using Performance Monitor, monitor the Bytes Sent/sec and Bytes Received/sec counters for the Server object.

Evaluation of Proposed Solution:
The proposed solution accomplishes which of the following objectives?

A. The Required Result only

B. The Required Result and both Optional Results

C. The Required Result and only one Optional Result

D. Only one Optional Result

E. Neither the Required Result nor any Optional Results

ANSWER KEY

1. A-E
2. E
3. B
4. C
5. C
6. D
7. E
8. B
9. B-D
10. A
11. C
12. A-E
13. D
14. E
15. D

ANSWERS & EXPLANATIONS

MONITOR SYSTEM PERFORMANCE USING VARIOUS TOOLS

1. From the following list, select all tools that can provide information about CPU utilization:

A. Performance Monitor

E. Task Manager

1. CORRECT ANSWER: A-E

Performance Monitor is a tool provided with Windows NT Workstation 4 that enables you to monitor a vast number of system components. The system's entire operation, as well as application performance, can be monitored, charted, logged, or displayed in a report. The Performance Monitor enables remote monitoring of other Windows NT 4 systems, assuming that administrative rights are available for the remote system.

Information is presented under the following three components:

- Performance monitoring items (such as the Processor, Memory, and so on) are categorized as objects.
- Each object has counters that can be monitored.
- There might be several instances of each counter.

An object is broken down into several counters, and counters are broken down into instances. There are three types of counters: instantaneous, averaging, and difference. Windows NT 4 now includes a total instance for most counters as well as individual instances for more detail. Instances shown might vary depending on the applications or features running. The number of objects available depends on the Windows NT features that are installed. A special set of TCP/IP counters shows up only if SNMP protocol is loaded along with Service Pack 1 or later. Disk performance counters show up only if `DISKPERF -y` is run. See the section "Pinpointing Disk Bottlenecks," later in this chapter, for additional information on using the `DISKPERF` command.

The objects found in the Performance Monitor might vary depending on the current configuration of Windows NT. For example, adding Peer Web Services adds additional counters for the HTTP and FTP services.

Performance Monitor is accessible from the Administrative Options (Common) program group on the Start menu.

Task Manager is another tool that can be used to provide a quick snapshot of processor utilization. In addition to providing information on CPU utilization, the Task Manager tool offers a quick overview of other key system resources, such as memory usage, the status of applications currently running, and processes in use on the system.

Task Manager can be accessed by the following methods:

- Right-click the taskbar and select Task Manager.
- Press Ctrl+Alt+Delete, and then select Task Manager.
- Press Ctrl+Shift+Esc.

2. Proposed Solution:
Install the application and monitor the following Performance Monitor counters: % Processor Time, % User Time, and % Interrupt Time. Use the Chart view to add the counters.

Save the data from Performance Monitor to a file using the Save Chart Setting from the File menu in Performance Monitor.

E. Neither the Required Result nor any Optional Results

2. CORRECT ANSWER: E

Although monitoring counters in Performance Monitor will give you a good indication of the processor activity on the system, it will not allow you to measure the impact that the new application has on the system. This can be measured only if a baseline is taken of the system before the application is installed.

A baseline is a snapshot of the system before any changes are made. A baseline is required to measure the impact of the changes after they are completed. In the example presented in the scenario, perhaps the processor was at 92 percent utilization before the application was installed. If this was the case, creating the baseline would have indicated that the application should have been installed on another system if available or that an additional system needed to be purchased to support the application.

Saving the results of a Performance Monitor session over a period of time creates a baseline. A particularly stressful time for the system, such as in the morning when many users are logging in or immediately after lunch when reports are being run, is the ideal time to start making a baseline. A baseline should also include times when the system is idle. By looking at the difference in performance during these times, you might be able to identify system bottlenecks or what areas could be tuned for optimal performance.

After the baseline is completed, make any necessary changes and then run Performance Monitor again. It is important, when judging the impact of the changes, to take the new measurements under similar conditions and loads. By comparing the two sets of data, you will be able to truly determine the impact of the changes.

The same procedure can be followed not only for new applications, but when performing changes to tune and optimize the operating system. By analyzing the before and after performance data, you can judge how effective your efforts were.

Monitoring the % User Time counter in the Processor object will enable you to determine how much processor time is, in fact, utilized by applications. However, the processor time is reported for all applications; there is not a way (unless the application installs specific counters into Performance Monitor) that the effect of one application can be observed. Had a baseline been created first, the effect of the new application on the % User Time counter could have been analyzed. The % Interrupt Time will not identify the effect of adding the new application. The % Interrupt Time identifies the time the processor is servicing interrupts. A large value for this counter could identify other system problems, such as faulty hardware or improper device drivers. The % Processor Time is a good counter to determine the overall load on the processor, which is a summation of counters such as % Interrupt Time and % User Time.

Because a baseline was not completed, the impact of the new application cannot be adequately determined. The Proposed Solution does not accomplish the Required Result.

When using the Chart view in Performance Monitor, you cannot save the actual recorded data, only the settings such as the objects and counters to be monitored. To save the data for later analysis, the desired objects must be enabled and the logging parameters, such as the update interval, must be set. From the View menu, select Log View. After you are in the Log view, select Log from the Options menu to select the file to which to save the data and the interval (in seconds) in which to take the data. Select Add to Log from the Edit menu to select the objects to be saved in the log file. Note that only objects, not individual counters, can be selected. After selecting the desired objects to monitor, select Log from the Options menu to start the logging. When the desired interval for logging is complete, select Log from the Options menu again to stop the logging.

When the log file is loaded into Performance Monitor at a later date through the Data From… option on the Log menu (you must be in Log view to access the Log menu), the logged data will be available for the Chart or Report view. Only the counters selected during logging can then be selected in the appropriate view, either Chart or Report.

After the data is loaded from the log file, the data can be saved as either a comma separated value (.CSV) or tab separated value (.TSV) file from the Export option on the File menu in either the Chart or Report view. The Proposed Solution does not accomplish either the first or second Optional Result.

3. You want to print a detailed summary of the current state of your system, including drivers, system services, and IRQ settings. Which tool do you use?

B. WinMSD

3. CORRECT ANSWER: B

The Windows NT Diagnostic application, available through the Administrative Tools (Common) program folder on the Start menu, provides the needed information on the operating system resources. The answer to the following question provides more information on the use and capabilities of Windows NT Diagnostic, also known as WinMSD.

4. Proposed Solution:
Use Performance Monitor to create a log over a period of three hours to monitor the memory utilization of the system. Log the Page Faults counter,

4. CORRECT ANSWER: C

WinMSD is the proper application to determine available system interrupts. Clicking the IRQ button on the System tab will enumerate which system interrupts are in use on the

Pages Input/sec counter, and Page Reads/sec counter in the Memory object.

Utilize WinMSD to determine what interrupts are in use by the system. In particular, check for the availability of IRQ 7.

Instruct the user to launch the Task Manager. Ask her to record the processor utilization reported by Task Manager every hour during business hours for three days.

C. The Required Result and only one Optional Result

workstation. In addition to providing information about system interrupt utilization and assignment, WinMSD is responsible for providing a summary report on the current status of the system. This utility displays nine categories of information, ranging from the services' status to the size of the current pagefile and the device drivers used on the system. The following list enumerates the available tabs within WinMSD and provides a brief description of each:

- *Version.* Shows the Licensing screen, which displays the registered owner and the CD key. This tab also lists the latest service pack installed on the workstation.
- *System.* Shows the type of computer and CPU chip used. The system BIOS date and version can also be found here.
- *Display.* Shows the display adapter BIOS information and the current adapter settings, including memory on the card and display drivers being used.
- *Drive.* Shows all local drives on the system. The properties of each drive reveal the usage in bytes and clusters.
- *Memory.* Shows the pagefile size and usage, displayed in kilobytes.
- *Services.* Shows all Windows NT services, along with their current status.
- *Resources.* Lists the four critical resources for each device: IRQ, I/O port, DMA, and memory. Information can also be listed per device.
- *Environment.* Shows the environment variables for the system as well as the local user.
- *Network.* Shows general information about the logon status, transport protocols, device settings of the network card, and overall statistics of network use.

WinMSD can also be used to provide similar information about remote machines.

The Proposed Solution accomplishes the first Optional Result.

To determine if the amount of installed memory on the system is causing a system bottleneck, use the Memory object to verify the amount of paging occurring on the system. In particular, the Page Faults counter, Pages Input/sec counter, and Page Reads/sec counter should be monitored. The Proposed Solution accomplishes the first Optional Result. If the memory counter indicates that the system memory might be causing a bottleneck, the %Usage counter of the Pagefile object should also be reviewed to determine the amount of pagefile utilization.

Periodically checking the Task Manager to determine processor utilization is not the best way to determine the average load on a processor over a period of time. The Proposed Solution does not accomplish the second Optional Result. It would have been more effective to monitor counters within the processor object at the same time Performance Monitor was run to monitor the memory utilization of the system.

5. You are looking at the Processes tab of Task Manager, but certain information regarding memory usage is not listed. How can you display more information in this window? (Choose all that apply.)

C. Use the View menu's Select Columns command.

5. CORRECT ANSWER: C

By using the Select Columns command available from the View menu in Task Manager, you can customize which columns are displayed within Task Manager. Table 6.1 lists the default columns available in the Processes tab when Task Manager is launched.

TABLE 6.1 DEFAULT-SELECTED COLUMNS IN THE PROCESSES TAB OF TASK MANAGER

Column	*Description*
Image Name	The process currently running
PID	Process identifier (a unique number)
CPU Usage	Current percentage of CPU's usage allocated to this process
CPU Time	Total time the process has used on the CPU
Memory Usage	The amount of memory allocated to this process

The following list enumerates the additional columns that you can view from the Processes tab within Task Manager.

- Memory Usage Delta
- Page Faults
- Page Faults Delta
- Virtual Memory Size
- Paged Pool
- Non-paged Pool
- Base Priority
- Handle Count
- Thread Count

6. Select the statement that best describes the relationship between counters, instances, and objects within Performance Monitor?

D. All objects are divided into counters. Each counter can be monitored for a particular instance of a component instance.

6. CORRECT ANSWER: D

Within Performance Monitor, an object is a basic component or subsystem within the operating system, such as a processor, memory, or disk. An instance is one or more physical realizations of that component. As an example, in a dual-processor system, there is one processor object; each individual processor will be an instance. In a system with two logical disks residing on one physical disk, there are two logical disk objects and one physical disk object.

A counter is used to determine the number of events occurring on a system for a particular instance. Within each logical disk object, for example, a counter measures the amount of time the device is servicing write requests to the device (the % Disk Write Time counter).

7. Proposed Solution: Set up a Performance Monitor alert of disk bytes written to disk.

E. Neither the Required Result nor any Optional Results

7. CORRECT ANSWER: E

Performance Monitor is a tool best used for tuning/optimizing Windows NT and identifying system bottlenecks. In this scenario, monitoring the disk counters, as well as the % Interrupt Time, might indicate if there is a disk controller problem; a better solution would be to use Event Viewer to review the System and Application event logs. If the system experiences disk read or write errors indicative of a disk or disk controller problem, the errors will be written to the System event log. Along the same lines, applications might also write errors to the Application event log if disk read or write errors occur. The Proposed Solution does not accomplish the Required Result.

Because the installation was a default installation of Windows NT Workstation, the DISKPERF counters have not been enabled. Without these counters enabled, Performance Monitor is not able to record any information for any of the physical or logical disk instances. The Proposed Solution does not accomplish the first Optional Result. The Proposed Solution should have included enabling the DISKPERF counters prior to monitoring the disk objects.

Monitoring only the % Interrupt Time counter in the processor object does not provide a good indication of processor activity. In order to determine if the processor is a system bottleneck, the % Processor Time, % Privileged Time, and % User Time counters in the processor object should be monitored.

The % User Time counter shows the amount of processor time spent executing non-idle thread processes running in the user mode, which typically covers user applications. The % Privileged Time shows the amount of time spent executing privileged or operating system tasks. The % Processor Time gives an indication of the overall activity level of the processor. The Proposed Solution does not achieve the second Optional Result.

8. You want to know the BIOS version and date for your computer. Which tool can you use to find out this information?

B. WinMSD

8. CORRECT ANSWER: B

The WinMSD application provides the BIOS version and date information for the workstation on the System tab.

9. When you're using Performance Monitor to set alerts on specific counter values, with what frequency can alerts be reported? (Choose all that apply.)

B. Each time the counter exceeds the threshold defined to cause the alert

D. The first time the counter exceeds the set value

9. CORRECT ANSWER: B-D

Alerts can be processed the first time they occur or every time the triggering event occurs. This is accomplished by switching to the Alert view in Performance Monitor and selecting the Add to Alert option from the View menu.

10. Proposed Solution:
Install Network Monitor to determine the amount of packets being received by the network adapter.

Using Performance Monitor, monitor the Bytes Received/sec and Bytes Sent/sec for the TCP object.

Using Performance Monitor, monitor the Connections Active for the TCP object.

A. The Required Result only

10. CORRECT ANSWER: A

Network Monitor is an additional utility than can be used to monitor the performance of an NT Workstation. Network Monitor acts as a software sniffer, enabling you to capture and view all the network traffic (i.e., frames) destined for and sent by the network adapter installed in the workstation. One important distinction is that the Windows NT Network Monitor will not operate in the promiscuous mode. That is, it will not capture all network traffic on the local segment, only that destined for or originating from the local network adapter. There is a version of the Network Monitor available with Microsoft's SMS product that will operate in the promiscuous mode. The Proposed Solution accomplishes the Required Result.

The TCP object does not contain counters to measure the amount of bytes sent and received. These counters are included in the Server service object. Remember that the Server service is the Windows NT service responsible for making shared resources on the local machine available to other networked machines. The Proposed Solution does not accomplish the second Optional Result.

The TCP object does contain a counter to measure the number of active connections as well as the number of rejected connections. A common reason for rejected connections is that the 10 inbound resource connection limit is exceeded with Windows NT Workstation. Because the Proposed Solution indicates that only the Active Connections object was monitored, it does not meet the first Optional Result.

11. You are using the Task Manager to monitor your CPU usage, but you want the chart to be updated more frequently. What can you do?

C. Change the Update Speed parameter in Task Manager.

11. CORRECT ANSWER: C

The update speed of the information presented in Task Manager's Performance tab can be altered by selecting the Update Speed option from the View menu. Be default, the value is set at Normal, but it can be changed to High, Low, or Paused.

12. Which two services must be running on your Windows NT 4.0 machine for Performance Monitor alerts to work properly?

A. Messenger service

E. Alerter service

12. CORRECT ANSWER: A-E

The Messenger service and Alerter service must be installed, configured and running on the Windows NT machine for Performance Monitor alerts to work properly.

13. You want to monitor the resources being used by remote users on your Windows NT 4 Workstation, and you want the option of disconnecting them from a resource. Which tool do you use?

D. Server applet (Control Panel)

13. CORRECT ANSWER: D

The Server applet in Control Panel enables you to monitor and disconnect Windows NT accounts utilizing shared resources on your Workstation.

14. You want to be able to easily start Performance Monitor and begin monitoring a pre-established group of objects and their counters. Which is the best method of doing this? (Choose one.)

E. Create a Settings file with all the settings, counters, and information you need to begin monitoring.

14. CORRECT ANSWER: E

The Settings file saves the object, counter, and instance information of the current configuration. This can be used to quickly begin monitoring several counters on a regular basis.

15. Proposed Solution:
Open Network Neighborhood and browse the local machine to determine what shares are available for the workstation.

Using Performance Monitor, monitor the Active Connections counter for the TCP object.

15. CORRECT ANSWER: D

Using Network Neighborhood to find the available shares does not reveal hidden shares established on the workstation. The Server Control Panel applet enumerates all the shares available on the workstation. The Proposed Solution does not accomplish the Required Result.

Using Performance Monitor, monitor the Bytes Sent/sec and Bytes Received/sec counters for the Server object.

D. Only one Optional Result

In addition to providing information on the available shares on a workstation and the number of connected users, the Server applet is also used to set up the Replication utility and the alert destinations for Windows NT Workstation 4.

Although Performance Monitor can be used to determine the number of active connections to the workstation through the TCP object, it does not indicate to which shares or resources the users are connected. Additionally, the TCP object identifies the number of connections established through TCP/IP only, not NetBEUI, NWLink or any other protocol loaded on the workstation. The Proposed Solution does not accomplish the first Optional Result.

Monitoring the Bytes Sent/sec and Bytes Received/sec counters for the Server object within Performance Monitor accurately shows the amount of information being processed by the Server service. The Proposed Solution accomplishes the second Optional Result.

FURTHER REVIEW

MONITOR SYSTEM PERFORMANCE USING VARIOUS TOOLS

This section reviews the tools available with Windows NT Workstation 4 to monitor system performance, and it expands upon the discussion of the use and analysis of results from each monitoring tool.

Task Manager

The Task Manager tool offers a quick overview of key system resources, such as memory and CPU usage, the status of applications currently running, and processes in use on the system.

There are three tabs available in Task Manager: the Applications tab, the Processes tab, and the Performance tab.

Task Manager Applications Tab

This tab displays all running applications and enables you to terminate applications. You might terminate an application from the Task Manager if a program crashes and cannot be shut down normally. The application might be "frozen" and unable to respond to commands, possibly using valuable system resources.

Task Manager Processes Tab

Each application may run several processes simultaneously. The Windows NT operating system runs several processes at a time. You can consider a process a subset of programming code used to run applications.

Windows NT services are also processes. They use system resources such as memory and CPU time. You can monitor each process in the Processes tab of the Task Manager. To free system resources for other applications and processes, you should close services not being used (see the section entitled "Running Windows NT Services").

Task Manager Performance Tab

The Performance tab displays a summary of memory, CPU usage, and general indicators. The first part of the Performance tab shows the CPU usage and CPU history. These indicators show the total usage of the CPU by either the operating system or an application. The CPU usage indicates the percentage of the CPU in use at the last update count. The history displays the last few updates. The default update time is approximately one second. You can change this value by using the Update Speed command in the View menu. Selecting a low update count allows for a longer time in the history window. Table 6.2 lists the four main categories in the Performance tab.

TABLE 6.2 MAIN CATEGORIES IN THE PERFORMANCE TAB

Category	*Description*
Totals	
Handles	The number of file handles opened on the system.
Threads	The total number of application threads in use by all applications.
Processes	Total number of processes in use by all applications.
Physical Memory	
Total	Actual RAM in the computer.
Available	Physical RAM available that can be allocated to a process.
File Cache	The amount of physical RAM used by the file cache.
Commit Charge	
Total	The total amount of memory allocated. This includes physical and virtual memory.
Limit	Total amount of memory the system can use before the pagefile needs to be increased. This is determined based on the current size of the pagefile, not the maximum or minimum necessarily.
Peak	The largest amount of memory that has been used this session.
Kernel Memory	
Total	The total amount of memory, both paged and nonpaged, being used by the kernel.
Paged	The amount of memory that the kernel is using and that can be swapped to the pagefile.
Nonpaged	The memory that cannot be paged while in use.

The Performance Monitor tool shows all these counters in much more detail. The Task Manager is used to obtain a quick overview of the system. Information cannot be logged or printed from the Task Manager.

Performance Monitor

The Performance Monitor takes the Task Manager to the next level of detail. The entire system's operations as well as the application's performance can be monitored, charted, logged, or displayed in a report. The Performance Monitor enables remote monitoring of other Windows NT 4 systems, assuming administrative rights are available for the remote system.

Performance Monitor is one of the best tools provided with Windows NT to measure system performance. There are two important things to understand about Performance Monitor. The first is when to use Performance Monitor, which is discussed in this section of the book. The second is how to interpret the output of Performance Monitor, which is discussed in the next set of practice questions.

Within Performance Monitor, an object is broken down into several counters, and counters are broken down into instances. There are three types of counters: instantaneous, averaging, and difference. Windows NT 4 now includes a total instance for most counters, as well as individual instances for more detail. Instances shown might vary depending on the applications or features running.

Objects found in the Performance Monitor might vary depending on the current configuration of Windows NT. Table 6.3 shows common objects that are always available.

TABLE 6.3 COMMON OBJECTS ALWAYS AVAILABLE IN THE PERFORMANCE MONITOR

Object	*Description*
Cache	The file system cache, an area of physical memory that holds recently used data
Logical Disk	Disk partitions and other logical views of disk space
Memory	Random access memory used to store code and data
Objects	Certain system software objects
Paging File	The file used to support virtual memory allocated by the system
Physical Disk	Hardware disk unit
Process	Software object that represents a running program
Processor	Hardware unit that executes program instructions
Redirector	File system that diverts file requests to network servers
System	Counters that apply to all system hardware and software
Thread	The part of a process that uses the processor

Performance Monitor Charts

The Performance Monitor can show the system's performance in an easy-to-read chart format. The default view is the Chart view, which is the easiest to use for most people. Data can be viewed in a chart format as live data or from a prerecorded log file. Live data must be monitored constantly and evaluated on the spot. A prerecorded log file can gather data for several hours or more and can be monitored at a more convenient time. Current or live data is explained in this section; log files are covered in a later section entitled "Using Logs."

To decide which data is going to be presented on the chart, use the Data From command on the Options menu. Two choices are presented: Current Activity (to view live data) and Log File (to open a previously recorded log file). Using the ellipsis button (...), you can browse the hard drive to find and obtain the log file.

Each charted value uses a scale shown at the bottom of the screen just before the counter name. A scale of 1.000 indicates that the counter was not scaled up or down. Imagine a point on the performance chart where the counter value is 50. A scale ratio of 0.100 shows that 50 has been multiplied by 0.1 (divided by 10) for a true value of 5. A ratio of 10 shows that the value was multiplied by 10 for a true value of 50. Multiply the value on the chart by the scale to get a true value.

Another useful option for easier viewing and analysis of performance charts is the grid option. Select Chart from the Options menu (or press Ctrl+O) to display the Chart Options dialog box. Here you can check or uncheck Vertical and Horizontal Grid Lines to control whether gridlines are displayed on your chart. You can also change the chart display from a graph to a histogram, as well as tweak and customize some other viewing preferences.

You can obtain further statistics on any chart line by clicking the counter name at the bottom of the screen. Just above the list of displayed counters are the last, average, minimum, and maximum values of the current item. To highlight a chart item on the screen, click the item name and press Ctrl+H. The emphasized counter is shown in a thick white line.

You cannot print charts from Performance Monitor, but you can export them to a tab separated value (.TSV) file or a comma separated value (.CSV) file. These files contain the data without the chart lines. Choose the Export Chart command from the File menu. You can open these files from a spreadsheet or database for analysis and further charting.

Performance Monitor Logs

In most cases, watching current data flowing across the screen is not a thorough analysis. Log files are designed to watch the system and record activity in a file that can be reviewed later. You can also use log files to compare the system's performance at different times. All object information that can be monitored live can also be logged to a file.

Creating a log and analyzing data from a log are two distinct processes. See the answer and explanation for question 2 for additional information of how to create, save, and analyze a log file with Performance Monitor.

When you log information with Performance Monitor, the update interval has a direct bearing on the size of the generated log file. The smaller the update time interval, the larger the file will be. Such a file will, however, offer a lot of detail. On the other hand, a larger interval will show a trend, but it might not reflect a specific problem. If a log is to run overnight, do not use a 15-second interval. Try using 15-minute (900-second) or 30-minute (1800-second) intervals instead.

If you create a new log file using the same name, it overwrites the old one. To stop a log file, use the same Log command in the Options menu. Stop the log only when all data has been collected. After a log file has been stopped, it cannot be restarted. You can view the log file after a log has been stopped. Viewing the log file while it is being created will stop the logging process.

The Time Window is a graphical tool in which you can drag to indicate the start and end of a section within the log file to be viewed. You can use a Time Window to view the data one hour at a time by continuously moving the Time Window graph. If bookmarks were recorded during the logging process, you can use them to mark the start or end of the Time Window. All other chart options, such as scales and gridlines (mentioned earlier in this chapter), apply to viewing logged data in the Chart view.

Performance Monitor Reports

The Report view displays data in a numeric format. With current data, it shows an average of the last three updates. When you're viewing data from a log file, it shows the average value for the Time Windows selected.

To view reports, choose the Reports command from the View menu or press Ctrl+R. To see the source of the data, select the Data From command in the Options menu. You must add each counter or instance to the report by using the Add Counter button or the Add to Report command on the Edit menu. To remove items from the report, select a value and press the Delete key.

The Report view cannot show trends or large fluctuations. You cannot print a report from Performance Monitor, but you can export it as a .CSV (comma separated value) file or a .TSV (tab delimited) file and open it in a spreadsheet or word processor.

In Report view, you have only one option: the update interval. The interval determines how often the report is updated with new information. This update interval can be set on a report displaying current data only, not logged data.

Using Alerts

The Alert view (which can be easily accessed from anywhere in Performance Monitor by pressing Ctrl+A) is very different from the Chart, Log, and Report views. No data is reported or displayed until a system passes a threshold set by the administrator. The administrator can set up to 1,000 alerts on a given system. The same objects, counters, and instances are used, and one other item is added as a condition. When an alert is generated, the system sends an administrative alert message or runs a program. You can set the alerts to react only the first time the threshold is attained or each and every time.

You might, for example, set one of the following conditions:

> Only alert the administrators if the computer's hard drive space falls below 10 percent free.

or

> Alert the administrators when the server's total logons are above 150.

In both of these cases, you can set up the system to inform the administrator of the situation via a message. It is important to note that two alerts cannot be set on the same value—for example, a high and low value alert. The alert's destination must be set separately using the Alert command in the Options menu. All alerts are sent to the same destination. You can enter the destination as either a user name or a computer name, and you can specify a program to run the first time or each time the condition occurs.

The following steps describe how to set up the alert's destination:

1. Change to the Alert view by choosing the Alerts command in the View menu.
2. Select the Options menu and choose Alerts.
3. Enter the user name or computer name you want Performance Monitor to notify in case of an alert.
4. Select Log Event in Application Log to enable this log feature for all alerts. Note that for the alerts to be generated from a computer, both the Alerter and Messenger services must be started.

For alerts to function, the Performance Monitor must be running. However, because this might slow down a workstation, it should be used for short-term monitoring and troubleshooting only.

Remote Monitoring with Performance Monitor

You can use the Performance Monitor to monitor other computers on the network. Each time a counter is added to a chart, log, report, or alert, the current computer is used. Any computer that can be remotely administered can be remotely monitored as well.

To select a remote computer to monitor, type the computer name in the Add Counter dialog box, or click the ellipsis (...) button next to the Computer Name field and select the specific computer on the network. The full computer name is usually preceded by two backslashes (\\). To add a counter for a computer named salesvr1, for example, you would type **\\salesvr1**. The person doing the remote monitoring must be a member of the Administrators group of the target computer. In a Windows NT domain environment, the group Domain-Admins is always a member of each workstation's local Administrators group. Thus, any member of that group can remotely administer or monitor the system.

Saving Performance Monitor Settings

Charts, reports, logs, and alerts are modified each time a counter is added or removed and each time options are set. You can save all these settings in a separate Settings file. This means that charts, reports, logs, or alerts will be generated one time. They can, however, be used several times on current data or several log files, which provides consistency for comparing systems or situations. To save the settings for the current view, choose the Save Settings command in the File menu or press Shift+F12. For example, to save the current Alert settings, you select Save Alert Settings from the File menu.

The Performance Monitor can be shut down and restarted quickly when a Settings file is opened. You can even move the Settings file from one computer to another. The Settings page stores the objects, counters, and instances for the computer on which they were set up. Just copying the file to another computer does not monitor the new computer; it just makes remote monitoring a little easier to set up.

Server Tool (Control Panel)

The Server tool can be found in the Control Panel. This tool is used to monitor network activity related to sharing folders or printers, to set up the Replication utility, and to set up alert destinations for Windows NT Workstation 4. The component of interest here is its capability to monitor the number of remote users and the types of access they are getting on the system.

The Server tool provides three methods of viewing remote users and their activity on the system. Those three methods basically offer the same information, but each has a slightly different focus. These methods are listed and described in Table 6.4.

TABLE 6.4 REMOTE USER MONITORING TOOLS IN THE SERVER TOOL

Button	*Description*
Users	The Users button lists all users remotely connected to the system. You can select a specific user to see a list of all the shares to which the user is connected. Additional information is available, such as how long the users have been connected and whether they are using the Guest account. From here, you can also disconnect any user from a share.
Shares	The Shares button shows the same information as the Users button, except the shares are listed first. You can select a specific share to see a list of all the users connected to it. You can also disconnect someone from a given share.
In Use	The In Use button goes one step further than the two previous items—it lists the resource to which a user is connected and the type of access. A list of files that may be opened with read-only permission is listed as such. You can also close off resources, which disconnects the current users.

The Server icon exists on all Windows NT Workstations and Servers. A Windows NT domain controller also includes a Server Manager icon that gives you access to the same tasks as the Server icon on all Windows NT systems in the domain.

Disconnecting a user or a share has little effect initially on remote users because Windows NT and Windows 95 use a persistent connection technique to reconnect lost connections as soon as the resource is needed. The feature for disconnecting a user is primarily used to close connections to systems after hours or to prepare for a backup in which all files must be closed. To permanently remove someone from a share, you must change the share permissions and then disconnect the user. When the persistent connection is attempted, the permissions are re-evaluated, and access is denied.

WinMSD Utility

The WinMSD (Windows Microsoft Diagnostics) utility is part of Windows NT Workstation 4 and can be run from the Start, Run command. The WinMSD utility does not provide any means for making changes to a system; it is a read-only utility.

WinMSD can generate a printed report with complete details from all tabs. However, this information is accurate only at the time WinMSD is started; it does not monitor or update information automatically while it's running. There is, however, a Refresh button at the bottom of the dialog box that you can use to update information.

WinMSD is very useful for comparing two systems. Network administrators can use WinMSD to view information about remote systems. (Slightly less information is available with remote viewing of WinMSD.)

Most of the information available in WinMSD can be configured through the Control Panel and the Registry Editor.

PRACTICE QUESTIONS

IDENTIFY AND RESOLVE A GIVEN PERFORMANCE PROBLEM

1. **This is a scenario question. First you must review the scenario, then review the required and optional results. Following that is a solution. You must pick the best evaluation of that solution.**

Scenario:
You have a Windows NT system that has been showing poor response time since you installed a new graphics-intensive application. You want to determine which system components are the bottlenecks.

Required Result:
Determine if the processor is the system bottleneck.

Optional Result:
Determine if the system is experiencing excessive paging.

Determine if the disk subsystem is the bottleneck.

Proposed Solution:
Enable the Page Faults counter in the Memory object.

Enable the % Privilege Time in the Processor object.

Enable the Disk Bytes/sec counter in the Physical Disk object.

Evaluation of Proposed Solution:
The proposed solution accomplishes which of the stated objectives?

A. The Required Result only

B. The Required Result and both Optional Results

C. The Required Result and only one Optional Result

D. Only one Optional Result

E. Neither the Required Result nor any Optional Results

2. **Which two objects are used to monitor disk activity?**

A. DiskPerf

B. Physical Disk

C. Hard Disk

D. Logical Disk

E. System

3. **The hard drive on your Windows NT 4 computer seems to be full. You investigate the C: drive using Explorer and find that there is very little software loaded. What could be using up so much hard drive space? (Choose all that apply.)**

A. The disk is fragmented.

B. There are several Recycle Bins at full capacity.

C. The Diskperf utility is active.

D. The size of a FAT partition is very large, using large clusters.

E. The wrong driver for the disk controller is loaded.

4. You need to monitor activity on your system. You suspect a lot of network activity. How can you substantiate your suspicions? (Choose all that apply.)

A. Use the Server service icon in the Control Panel.

B. Use the Performance Monitor and make sure DiskPerf is enabled.

C. Use the Task Manager's Network tab.

D. Use the System Control Panel applet.

E. Use the Server icon in the Control Panel.

5. This is a scenario question. First you must review the scenario, then review the required and optional results. Following that is a solution. You must pick the best evaluation of that solution.

Scenario:
You have added a new SCSI adapter that appears on the Hardware Compatibility List for a Windows NT Workstation, and you've loaded what you thought to be the correct drivers that were included with the SCSI card. When you reboot the system, a dialog box appears, indicating a driver failed to load.

Required Result:
Restore the system to the stable state it was in before the new driver was loaded.

Optional Result:
Attempt to determine what the failure was.

Load the correct driver.

Proposed Solution:
Log on to the system and select Shutdown from the Start menu.

When the system reboots, select the Last Known Good configuration.

Log in and open the Event Viewer application to verify that it was in fact the new driver causing the error message.

Because the SCSI card is on the Hardware Compatibility List, use the Microsoft supplied driver for the adapter.

Evaluation of Proposed Solution:
The proposed solution accomplishes which of the following objectives?

A. The Required Result only

B. The Required Result and both Optional Results

C. The Required Result and only one Optional Result

D. Only both Optional Results

E. Neither the Required Result nor any Optional Results

6. You have lost your emergency repair disk. You can create a new one from which of the following?

A. Any Windows NT 4 Workstation computer.

B. Any Windows NT 4 Workstation or Windows NT 4 Server computer.

C. Any computer, as long as you use the Windows NT 4 Workstation CD-ROM.

D. An emergency repair disk can only be created during Windows NT Setup.

E. Only the Windows NT 4 computer for which you need the disk.

7. This is a scenario question. First you must review the scenario, then review the required and optional results. Following that is a solution. You must pick the best evaluation of that solution.

Scenario:
You have a Windows NT Workstation on which a new application has been installed. When you try to launch the application, a dialog box appears, stating the program cannot initialize due to a logon validation error. Another dialog box immediately appears, stating there is not enough virtual memory.

Required Result:
Attempt to determine why the security error appeared.

Optional Result:
Increase the amount of virtual memory available to the system.

Determine if the amount of memory installed in the workstation is causing a performance bottleneck.

Proposed Solution:
Utilize the Event Viewer to review the System, Application, and Security logs for the system.

Utilize the WinMSD application to increase the amount of virtual memory available to the system.

Use Performance Monitor to log the Page Faults, Page Inputs/sec, and Page Reads/sec counters in the Memory object for a period of time.

Evaluation of Proposed Solution:
The proposed solution accomplishes which of the following stated objectives?

A. The Required Result only

B. The Required Result and both Optional Results

C. The Required Result and only one Optional Result

D. Only both Optional Results

E. Neither the Required Result nor any Optional Results

8. How can you free up system memory without restarting the system? (Choose all that apply.)

A. Close any applications or files that are not required.

B. Minimize all background applications.

C. Run a 16-bit application in its own memory address space.

D. Increase the size of the pagefile.

E. From the command line, run the memfree.som utility.

9. From the following list of performance counters, which can be used to determine excessive processor time spent in Privileged Processor Mode? (Choose all that apply.)

A. % User Time

B. % DPC Time

C. % Processor Time

D. % Idle Time

E. % Privileged Time

10. Which of the following is *not* a feature of Windows NT 4 automatic optimization?

A. Disk space quota management

B. Process and thread prioritizing

C. Symmetric multiprocessing

D. Avoiding physical memory fragmentation

E. Automatic conversion to NTFS for large volumes

11. This is a scenario question. First you must review the scenario, then review the required and optional results. Following that is a solution. You must pick the best evaluation of that solution.

Scenario:
You are monitoring a Windows NT Workstation with Performance Monitor. You are monitoring the % Processor Time counter from the Processor object and the Average Disk Queue Length from the Logical Disks object. The disk performance counters have been enabled.

The % Processor Time counter normally averages around 40 percent, but when you load an application, the % Processor Time spikes to 100 percent.

The Average Disk Queue length never drops below four.

Required Result:
Determine if the processor is a system bottleneck and provide resolution if it is.

Optional Result:
See if the amount of installed system memory is a bottleneck and provide resolution if it is.

Determine if the disk subsystem is a system bottleneck and provide resolution if it is.

Proposed Solution:
Because the % Processor Time counter remains below 40 percent, the processor is not a bottleneck. A spike in excess of 80 percent when an application first initializes is no need for concern, as long as the counter returns to a steady state.

A large steady state number for disk queue length is an indication of excessive paging. If excessive paging is occurring, there is not enough system memory. The disk system is not a bottleneck, but its performance is being hindered due to excessive paging. More memory should be added to the system and then Performance Monitor should be used to analyze system performance again.

Evaluation of Proposed Solution:
The proposed solution accomplishes which if the following objectives?

A. The Required Result only

B. The Required Result and both Optional Results

C. The Required Result and only one Optional Result

D. Only one Optional Result

E. Neither the Required Result nor any Optional Results

12. You are using Performance Monitor to analyze your system processor. Based on

the System object's System Processor Queue counter, which of the following conditions indicate your processor is too slow? Select all that apply.

A. The Processor Queue Length never drops below 8.

B. The Processor Queue Length drops below 2.

C. The Processor Queue Length does not fluctuate.

D. The Processor Queue Length is always greater than 2.

E. The Processor Queue Length rises quickly and slowly decreases to a steady state value of 2.

ANSWER KEY

1. E
2. B-D
3. A-B-D
4. B-E
5. D
6. E
7. C
8. A-B
9. B-E
10. A-E
11. C
12. D-E

ANSWERS & EXPLANATIONS

IDENTIFY AND RESOLVE A GIVEN PERFORMANCE PROBLEM

1. **Proposed Solution:**
   Enable the Page Faults counter in the Memory object.

   Enable the % Privilege Time in the Processor object.

   Enable the Disk Bytes/sec counter in the Physical Disk object.

   E. Neither the Required Result nor any Optional Results

1. CORRECT ANSWER: E

Monitoring only the % Privilege Time counter in the Processor object will indicate the amount of processor time dedicated to performing system tasks. To determine if the processor is a system bottleneck, you should also monitor the % Processor Time and % User Time counters. Monitoring these three counters enables you to determine the amount of overall processor load, as well as the amount of time dedicated to operating system tasks and user tasks. The Proposed Solution does not accomplish the Required Result.

To determine if the system is experiencing excessive paging, monitor the Page Fault, Pages Input/sec, and Page Reads/sec counters in the Memory object with Performance Monitor. The Page Fault counter indicates the number of hard and soft page faults per second. See the "Further Review" section for more information on hard and soft page faults. The Page Inputs/sec counter indicates the number of pages swapped into memory from the disk per second to satisfy the page faults. Finally, the Page Reads/sec indicates the number of times pages are transferred from the swap file to memory. This counter can also be used to determine if the disk subsystem is causing a bottleneck with the Virtual Memory Manager. The Proposed Solution does not accomplish the first Optional Result.

To determine if the disk subsystem is causing a system bottleneck, monitor the % Disk Time, Avg. Disk Queue Length, Current Disk Queue Length, Avg. Disk sec/Transfer, Disk Bytes/sec, Avg. Disk Bytes/Transfer, and Disk Transfers/sec counters within both the Physical and Logical Disk objects. Monitoring only a single disk counter does not give a good enough indication of disk performance. The Proposed Solution does not accomplish the second Optional Result.

2. Which two objects are used to monitor disk activity?

B. Physical Disk

D. Logical Disk

2. CORRECT ANSWER: B-D

The Physical Disk object contains counters to measure activity with the actual hard disks installed in the workstation. The Logical Disk object contains counters to measure the performance and activity of the logical disks associated with each physical disk. There can be multiple Logical Disk objects defined for a single Physical Disk object.

3. The hard drive on your Windows NT 4 computer seems to be full. You investigate the C: drive using Explorer and find very little software loaded. What could be using up so much hard drive space? (Choose all that apply.)

A. The disk is fragmented.

B. There are several Recycle Bins at full capacity.

D. The size of a FAT partition is very large, using large clusters.

3. CORRECT ANSWER: A-B-D

Fragmentation, especially on FAT formatted partitions can seriously affect disk performance and waste space by using excessive amounts of clusters to store files. Although Microsoft claims that NTFS does not fragment, a large market for NTFS defragmentation utilities has been carved out by such products as Diskeeper from Executive Software. Regardless of the file system, periodic defragmentation can improve disk performance and increase the amount of available space.

The Recycle Bin utility, even though it is often helpful, can invisibly consume an enormous amount of disk space. Periodically cleaning out the Recycle Bin can free up wasted disk space. Also, the amount of disk space reserved for use by the Recycle Bin can be set by right-clicking on the Recycle Bin and selecting Properties from the resulting context menu. Another area to periodically check and clean up is the <WinNT_Root>\temp folder.

When FAT is used as the file system, the cluster size is directly proportional to the volume size. On large volumes, the cluster size can reach 16KB. When a 4KB file is stored on a volume with 16KB cluster sizes, the file consumes 16KB of disk space. In the same manner, a 17KB file occupies 32KB. Large cluster sizes can quickly add up to a lot of wasted disk space. Converting the file system on large volumes from FAT to NTFS will recover most of the wasted space. See Chapter 2, "Installation and Configuration," for more information on file system selection, especially in a dual-boot environment.

4. You need to monitor activity on your system. You suspect a lot of network activity. How can you substantiate your suspicions? (Choose all that apply.)

B. Use the Performance Monitor and make sure DiskPerf is enabled.

E. Use the Server icon in the Control Panel.

4. CORRECT ANSWER: B-E

By using the disk counter in Performance Monitor, you will be able to tell if there is disk activity caused by network file and print traffic originating from and addressed to the workstation, especially if there are no open applications on the workstation in question.

The Server applet in Control Panel will also help you to identify how many users are connected to the workstation and what shares are being accessed.

5. Proposed Solution:
Log on to the system and select Shutdown from the Start menu.

When the system reboots, select the Last Known Good configuration.

Log in and open the Event Viewer application to verify that it was in fact the new driver causing the error message.

Because the SCSI card is on the Hardware Compatibility List, use the Microsoft supplied driver for the adapter.

D. Only both Optional Results

5. CORRECT ANSWER: D

The Last Known Good configuration is a safety feature built into Windows NT Workstation and Windows NT Server that enables you to back out of changes committed since the last good boot in the event those changes cause errors in the initialization of the operating system. The Last Known Good option can also fix boot problems if the boot process is stable enough to reach the point where the Last Known Good configuration option can be used. For other boot problems, see Chapter 7, "Troubleshooting."

The key to using the Last Known Good configuration is having a good configuration to restore. During the boot process, the old Registry values are saved and not written over by the new Registry settings used during the boot process until the user logs on to the system. In effect, by logging into Windows NT, you are indicating to the operating system that the boot was good. At that point, the Registry values used to boot the operating system are written over the saved setting. The current configuration would now become the Last Known Good configuration for the next boot. Because you logged on to the workstation with the boot errors in the scenario, the Proposed Solution does not accomplish the Required Result. Instead of completing the logon process, you should have clicked the reboot button on the logon dialog box to restart the system and then selected the Last Known Good configuration.

Viewing the System Event Log will help you to identify the cause of the failure. The System Log is opened with the Event Viewer application, accessible from the Administrative Options (Common) program group on the Start menu. The Proposed Solution accomplishes the first Optional Result.

When a device appears on the HCL, it is wise to use the Microsoft-supplied driver for 100 percent compatibility with Windows NT. This does not always guarantee that all the features available with the hardware device will be available, but rather the device will be compatible with Windows NT. The HCL needs to be carefully read, as often there are footnotes indicating which driver should be utilized. The Proposed Solution accomplishes the second Optional Result.

6. You have lost your emergency repair disk. You can create a new one from which of the following?

E. Only the Windows NT 4 computer for which you need the disk.

6. CORRECT ANSWER: E

The ERD contains part of the system Registry and is therefore unique to each system. The ERD also contains the local SAM database and file/folder permission information. The ERD should be updated periodically to maintain account and permission information in the event the ERD process must be performed on the system. Additionally, whenever system changes are completed, such as adding new software, the ERD should be updated. The ERD can be updated by running the RDISK utility with the `/s` switch. By default, only system information, not the account and security information, is written to the repair disk. The ERD must fit on only one diskette because RDISK does not have the capability to write repair information to multiple floppies. In the case where a large SAM database exists, the information could not be contained on a single floppy. The repair information is written by RDISK first to the \REPAIR folder in the Windows NT System folder. You are then prompted to write the information to floppy. This option can be dismissed, in effect only updating the \REPAIR folder.

There are no entries in any of the program groups for the RDISK utility. It should be run from the command line or the Run dialog box from the Start menu.

7. Proposed Solution:
Utilize the Event Viewer to review the System, Application, and Security logs for the system.

Utilize the WinMSD application to increase the amount of virtual memory available to the system.

Use Performance Monitor to log the Page Faults, Page Inputs/sec, and Page Reads/sec counters in the Memory object for a period of time.

C. The Required Result and only one Optional Result

7. CORRECT ANSWER: C

Although there are no hard and fast requirements for applications to log specific errors or events to the Event Log, utilizing Event Viewer to check the system logs, especially the Application log and the Security log, is a good start in determining why the application could not initialize. Unless Auditing is turned on, the Security log might not have any entries. The Proposed Solution accomplishes the Required Result.

WinMSD is a diagnostic tool that only produces output; that is, it can be used only to view system configuration settings, not to alter them. The virtual memory setting is configured through the Performance tab in the System Control Panel applet. The Proposed Solution does not accomplish the first Optional Result.

To monitor the installed system memory to determine if it is a system bottleneck, the Page Faults, Page Inputs/sec, and Page Reads/sec counters in the memory object should be analyzed for a period of time with Performance Monitor. The Proposed Solution accomplishes the second Optional Result.

8. How can you free up system memory without restarting the system? (Choose all that apply.)

A. Close any applications or files that are not required.

B. Minimize all background applications.

8. CORRECT ANSWER: A-B

Open applications require system memory to run. Closing the applications frees the memory occupied by the applications. Additionally, maximized or full window applications require greater memory (from the GDI subsystem) when running. Minimizing these applications frees up the system memory required to window these applications.

9. From the following list of performance counters, which can be used to determine excessive processor time spent in Privileged Processor Mode? (Choose all that apply.)

B. % DPC Time

E. % Privileged Time

9. CORRECT ANSWER: B-E

The % DPC Time counter in the Processor object measures the time spent servicing deferred procedure calls, which are interrupts with a lower priority. The %DPC Time is a component of the % Privileged Time counter.

10. Which of the following is not a feature of Windows NT 4 automatic optimization?

A. Disk space quota management

E. Automatic conversion to NTFS for large volumes

10. CORRECT ANSWER: A-E

Windows NT has no built-in capabilities to manage user disk quotas. A utility, CONVERT.EXE, is provided by Windows NT to convert from FAT to NTFS volumes; however, the conversion must be user-initiated.

11. Proposed Solution:

Because the % Processor Time counter remains below 40 percent, the processor is not a bottleneck. A spike in excess of 80 percent when an application first initializes is no need for concern, as long as the counter returns to a steady state.

A large steady state number for disk queue length is an indication of excessive paging. If excessive paging is occurring, there is not enough system memory. The disk system is not a bottleneck, but its performance is being hindered due to excessive paging. More memory should be added to the system and then Performance Monitor should be used to analyze system performance again.

A. The Required Result only

11. CORRECT ANSWER: A

Microsoft recommends that the % Processor Time should never exceed 90 percent for a single processor system for any long period of time. It is a normal system characteristic to see processor spikes above the 80 percent range when an application is launched. The Proposed Solution is correct in that the processor is not a significant system bottleneck. The Required Result is accomplished.

A constant large number for the disk queue counter is a sign of a disk subsystem bottleneck. Because the requests to access the paging file appear in the queue with all other disk requests, using the Disk Queue Length to judge the effect of memory on system performance is not a good idea. With Performance Monitor, there is no way to tell if the majority of requests in the queue are for paging file access. A large disk queue is a sign that the disk subsystem may be a performance bottleneck. The counters in the Paging File object (such as % Usage) and counters such as Page Faults, Pages Input/sec, and Page Reads/sec from the Memory object should be combined with the Logical Disk counters to determine if the disk subsystem or the system memory is causing the bottleneck. The Proposed Solution does not accomplish the second Optional Result.

As stated above, counters from the Page File and Memory objects should be used to determine the effect the amount of installed memory has on system performance. Although adding memory will usually increase performance on an NT system, memory alone cannot overcome other serious system bottlenecks. The Proposed Solution does not accomplish the first Optional Result.

12. You are using Performance Monitor to analyze your system processor. Based on the System object's System Processor Queue counter, which of the following conditions indicate your processor is too slow? Select all that apply.

D. The Processor Queue Length is always greater than 2.

E. The Processor Queue Length rises quickly and slowly decreases to a steady state value of 2.

12. CORRECT ANSWER: D-E

Microsoft suggests a Processor Queue Length of greater than two is a strong indication of a processor bottleneck. Also, spikes in the queue length that slowly dissipate are a sign that the processor has trouble keeping up with the demands of the system.

FURTHER REVIEW

IDENTIFY AND RESOLVE A GIVEN PERFORMANCE PROBLEM

The Task Manager and Performance Monitor are used to determine whether performance is suffering in any way and to test the effect of performance and tuning changes implemented to a system.

The major components that can be monitored and enhanced fall under the following four categories:

- Memory
- Processor
- Disks
- Network

These items are discussed in the following sections.

Creating a Baseline Log

To determine if a bottleneck does in fact exist, or to determine the effects of a new application, it is necessary to create a baseline log by using the Log feature within Performance Monitor (as explained in the preceding sections of this chapter). A log file does not have to be very large to show pertinent information, as long as the log was created while the system was being used in its normal or basic state. You can create a baseline log for each object individually or for a complete set. Creating a complete set gives you more flexibility, but the file will be larger. The following sections show which counters to follow and log to pinpoint possible bottlenecks and system deficiencies.

Pinpointing Memory Bottlenecks

The amount of physical memory (RAM) in a computer is probably the most significant factor when it comes to system performance. More is definitely better in respect to memory. The amount of RAM depends on the typical use of the workstation (running applications or sharing folders) and the expectations of the user.

Windows NT Workstation 4 uses a virtual memory mechanism to store and retrieve information for the processor. Along with real memory capacity (that is, the amount of physical RAM), Windows NT also makes use of a pagefile system. As soon as Windows NT Workstation runs out of RAM to store information, it makes up virtual memory by using space on the hard drive. The action of moving information between the pagefile and physical memory is called *paging*.

If information cannot be retrieved from physical memory, the system returns a *page fault*. Two kinds of page faults can occur:

- *Soft page fault.* The information is found in physical RAM, but it is in a different location.
- *Hard page fault.* The information must be retrieved from the pagefile on the hard disk, which takes more time and resources.

You should monitor the size of the pagefile to see if it is always increasing. Excessive paging might just be a short-term phenomenon and could be due to a one-time increase in demand. However, if the pagefile is constantly pushing the upper limits, there might be cause for concern. The pagefile can grow to its maximum size as more space is needed. The default size of the pagefile is based on the amount of physical RAM that was present when Windows NT Workstation was installed. The installation procedure creates a pagefile with a minimum size of RAM plus 11MB, and a maximum of RAM plus 11MB plus 50MB.

All Microsoft documentation shows the pagefile calculation to be RAM plus 12MB for the minimum and RAM plus 12MB plus 50MB for the maximum on Windows NT Workstation. On the exam, always quote Microsoft's numbers. There is never a choice of answers showing 11MB and 12MB; only 12MB is listed.

The Memory object is definitely of interest, but you cannot forget that Windows NT Workstation uses logical disks to create a pagefile (used as virtual memory) as well as processor time to perform the paging. The Performance Monitor objects of interest in monitoring and pinpointing memory bottlenecks are:

- Memory
- Paging File
- Process
- Logical Disk
- Processor

These items are listed in order of importance and, if monitored as a group, indicate whether a bottleneck has occurred due to lack of physical memory. As you should remember, when you select an object for a log, all the counters and instances are included as well.

The Memory Object

From the Memory object, three specific counters should be monitored:

- *Page Faults.* Includes soft and hard page faults. Microsoft suggests that a count of more than five page faults per second on an ongoing basis is problematic.
- *Pages Input/sec.* Represents the number of pages the system had to retrieve from the hard drive to satisfy page faults.
- *Page Reads/sec.* Shows the number of times per second that pages are transferred into memory from the pagefile. This indicator can also be used to show a disk bottleneck that might be created by a memory shortage.

The Paging File Object

You should monitor the size of the pagefile to see whether it is always increasing. Excessive paging might just be a short-term phenomenon and could be due to a one-time increase in demand. The following two counters are used by the Paging File object to monitor pagefile activity:

- *% Usage.* The percentage of the paging file in use.
- *% Usage Peak.* The peak usage of the page file, measured as a percentage.

The Process Object

The Process object offers two useful counters for monitoring pagefile performance:

- *Page File Bytes.* Shows the current amount of the pagefile being used, in bytes.
- *Pool Nonpaged Bytes.* Represents the amount of physical memory an application is using that cannot be moved to the pagefile. If this number keeps increasing while an application runs, it can indicate that an application is using up physical memory.

The Logical Disk Object

The Logical Disk object does not have the same significance that the previous objects do, but it might help point out inefficiencies with the disks instead of memory. The pagefile is stored on one or more physical disks. The Logical Disk object provides one important counter that might be of use.

Average Disk Queue Length shows the number of entries waiting to be read or written to the disk. Pagefile items fall into the queue like any other requests. If the queue is too slow and cannot process paging requests fast enough, the system appears to be slow due to paging when, in fact, it is the disk that cannot handle the request. This number should be less than two in an optimum scenario.

The Processor Object

The counters to follow for the processor are:

- *% Processor Time.* Shows just how busy the processor is performing all tasks.
- *% Privilege Time.* Excludes all tasks being performed for applications.
- *DPC Rate.* DPC stands for Deferred Procedure Call. These are tasks that are placed in a queue and are waiting to be processed.

Pinpointing Processor Bottlenecks

The processor (CPU) of any computer is always busy processing information. Even when no real process is running, Windows NT runs an idle process. Most counters take this idle process into account and display information on all processes except the idle process. A bottleneck might occur if too many items are waiting in a queue to be processed at one time or if an item takes a long time to make it through the queue.

A main component of CPU usage, besides processor utilization as discussed previously in this chapter, is the queue of items waiting to be processed. Microsoft's guideline on the queue is that it should contain no more than two entries most of the time. In a multiprocessor system, there can be two types of processing: synchronous and asynchronous. Windows NT Workstation uses a synchronous environment in which all processors can be used simultaneously. Several single-threaded applications can share a processor, and multithreaded applications can run several threads on one processor or can spread the threads across processors.

The objects and counters listed in Table 6.5 can be monitored to determine a possible processor bottleneck.

TABLE 6.5 OBJECTS AND COUNTERS USED TO MONITOR PROCESSOR BOTTLENECKS

Object	*Counter*	*Description*
Processor	% Processor Time	The total amount of time the processor is busy, excluding the idle process. This includes user-processing and privilege-processing time. This counter should be below 90 percent over time.
System	Processor Queue Length	The number of threads waiting to be processed by all processors on the system. This does not include threads being processed.

The solution to resolving CPU bottlenecks depends on the number of processors, as well as their speed and the type of applications (single-threaded or multithreaded) being run on the system.

Pinpointing Disk Bottlenecks

Disk performance affects many components of Windows NT Workstation 4. The pagefile system runs off a disk, the processor is busy searching or seeking for information on a disk, and file sharing uses the disk along with disk caching to provide information to clients.

These same components can create disk bottlenecks due to their limitations. When at all possible, eliminate memory or CPU bottlenecks before trying to monitor disk performance. All components such as memory, CPU, caches, and disks must work together to accomplish proper overall system throughput. Calculating the speed of a disk might not be very relevant because a faster disk might not enable the overall system to perform faster if other bottlenecks are present.

The most important objects and counters are not available by default in Windows NT Workstation 4. They must be activated with the DiskPerf utility. If they are needed, you can activate them and then deactivate them after completing the analysis. Table 6.6 shows the DiskPerf utility and its switches.

TABLE 6.6 DISPERF.EXE AND ITS SWITCHES

Command	*Description*
`diskperf`	Shows whether the DiskPerf objects are active
`diskperf -y`	Activates the disk counters
`diskperf -ye`	Activates the disk counters on mirror, stripe sets, and other noncontiguous partition sets
`diskperf -n`	Deactivates disk counters

Only a member of the Administrators groups can run the DiskPerf utility on a stand-alone Windows NT Workstation 4. If you are activating or deactivating counters with the DiskPerf utility, you must restart the computer for the change to take effect.

After the appropriate objects and counters have been activated, two objects are available:

- *Physical Disk.* Refers to the actual hard drive placed in the system.
- *Logical Disk.* Refers to subsets of the physical disks.

Two types of possible bottlenecks exist when it comes to disks: the amount of disk space available and the access time of the disk. The counters used and the necessary solutions differ greatly.

The second area of concern is the efficiency at which requests are being handled by the hard drive and the overall use of the hard drive. Microsoft makes the following three recommendations regarding use of a typical hard drive:

- Disk activity should not be above 85 percent usage as shown by the % Disk Time counter in the Physical Disk or Logical Disk object.
- The number of requests waiting in the queue should not exceed two, as shown in the Current Disk Queue Length counter of the Physical Disk or Logical Disk object.
- Paging should not exceed five page faults per second, as shown in Page Reads/Sec, Pages Input/Sec, and Page Faults counters of the Memory object.

Monitoring drives for a comparison is fairly simple as long as the same conditions apply to both disks. Certain factors might affect how one disk performs compared to another. Examples of those factors include the file system (FAT versus NTFS), the type of disk (IDE versus SCSI), and the type of controller card. Table 6.7 shows a list of common counters used to determine the cause of a bottleneck.

TABLE 6.7 DISK BOTTLENECK COUNTERS

Object	*Counter*
Logical Disk/Physical Disk	% Disk Time
Logical Disk/Physical Disk	Avg. Disk Queue Length
Logical Disk/Physical Disk	Current Disk Queue Length (known in previous versions as Disk Queue Length)
Logical Disk/Physical Disk	Avg. Disk sec / Transfer
Logical Disk/Physical Disk	Disk Bytes / sec
Logical Disk/Physical Disk	Avg. Disk Bytes / Transfer
Logical Disk/Physical Disk	Disk Transfers / sec
Logical Disk/Physical Disk	% Free Space
Logical Disk/Physical Disk	Free Megabytes

You can use several other counters to interpret disk activity. This might not necessarily show a bottleneck, but it can help you understand how the system resources are being used by certain applications.

Pinpointing Network Bottlenecks

You can monitor network activity only on a system connected to the network. Network terminology is used throughout this chapter, and there is an expectation of networking basics on the part of the reader. Non-networked systems do not require monitoring of network activities; therefore, some readers can skip this section. Typically a Windows NT Workstation's primary function is not that of a file or print server, and the number of requests made to the system does not have any negative effects.

You have two main tools to monitor network activity on the system:

- The Performance Monitor offers counters that can monitor the number of bytes transmitted, as well as errors encountered over several protocols, the Server service, and the Redirector service (client).
- The Server tool in the Control Panel can display all the shares on a system, as well as which user at which computer is connected to that share.

The Performance Monitor counters are not all initially present for network monitoring. Some counters that deal specifically with TCP/IP network traffic are not installed and must be added separately. Installing the SNMP (Simple Network Management Protocol) service adds the TCP/IP counters. Only the network or system administrator can add network services.

After the SNMP service is loaded, a TCP/IP system has five additional counters available: TCP, UDP, IP, ARP, and ICMP. The full detail of these counters is beyond the scope of this book. The focus here is on counters that show information about data transmission.

Regardless of the network protocol being used, there are counters to monitor simple read or write requests from the network card. These counters are always available under the Redirector and Server objects. Individual protocol counters are under the protocol name itself. Table 6.8 displays a list of relevant counters from various objects used to monitor network activity on the system.

TABLE 6.8 NETWORK COUNTERS

Object	*Counter*	*Description*
Server	Bytes Total/sec	The total activity of the system as a peer server on the network.
Server	Files Opened Total	The total number of files opened by remote systems. This calculates the number of I/O requests.
Server	Errors Access Permission	The number of client requests that have failed. A remote user might be attempting to access resources that have been restricted. The system must process these requests, using system resources for nothing. It might also identify possible hackers trying to gain access to the system.
Redirector	Bytes Total/sec	The client portion of the network initiated by the local system.
NetBEUI	Bytes Total/sec	The NetBEUI protocol only. This can be useful in determining which protocols are not used much and can be removed.
TCP	Segments/sec	The amount of information is being handled by the TCP/IP protocol.
NWLink	Bytes Total/sec	There are three objects for NWLink: IPX, SPX, and NetBIOS. All three have the same counter of bytes transferred per second using the NWLink protocol.

Monitoring with the Event Viewer

A part of the operating system is constantly monitoring for possible errors committed by either applications or other parts of the operating system. Event monitors are always active and keep track of these errors in the following three separate logs, which you can view with the Event Viewer. It should be noted that only 32-bit applications can log errors in the Application log.

- *System log.* Reports errors originating from the operating system, including services and devices.
- *Security log.* Tracks errors during security auditing. Not relevant in performance monitoring, but when security auditing is active, writing events to the Security log does take up resources.
- *Application log.* Keeps track of 32-bit application errors.

Reading Event Viewer Logs

In both the System and Application logs, Windows NT categorizes the entries as Information, Warning, or Error. In the Security log, it records Success or Failure to perform the activity sections. The Event Viewer records three general types of events:

- *Information.* Mostly information about successful activities.
- *Warnings.* The results of critical errors. (However, the system can still function properly.)
- *Errors.* Error message indicating that a service or device failed to start properly. The system might still function, but none of the dependent features are available. You should address these errors quickly.

Understanding the error codes and types can make it easier to solve the problem. You can expand any log entry by double-clicking anywhere on the line.

The Event Viewer logs provide extended information on each event, including the date and time of the event, the computer originating the event, the source of the event, and its type and category.

Filtering for Events

The size of a current log or an archive file can make it very difficult to find a specific problem. Using a filter can remove from the view all events that do not match certain criteria. You can set criteria based on time, type of event, source of event, category, and event ID.

Windows NT performs the filter only on the currently displayed information. The log might need to be refiltered if new information is added during the analysis. The full list of events does not have to be displayed between filtered views; the system always bases the filter criteria on all events currently in the log.

Managing Log Settings

All three logs have settings that you can manage separately. Using the Log Settings command on the Log menu, you can set the size of each log as well as the actions to be taken when a log is full. The default values for a log are that it can use up to 512KB of disk space to store events and that entries are removed when they have been in the log for seven days. Three options can be set to clear out logs: Overwrite Events as Needed, Overwrite Events Older Than X Days, and Do Not Overwrite Events (Clear Log Manually). The system warns with a message box that the log is full, except when the option Overwrite Events as Needed is used. If the log is full and is not cleared manually, new events cannot be logged.

A larger log keeps track of more information, but it also uses more system resources. Clearing and saving logs is a more efficient method of tracking events and possible trends.

Archiving and Retrieving a Log

The file format used is an .EVT file format and can be viewed only from the Event Viewer. *Archiving a log* refers to saving the event log in a separate file. You can do this while clearing the log or by using the Save As command in the Log menu. The Event Viewer is a 32-bit utility. Its Save As routine uses all the standard 32-bit saving features, such as long filenames and Create New Folder. All three logs must be saved separately.

To open an archived log file, choose Open from the Log menu and select the appropriate .EVT file. An archive file contains only one of the three types of logs. When you open an archive file, the system prompts for the type of log you want to open.

PRACTICE QUESTIONS

OPTIMIZE SYSTEM PERFORMANCE IN VARIOUS AREAS

1. Select all of the following factors that affect disk performance? (Choose all that apply.)

A. The partition format type (FAT, NTFS)

B. Type of disk interface (SCSI, IDE, EIDE, etc.)

C. The length of the disk controller cable

D. The DiskPerf utility

E. The names of the files

2. Your Windows NT 4 Workstation alerts you that virtual memory is too low. Where can you increase virtual memory?

A. Disk Administrator

B. WinMSD application

C. Device Manager

D. File Explorer

E. System applet in Control Panel

3. How many pagefiles can be created per disk?

A. 1

B. 2

C. 4

D. 32

E. 64

4. This is a scenario question. First you must review the scenario, then review the required and optional results. Following that is a solution. You must pick the best evaluation of that solution.

Scenario:
You are running a mission-critical application on your Windows NT Workstation 4 system. The system is a dual-processor system with two physical drives with two logical drives contained on each physical drive.

Required Result:
Ensure the application receives as much processor time as possible.

Optional Result:
Increase the amount of virtual memory available to the system.

Maximize access to the pagefile.

Proposed Solution:
Restart the application with the `/realtime` switch.

Use the System applet in Control Panel to set the new desired virtual memory size.

Use the System applet in Control Panel to create two page files, one on each logical volume on the first physical disk.

Evaluation of Proposed Solution:
The proposed solution accomplishes which of the following objectives?

A. The Required Result only

B. The Required Result and both Optional Results

C. The Required Result and only one Optional Result

D. Only one Optional Result

E. Neither the Required Result nor any Optional Results

5. Your Windows NT Workstation 4 is equipped with 64MB of RAM. What is the recommended total paging file size?

A. 64MB

B. 128MB

C. 76MB

D. 96MB

E. 32MB

6. This is a scenario question. First you must review the scenario, then review the required and optional results. Following that is a solution. You must pick the best evaluation of that solution.

Scenario:
You are preparing to install Windows NT Workstation with three identical 2GB hard disks.

Required Result:
Maximize disk performance.

Optional Result:
Maximize available disk space with the chosen configuration.

Maximize fault tolerance of the disk subsystem.

Proposed Solution:
Install Windows NT Workstation, placing the operating system on the first physical disk. Format the disk with the FAT file system.

Create a volume set with the two remaining physical disks. Format the volume set with NTFS.

Evaluation of Proposed Solution:
The proposed solution accomplishes which of the following stated objectives?

A. The Required Result only

B. The Required Result and both Optional Results

C. The Required Result and only one Optional Result

D. Only one Optional Result

E. Neither the Required Result nor any Optional Results

7. Which are valid methods of recovering from configuration changes? (Choose all that apply.)

A. Using the emergency repair disk

B. Using Windows NT's Backup to store the Registry

C. Using the Last Known Good configuration

D. Using hardware profiles

E. All of the above

8. Select all the correct statements about creating a new hardware profile with Windows NT Workstation.

A. All device-related information is reconfigured from scratch to provide a fresh profile.

B. The entire Registry is copied over to the new profile.

C. The profile begins as an identical copy of the current configuration, and changes are made as needed.

D. Device drivers must be reinstalled.

E. By default, only devices installed as part of the original Windows NT installation are available in the new profile.

9. You have just created a new hardware profile. When you reboot and choose your new profile, the profile fails and the system crashes. What should you do first to enable yourself to access your Windows NT 4 Workstation again?

A. You must install a fresh copy of Windows NT 4 Workstation.

B. You must reboot the computer and choose the original configuration.

C. You must restore the Registry.

D. Start the Windows NT Setup and select Repair an Existing Copy of Windows NT Workstation from the available installation options.

E. You must use the emergency repair disk to repair your Windows NT installation.

10. What is stored in a hardware profile?

A. Security information from the Registry

B. A copy of the HKEY_CURRENT_USER Registry key

C. Device and device-related information

D. A copy of the HKEY_LOCAL_MACHINE Registry key

E. A copy of the HKEY_CURRENT_CONFIG Registry key

11. Select all the recommended tools that should be used to modify the current hardware profile in use.

A. Registry Editor

B. The Control Panel Device applet

C. The Control Panel Services applet

D. The System Policy Editor

E. All of the above

12. You want to test several new settings for your experimental video devices on your Windows NT 4 graphics workstation. You are unsure if your new hardware settings work properly. What are the best options for safely testing the new settings?

A. Back up the Registry before attempting to change the settings.

B. Create an emergency repair disk, make the changes to the settings, and use the ERD if necessary.

C. Create a new hardware profile for experimenting with the new settings.

D. Make any necessary changes and rely on the Last Known Good configuration if the settings damage the system.

E. Restart Windows NT Workstation, selecting the VGA Mode option from the boot loader menu.

13. **This is a scenario question. First you must review the scenario, then review the required and optional results. Following that is a solution. You must pick the best evaluation of that solution.**

Scenario:
You have a new installation of Windows NT Workstation to which no applications have been added and no configuration changes have been made. The workstation will be used for Internet application development with Active Server Pages. The system is connected to a network that is running both TCP/IP and IPX/SPX. The system has two physical disks installed, with one logical disk on each physical disk.

Primary Result:
Maximize paging performance.

Optional Results:
Maximize system performance.

Maximize network performance.

Proposed Solution:
Place the paging file on a separate volume from the operating system.

Disable any unneeded services.

Adjust the binding order to maximize the performance of IPX/SPX.

Evaluation of Proposed Solution:
The proposed solution accomplishes which of the stated objectives?

A. The Required Result only

B. The Required Result and both Optional Results

C. The Required Result and only one Optional Result

D. Only one Optional Result

E. Neither the Required Result nor any Optional Results

ANSWER KEY

1. A-B-D
2. E
3. A
4. D
5. C
6. E
7. E
8. C
9. B
10. C
11. B-C-D
12. C-E
13. C

ANSWERS & EXPLANATIONS

OPTIMIZE SYSTEM PERFORMANCE IN VARIOUS AREAS

1. Select all of the following factors that affect disk performance. (Choose all that apply.)

A. The partition format type (FAT, NTFS)

B. Type of disk interface (SCSI, IDE, EIDE, etc.)

D. The DiskPerf utility

1. CORRECT ANSWER: A-B-D

The type of partition format, combined with the size of the partition, affects disk performance. For volumes less than 400MB in size, FAT will yield better disk performance; for volumes in excess of 400 MB, the inverse is true.

The type of disk interface affects disk performance. Traditionally, SCSI interfaces have exceeded the performance delivered by IDE; however, the newer IDE interfaces, such as ATA and EIDE, are closing the performance gap for access times. Many SCSI controllers also have built-in processors dedicated to handle disk I/O, thereby freeing the CPU from these tasks and enhancing overall performance.

Running any type of program that monitors the system activities, such as disk performance, will obviously affect the performance of the device in some way. Microsoft states that the use of DiskPerf does affect the disk performance, but the effects are negligible on Pentium class machines. It should also be noted that if the disk performance needs to be monitored and the DiskPerf utility is not activated, the machine must be rebooted.

2. Your Windows NT 4 Workstation alerts you that virtual memory is too low. Where can you increase virtual memory?

E. System applet in Control Panel

2. CORRECT ANSWER: E

Virtual memory is set through the Performance tab in the System Control Panel applet. From the Performance tab, click the Change button in the Virtual Memory section. From this dialog box, you can set the size and location of the paging files. After completing the desired changes, click the Set button to commit the changes. A system reboot will be required to effect the changes.

3. How many pagefiles can be created per disk?

A. 1

3. CORRECT ANSWER: A

Only one pagefile can be created on each disk. Placing pagefiles on multiple disks can help boost paging performance if the disks are connected to multiple controllers or if a single controller with multiple disks can simultaneously process multiple I/O requests.

4. Proposed Solution:
Restart the application with the `/realtime` switch.

Use the System applet in Control Panel to set the new desired virtual memory size.

Use the System applet in Control Panel to create two page files, one on each logical volume on the first physical disk.

D. Only one Optional Result

4. CORRECT ANSWER: D

Although starting the application with the `/realtime` switch will ensure the application gets as much processor time as possible, the scenario stated the application was mission-critical. Typically, the `/realtime` priority is reserved for operating system components that cannot be swapped to disk. Starting applications at this priority will jeopardize system stability, which is an undesirable characteristic of a system running a mission-critical application. The Proposed Solution does not accomplish the Required Result. Instead, you should have used the Performance tab in the System applet in Control Panel to boost the priority of foreground applications and ensure the application always remains a foreground application.

The amount of virtual memory allocated to a system is controlled through the Performance tab in the System Control Panel applet. The Proposed Solution accomplishes the first Optional Result.

Although creating multiple page files will increase paging performance on a system, placing them on the same physical drive will not enhance performance, because all requests will still go through the same channel on the disk controller. To optimize the paging performance, the pagefiles should be distributed across both disks. A greater performance gain is realized if the disks are on separate disk controllers or if they are on a single controller that separates the disk onto separate channels. The Proposed Solution does not accomplish the second Optional Result.

5. Your Windows NT 4 Workstation is equipped with 64MB of RAM. What is the recommended total paging file size?

C. 76MB

5. CORRECT ANSWER: C

Microsoft recommends that the optimal pagefile size be the amount of installed RAM + 12MB.

**6. Proposed Solution:
Install Windows NT Workstation, placing the operating system on the first physical disk. Format the disk with the FAT file system.**

Create a volume set with the two remaining physical disks. Format the volume set with NTFS.

E. Neither the Required Result nor any Optional Results

6. CORRECT ANSWER: E

Disk performance in a volume set is not maximized because the data is written sequentially to the volume set. A volume set is simply a method to combine areas of free space into one logical volume. On the other hand, creating a stripe set out of the two volumes would increase disk I/O performance because the data is uniformly written across each member of the stripe set in 64KB blocks. The Proposed Solution does not accomplish the Required Result.

The FAT file system is less efficient for larger partitions when compared to NTFS due to the dependency of FAT cluster size on overall volume size. To maximize the available disk space, both the operating system partition and the volume set should be formatted with the NTFS file system. The Proposed Solution does not accomplish the first Optional Result.

Although stripe sets offer increased performance, both volume sets and stripe sets are less fault-tolerant than if the disks were formatted and used individually. If a member of either a stripe set or volume set fails, the entire volume or stripe set will be corrupt. In effect, a volume or stripe set is dependent upon two components, thereby decreasing fault tolerance. The only way to restore in a volume or stripe set failure is to replace the faulty member, rebuild and reformat the stripe or volume set, and restore from tape backup. The Proposed Solution does not accomplish the second Optional Result.

7. Which are valid methods of recovering from configuration changes? (Choose all that apply.)

E. All of the above

7. CORRECT ANSWER: E

Using the Emergency Repair Disk, Windows NT's backup, the Last Known Good configuration, and hardware profiles are all valid methods of recovering from system configuration changes.

8. Select all the correct statements about creating a new hardware profile with Windows NT Workstation.

C. The profile begins as an identical copy of the current configuration, and changes are made as needed.

8. CORRECT ANSWER: C

When you create a new hardware profile, the new profile will appear as an identical copy of the existing hardware profile; that is, parts of the Registry relating to devices and device configuration are copied to the new profile. You may then make device configuration changes with the appropriate Window's NT tools that are then saved as part of the new hardware profile.

9. You have just created a new hardware profile. When you reboot and choose your new profile, the profile fails and the system crashes. What should you do first to enable yourself to access your Windows NT 4 Workstation again?

B. You must reboot the computer and choose the original configuration.

9. CORRECT ANSWER: B

When you're using hardware profiles, selecting the original configuration during the Windows NT Workstation boot process will enable you to recover from improper device configuration in the current hardware profile.

After the test profile is thoroughly tested, you can enable that profile as default by deleting the original configuration profile and renaming the test profile as the original configuration profile. This action is accomplished through the Hardware Profiles tab in System Control Panel applet.

10. What is stored in a hardware profile?

C. Device and device-related information

10. CORRECT ANSWER: C

All Registry information related to device and device configuration information, which might be pulled from numerous Registry keys, is stored in the hardware profile.

11. Select all the recommended tools that should be used to modify the current hardware profile in use.

B. The Control Panel Device applet

C. The Control Panel Services applet

D. The System Policy Editor

11. CORRECT ANSWER: B-C-D

As with all Windows NT configuration tasks, the Registry Editor should not be used unless absolutely needed and explicitly stated by Microsoft. If the Registry editor needs to be used, you should have detailed instructions from Microsoft, such as those found in the TechNet or Knowledge Base reference materials, to make very specific Registry changes. Otherwise, the Control Panel applets and other Microsoft tools should be used to perform configuration changes.

12. You want to test several new settings for your experimental video devices on your Windows NT 4 graphics workstation. You are unsure if your new hardware settings will work properly. What are the best options for safely testing the new settings?

C. Create a new hardware profile for experimenting with the new settings.

D. Make any necessary changes and rely on the Last Known Good configuration if the settings damage the system.

E. Restart Windows NT Workstation, selecting the VGA Mode option from the boot loader menu.

12. CORRECT ANSWER: C-E

When dealing with video hardware, the VGA boot option is a good choice for rebooting the system when video adapter settings do not work. If you boot with this option, the video setting is temporarily reset to VGA (640x480 resolution, 256 colors). Although this option does not enable you to recover from faulty device drivers or settings, it will enable you to reboot when the video setting are incompatible with the video card or monitor.

The easiest method for testing all adapter and hardware settings, not just video hardware, is using hardware profiles. Hardware profiles are easier to use than Registry backups, although regular backups should be completed in the event there is a hardware failure. Additionally, using the ERD requires that Services Packs be reinstalled, and, if the ERD is not regularly updated, it becomes necessary to re-create user accounts and reassign file and folder permissions.

13. Proposed Solution:

Place the paging file on a separate volume from the operating system.

Disable any unneeded services.

Adjust the binding order to maximize the performance of IPX/SPX.

C. The Required Result and only one Optional Result

13. CORRECT ANSWER: C

Placing the paging file on a separate volume from the operating system increases performance by eliminating disk request contention for both the operating system and the Virtual Memory Manager. The Proposed Solution accomplishes the Required Result.

Disabling any unneeded services using the Services applet in Control Panel will increase system performance by freeing system resources used by the unneeded services. The Proposed Solution accomplishes the first Optional Result.

Because the scenario stated that the workstation will be used for Internet development, the TCP/IP protocol should be given priority over the IPX/SPX protocol. The Proposed Solution does not accomplish the second Optional Result.

FURTHER REVIEW

OPTIMIZE SYSTEM PERFORMANCE IN VARIOUS AREAS

Microsoft has shipped Windows NT Workstation 4 optimized for the majority of users working in a typical environment. The improvement in performance might be slim (about two percent), and it could require a lot of work and money to make it happen.

Experimenting with the system configuration can be hazardous. In all cases, you should perform a backup of critical system files and settings before making any changes. The effect of the changes should also be monitored and compared with a baseline log that you created before the changes were implemented. (See the section entitled "Creating a Baseline Log," earlier in this chapter.)

Making a Safe Recovery

You can make a safe recovery if you took the proper steps before making any major changes to the system. Several methods enable users to recover from system configuration changes:

- Creating an emergency repair disk
- Using Windows NT's Backup to store the Registry
- Using Last Known Good configuration
- Creating hardware profiles

Emergency Repair Disk (ERD)

The best way to make a copy of all necessary Registry files is to create and maintain an *emergency repair disk* (ERD). The disk includes all hardware and software configuration items, as well as security account database information. You can use this disk to restore a corrupted Registry. The backup copy of these files can be stored in two locations when an ERD is created. The disk has a copy, and the %winroot%\repair folder has a second identical copy. However, the copy on the hard drive is not very useful if the system has crashed.

The RDISK utility presents two options: Update Repair Info and Create Repair Disk. Update Repair Info updates the repair folder and then prompts you to create a disk. Create Repair Disk creates a disk without updating the repair folder. You should create and maintain an emergency repair disk. You should also have a backup copy of the disk on a system dealing with critical information.

Hardware Profiles

Creating a hardware profile is one of the safest and fastest methods for making and testing changes to a system without running the risk of losing system integrity. Hardware profiles are also used to control when the network settings are loaded on laptops that might be connected to the network or when they are set up to run as a stand-alone. You can quickly change this setting by using the Properties button of the profile.

After multiple hardware profiles exist, Windows NT displays a prompt prior to logon (but after the

Boot.ini displays the list of operating systems), asking which hardware profile is to be used for this session. If no choice is made, the system has a timeout of 30 seconds and then loads the default profile. Note that you can modify the timeout period as well as the default choice in the system's Properties dialog box.

The hardware profiles are easier to use than the ERD. However, the ERD might still be needed if any changes made to the system corrupt the Registry. The hardware profiles are stored in the Registry.

Using the Last Known Good Configuration

A temporary copy of the hardware's original profile is made after a successful logon. This temporary copy is called the Last Known Good configuration. It is replaced each time the user logs on.

Configuration changes are written to the Registry in the Current Control Set. Upon successful logon, a copy of this Control Set is copied to the LastKnownGood set. This set can be retrieved when a system is restarted after failed configuration changes. During the startup procedure, Windows NT displays the message `Press the space bar now to load Last Known Good Configuration`. This message appears for a short time only. If you choose to load the Last Known Good configuration, it replaces the last set that failed. All the changes to the system made during the last session are lost.

The Last Known Good configuration is updated after the user logs on using the Ctrl+Alt+Del logon sequence. Always wait for the system to load all devices and services before you log on. If a device or service fails, Windows NT displays an error message. Then you can turn off the system's power and restart with the Last Known Good configuration still intact. Because the Last Known Good configuration is not always reliable, hardware profiles and emergency repair disks are recommended as well.

Configuring the Operating System

You can tune several aspects of Windows NT. Having faster hardware is always an asset, but it is not always realistic in the short term. From the operating system's perspective, Windows NT is a set of services that run devices to provide resources to the user. You can tune these items quickly, without having to upgrade or invest a large amount of money. The following sections cover these components:

- "Windows NT Services"
- "Windows NT Device Drivers"
- "Virtual Memory"

Windows NT Services

Windows NT Workstation 4 is made up of a series of services that run with each other to provide the operating system. A default set of services is loaded with a typical installation, and the user or applications can install additional services. Not all services are necessary to run Windows NT Workstation 4. The default set of services is chosen to satisfy the needs of most common users and systems.

Windows NT Devices

Devices, like services, can be disabled on a per-hardware profile basis. Most devices that are set up initially are required to run the hardware attached or included in the system. During normal operation of the system, some devices might not be used. They are wasting system resources and should be disabled through the Devices applet in Control Panel.

Virtual Memory

You can almost always add physical memory to a computer with positive results. *Memory is the single most significant factor in overall system performance.* Adding more memory might not be possible in the short term for several reasons. For instance, the cost of upgrading can be a barrier, or the system might not have any space to quickly add additional RAM.

There are alternatives to purchasing more memory. After Windows NT has been tuned to make the best use of its current memory levels, you can do several things to increase the efficiency of the pagefile:

- On a system with several hard drives, move the pagefile to a drive that is faster or is not used as much to improve read and write requests.
- Create additional pagefiles stored on different drives, and the read/write operations could be handled faster depending on the hardware.

If a pagefile is moved from its initial default location, you will no longer be able to dump the memory contents to a debug file in the event of a system crash.

You can make all changes to the pagefile from the Performance tab of the System Properties dialog box. Select the Change button in the Virtual Memory section. The maximum size of the pagefile could be left intact. The recommendation is to always keep a 50MB buffer between the minimum and maximum sizes. This buffer ensures that the pagefile can grow to accommodate short-term demands.

Disk Usage

In addition to pagefile activity, the disks are used constantly by the operating system to read information and write data. The speed and efficiency of the drive is important, and hardware issues are very important when selecting a type and speed of hard drive.

Hardware Selection

Hard drive and controller types can make a big difference in regards to performance. SCSI hard disks, for instance, are much faster than IDE hard disks. Using a 32-bit controller card instead of a 16- or 8-bit controller will have significant impact on the system, too. Although these options improve performance, they might not be realistic in the short term. The cost of these new controller cards might prevent an upgrade.

Disk Partitioning and Format

You can partition each hard drive into different sizes and format them using FAT or NTFS. Large partitions might be easier to use because a single drive letter references them. It is not always better to use one logical disk per physical disk. The size and format of the partition determines the size of the cluster that's used for storage. A *cluster* is the smallest storage unit on a hard drive.

There are several points to consider when choosing partition and disk format options:

- FAT partitions typically have larger cluster sizes, which means that smaller amounts of data can inefficiently take up more space than they actually require.
- NTFS partitions are not bound by the same cluster size limitation that FAT partitions are.
- Partitions larger than 512MB should be converted to NTFS to reduce the size of the cluster that's used.
- Partitions smaller than 512MB can be converted to NTFS, but because NTFS requires additional space to operate, it might in fact offer less disk space.

Disk Access

You should be aware of several disk access issues when optimizing your Windows NT Workstation 4 system:

- It is often inefficient to store the operating system, pagefile, programs, and data on a single hard drive.
- Placing the operating system on a separate partition improves the I/O request.
- When a pagefile is used constantly, it should be placed on a partition other than the one on which the operating system is located.
- Applications and data files should share the same physical disk so the hard disk does not have to search multiple locations.
- You should never compress heavily used files and programs that access the hard disk frequently. Compression under NTFS was designed for the Windows NT Workstation and does not have a major impact, but it can be noticeable in some cases.

Disk Fragmentation

Fragmentation occurs in all cases when the operating system saves, deletes, and moves information on a hard drive. A file is fragmented if it is stored in several nonconsecutive clusters on the hard drive. Windows NT attempts to store information in the first continuous block of clusters. When a continuous block is not available, the file is stored in several nonconsecutive blocks. A disk can be fragmented even if files are not fragmented. There might be unused clusters in areas that are not large enough to store any one complete file. Fragmentation slows down disk access time because the read heads must move to several locations on the disk to read one file.

Currently, Windows NT Workstation 4 does not offer a defragmentation tool. There are third-party disk utilities that can do the job. There are also several methods you can use to help reduce fragmentation, especially on multi-user workstations:

- Move information between drives. From within Windows NT, moving large amounts of information from one drive to another and back again re-creates a larger continuous block of clusters that will store data more efficiently.
- Reduce the size of the Recycle Bin; the deleted files it stores can take up a large percentage of your hard disk.

- Use only one hard drive for the Recycle Bin.
- Delete unused user profiles.

All improvements in performance come at a price. As you learned earlier, there will always be faster and newer hardware available. Changing Windows NT's internal configuration might improve performance slightly, but in some cases, it will do so at the expense of losing a service or resource. Always consider the repercussions of a change before implementation, and be prepared to reverse the change if problems occur. The basic configuration generated with a standard installation might be more than adequate for most systems.

CHAPTER SUMMARY

Monitoring and optimization is a critical skill to possess in the long-term management and maintenance of any Windows NT Workstation installation. Although Windows NT Workstation is designed to be self-tuning, it does not properly tune itself for all situations and applications. You must be able to carefully and accurately analyze the system, determine the system bottlenecks, recommend solutions, and verify those solutions when supporting Windows NT Workstation. An improperly tuned system will not make efficient use of resources and can have such far-reaching effects as decreasing user productivity.

A true support professional, and a Microsoft Certified Professional, must understand the intricacies of tuning a Windows NT system and understand how to continually monitor the system for new bottlenecks as users expect more and more from their workstations.

CHAPTER 7

Troubleshooting

It is inevitable, no matter how well an operating system or an application is designed, that something will go wrong at one point or another. Part of being a network professional, IT support person, or Microsoft Certified Professional is using your troubleshooting skills to identify the problem and using the skills you learned in all the previous chapters of this book to resolve the problem.

OBJECTIVES

Choose the appropriate course of action to take when the boot process fails.

Choose the appropriate course of action to take when a print job fails.

Choose the appropriate course of action to take when the installation process fails.

Choose the appropriate course of action to take when an application fails.

Choose the appropriate course of action to take when a user cannot access a resource.

Modify the Registry using the appropriate tool in a given situation.

Implement advanced techniques to resolve various problems.

PRACTICE QUESTIONS

CHOOSE THE APPROPRIATE COURSE OF ACTION TO TAKE WHEN THE BOOT PROCESS FAILS

1. **This question is based on the following scenario. Review the scenario first, followed by the objectives and the proposed solution. Then evaluate the proposed solution by choosing the best answer.**

   Scenario:
   You have a Windows NT Workstation (Service Pack 3 installed) that generates the blue screen stop message during the boot process.

   Required Result:
   Attempt to recover the NT Workstation installation.

   Optional Results:
   After it is recovered, update the \REPAIR directory in the Windows installation directory.

   Update the emergency repair disk.

   Proposed Solution:
   Reinstall Windows NT Workstation. During the installation, select Repair an Existing Windows NT Installation from the setup menu options.

   From the command line, run RDISK.EXE with the /s switch. When you're asked if you would like to update the repair disk, click Yes.

   Evaluation of Proposed Solution:
   The proposed solution accomplishes which of the following stated objectives?

   A. The Required Result only

   B. The Required Result and both Optional Results

   C. The Required Result and only one Optional Result

   D. Only both Optional Results

   E. Neither the Required Result nor any Optional Results

2. **Which of the following files are not on the emergency repair disk?**

   A. NTSYSTEM.DA_

   B. SETUP.LOG

   C. CONFIG.NT

   D. NTUSER.DA_

   E. HRDWR.DA_

3. **Which of the following choices is *not* available from the Emergency Repair Process menu?**

   A. Inspect Registry Files

   B. Verify Windows NT System Files

   C. Open Event Viewer

   D. Inspect Startup Environment

   E. Convert the Existing File System to NTFS

4. **This question is based on the following scenario. Review the scenario first, followed by the objectives and the proposed solution. Then evaluate the proposed solution by choosing the best answer.**

Scenario:
You have changed the video settings on a Windows NT Workstation. When you reboot, the login screen appears scrambled. When you reboot to invoke the VGA boot option, there is no listing for the VGA option in the boot loader menu. The system partition is formatted with the FAT file system.

Required Result:
Verify the integrity of the boot loader initialization file.

Optional Results:
Add an entry in the boot loader initialization file to enable the VGA only boot option.

Correct the video problem.

Proposed Solution:
Boot the system from a DOS bootable floppy disk. Ensure some type of ASCII editor, such as Microsoft's EDIT.COM, is on the disk.

Change directories to the root drive of the Windows NT installation volume. Change the attributes on the file BOOT.INI to remove the hidden and read-only attributes of the file.

Within the BOOT.INI file, ensure there is a [boot loader] and an [operating systems] section. Ensure the [boot loader] section has a default= and timeout= section.

In the BOOT.INI file, copy the line from the [operating systems] section similar to the following:

```
multi(0)disk(0)rdisk(0)
➥partition(1)\WINNT="Windows NT
➥Server Version 4.00"
```

Edit the new entry you created in the [operating systems] section to look similar to the following:

```
multi(0)disk(0)rdisk(0)
➥partition(1)\WINNT="Windows NT
➥Server Version 4.00 [VGA]" /sos
```

Save the BOOT.INI file and reset the hidden and read-only attributes on the file.

When the workstation reboots, reconfigure the display settings with the Display applet in Control Panel.

Evaluation of Proposed Solution:
The proposed solution accomplishes which of the following stated objectives?

A. The Required Result only

B. The Required Result and both Optional Results

C. The Required Result and only one Optional Result

D. Only one Optional Result

E. Neither the Required Result nor any Optional Results

5. **This question is based on the following scenario. Review the scenario first, followed by the objectives and the proposed solution. Then evaluate the proposed solution by choosing the best answer.**

Scenario:
You have installed a UPS on COM port 1. When you boot the system, a message appears indicating communications could not be established with the UPS, and the system shuts down after five minutes. The system partition is formatted with the NTFS file system.

Required Result:
Disable the UPS service.

Optional Results:
Reconfigure Windows NT Workstation to enable the use of the UPS.

Re-enable the UPS service and verify correct functionality.

Proposed Solution:
Immediately after the system boots, open the Services applet in Control Panel, select the UPS service, click the Startup button, and click the Disabled button. Reboot the system.

Edit the BOOT.INI file and add the `/NoSerialMice:COM1` switch to the end of all the Windows NT Workstation boot paths.

Using the Services applet in Control Panel, re-enable the UPS service to start at bootup. Reboot the system.

Evaluation of Proposed Solution:
The proposed solution accomplishes which of the following stated objectives?

A. The Required Result only

B. The Required Result and both Optional Results

C. The Required Result and only one Optional Result

D. Only one Optional Result

E. Neither the Required Result nor any Optional Results

6. **The user screen switches into GUI mode after which phase of startup?**

A. Kernel Initialization

B. Services Load

C. Windows Start

D. Win32 subsystem

E. Boot Load completion

7. **This question is based on the following scenario. Review the scenario first, followed by the objectives and the proposed solution. Then evaluate the proposed solution by choosing the best answer.**

Scenario:
You have just added a new sound card adapter to a Windows NT Workstation. When you installed the sound card, it required you to supply a free Interrupt Request during the configuration. When you reboot, the system message appears, indicating a driver or service failed to start.

Required Result:
Use the Last Known Good configuration during the boot process to recover from the configuration error.

Optional Results:
Determine what component caused the error to be generated.

Take the appropriate course of action to repair the problem and verify that the solution corrected the problem.

Proposed Solution:
When the logon dialog box appears, click the Shutdown button without logging into Windows NT Workstation. When the system reboots, press the Spacebar when prompted to invoke the Last Known Good configuration.

Open the System Control Panel applet, select the Resources tab, and find a free IRQ resource.

Reconfigure the sound card to use a known free IRQ.

Evaluation of Proposed Solution:
The proposed solution accomplishes which of the following stated objectives?

A. The Required Result only

B. The Required Result and both Optional Results

C. The Required Result and only one Optional Result

D. Only one Optional Result

E. Neither the Required Result nor any Optional Results

8. **Which of the following is responsible for building the hardware list during boot operations?**

   A. HAL.DLL

   B. NTLDR

   C. NTOSKRNL.EXE

   D. NTDETECT.COM

   E. NTSYSTEM.COM

9. **Which of the following are files needed during an Intel-based boot, but are not needed for a RISC boot operation?**

   A. NTDETECT.COM

   B. NTLDR

   C. OSLOADER.EXE

   D. NTOSKRNL.EXE

   E. BOOT.INI

10. **Which two files are common to RISC-based boots, as well as Intel-based boots?**

   A. OSLOADER.EXE

   B. HAL.DLL

   C. NTDETECT.COM

   D. NTOSKRNL.EXE

   E. BOOT.INI

11. **Which of the following system files are located in the <winnt_root>\SYSTEM32 directory of an Intel Windows NT system?**

   A. HAL.DLL

   B. NTLDR

   C. NTOSKRNL.EXE

   D. NTDETECT.COM

   E. OSLOADER.EXE

12. **This question is based on the following scenario. Review the scenario first, followed by the objectives and the proposed solution. Then evaluate the proposed solution by choosing the best answer.**

Scenario:
You have a Windows NT Workstation that stops during the boot process with the following message:

```
Windows NT could not start because
➥the following file is missing or
➥corrupt:
\<winnt root>\system32\ntoskrnl.exe
➥Please re-install a copy of the
➥above file.
```

The system partition is FAT formatted. Windows NT is installed in the \NT4 folder on the D: drive (the first logical partition on the second disk drive).

Required Result:
Locate and open the boot loader configuration file.

Optional Results:
Verify the path used to start the operating system in the boot loader configuration file.

Replace any missing Windows NT boot files.

Proposed Solution:
Boot the system from a DOS bootable floppy disk. Ensure some type of ASCII editor, such as Microsoft's EDIT.COM, is on the disk.

Change directories to the root drive of the Windows NT installation volume. Change the attributes on the file BOOT.INI; remove the hidden and read-only attributes of the file.

Within the BOOT.INI file, ensure there is a [boot loader] section and an [operating systems] section. Ensure the [boot loader] section has a default= and timeout= section. Ensure the default entry appears as:

```
multi(0)disk(1)rdisk(0)
➥partition(1)\NT4
```

In the BOOT.INI file, ensure the [operating systems] section has a line such as the following:

```
multi(0)disk(1)rdisk(0)
➥partition(1)\NT4="Windows NT
➥Server Version 4.00"
```

Save the BOOT.INI file, and reset the hidden and read-only attributes on the file.

Run Windows NT Setup from the Windows NT Workstation boot disks and select the Repair option from the installation menu.

When the workstation reboots, apply the latest service pack.

Evaluation of Proposed Solution:
The proposed solution accomplishes which of the following stated objectives?

A. The Required Result only

B. The Required Result and both Optional Results

C. The Required Result and only one Optional Result

D. Only both Optional Results

E. Neither the Required Result nor any Optional Results

13. On Intel x86-based computers, what is the name of the file loaded by the boot sector of the active partition?

A. NTLDR

B. IO.SYS

C. BOOT.INI

D. MSDOS.SYS

E. BOOTSECT.DOC

14. From the following, select all of the ways in which the Automatic Recovery and Restart capability can be enabled in Windows NT.

A. With the `/crashdebug` switch in the BOOT.INI file.

B. With the `/recovery` switch in the BOOT.INI file.

C. Via the System application in the Control Panel.

D. Through the Server Control Panel applet.

E. The Automatic Recovery and Restart capability cannot be enabled in Windows NT.

ANSWER KEY

1. D
2. A-E
3. C-E
4. C
5. B
6. D
7. A
8. D
9. A-B-E
10. B-D
11. C
12. B
13. A
14. A-C

ANSWERS & EXPLANATIONS

CHOOSE THE APPROPRIATE COURSE OF ACTION TO TAKE WHEN THE BOOT PROCESS FAILS

1. Proposed Solution:

- **Reinstall Windows NT Workstation. During the installation, select Repair an Existing Windows NT Installation from the setup menu options.**
- **From the command line, run RDISK.EXE with the /s switch. When you're asked if you would like to update the repair disk, click Yes.**

D. Only both Optional Results

1. CORRECT ANSWER: D

Using the repair disk in conjunction with the Windows NT Setup application is the first step in attempting to recover a bootable Windows NT Workstation installation. If RDISK was run regularly to keep the repair information current, the original system files will be placed in the Windows system directory, overwriting any service packs or updated files. At the very least, when a Windows NT Workstation is recovered, the most current service pack must be reinstalled. The Proposed Solution does not accomplish the Required Result.

By using RDISK.EXE from the command line, you can update the \REPAIR directory in the Windows NT system folder, as well as create an ERD. Using the /s switch forces RDISK to also back up security and account information. The Proposed Solution accomplishes both Optional Results.

2. Which of the following files are not on the emergency repair disk?

A. NTSYSTEM.DA_

E. HRDWR.DA_

2. CORRECT ANSWER: A-E

The ERD contains the following files:

- *autoexec.nt* and *config.nt.* The two files responsible for a virtual DOS machine. They correspond to the autoexec.bat and config.sys files on MS-DOS. The first file runs a batch file; the second sets an environment.
- *default._.* The compressed copy of the system's default profile.
- *ntuser.da_.* The compressed copy of the ntuser.dat file, which stores user profiles.
- *sam._.* The compressed copy of the SAM hive of the Registry, with a copy of the Windows NT accounts

database. A workstation SAM doesn't contain as much information as a server (especially a domain server) SAM does. Missing is information about other machine and user accounts that the workstation doesn't know about. This file is included only when RDISK is run with the /s switch.

- *security._*. The compressed copy of the Security hive with SAM and security policy information for your workstation's users. This file is included only when RDISK is run with the /s switch.
- *setup.log*. A text file with the names of the Windows setup and installation files and checksums for each file. The file is used to determine whether essential system files are either missing or corrupt. If this is the case, it replaces them in a recovery operation.
- *software._*. A compressed copy of the Software hive with information about installed programs and associated files and configuration information for those programs.
- *system._*. A compressed copy of the System hive of the Registry. This hive contains the Windows NT control set.

3. Which of the following choices is *not* available from the Emergency Repair Process menu?

C. Open Event Viewer

E. Convert the Existing File System to NTFS

3. CORRECT ANSWER: C-E

Event Viewer is a GUI application that requires a fully functional environment to use.

File system conversion is accomplished with the command line utility CONVERT.EXE.

4. Proposed Solution:

- **Boot the system from a DOS bootable floppy disk. Ensure some type of ASCII editor, such as Microsoft's EDIT.COM is on the disk.**

4. CORRECT ANSWER: C

When the system partition is formatted with the FAT file system, you can directly edit the Windows NT Boot Manager initialization file, BOOT.INI. BOOT.INI is a hidden, read-only file; its attributes must be changed before the file can be changed in any ASCII text editor.

- **Change directories to the root drive of the Windows NT installation volume. Change the attributes on the file BOOT.INI to remove the hidden and read-only attributes of the file.**
- **Within the BOOT.INI file, ensure there is a [boot loader] and an [operating systems] section. Ensure the [boot loader] section has a default= and timeout= section.**
- **In the BOOT.INI file, copy the line from the [operating systems] section similar to the following:**

```
multi(0)disk(0)rdisk(0)
➥partition(1)\WINNT=
➥"Windows NT Server
➥Version 4.00"
```

- **Edit the new entry you created in the [operating systems] section to look similar to the following:**

```
multi(0)disk(0)rdisk(0)
➥partition(1)\WINNT=
➥"Windows NT Server
➥ Version 4.00 [VGA]
➥" /sos
```

- **Save the BOOT.INI file and reset the hidden and read only attributes on the file.**
- **When the workstation reboots, reconfigure the display settings with the Display applet in Control Panel.**
- **Save the BOOT.INI file and reset the hidden and read-only attributes on the file.**
- **When the workstation reboots, reconfigure the display settings with the Display applet in Control Panel.**

C. The Required Result and only one Optional Result

The BOOT.INI file has two sections, the [boot loader] section and the [operating systems] section. The [boot loader] section contains the length of time Boot Loader will wait before starting the operating system listed as default, also in the [boot loader] section. The [operating systems] section contains the operating systems that will appear on the Boot Loader menu.

The paths in the BOOT.INI file might look a bit strange. They are in the ARC notation, which denotes the physical path to the partition. In the path presented in the scenario, this line

```
multi(0)disk(0)rdisk(0)partition(1)\WINNT
```

can be interpreted as follows:

> Windows NT is located in the WINNT folder, on the first partition (partition(1), partition numbering is "1"-based) on the first disk device (rdisk(0), physcial disk devices are "0"-based) in the first disk drive (disk(0), disks are "0"-based) on the first disk controller (multi(0), controllers are "0"-based).

In the [operating systems] section, the text string following the ARC path is the entry displayed on the Boot Manager menu for the ARC path.

Because the Proposed Solution indicated the BOOT.INI file should be opened and reviewed, the Proposed Solution accomplishes the Required Result.

In order to invoke the VGA option, the `/BASEVIDEO` switch must be used, appended to the ARC path string. The Proposed Solution uses the `/sos` switch, which is used to enumerate each device driver as it is loaded. By default, the Windows NT installation program creates the "Windows NT Workstation Version 4.00 [VGA]" Boot Loader entry with both the `/sos` switch and the `/BASEVIDEO` switches. The Proposed Solution does not accomplish the first Optional Result.

The Display applet in Control Panel is used to reconfigure the video settings on any NT Workstation 4 computer. The Proposed Solution accomplishes the second Optional Result.

5. **Proposed Solution:**
   - **Immediately after the system boots, open the Services applet in Control Panel, select the UPS service, click the Startup button, and click the Disabled button. Reboot the system.**
   - **Edit the BOOT.INI file and add the `/NoSerialMice:COM1` switch to the end of all the Windows NT Workstation boot paths.**
   - **Using the Services applet in Control Panel, re-enable the UPS service to start at bootup. Reboot the system.**

   B. The Required Result and both Optional Results

5. CORRECT ANSWER: B

The UPS service should be stopped from Control Panel using the Services applet. The Proposed Solution accomplishes the Required Result.

When Windows NT boots, it sends a query signal out to all serial ports in order to attempt to detect an attached mouse. Many UPSs interpret this signal as a shutdown signal and begin shutdown procedures. Windows NT can be forced to not perform this test with the following switch in BOOT.INI:

```
/NoSerialMice:ComX
```

where:

X is the desired serial port where the UPS is attached.

The Proposed Solution accomplishes the first Optional Result.

Services are restarted through the System applet in Control Panel. The Proposed Solution accomplishes the second Optional Result.

6. **The user screen switches into GUI mode after which phase of startup?**

   D. Win32 subsystem

6. CORRECT ANSWER: D

The GUI appears after the Win32 subsystem starts. When the Win32 subsystem starts, the WINLOGON process is invoked, displaying the Press CTRL+ALT+DEL to Log On dialog box.

7. **Proposed Solution:**
   - **When the logon dialog box appears, click the Shutdown button without logging into Windows NT Workstation. When the system reboots, press the Spacebar when prompted to invoke the Last Known Good configuration.**
   - **Open the System Control Panel applet, select the Resources tab, and find a free IRQ resource.**
   - **Reconfigure the sound card to use a known free IRQ.**

   A. The Required Result only

7. CORRECT ANSWER: A

When the boot process fails, you must be sure not to log in to the operating system during the troubled boot. Windows NT will not overwrite the Current control set with the boot parameters until the logon is complete. In effect, completing the logon process is an indication to the operating system that the boot was trouble-free and the parameters used to boot the system should be used permanently. By canceling the logon with the Shutdown button, you can still invoke the previous configuration that did not cause an error in the boot process. The Proposed Solution accomplishes the Required Result.

Although the boot error occurred immediately after the sound card installation, it is not necessarily the sound card causing the boot failure. The Proposed Solution immediately assumed it was an IRQ conflict with the sound card that caused the boot error. The Event Log should be consulted first to determine if in fact it was the sound card driver that failed to load. The Proposed Solution does not achieve the first Optional Result.

Assuming it was the sound card driver causing an interrupt conflict, the WinMSD utility should be used to determine which interrupts are free, not the System Control Panel applet. The System applet does not display free/used system resources. The required information could be found on the Resources tab of the WinMSD application. The Proposed Solution does not accomplish the second Optional Result.

8. Which of the following is responsible for building the hardware list during boot operations?

D. NTDETECT.COM

8. CORRECT ANSWER: D

NTDETECT.COM is the Windows NT Workstation boot file that is responsible for detecting the hardware installed in the system and available to Workstation.

9. Which of the following are files needed during an Intel-based boot that are not needed for a RISC boot operation?

A. NTDETECT.COM

B. NTLDR

E. BOOT.INI

9. CORRECT ANSWER: A-B-E

The firmware on a RISC system takes care of the functionality provided by the BOOT.INI, NTDETECT.COM, and NTLDR Intel boot files.

10. Which two files are common to RISC-based boots, as well as Intel-based boots?

B. HAL.DLL

D. NTOSKRNL.EXE

10. CORRECT ANSWER: B-D

NTDETECT.COM and BOOT.INI are only required for booting Windows NT on an Intel platform. OSLOADER.EXE is used only on RISC boots. HAL.DLL and NTOSKRNL.EXE are common to the boot process on both platforms.

11. Which of the following system files are located in the <winnt_root>\SYSTEM32 directory of an Intel Windows NT system?

C. NTOSKRNL.EXE

11. CORRECT ANSWER: C

NTOSKRNL.EXE, the Windows NT operating system kernel resides in the <winnt_root>\System32 directory on both Intel and RISC platforms.

12. Proposed Solution:

- **Boot the system from a DOS bootable floppy disk. Ensure some type of ASCII editor, such as Microsoft's EDIT.COM, is on the disk.**
- **Change directories to the root drive of the Windows NT installation volume. Change the attributes on the file BOOT.INI; remove the hidden and read-only attributes of the file.**
- **Within the BOOT.INI file, ensure there is a [boot loader] section and an [operating systems] section. Ensure the [boot loader] section has a default= and timeout= section. Ensure the default entry appears as:**

```
multi(0)disk(1)rdisk(0)
➥partition(1)\NT4
```

- **In the BOOT.INI file, ensure the [operating systems] section has a line such as the following:**

```
multi(0)disk(1)rdisk(0)
➥partition(1)\NT4=
➥"Windows NT Server
➥Version 4.00"
```

- **Save the BOOT.INI file, and reset the hidden and read-only attributes on the file.**
- **Run Windows NT Setup from the Windows NT Workstation boot disks and select the Repair option from the installation menu.**
- **When the workstation reboots, apply the latest service pack.**

B. The Required Result and both Optional Results

12. CORRECT ANSWER: B

When the system partition is FAT formatted, booting with a DOS floppy will enable your access to the boot files. The boot error presented in the scenario is indicative of one of two problems: The boot.ini file is corrupt (either it's pointing to the wrong folder for starting the operating system, or it's missing completely), or the NTOSKRNL.EXE file is missing or corrupt.

The first step in diagnosing this problem is to verify the contents of the boot.ini file. This is accomplished by changing the file attribute of the boot.ini file from hidden, read-only and opening the file with any ASCII text editor. The Proposed Solution accomplishes the Required Result.

Because the scenario stated Windows NT was installed in the NT4 folder on the D: drive, the ARC path should be configured for the first partition, on the first disk device configured on the second physical disk drive controlled by the first adapter. The ARC path would be:

```
multi(0)disk(1)rdisk(0)partition(1)\NT4
```

The Proposed Solution accomplishes the first Optional Result.

After the boot.ini file is eliminated as the possible cause of the boot error, you should run Windows NT Setup, invoking the Repair option in the Setup menu to replace the corrupt files. After the installation is repaired, the latest service pack should be applied. The Proposed Solution accomplishes the second Optional Result.

13. On Intel x86-based computers, what is the name of the file loaded by the boot sector of the active partition?

A. NTLDR

13. CORRECT ANSWER: A

Similar in nature to the IO.sys file in MS-DOS, the NTLDR file is used to begin the initialization of the operating system. NTLDR first loads a mini-OS and changes the memory model to a flat 32-bit structure. NTLDR next loads the BOOT.INI file and displays the Boot Manager menu. After Windows NT is selected as the operating system, NTLDR loads NTDETECT.COM which begins building the HKEY_LOCAL_MACHINE\Hardware hive in the Registry. Finally, NTLDR loads NTOSKRNL.EXE and HAL.DLL to build the SYSTEM hive in the Registry. At this point, control is passed to NTOSKRNL.EXE to finish the boot process.

If Windows NT is not selected as the operating system to start, NTLDR will load the BOOTSECT.DOS file to boot the alternate operating system.

14. From the following, select all of the ways in which the Automatic Recovery and Restart capability can be enabled in Windows NT.

A. With the `/crashdebug` switch in the BOOT.INI file

C. Via the System application in the Control Panel

14. CORRECT ANSWER: A-C

When used with the BOOT.INI file, the `/crashdebug` switch enables the operating system to automatically restart after a crash. Additionally, this option can be (and should be) configured through the Startup/Shutdown tab in the System Control Panel applet.

FURTHER REVIEW

CHOOSE THE APPROPRIATE COURSE OF ACTION TO TAKE WHEN THE BOOT PROCESS FAILS

If you know that your workstation's hardware is functioning correctly, the failure of Windows NT Workstation to start up properly and load the Windows NT shell could be a boot process problem. The key to solving problems of this type is to understand the logical sequence that your workstation uses when starting up. Windows NT shows you various boot sequence errors, the meaning of which should help you determine the problem with your system. You also can diagnose the boot.ini file to determine the nature of any potential problems, and you can apply your emergency repair disks to boot your system and repair common boot process failure problems.

The Boot Sequence

The boot sequence initiates when the hard drive's *Master Boot Record (MBR)* is read into memory and begins to load the different portions of the Windows NT operating system. Windows NT Workstation runs on different microprocessor architectures. The exact boot sequence depends on the type of microprocessor on which you have installed Windows NT Workstation.

Intel-Based Boot Sequence

Windows NT loads on an Intel x86 computer by reading a file called the *NTLDR*, or *NT Loader*, into memory from the boot sector of the startup or active partition on your boot drive. The NTLDR is a hidden system file set to be read-only. NTLDR is located in the root folder of your system partition and can be viewed in the Windows NT Explorer when you set the View All File Types option.

RISC-Based Boot Sequence

A *RISC computer* contains the NTLDR software as part of its BIOS. Therefore, the boot phase of a RISC-based computer is both simpler and faster than the boot phase of an Intel x86 computer. A RISC computer keeps its hardware configuration in its BIOS, which obviates the need for the ntdetect.com file. Another item kept in firmware is the list of any valid operating systems and how to access them. This means that a RISC computer also doesn't use a boot.ini file.

A RISC computer boots by loading a file called osloader.exe. After reading the hardware configuration from the BIOS and executing, osloader.exe hands off the boot process to the ntoskrnl.exe. Then the hal.dll is loaded, followed by the system file, which ends the RISC Windows NT boot process.

Creating a Memory Dump

When you encounter a blue screen error, you might need to take a memory dump of your system for diagnostic purposes. A *memory dump* is a copy of the data held in RAM. To save that file, you need free disk space equal to that of your installed RAM plus an additional 1MB of space.

To take a memory dump, check the Write Debugging Information To and Overwrite Any Existing Files check boxes in the Startup/Shutdown tab of the System Control Panel. Close that Control Panel and confirm any alerts about page file size should they occur. Then reboot your computer. The memory dump file is written to the location displayed in the Startup/Shutdown tab's text box.

The Load Process

After the boot portion of the operating system loads, your device drivers load, and the boot process is handed off to the operating system kernel. In Windows NT, this portion of the startup occurs when the screen turns a blue color and the text shrinks. At that point, the kernel is initializing, and the operating system begins to read various hives in the Windows NT Registry. One of the first hives read is the CurrentControlSet, which is copied to the CloneControlSet and from which a HARDWARE key is written to RAM. The System hive is read to determine whether additional drivers need to be loaded into RAM and initialized. This ends the kernel initialization phase.

The Session Manager reads the System hive in the Registry to determine which programs must run before Windows NT is loaded. Commonly, the AUTOCHK.EXE program (a stripped down version of CHKDSK.EXE) runs and reads the file system. Other programs defined in the HKEY_LOCAL_MACHINE\SYSTEM\CurrentControlSet\Control\Session Manager\BootExecute key are run, and a page file is then created in the location stored in the HKEY_LOCAL_MACHINE\SYSTEM\CurrentControlSet\Control\Session Manager\Memory Management key.

The Software hive is read, and the Session Manager loads other required subsystems as defined in the HKEY_LOCAL_MACHINE\SYSTEM\CurrentControlSet\Control\Session Manager\Subsystems\Required key. This ends the portion of the boot process in which services are loaded into RAM.

After services are loaded, the Windows WIN32 Subsystem starts to load. This is where Windows NT Workstation switches into a graphics (GUI) mode. The WINLOGON module runs, and the Welcome dialog box appears. WINLOGON runs under the lsass.exe process. The Windows operating system is still loading at this point, but the user can enter the user name, domain, and password to initiate the logon process. After the service controller (SERVICES.EXE) loads and initializes the computer browser, workstation, server, spooler, and so on, the request for logon is passed to the domain controller for service.

The SERVICES.EXE program is a central program in the Windows NT operating system. It initializes various system DLL files. Should this file be damaged, you must reinstall Windows NT Workstation.

A successful logon is considered the completion of the boot process. To mark the event, Windows NT Workstation updates the LastKnownGood control set key in the Registry with information about what was loaded and the system configuration at startup.

Last Known Good Recovery

The *Last Known Good configuration* provides a method for recovering your preceding system setup. When you create a specific configuration for Windows NT, that information is stored in a particular control set. The LastKnownGood control set enables you to recover from a boot process error—provided that you use this method immediately after discovering the error on the first boot up attempt and you do not log on a second time. Subsequent boots (if they proceed and you log on to the system again) remove this option as a recovery method.

The information contained in the LastKnownGood configuration is stored in the Registry in the HKEY_LOCAL_MACHINE\SYSTEM\CurrentControlSet key. To boot to the Last Known Good configuration, follow these steps:

1. Press Ctrl+Alt+Delete to bring up the logon dialog box. Click the Shutdown button. If the button is not available, turn the machine off. Do not log on, as the Last Known Good configuration will be overwritten with incorrect values.

2. Restart the machine. During the boot process, press the Spacebar when prompted to invoke the Last Known Good configuration. When the boot process is finished, log on as normal. You may now fix the problem using the necessary means. Checking the log files with the Event Viewer application may help you identify the problem causing the boot error.

When a critical system error is encountered, Windows NT Workstation defaults to the Last Known Good configuration on its own. This defaulting doesn't always occur but is a frequent occurrence. If basic operating system files are damaged, you must boot using a boot floppy and recover your system as described in the next few sections.

Boot Sequence Errors

The most common boot sequence errors occur when the operating system components required for the boot process cannot be found or are corrupted. Often a modification of the boot.ini file leads to a failure to boot properly. If you or your client have recently made a modification to the startup files, you should suspect that first.

Catastrophic hardware failure is not a common problem, but it is occasionally encountered—particularly in older equipment. If a hard drive stops operating, it will be obvious because your computer makes different sounds when no disk is being accessed. Also, when you open the case of the computer and listen to it, you won't hear the hard drive spin up and achieve its operating speed.

Much less obvious are hardware errors that damage the capability of your system to start up without appearing to noticeably alter the performance of your system. For example, if your hard drive develops a bad disk sector (which contains the operating system components responsible for booting your computer), the computer appears to function correctly. You can solve this problem by re-establishing the boot files on another portion of your hard drive.

BOOT.INI Error Messages

The following error messages appear when there is a problem with the boot.ini file. If you get one of these error messages and the Windows shell doesn't load, you should suspect the boot.ini file and use a boot disk or an *emergency repair disk (ERD)* to repair the boot.ini file. Later in this chapter, you learn how to create an ERD. This message indicates that the Windows NT Loader file is either damaged or corrupted:

```
BOOT: Couldn't find NTLDR
Please insert another disk
```

Typically, the error with the NTLDR file occurs early on in the boot process. When you see a repeated sequence of error messages indicating that Windows NT Workstation is checking hardware, the error is a problem with the ntdetect.com file. These messages appear as follows:

```
NTDETECT V1.0 Checking Hardware÷
NTDETECT V1.0 Checking Hardware÷
NTDETECT V1.0 Checking Hardware÷
```

It is possible for Windows NT to load even if the boot.ini file is missing. If that is the case, the NTLDR starts Windows NT loading files it finds in the <default>\WINNT folder. If the operating system was installed in another location, an error message appears, indicating that the ntoskrnl.exe file is missing or corrupt.

When there is a problem with the boot sector, the following error message appears during startup:

```
I/O Error accessing boot sector file
Multi(0)disk(0)rdisk(0)partition(1):\boots
➥ect.dos
```

This error message could indicate a problem with your hard drive. You should boot from a Windows NT boot disk and run the RDISK utility.

Windows NT Workstation also posts a more specific message when it can determine that the error occurs when it tries to locate the boot sector is hardware-related. The operating system checks hardware (as you have just seen) by testing it during startup. Failure to respond to one of these tests generates the following message:

```
OS Loader V4.00
Windows NT could not start because of a
➥computer disk hardware configuration
➥problem.
Could not read from the selected boot
➥disk. Check boot path and disk hardware.
Please check the Windows NT
➥documentation about hardware disk
➥configuration and your hardware reference
➥manuals for additional information.
```

The preceding message indicates that the pointer in the boot.ini file that locates the Windows NT operating system references either a damaged or non-existing device or a partition that doesn't contain a file system Windows NT can access with the boot loader.

Finally, you might see a STOP error when the Windows NT loader cannot resolve the appropriate partition that contains your operating system files. This error takes the following form:

```
STOP: 0x000007E: Inaccessible Boot Device
```

This error appears when the hard disk controller has difficulty determining which device is the boot device—for example, this occurs if your computer contains an Adaptec SCSI disk controller, and there is an ID number conflict. Another instance in which this error occurs is when the Master Boot Record (MBR) is corrupted by a virus or a disk error.

If your system proceeds through the load phase and boots correctly but still seems to be malfunctioning, you should check the System Event Log to see whether any system messages were written to the log.

The *System Event Log* can display errors, warnings, or informational events that explain the conditions leading to an anomaly due to an error in the boot sequence. Use the Event Viewer program in the Administrative Tools folder on the Program submenu of the Start menu to view the System Log. Choose the System Log command on the Log menu to open the System Log.

Boot Disk Recovery

If your hard disk boot partition fails, you can boot from a floppy disk, provided you've created a Windows NT boot disk prior to the occurrence of the error condition. If you have installed a multi-partition system and your boot partition contains Windows NT, you can also use your boot disk to start up. After you have started your system using the floppy disk, you can perform procedures to test and repair any errors that exist.

Most computers are started from their floppy disk drives—commonly given the volume label A. If your computer is configured to start up from your hard drive, you must change this in your computer's BIOS setup. Press the keystroke displayed in the startup sequence to open your computer's setup. Then change the boot sequence to start up from the floppy disk drive prior to attempting to boot from a floppy boot disk.

A Windows NT boot disk is simply a floppy disk formatted in Windows NT (it must be formatted from within Windows NT to function properly) that contains the NTLDR, NTDETECT.COM, and ntbootdd.sys files. BOTSECT.DOS should also be included if you want to boot to another operating system such as DOS or Windows 95.

The Emergency Repair Disk (ERD)

When a portion of the Windows NT Registry becomes corrupted, your workstation can become unstable and crash. In some instances, these errors even prevent you from starting your computer and booting the Windows NT operating system itself. You can repair the Windows NT Registry if you have created an ERD that contains the important system Registry information.

You are prompted to create an ERD when you install Windows NT Workstation. If you prefer, you can create an ERD at a later time. Regardless of whether you choose to create an ERD, the appropriate files are copied to the %systemroot%\Repair directory.

These files are copied into the folder %systemroot%\REPAIR, after which, the RDISK utility prompts you for a floppy disk on which to create an ERD. The information in the REPAIR folder is copied onto this disk.

The ERD is useful only if you update it on a regular basis. You should consider updating the ERD before performing any major software installations or upgrades, making any changes to your security policy, or changing the hardware configuration of your workstation.

If this information is not current on your ERD, the restoration you can perform using the ERD is of limited value. The ERD doesn't take the place of a full volume backup—it saves only data that can help re-establish your system configuration based on information contained in the Registry.

The importance of using the `/S` switch for the RDISK program is worth noting. This switch updates the DEFAULT, SECURITY, and SAM changes when using RDISK. Without the `/S` switch, changes to your account information are not noted. If you have a lot of accounts, updating this information can take some time. Because the ERD cannot span multiple disks, the `/S` switch is often used when updating the \REPAIR folder, but it cannot be used to create a floppy ERD if the SAM information will not fit onto a single floppy.

Restoring Your System by Using the ERD

When you use the ERD to repair a damaged Windows NT Workstation, the procedure essentially reinstalls the sections of the operating system that are required for your particular setup. The data that you copied to the ERD contained in the Windows NT Registry determines which files need to be replaced and how the configuration should be re-established. The ERD performs the following tasks, among others:

- Runs CHKDSK to determine the validity of the partition containing your Windows NT system files
- Determines whether the individual files on a system partition are valid, as determined by the use of a checksum
- Restores missing or corrupt files from your Windows NT installation disks
- Replaces your default System and Security Registry hives
- Replaces the Security Account Manager hives
- Reinstalls the files responsible for booting your system in the Boot Loader (boot.ini, NTLDR, ntbootdd.sys, and ntdetect.com)

Before you begin to restore your system, make sure you have a set of Windows NT Setup floppy disks available. To restore Windows NT Workstation on an Intel x386 system, boot the system with the Windows NT boot floppies. When the installation menu appears, select the R option to perform a repair on an existing Windows NT installation. You will be prompted for your ERD. If you do not have the ERD, Windows NT will attempt to retrieve the information from the \REPAIR folder in the Windows NT directory in the workstation.

You can choose the following four main options to repair in the recovery process:

- *Inspect Registry Files.* By using your ERD, you can repair corrupt portions of the Registry. You can select to repair any or all of the following hives: Default, Security/SAM, Software, and System. Changes to the Registry do not require the use of the Windows NT installation CDs.
- *Inspect Startup Environment.* Any boot files are inspected, dissected, and potentially rejected. Because all default boot files are equivalent, you can use any ERD to replace startup files.
- *Verify Windows NT System Files.* This option compares any system file (with the system attribute) in the Windows NT directory and any subdirectories and verifies them using the checksum values in the setup.log file. You need your installation disks to perform this repair.
- *Inspect Boot Sector.* Often the boot sector becomes invalid when you upgrade MS-DOS or Windows 95 by using the SYS command. Use an ERD (any ERD) and the installation disks to repair this problem.

Each ERD that you create is specific to the type of computer (vendor and CPU type) on which it is created. An ERD that you create on one system does not work on another system. The process of restoring a RISC system containing the Windows NT Workstation as its operating system is similar in concept to the procedure previously described. The individual sequence differs, however, depending on the specific manufacturer of your system.

After the repair is complete, remove the ERD and reboot your system. Creating and maintaining an ERD is one of the most effective troubleshooting tools that you have in your arsenal. It cures a host of ills. It is only effective, however, if you remain diligent about updating it whenever a workstation's configuration changes.

PRACTICE QUESTIONS

CHOOSE THE APPROPRIATE COURSE OF ACTION TO TAKE WHEN A PRINT JOB FAILS

1. **This question is based on the following scenario. Review the scenario first, followed by the objectives and the proposed solution. Then evaluate the proposed solution by choosing the best answer.**

   Scenario:
   You receive several calls from a user who cannot print to a local shared printer on a Windows NT Workstation. When you visit the user's work area, other users mention that their print jobs are also garbled, and often the print jobs never complete. Another user complains that she cannot print from MS-DOS-based applications. The printer server is a Windows NT Workstation with 128MB of RAM. There's 100MB available on the C: drive and 2.12GB available on the D: drive.

   Required Result:
   Install the correct print drivers on the Windows NT Workstation print server and the users' NT Workstations.

   Optional Results:
   Identify and resolve the problem causing the Windows-generated print jobs to not produce any output.

   Identify and resolve the problem of DOS-based applications not printing to the networked printer.

   Proposed Solution:
   Upon inspecting the print server, you find the drivers loaded for the specific printer were incorrect. You load the correct drivers from the manufacturer's CD and manually load the drivers onto all the users' workstations.

   You find the spool directory is in its default location. You change the spool directory to point to a folder on the D: drive because it has more free space.

   With the NET USE command, map the LPT1 port of the DOS application user's machine to point to the print server.

   Evaluation of Proposed Solution:
   Which of the following stated objectives does the proposed solution accomplish?

   A. The Required Result only
   B. The Required Result and both Optional Results
   C. The Required Result and only one Optional Result
   D. Only both Optional Results
   E. Neither the Required Result nor any Optional Results

2. **What priority level is assigned to the print Spooler service by Windows NT Workstation?**

   A. 1
   B. 3
   C. 7
   D. 15
   E. 23

3. **Which of the following is a potential solution to problems with printing from**

non-Windows-based applications to a printer that works fine in Windows?

A. Install additional printer drivers specifically designed for the non-Windows application.

B. Elect to use RAW data instead of EMF.

C. Stop spooling services and send data directly to the printer.

D. Configure the printer on a different port.

E. Enable DOS printing from the Printer Property menu.

4. **Files in the printer spool should have which two of the following extensions?**

A. .TXT

B. .SHD

C. .SHT

D. .SPL

E. .RAW

5. **When are the files in the printer spool cleared?**

A. When the system is rebooted

B. When the workstation is shut down

C. When the job finishes printing

D. When an administrator empties the spool

E. When the Spooler service is stopped

6. **If a print job appears to be stuck in the printer after you recover from a system crash, and you cannot delete it, what should you do?**

A. Reboot the computer until the problem goes away.

B. Stop the Spooler service in Control Panel Services and delete the files for that job in the spool directory.

C. Relocate the spool directory and delete the old directory.

D. Use Regedit to change stuck job parameters.

E. Manually delete all files from the spool directory.

7. **This question is based on the following scenario. Review the scenario first, followed by the objectives and the proposed solution. Then evaluate the proposed solution by choosing the best answer.**

Scenario:
You have a Windows NT Workstation dedicated as a network print server. The workstation user has been complaining that there seems to be a high number of print jobs coming through. Additionally, many users are complaining that large print jobs are causing them to wait long periods of time for their print jobs.

Required Result:
Determine which users are actually sending print jobs to the print server.

Optional Results:
Reserve the printer for printing large print jobs during off-peak times.

Increase the responsiveness of the print server.

Proposed Solution:
Enable logging on the selected printer.

Install an identical print device and create a printer pool.

Increase the priority of the Spooler service from its default Normal priority to a priority of 9.

Evaluation of Proposed Solution:
The proposed solution accomplishes which of the following stated objectives?

A. The Required Result only

B. The Required Result and both Optional Results

C. The Required Result and only one Optional Result

D. Only both Optional Results

E. Neither the Required Result nor any Optional Results

ANSWER KEY

1. D
2. C
3. A
4. B-D
5. C
6. B
7. C

ANSWERS & EXPLANATIONS

CHOOSE THE APPROPRIATE COURSE OF ACTION TO TAKE WHEN A PRINT JOB FAILS

1. Proposed Solution:

- **Upon inspecting the print server, you find the drivers loaded for the specific printer were incorrect. You load the correct drivers from the manufacturer's CD and manually load the drivers onto all the users' workstations.**
- **You find the spool directory is in its default location. You change the spool directory to point to a folder on the D: drive because it has more free space.**
- **With the NET USE command, map the LPT1 port of the DOS application user's machine to point to the print server.**

D. Only both Optional Results

1. CORRECT ANSWER: D

When it is used as a print server, Windows NT Workstation (or Server) will automatically check the driver files on the client machine when the client machine submits a print job. If the correct drivers are not loaded, or if an older version of the driver is loaded on the client, the print server will automatically update the driver files on the workstation for Windows 95, Windows 98, and Windows NT clients. The Proposed Solution specifies that the administrator manually loaded the driver files on the client's machine, which was an unnecessary step. The Proposed Solution does not accomplish the Required Result.

Although changing the printer driver on the server might clear up the problem with print jobs not producing any output, the spool directory should always be located on the volume with the greatest amount of free space. Additionally, because some users received garbled output and others did not receive any output, the amount of disk space available to the printer spooler should be suspected. One of the most critical components in print server configuration is the amount of free disk space available to concurrently spool print jobs submitted by network clients.

By default, the spool directory points to the folder \<winnt_root>\SYSTEM32\SPOOL\PRINTERS. Changing the spool directory to the volume with the greatest amount of free space should be done to optimize the printing process. Selecting the desired printer in the Printers Control Panel applet and selecting Properties… from the File menu enables you to change the spool directory. The spool directory can also be changed through the Advanced tab in the Properties window. The Proposed Solution accomplishes the first Optional Result.

DOS-based applications will typically attempt to connect to printers through the LPT ports installed on the workstation. If you map the output of the LPT1 port to the network printer via the `NET USE` command, the DOS application should be able to generate printed output by printing to the LPT port. The Proposed Solution accomplishes the second Optional Result.

2. What priority level is assigned to the print Spooler service by Windows NT Workstation?

C. 7

2. CORRECT ANSWER: C

As with other applications, Windows NT Workstation runs the printer Spooler service at the normal priority of 7.

3. Which of the following is a potential solution to problems with printing from non-Windows-based applications to a printer that works fine in Windows?

A. Install additional printer drivers specifically designed for the non-Windows application.

3. CORRECT ANSWER: A

Non-Windows-based applications—for example, MS-DOS-based applications—require their own printer drivers if the application requires any kind of formatted output other than plain ASCII text.

Typically these applications will print to the LPT port assigned to the computer. If you need to print to a network printer, use the `NET USE` command to map the local LPT port to the network printer.

4. Files in the printer spool should have which two of the following extensions?

B. .SHD

D. .SPL

4. CORRECT ANSWER: B-D

When a document prints, two files are created for the print job in the spool directory (which is, by default, print <winnt_root>\ SYSTEM32\SPOOL\PRINTERS). One of the files, which has an .SPL extension, is the actual print job spool file. The other file, which has an .SHD extension, is a shadow file that contains information about the job, including its owner and priority.

5. When are the files in the printer spool cleared?

C. When the job finishes printing

5. CORRECT ANSWER: C

Normally, the files associated with a particular print job are cleared when the job finishes printing. If the job does not terminate or the spool file gets jammed, the files might never be deleted unless they're specifically deleted by the administrator. Periodically, the administrator should check the date on files in the spool directory. Any files with dates other than the current date can safely be deleted from the folder.

6. If a print job appears to be stuck in the printer after you recover from a system crash, and you cannot delete it, what should you do?

B. Stop the Spooler service in Control Panel Services and delete the files for that job in the spool directory.

6. CORRECT ANSWER: B

When a job is stuck in the spooler, the Spooler service should be stopped by using the Services applet in Control Panel. This eliminates any additional print jobs from being spooled. The spooler directory contents should then be emptied using Windows NT Explorer. After the spool directory is cleaned out, the Spooler service should be restarted. The consequence of this action is that any other print jobs that were spooled after the jammed job are also deleted. After the Spooler service is restarted, those jobs have to be resubmitted.

7. Proposed Solution:

- **Enable logging on the selected printer.**
- **Install an identical print device and create a printer pool.**
- **Increase the priority of the Spooler service from its default Normal priority to a priority of 9.**

C. The Required Result and only one Optional Result

7. CORRECT ANSWER: C

Enabling logging on a printer is the simplest way to determine which users are accessing the printer. Printer logging is enabled through the Security tab of the printer properties. In this case, you should enable logging of the Print event for the Everyone group to determine which users are accessing the printer. The Proposed Solution accomplishes the Required Result.

A printer pool will load balanced print jobs between identical print devices, thereby processing print jobs faster, but it will do nothing to schedule certain print jobs to run during off-peak hours. To schedule jobs, you must enable printer scheduling by creating multiple printers for one print device and setting the hours of availability appropriately for each printer. See Chapter 3, "Managing Resources," for more information on printer pooling and printer scheduling. The Proposed Solution does not achieve the first Optional Result.

As with all other background processes, Windows NT assigns the print Spooler service a priority of 7. If you boost this priority to 9, which is consistent with foreground applications, the performance of the print spooler will be increased. This should be done only if the workstation is serving as a print server. Boosting the priority can also be done temporarily to speed the printing of a large document on a normal workstation.

To change the priority of the Spooler service, open the RegEdit32 application and change the value of the PriorityClass of type REG_DWORD in the following key:

```
HKEY_LOCAL_MACHINE\System\CurrentControlSet\Control\
➥Print
```

Set that value to the priority class required. A value of 0, or no value entered, is substituted with the default value of a background process of 7 for Windows NT Workstation.

The Proposed Solution accomplishes the second Optional Result.

FURTHER REVIEW

CHOOSE THE APPROPRIATE COURSE OF ACTION TO TAKE WHEN A PRINT JOB FAILS

One of the benefits of Windows printing is that the operating system handles all print job output in a standardized manner, regardless of the application from which you are printing. Windows NT, being a network operating system, enables you to define network printers that are available as shared resources to which other Windows NT Workstations can print. Any client or server on a network can serve as the print server to a network printer. Additionally, you can have local printers that are not shared resources to other network computers, but that you need to manage and troubleshoot.

The centralization of printing services is a beautiful thing. A single standardized print model under Windows replaces the individual print models of applications under MS-DOS, and it is more easily understood. The down side is that when problems do arise, they affect your entire application suite and maybe an entire workgroup.

Keep in mind that Windows still retains the older model for printing MS-DOS applications that run in Windows NT Workstation from the command prompt. These applications require their own printer drivers to print anything other than ASCII output. If you are using WordPerfect 5.1, for example, you must have both a WordPerfect and a printer driver installed. Some MS-DOS applications require that you turn on the printer port by using a command such as the following prior to printing:

```
NET USE LPT1: \\servername\printername
```

Understanding the Windows Print Subsystem

The Windows printing subsystem is modular and works hand-in-hand with other subsystems to provide printing services. When a printer is local and a print job is specified by an application, data is sent to the *Graphics Device Interface (GDI)* to be rendered into a print job in the printer language of the print device. The GDI is a module between the printing subsystem and the application requesting the printing services. This print job is passed to the *spooler*, which is a .DLL. The print job is written to disk as a temporary file so that it can survive a power outage or a reboot. Print jobs can be spooled using either the RAW or the EMF printer language.

The client side of the print spooler is winspool.drv, and that driver makes a *Remote Procedure Call (RPC)* to the spoolss.exe server side of the spooler. When the printer is attached to the same computer as the spooler, both files are located on the same computer. When the printer is attached to a Windows NT Workstation in a peer-to-peer relationship, those files are located on different computers.

Spoolss.exe calls an API that sends the print job to a route (spoolss.dll). Spoolss.dll then sends the print job to the computer with the local printer. Finally, the localspl.dll library writes the file to disk as a spooled file. At this point, the printer is polled by the localspl.dll to determine whether the spooled print job can be processed by the printer, and the print job is altered if necessary.

The print job is then turned over to a separator page processor and despooled to the print monitor. The print device receives the print job and raster image processes it to a bitmap file that is then sent to the print engine for output.

Network Printer Process

For network printers, the process is very much the same as the process for locally defined printers; however, client requests and server services are more clearly defined and separate. The routers found in the spooler modules—winspool.drv, spoolss.exe, and spoolss.dll—are identical to the ones used for a local printer. A local print provider on the client localspl.dll is matched to a remote print provider (win32sp.dll for Windows print servers or nwprovau.dll for NetWare print servers) on the server side. In a network printer process, the print processors and print monitors might use several different server DLLs, each one of which is required by a supported operating system.

Multiple Virtual Printer Setup

Generally, you install a printer by using the Add Printer Wizard that you find in the Printers folder accessed from the Settings submenu of the Start menu. With the help of the wizard, you can create a virtual printer with a name that you provide. You can create any number of virtual (or logical, if you will) printers that use the same physical printer for a number of purposes. If you want to print to a different printer, have different security schemes, or provide different access times, having multiple virtual printers provides a means to do this. You can manipulate printers by any of the following means:

- Double-click on the printer to see spooled jobs, provided you have the privilege to do so.
- Right-click on a printer to view a shortcut menu that provides several options. You can use this menu to delete a printer that no longer exists, for example. You can use the Default Printer command to set the default printer for a Windows NT Workstation from the shortcut menu.
- Right-click on a printer and select the Properties command from the shortcut menu to access the printer's properties sheet and control any number of settings.

Printers as Shared Resources

Network printers are shared resources. You must own the printer (have created or installed it), be an administrator, or be assigned the rights to use a printer in some way to be able to view, modify, and use a printer. An owner or an administrator can assign different levels of rights. You assign shared rights by using the Sharing command on a printer's shortcut menu, which brings up the Sharing tab of the printer's Properties dialog box.

Creating additional printer shares for the same physical printer proves useful for the following reasons:

- Each share can have different printer setups.
- You can assign different access privileges to groups of users.
- Each group can have different printing priorities.

- You can control access to the printer at different times for each group.
- You can use one share name for a network printer and another share name for a local printer.

If users cannot see a printer, they might not have been given the right to access that printer. An administrator should be able to view and modify printers on any Windows NT Workstation.

Solving Print Spooler Problems

Any print job spooled to a printer is written as a temporary file to the folder %systemroot%\System32\Spool\Printers. The file is deleted after the printer indicates that the job has been printed. The most common print spool problem is a lack of available disk space. If you print high-resolution graphics, you might have print jobs as large as 20MB to 80MB per file for a 32-bit image at standard page size. Not surprisingly, it does not take many of such print jobs to overwhelm the typical Windows NT Workstation configuration.

When you print to the spooler, two files are created for each print job. The .SPL file is the actual print job spool file. The second file is a shadow file, given the .SHD extension. The shadow file contains additional information about the print job that is not part of the print job itself, such as owner, priority, and so forth. If your computer crashes, .SPL and .SHD files remain in the default spool file until the service restarts and they are processed and printed. After being printed, these files are deleted from disk. Should your spooled files become corrupted, they will be orphaned and remain in the spool folder, taking up valuable space.

You can print directly to a printer from your application by turning off the print spooling feature. Before you print, open the Scheduling tab of the printer's Properties dialog box and select the Print Directly to the Printer option button. When the printer next becomes available, your document prints. Until that time, you cannot use the application that originated the print job. You can, however, switch to another application and continue working until your printing application becomes available.

Print Spool Event Logging

You can enable event logging to your spooler by adding a check mark to the Log Spooler Error Events, Log Spooler Warning Events, or Log Spooler Information Events check boxes on the Advanced tab.

PRACTICE QUESTIONS

CHOOSE THE APPROPRIATE COURSE OF ACTION TO TAKE WHEN THE INSTALLATION PROCESS FAILS

1. **This question is based on the following scenario. Review the scenario first, followed by the objectives and the proposed solution. Then evaluate the proposed solution by choosing the best answer.**

   Scenario:
   During the Network Setup portion of Windows NT Workstation installation, the network failed to start. You specified the workstation should use the TCP/IP networking protocol with DHCP on an NE2000-compatible adapter. The workstation is joining the WebWorks domain. There are two other machines configured on the local segment.

   Required Result:
   Find the cause of the problem.

   Optional Results:
   Manually configure the IP settings for the workstation.

   Verify the adapter settings.

   Proposed Solution:
   Using one of the other machines on the subnet, ping the domain controller to ensure it is active and available.

   Click the Back button on the Setup dialog box until the adapter configuration information appears. Click the Detect Adapter button to verify the settings are correct.

   After the adapter settings are confirmed, manually enter an IP address and a default gateway for the machine.

   Evaluation of Proposed Solution:
   The proposed solution accomplishes which of the following stated objectives?

   A. The Required Result only

   B. The Required Result and both Optional Results

   C. The Required Result and only one Optional Result

   D. Only both Optional Results

   E. Neither the Required Result nor any Optional Results

2. **During the installation of Windows NT Workstation, you proceed to the point where Setup will begin copying files from the NT CD, but then you continually receive the following message: `Please insert Windows NT into your CD-ROM.` What should be your next step?**

   A. Boot to a different operating system and run WINNT from there.

   B. Clean the CD-ROM.

   C. Verify the local computer has a unique name in the Control Panel.

   D. Call Microsoft Sales to replace the CD.

   E. Create another set of boot disks for the installation.

3. Which of the following should be one of the first steps taken to resolve an error of insufficient disk space during a Windows NT installation on a dual-boot operating system?

A. Boot to a different operating system and run WINNT from there.

B. Compress all available disk space under the alternate operating system partitions.

C. Verify the local computer has a unique name in the Control Panel.

D. Install Windows NT Workstation on a different partition.

E. Boot to the alternative operating system and delete any unnecessary files, and then start the Windows NT installation again.

4. To install Windows NT 4 on a previous version of Windows NT Workstation and keep all settings, what should you do?

A. Install in the same directory the old version was in.

B. Install in a new directory.

C. Do nothing; it will automatically find and install over the old version.

D. Run the MIGRATE utility.

E. This is not possible. Windows NT will always install a fresh copy.

5. How do you create a dual-boot machine with a previous version of Windows NT?

A. Install in the same directory the old version was in.

B. Install in a new directory.

C. Do nothing; it will automatically find and install over the old version.

D. Run the MIGRATE utility.

E. Windows NT Workstation 4 cannot co-exist with previous versions of Windows NT.

ANSWER KEY

1. E
2. A
3. D-E
4. A
5. B

ANSWERS & EXPLANATIONS

CHOOSE THE APPROPRIATE COURSE OF ACTION TO TAKE WHEN THE INSTALLATION PROCESS FAILS

1. Proposed Solution:

- **Using one of the other machines on the subnet, ping the domain controller to ensure it is active and available.**
- **Click the Back button on the Setup dialog box until the adapter configuration information appears. Click the Detect Adapter button to verify the settings are correct.**
- **After the adapter settings are confirmed, manually enter an IP address and a default gateway for the machine.**

E. Neither the Required Result nor any Optional Results

1. CORRECT ANSWER: E

When you're installing the network components of Windows NT, the network failing to start is indicative of an adapter, protocol configuration, or connectivity problem. Because there are already two configured workstations on the local segment, it is easiest to diagnose the connectivity problem. When installing the TCP/IP protocol, you must specify an IP address and subnet mask. If a requirement to communicate outside of the local segment exists, the default gateway must also be specified. Because the installation will be using DHCP, the DHCP server is responsible for supplying this information. The first logical step would be to use one of the existing workstations to ping the DHCP server to test for availability and connectivity. Pinging the domain controller will have no effect on starting the network until the domain information is configured with the Windows NT Workstation, which occurs *after* the network is started. The Proposed Solution does not accomplish the Required Result.

When configuring the TCP/IP protocol manually, at a minimum, you must supply an IP address and subnet mask. The Proposed Solution does not accomplish the first Optional Result.

During the setup of the network components, you are free to use the Back and Next buttons to change the information requested by Setup to configure the desired network components. A common network adapter is the NE2000-compatible adapter. Because Windows NT does not support Plug and Play, the information required to configure the adapter (mainly the IRQ and I/O memory settings) must be supplied manually. Although the adapter might be detected, its settings cannot be. The Proposed Solution does not accomplish the second Optional Result.

2. During the installation of Windows NT Workstation, you proceed to the point where Setup will begin copying files from the NT CD, but then you continually receive the following message: `Please insert Windows NT into your CD-ROM`. What should be your next step?

A. Boot to a different operating system and run WINNT from there.

2. CORRECT ANSWER: A

This message commonly occurs when Windows NT is unable to recognize your CD-ROM. An incompatible CD-ROM drive or CD-ROM controller, such as an unsupported SCSI controller, most often causes this problem.

This problem can be overcome by booting the system with an operating system that does support the installation, such as DOS, and starting the setup using WINNT.EXE with the `/b` switch. However, it is important to realize that if Windows NT is set up in this manner, the CD-ROM drive probably will not be available after the installation is complete.

3. Which of the following should be one of the first steps taken to resolve an error of insufficient disk space during a Windows NT installation on a dual-boot operating system?

D. Install Windows NT Workstation on a different partition.

E. Boot to the alternative operating system and delete any unnecessary files, and then start the Windows NT installation again.

3. CORRECT ANSWER: D-E

If you're configuring a dual-boot system and there is not enough free disk space, Windows NT should be installed on an alternate partition. If an alternate partition is not available, you can try to free enough disk space for the installation by booting to the alternate operating system and making more room on the partition. Compression routines from the alternate operating system should not be used because the partition will no longer be accessible to Windows NT.

4. To install Windows NT 4 on a previous version of Windows NT Workstation and keep all settings, what should you do?

A. Install in the same directory the old version was in.

4. CORRECT ANSWER: A

Install Windows NT 4 in the same directory that contains the version of Windows NT you want to upgrade. Windows NT Setup will detect the previous version and prompt you to upgrade the existing installation. When a pervious version of Windows NT is upgraded, all security settings, applications, and user settings are maintained.

5. How do you create a dual-boot machine with a previous version of Windows NT?

B. Install in a new directory.

5. CORRECT ANSWER: B

When NT Workstation Setup runs, the existing installation will be detected and you will be prompted to upgrade the existing installation or install a fresh copy, overwrite the installation, or install to a different directory in order to maintain both versions on the same computer.

FURTHER REVIEW

CHOOSE THE APPROPRIATE COURSE OF ACTION TO TAKE WHEN THE INSTALLATION PROCESS FAILS

The Windows NT Setup program makes installation errors much less common than they used to be. Several categories of errors might still occur after an installation has been made, but they are also easier to track down and eliminate.

Disk Configuration Errors

The best way to ensure that you are using hardware compatible with Windows NT Workstation is to check the *Hardware Compatibility List (HCL)* to see whether the device is approved for use and supported.

If you have inherited a configuration with a nonsupported SCSI device adapter, you might not be able to boot your newly installed Windows NT Workstation operating system. In that instance, boot to a different operating system and try starting WINNT from the installation CD. You can also use a network installation to try to rectify the problem. Short of these solutions, you might be forced to replace the adapter with one recommended on the Hardware Compatibility List.

Cannot Connect to a Domain Controller Error

The error message `Cannot Connect to a Domain Controller` is one of the more common error messages you might see when you install Windows NT Workstation, change your hardware configuration, or change network settings. There are a number of explanations for this problem.

Carefully verify that you are entering the correct user name and password and that the Caps Lock key is not on. The next thing you should check is that the account name you are using is listed in User Manager for Domains on the primary domain controller. An incorrect password generates a different error message than does the lack of a user account.

You should also check to see whether the machine account has been added to the User Manager for the primary domain controller. Next, open the Network Control Panel and check that the network bindings are properly installed on the Bindings tab. Some bindings such as TCP/IP require not only computer names, but IP addresses and subnet masks as well. If there is a conflict on the network with two machines having the same IP address, you get an error message. Failure to enter the subnet mask (or entering an incorrect subnet mask) also leads to your workstation being unable to find and connect to a domain controller and have its network identity properly verified.

The failure to connect to a domain controller is such a common problem that it is really unfortunate the message isn't more descriptive of the problem.

PRACTICE QUESTIONS

CHOOSE THE APPROPRIATE COURSE OF ACTION TO TAKE WHEN AN APPLICATION FAILS

1. Which type of application is least likely to crash on Windows NT Workstation?

A. MS-DOS-based

B. Windows 16-bit

C. Windows 32-bit

D. Real mode

E. Protected mode

2. How can the Task Manager be opened?

A. Click on the Task Manager button in the Windows NT Security dialog box.

B. Right-click on the status bar and select Task Manager from the resulting context menu.

C. Select Task Manager from the Control Panel.

D. Right-click on the desktop and choose Task Manager from the menu.

E. Choose Task Manager from the Administrative Tools (Common) program group on the Start menu.

3. Which of the following services are part of Internet Information Server?

A. HTTP (WWW)

B. FTP

C. Gopher

D. VRML

E. Internet

4. Closing a 32-bit runaway application can involve closing which one of the following?

A. The desktop

B. The entire session

C. The errant thread

D. Windows NT Workstation

E. Application Manager

5. This question is based on the following scenario. Review the scenario first, followed by the objectives and the proposed solution. Then evaluate the proposed solution by choosing the best answer.

Scenario:

You have a Windows NT Workstation installation. You install a new device that requires a driver to run as a service to operate correctly. You install the device driver and reboot the system. When you attempt to log on, you receive a message that states a service or driver failed to initialize.

Required Result:

Determine which service caused the error to be generated.

Optional Results:

Configure the service to be started manually in the Original Configuration hardware profile.

Configure the service to start automatically in the NewDevice Configuration hardware profile.

Proposed Solution:
After the system boots, run the Event Viewer application to determine if the newly added device driver caused the error.

Create a new hardware profile using the Hardware Profiles tab in the System Control Panel applet.

Use the Devices applet in Control Panel to disable the new device driver in the Original Configuration profile. Also, use Service Manager to change the startup of the new device driver to Manual in the newly created profile.

Evaluation of Proposed Solution:
The proposed solution accomplishes which of the following objectives?

A. The Required Result only

B. The Required Result and both Optional Results

C. The Required Result and only one Optional Result

D. Only both Optional Results

E. Neither the Required Result nor any Optional Results

6. **Alex is attempting to set a service to start automatically when his workstation starts. He calls the system administrator, who tells him this can be accomplished from where?**

A. Control Panel, Network

B. Control Panel, Services

C. Control Panel, System

D. Control Panel, Devices

E. The WinMSD application

ANSWER KEY

1. C
2. B
3. A-B-C
4. E
5. C
6. B

ANSWERS & EXPLANATIONS

CHOOSE THE APPROPRIATE COURSE OF ACTION TO TAKE WHEN AN APPLICATION FAILS

1. Which type of application is least likely to crash on Windows NT Workstation?

C. Windows 32-bit

1. CORRECT ANSWER: C

Win32 applications are less likely to crash under Windows NT Workstation because each is run in its own protected memory space.

MS-DOS applications are also run in their own memory spaces (in their own NTVDMs to be exact); however, if an application attempts to directly access hardware for which NT does not provide a virtual device driver, the application might behave erratically or stop responding all together.

Win16 applications, by default, are all started in a single NTVDM running the Windows on Windows (WOW) subsystem to emulate the cooperative multitasking environment for which they were designed. Because these applications share a common message queue, the failure of one application could jam the message queue, causing the other applications to become unresponsive.

2. How can the Task Manager be opened?

B. Right-click on the status bar and select Task Manager from the resulting context menu.

2. CORRECT ANSWER: B

Right-clicking on the taskbar and selecting Task Manager from the resulting context menu starts the Task Manager system application. Alternatively, Task Manager can be started by the following methods:

- Press Ctrl+Alt+Delete, and then select Task Manager.
- Press Ctrl+Shift+Esc.

3. Which of the following services are part of Internet Information Server?

A. HTTP (WWW)

B. FTP

C. Gopher

3. CORRECT ANSWER: A-B-C

By default, Internet Information Server is comprised of three distinct services. The HTTP service responds to HTTP requests, the FTP service responds to FTP requests, and the Gopher service provides index and search services.

4. Closing a 32-bit runaway application can involve closing which one of the following?

C. The errant thread

4. CORRECT ANSWER: C

Because Win32 applications run in their own private, protected memory spaces, closing an errant Win32 application only involves closing the thread within the application that caused the problem, which will usually result in application termination.

5. Proposed Solution:

- **After the system boots, run the Event Viewer application to determine if the newly added device driver caused the error.**
- **Create a new hardware profile using the Hardware Profiles tab in the System Control Panel applet.**
- **Use the Devices applet in Control Panel to disable the new device driver in the Original Configuration profile. Also, use Service Manager to change the startup of the new device driver to Manual in the newly created profile.**

C. The Required Result and only one Optional Result

5. CORRECT ANSWER: C

By using Event Viewer to view the Application and System logs, you can identify which service or driver failed to load. Event Viewer is accessible from the Administrative Tools (Common) program group from the Start menu. The Proposed Solution accomplishes the Required Result.

Creating another hardware profile will enable you to safely run the device driver as a service until the bugs are worked out of the new installation. Hardware profiles are created through the System Control Panel applet by accessing the Hardware Profiles tab. The Proposed Solution accomplishes the first Optional Result.

Service startup in the various hardware profiles is configured through the Services applet in Control Panel, not through the Devices applet. The Proposed Solution does not accomplish the second Optional Result.

6. Alex is attempting to set a service to start automatically when his workstation starts. He calls the system administrator, who tells him this can be accomplished from where?

B. Control Panel, Services

6. CORRECT ANSWER: B

Service startup behavior is controlled through the Services applet in Control Panel. The startup options for services are Automatic, Manual, and Disabled.

FURTHER REVIEW

CHOOSE THE APPROPRIATE COURSE OF ACTION TO TAKE WHEN AN APPLICATION FAILS

Unlike in MS-DOS and earlier versions of Windows, an application failure won't bring your Windows NT system to a complete halt. Most application failures are recoverable, and in many cases you won't even need to reboot your computer to re-establish a working configuration. That is not to say that a system crash is impossible. It happens very infrequently, however.

Most often, the worst culprits are applications written for MS-DOS or 16-bit Windows applications. These programs tend to crash more frequently than 32-bit Windows applications—which is a good reason to upgrade.

If you have a malfunctioning application, bring up the Task Manager and close the process. You can access the Task Manager by using either your mouse or your keyboard (useful in case one or the other is hung up by a malfunction). To use your keyboard to close an application, complete the following steps:

1. Press Ctrl+Alt+Delete to open the Windows NT Security dialog box.
2. Click on the Task Manager button to open the Task Manager.
3. Click on the Applications tab.
4. Select the offending application and click on the End Task button.
5. Close the Task Manager.

You can also open the Task Manager by right-clicking the taskbar and selecting the Task Manager command.

If you need to end a 16-bit Windows or MS-DOS application, you must close the entire session. When you close a 32-bit Windows application, only the process or thread must be closed.

Using the Application Log

Many errors are logged into the Application log for native Windows NT applications. The developer of the application determines the events that are logged, their codes, and meanings. Often, an application's manual or online Help system documents the events that are to be logged in the Application log, as well as your ability to control which events are noted.

Service Failures

Many applications run as *services* on Windows NT Workstation. Internet Information Server's three applications (WWW, FTP, and Gopher), for example, all are services. Services are started, stopped, and paused from within either their central administrative tool (for IIS, that tool is the Internet Service Manager) or the Services Control Panel. If you want to configure a service so that it runs automatically when your workstation boots, more often than not you will set this behavior in the Services Control Panel.

Sooner or later, you will see this infamous error message and instruction when your Windows NT Workstation starts up after the load phase:

```
One or more services failed to start.
Please see the Event Viewer for details.
```

Although the error message doesn't tell you anything useful, the Event Viewer does. Open the System log and look under the Event heading for the event code that has a value of 6005. That event is an informational message that indicates the EventLog service has started up. Any event prior to that is a boot event and should be resolved. Double-click on the event message to view an Event Detail dialog box.

PRACTICE QUESTIONS

CHOOSE THE APPROPRIATE COURSE OF ACTION TO TAKE WHEN A USER CANNOT ACCESS A RESOURCE

1. **What is the most likely cause of a failure to log on to a network from a workstation you have used in the past?**
   A. The account has expired.
   B. Incorrect user name.
   C. Incorrect media.
   D. Incorrect frame type.
   E. Caps Lock key is enabled.

2. **If you cannot log on to a server from a workstation you were using earlier, but you are certain that the user name and password are correct, what should you check next?**
   A. Verify that you are logging on to the correct domain or workgroup.
   B. Check the media.
   C. Verify frame types.
   D. Look for CRC errors.
   E. Ensure the WINLOGON process is running on the server.

3. **If you cannot log on to the network from a workstation you have used earlier, but you are certain that the user name, password, and domain name are correct, what is the next logical step to try?**
   A. Shut down the network and begin an emergency repair procedure.
   B. Verify that the proper permissions are stored in the SAM database.
   C. Attempt to log on using another account.
   D. Look for CRC errors.
   E. Ensure the Server service is active by pinging the workstation from another computer on the network.

4. **If you cannot log on to a workstation using any account, what is the next logical step in solving the problem?**
   A. Repair the accounts database by using the emergency repair process.
   B. Verify the proper permissions are stored in the SAM database.
   C. Look for CRC errors.
   D. Verify frame types.
   E. Verify the Server service is running by pinging the workstation from another computer on the network.

5. **If a user can't access a file, a share, a printer, or any other resource, what should you check?**
   A. The resource permissions
   B. User group membership
   C. The Server service on the client workstation
   D. The Workstation service on the client workstation
   E. All of the above

6. **If you suspect a logon problem from a workstation in a Microsoft Domain environment, you should check the Control Panel Services application to ensure that which of the following services are running properly?**

   A. The NetLogon service

   B. The Server service

   C. The Workstation service

   D. The Bindings service

   E. The User service

7. **This question is based on the following scenario. Review the scenario first, followed by the objectives and the proposed solution. Then evaluate the proposed solution by choosing the best answer.**

   Scenario:
   Heidi calls you stating that she cannot log on to her Windows NT Workstation.

   Required Result:
   Provide the user with directions for troubleshooting the problem from the workstation.

   Optional Results:
   Ensure the account is not locked out.

   Reset Heidi's password.

   Proposed Solution:
   Ask the user to ensure the Domain: selection in the Logon dialog box is set to WebWorks and not the local machine.

   Log on to the workstation with your administrator account.

   From the command line run the command:

   ```
   setpass heidi password
   ```

   Open User Manager, double-click on the account, and ensure the Account Locked Out box is not checked.

   Evaluation of Proposed Solution:
   The proposed solution accomplishes which of the following stated objectives?

   A. The Required Result only

   B. The Required Result and both Optional Results

   C. The Required Result and only one Optional Result

   D. Only one Optional Result

   E. Neither the Required Result nor any Optional Results

8. **If a user cannot access a file, a share, a printer, or any other resource on your workstation only, what should you check?**

   A. The resource permissions

   B. User group membership

   C. The Server service on your workstation

   D. The Workstation service on the client workstation

   E. The Server service on the client's workstation

ANSWER KEY

1. E	4. A	7. D
2. A	5. A-B-D	8. A-B-C
3. C	6. A	

ANSWERS & EXPLANATIONS

CHOOSE THE APPROPRIATE COURSE OF ACTION TO TAKE WHEN A USER CANNOT ACCESS A RESOURCE

1. What is the most likely cause of a failure to log on to a network from a workstation you have used in the past?

E. Caps Lock key is enabled.

1. CORRECT ANSWER: E

The most likely cause of login failure is the Caps Lock key being enabled. Because NT passwords are case sensitive but are never displayed onscreen, the most common reason for failed logons is that the correct password was entered in the wrong case.

2. If you cannot log on to a server from a workstation you were using earlier, but you are certain that the user name and password are correct, what should you check next?

A. Verify that you are logging on to the correct domain or workgroup.

2. CORRECT ANSWER: A

When logging on to a Windows NT Workstation, you have the option of authenticating to a domain or the local workstation, depending upon the entry in the Domain: drop-down list in the Logon dialog box. By default, the value is "remembered" from the last logon. If another user has used the workstation since your last session, however, the security authority (i.e., the workstation or a domain) could have been changed.

3. If you cannot log on to the network from a workstation you have used earlier, but you are certain that the user name, password, and domain name are correct, what is the next logical step to try?

C. Attempt to log on using another account.

3. CORRECT ANSWER: C

The quickest way to diagnose logon problems with a particular account is to eliminate as many variables as possible. In this case, it is easy to eliminate the workstation and network by logging in with another account. If that account is authenticated successfully, the original account should be checked for such things as account expiration or account lock out. If the second account cannot log in either, you should begin suspecting a problem with the workstation.

4. If you cannot log on to a workstation using any account, what is the next logical step in solving the problem?

A. Repair the accounts database by using the emergency repair process.

4. CORRECT ANSWER: A

If no accounts can be authenticated by the workstation, you are effectively locked out. The only alternative is to repair the accounts database using Windows NT Setup and the ERD. You do update your ERD on a regular basis, don't you?

5. **If a user can't access a file, a share, a printer, or any other resource, what should you check?**

   A. The resource permissions

   B. User group membership

   D. The Workstation service on the client workstation

5. CORRECT ANSWER: A-B-D

If a user cannot access a resource, the obvious first step is to check the permissions on the resource. If there are any No Access permissions, the user account should be checked for membership in any of the groups assigned the No Access permission to the resource.

Another area to check is the Workstation service on the client computer. The Workstation service is responsible for enabling the local workstation to attach to network resources. If this service is disabled or stopped, the workstation will not be able to access any network resources.

6. **If you suspect a logon problem from a workstation in a Microsoft Domain environment, you should check the Control Panel Services application to ensure that which of the following services are running properly?**

   A. The NetLogon service

6. CORRECT ANSWER: A

When a user attempts to log on to a workstation by authenticating to a domain controller, the information is passed to the NetLogon service that is responsible for authenticating the user with the domain controller. If the user is completing a local logon, the WinLogon service authenticates the user with the workstation's SAM database.

7. **Proposed Solution:**

   - **Ask the user to ensure the Domain: selection in the Logon dialog box is set to WebWorks and not the local machine.**
   - **Log on to the workstation with your administrator account.**
   - **From the command line run the command:**

     ```
     setpass heidi password
     ```

   - **Open User Manager, double-click on the account, and ensure the Account Locked Out box is not checked.**

   D. Only one Optional Result

7. CORRECT ANSWER: D

Two of the most common errors that prevent users from logging on to a Windows NT Workstation are an improper authenticating authority and an invalid password caused by the Caps Lock key being enabled. Because the Proposed Solution only mentions checking one of these possible errors, the Proposed Solution does not achieve the Required Result.

The account lockout status is determined by accessing the properties of the account through User Manager. The Proposed Solution accomplishes the first Optional Result.

User passwords are reset through User Manager. Windows NT does not provide any command line utilities for changing, checking, or resetting a user's password. The Proposed Solution does not accomplish the second Optional Result.

8. If a user cannot access a file, a share, a printer, or any other resource on your workstation only, what should you check?

A. The resource permissions

B. User group membership

C. The Server service on your workstation

8. CORRECT ANSWER: A-B-C

If a user cannot access a resource, the obvious first step is to check the permissions on the resource. If there are any No Access permissions set, the user account should be checked for membership in any of the groups assigned the No Access permission to the resource.

Another area to check is the Server service on the resource-providing computer. The Server service is responsible for enabling remote workstations to connect to shared resources on the local workstation. If this service is disabled or stopped, the workstation will not be able to provide access to any network resources.

FURTHER REVIEW

CHOOSE THE APPROPRIATE COURSE OF ACTION TO TAKE WHEN A USER CANNOT ACCESS A RESOURCE

Windows NT's security system controls access to network resources through user and machine accounts. Your logon to a particular domain or machine is validated by a domain controller or the local workstation that provides you with certain privileges and rights as registered in the Security Accounts Manager (SAM) database. When this security process breaks down, the user is not able to access resources. The following sections discuss some common reasons why users cannot successfully access local or remote resources.

Password Issues

A password enables you to log on to a particular user account. To log on successfully, you must know both the user name and the exact password. The important thing to know about passwords is that they are *case sensitive*.

To protect passwords, Windows NT has an option that enables you to retire a password after a certain period of time. You can also set an option that requires Windows NT Workstation users to change the assigned password the first time they log on to the system. Users logging on after that time are required to change their passwords.

Additionally, Windows NT domain controllers enable you to set a lockout policy that will lock out accounts after a certain number of incorrect logon attempts. If a user is unable to log on, a check should be completed to ensure the account is not locked out. This can be accomplished with User Manager.

Accessing Shared Resources

Accessing files, shared folders (or simply shares), printer shares, and other shared resources requires resource permissions. To create a share for an object, typically you right-click on the object and select the Sharing command. In many instances, the Sharing tab of the object's properties sheet appears and enables you to specify users, groups, and access privileges that are allowed.

The person who creates the resource "owns" the resource and has full privileges to it. The administrator also has full access to resources and can take ownership of them. When an administrator takes ownership of a resource, the original owner's access to the resource is denied. This is a safety mechanism to make it obvious that ownership has been removed and that the resource has been fully taken over.

When users can't access a shared resource, they might not have the privileges required to do so. Try logging on under a different account to attempt to access that resource. If the resource has been accessed in the past with a particular user account, make sure that the resource is spelled correctly and that it has been located properly.

Because management of shared resources is one of the central tasks for which an administrator is expected to be responsible, this topic is likely to be on the exam. The inability to access a share is one of the most common problems requiring resolution by an administrator.

PRACTICE QUESTIONS

MODIFY THE REGISTRY USING THE APPROPRIATE TOOLS IN A GIVEN SITUATION

1. **The System tab in the Windows NT Diagnostics box displays information stored in the Registry under which hive?**

   A. HKEY_LOCAL_MACHINE\SOFTWARE

   B. HKEY_LOCAL_MACHINE\HARDWARE

   C. HKEY_LOCAL_MACHINE\SOFTWARE\MICROSOFT\WINDOWS NT\CurrentVersion

   D. HKEY_LOCAL_MACHINE\SYSTEM

   E. HKEY_CLASSES_ROOT

2. **This question is based on the following scenario. Review the scenario first, followed by the objectives and the proposed solution. Then evaluate the proposed solution by choosing the best answer.**

   Scenario:
   A Windows NT Workstation 4 user calls you, stating that she was trying to change the Registered User Name of the Windows NT installation. In the process, she inadvertently deleted the HKEY_LOCAL_MACHINE\HARDWARE\RESOURCEMAP key.

   Required Result:
   Restore the missing Registry hive.

   Optional Results:
   Change the registered user name.

   Change the source path from E:\I386 to D:\I386 for the installation files when installing new Windows NT components.

   Proposed Solution:
   Reboot the system and invoke the Last Known Good configuration.

   Use the System Control Panel applet to change the user name.

   Edit the Registry directly, changing the value of HKEY_LOCAL_MACHINE\SOFTWARE\Microsoft\Windows NT\CurrentVersion\SourcePath key from "E:\I386" to "D:\I386".

   Evaluation of Proposed Solution:
   The proposed solution accomplishes which of the following stated objectives?

   A. The Required Result only

   B. The Required Result and both Optional Results

   C. The Required Result and only one Optional Result

   D. Only one Optional Result

   E. Neither the Required Result nor any Optional Results

3. **Version information is stored in the Windows NT 4 Registry under which hive?**

   A. HKEY_LOCAL_MACHINE\SOFTWARE

B. HKEY_LOCAL_MACHINE\SOFTWARE\MICROSOFT\WINDOWS NT

C. HKEY_LOCAL_MACHINE\SOFTWARE\MICROSOFT\WINDOWS NT\CurrentVersion

D. HKEY_LOCAL_MACHINE\SYSTEM

E. HKEY_CLASSES_ROOT

4. **Service information is stored in the Windows NT Registry under which hive?**

A. HKEY_LOCAL_MACHINE\SOFTWARE

B. HKEY_LOCAL_MACHINE\SOFTWARE\MICROSOFT\WINDOWS NT

C. HKEY_LOCAL_MACHINE\SOFTWARE\MICROSOFT\WINDOWS NT\CurrentVersion

D. HKEY_LOCAL_MACHINE\SYSTEM

E. HKEY_CLASSES_ROOT

5. **By default, members of which groups can access the Registry?**

A. Administrators

B. Power Users

C. Users

D. Replicator

E. Backup Operators

6. **Select all of the tools that can be used to directly edit entries in the Registry.**

A. Task Manager

B. Regedit

C. User Manager

D. Regedt32

E. Control Panel

7. **Where is the Registry Editor started?**

A. From the Control Panel

B. Under Administrative Utilities

C. From the Run command

D. As a choice on the menu that appears when you press Ctrl+Alt+Del

E. From the System Control Panel applet

8. **Which of the following is a graphical—and limiting—version of the Registry Editor that is found in the Administrative Tools folder?**

A. Windows NT Diagnostics program

B. Performance Monitor

C. Network Monitor

D. Task Manager

E. User Manager

9. **This question is based on the following scenario. Review the scenario first, followed by the objectives and the proposed solution. Then evaluate the proposed solution by choosing the best answer.**

Scenario:

You have a Windows NT Workstation user that calls you about changing the default behavior of the Windows NT Logon dialog box to not show the last user that logged on. The user tried to edit the Registry and thinks he might have deleted a key.

Required Result:
Restore the Registry.

Optional Results:
Inform the user of where the key resides to change the default behavior of the Windows NT Logon dialog box.

Inform the user of the proper way to edit the Registry key.

Proposed Solution:
From REGEDT32, choose Restore All from the Registry menu.

Tell the user the key is HKEY_LOCAL_MACHINE\SOFTWARE\Microsoft\Windows NT\CurrentVersion\WinLogon\DefaultUserName.

Tell the user to change the value of the key to "" to disable the display of the user name in the Windows NT Logon dialog box.

Evaluation of Proposed Solution:
The proposed solution accomplishes which of the following stated objectives?

A. The Required Result only

B. The Required Result and both Optional Results

C. The Required Result and only one Optional Result

D. Only one Optional Result

E. Neither the Required Result nor any Optional Results

10. By default, on most systems the Registry file is located where?

A. C:\

B. C:\WINNT

C. C:\WINNT\SYSTEM32

D. C:\WINNT\SYSTEM32\DRIVERS

E. C:\WINNT\SYSTEM\REGISTRY

ANSWER KEY

1. B
2. C
3. B
4. D
5. A-B
6. B-D
7. C
8. A
9. E
10. B

ANSWERS & EXPLANATIONS

MODIFY THE REGISTRY USING THE APPROPRIATE TOOLS IN A GIVEN SITUATION

1. The System tab in the Windows NT Diagnostics box displays information stored in the Registry under which hive?

B. HKEY_LOCAL_MACHINE\HARDWARE

1. CORRECT ANSWER: B

The System tab in WinMSD displays information stored in the HKEY_LOCAL_MACHINE\HARDWARE key, which contains information about the hardware devices available to Windows NT.

2. Proposed Solution:

- **Reboot the system and invoke the Last Known Good configuration.**
- **Use the System Control Panel applet to change the user name.**
- **Edit the Registry directly, changing the value of HKEY_LOCAL_MACHINE\SOFTWARE\Microsoft\Windows NT\CurrentVersion\SourcePath key from "E:\I386" to "D:\I386".**

C. The Required Result and only one Optional Result

2. CORRECT ANSWER: C

Rebooting the workstation and invoking the Last Known Good configuration will restore the Registry, effectively undoing any changes completed since the last successful boot. The Proposed Solution accomplishes the Required Result.

The user name associated with the Windows NT installation cannot be changed with the System applet; it can only be changed by directly editing the Registry. The Proposed Solution does not achieve the first Optional Result.

The source path for Windows NT installation files must also be changed by directly editing the Registry key listed in the Proposed Solution. The Proposed Solution accomplishes the second Optional Result.

3. Version information is stored in the Windows NT 4 Registry under which hive?

B. HKEY_LOCAL_MACHINE\SOFTWARE\MICROSOFT\WINDOWS NT

3. CORRECT ANSWER: B

HKEY_LOCAL_MACHINE\SOFTWARE\MICROSOFT\WINDOWS NT\CurrentVersion stores information about the current version of Windows NT on the machine.

4. Service information is stored in the Windows NT Registry under which hive?

D. HKEY_LOCAL_MACHINE\SYSTEM

4. CORRECT ANSWER: D

HKEY_LOCAL_MACHINE\SYSTEM\CurrentControlSet\Services stores information about the current services available to Windows NT on the machine.

5. By default, members of which groups can access the Registry?

A. Administrators

B. Power Users

5. CORRECT ANSWER: A-B

Power Users and Administrators, by default, are the only groups that can access the Registry. The Backup Operators group members can access the Registry for purposes of conducting backup and restore operations.

6. Select all of the tools that can be used to directly edit entries in the Registry.

B. Regedit

D. Regedt32

6. CORRECT ANSWER: B-D

REGDIT and REGEDT32 are the only two tools included with Windows NT Workstation that enable you to directly edit the Registry. Control Panel and User Manager provide an application interface to the Registry, but they do the actual modifications for you.

7. Where is the Registry Editor started?

C. From the Run command

7. CORRECT ANSWER: C

Because the Registry Editor is such a powerful tool, Microsoft made sure curious users would not be able to easily access a tool to edit the Registry.

8. Which of the following is a graphical—and limiting—version of the Registry Editor that is found in the Administrative Tools folder?

A. Windows NT Diagnostics program

8. CORRECT ANSWER: A

WinMSD, found in the Administrative Tools (Common) program folder on the Start menu, is a graphical read-only version of a Registry editing tool.

9. Proposed Solution:

- **From REGEDT32, choose Restore All from the Registry menu.**
- **Tell the user the key is HKEY_LOCAL_MACHINE\SOFTWARE\Microsoft\Windows NT\CurrentVersion\WinLogon\DefaultUserName.**
- **Tell the user to change the value of the key to "" to disable the display of the user name in the Windows NT Logon dialog box.**

E. Neither the Required Result nor any Optional Results

9. CORRECT ANSWER: E

After a Registry key is deleted or altered with REGEDT32, there is no way to undo the changes. The only way to restore the Registry is to reboot the system and invoke the Last Known Good configuration. If the Registry keys are saved, they can be restored to the current Registry with REGEDT32 (via the Restore option from the Registry menu). The Proposed Solution does not accomplish the Required Result.

The Registry key that can be used to change the default behavior of the WinLogon process is located in the following key:

HKEY_LOCAL_MACHINE\SOFTWARE\Microsoft\Windows NT\CurrentVersion\WinLogon\DONTDISPLAYLASTUSERNAME

The key should be set to a value of 1 to change the default behavior. The Proposed Solution does not accomplish the first Optional Result.

The key specified in the Proposed Solution contains the user name of the last user to successfully log on to the system.

The Registry should never be edited directly if there is a utility that will accomplish the same task. The C2 Security Configuration Tool, available in the Windows NT Workstation Resource Kit, will automatically change the default behavior of the Windows NT Logon dialog box. The Proposed Solution does not accomplish the second Optional Result.

10. By default, on most systems the Registry file is located where?

B. C:\WINNT

10. CORRECT ANSWER: B

The default location of the Registry is C:\WINNT.

FURTHER REVIEW

MODIFY THE REGISTRY USING THE APPROPRIATE TOOLS IN A GIVEN SITUATION

Windows NT 4 introduced the Registry database to this operating system, building on an early version in Windows NT 3.1 that stored OLE location information on object servers. The first complete Registry appeared in Windows 95, although the Windows 95 and Windows NT Registry differ significantly enough to prevent a direct upgrade from Windows 95 to Windows NT. The Registry is a database of settings and parameters. Among the features set by the Registry are the nature of the interface, operating system hardware and software settings, user preferences, and other settings. Prior to Windows NT Workstation and Server 3.51, these settings appeared as sections and lines in various .INI files.

The Registry is hierarchical, and each branch is referred to as a *hive*. Individual sub-branches are called *keys*, which are actually binary files. The top or first key of a hive is the *primary key*; each key is composed of subkeys that take value entries. Most Registry entries are permanent, although some are session-dependent, transient, and never written to disk. An example of a *transient key* is the HKEY_LOCAL_MACHINE\Hardware, which is generated by automatic hardware detection by the Hardware Recognizer (ntdetect.com for Intel computers). Another transient value is the information written as part of a logon for a session, including security tokens.

Only members of the Administrators or Power Users group can access the Registry by default. You can assign other users rights to modify all or part of the Registry by hives, but you should think long and hard before doing so. The potential to compromise security or corrupt an installation is high. By default, any user can see the Registry files, but cannot edit, delete, or copy Registry files without specific permission to do so.

Modifying the Registry

You use the Registry Editor to view and modify the Windows NT Registry. Of the two versions of the Registry Editor, regedt32.exe and regedit.exe, the former is more generally useful and offers more options.

Whenever you change a setting in a Control Panel or alter your desktop, you are writing changes to the Registry associated with the user account profile with which you logged on. If you want to view Registry information relating to services, resources, drivers, memory, displays, or network components, you can use the Windows NT Diagnostics program (WINMSD). This utility is found in the <System Root>\System32 folder, or in the Administrative Tools folder on the Programs submenu of the Start menu.

When you alter a value in the Registry using the Registry Editor, the changes you can make are unlimited and can be hazardous to your computer's health. The only recovery method that you can count on in that instance is to reinstall Windows NT or use the repair disk.

The five root keys and their subtrees are as follows:

- *HKEY_CLASSES_ROOT.* This subtree stores OLE, file, class, and other associations that enable a program to launch when a data file is opened. Although the HKEY_CLASSES_ROOT is displayed as a root key, it is actually a subkey of HKEY_LOCAL_MACHINE\Software.
- *HKEY_CURRENT_USER.* All user settings, profiles, environment variables, interface settings, program groups, printer connections, application preferences, and network connections for each user are stored in the subkeys of this root key.
- *HKEY_LOCAL_MACHINE.* This subkey contains information that identifies the computer on which the Registry is stored. Information in this key includes settings for hardware such as memory, disk drives, network adapters, and peripheral devices. Any software that supports hardware—device drivers, system services, system boot parameters, and other data—also is contained in this subkey.
- *HKEY_USERS.* All data on individual user profiles is stored in this subkey. Windows NT stores local profiles in the Registry, and the values are maintained in this subkey.
- *HKEY_CURRENT_CONFIG.* The current configuration for software and any machine values are stored in this key. Among the settings stored in this root key are display device setup and control values required to restore the configuration when the program launches or your computer starts up.

When the system loads the Registry, most of the data is contained in the HKEY_LOCAL_MACHINE and HKEY_USERS keys. As an example of the kinds of changes you can make, individual settings that you make in the Control Panels are written back to different keys in the Registry. You can modify those settings directly. Table 7.1 shows you the location of the different Control Panel settings. When you install a program using the Add/Remove Programs Control Panel, the data isn't written directly to the Registry, but the installer creates Registry entries in the Software hive.

TABLE 7.1 CONTROL PANEL RELATIONS TO REGISTRY KEYS

Control Panel	*Registry Data Location*
Accessibility Options	HEKY_CURRENT_USER\Control Panel\Accessibility
Add/Remove Software	HEKY_CURRENT_USER\Console\Application Console
Date/Time	HKEY_LOCAL_MACHINE\System\CurrentControl Set\Control\TimeZoneInformation
Devices	HKEY_LOCAL_MACHINE\System\CurrentControlSet\Services
Display (Machine settings)	HKEY_LOCAL_MACHINE\Hardware\ResourceMap\Video
Display (User settings)	HKEY_CURRENT_USER\Control Panel\Desktop
Fast Find	HKEY_LOCAL_MACHINE\Software\Microsoft\Shared Tools\Fast Find
Fonts	HKEY_LOCAL_MACHINE\Software\Microsoft\Windows NT\CurrentVersion\Fonts

Control Panel	*Registry Data Location*
Internet	HKEY_LOCAL_MACHINE\Software\Microsoft\Windows\CurrentVersion\Internet Settings
Keyboard	HKEY_CURRENT_USER\Control Panel\Desktop
Mail	Several locations
Modems	HKEY_LOCAL_MACHINE\Software\Microsoft\Windows\CurrentVersion\Unimodem
Mouse	HKEY_CURRENT_USER\Control Panel\Mouse
Multimedia	HKEY_LOCAL_MACHINE\Software\Microsoft\Windows\Multimedia
Network	Several locations
PC Card	HKEY_LOCAL_MACHINE\Hardware\Description\System\PCMCIA PCCARDs
Ports	HKEY_LOCAL_MACHINE\Hardware\ResourceMap
Printers	HKEY_CURRENT_USER\Printers
Regional Settings	HKEY_CURRENT_USER\ControlPanel\International
SCSI Adapters	HKEY_LOCAL_MACHINE\Hardware\ResourceMap\ScsiAdapter
Server	Several locations
Services	HKEY_LOCAL_MACHINE\System\CurrentControlSet\Services
Sounds	HKEY_CURRENT_USER\AppEvent\Schemes\Apps\Default
System	Several locations
Tape Devices	HKEY_LOCAL_MACHINE\Hardware\ResourceMap\OtherDrivers\TapeDevices
Telephony	HKEY_LOCAL_MACHINE\Software\Microsoft\Windows\CurrentVersion\Telephony
UPS	HKEY_LOCAL_MACHINE\System\CurrentControlSet\Services\UPS

Backing Up the Registry

The most important thing you can do to protect your investment in your system's configuration is to back up the Registry files. When you create an ERD, as described earlier in this chapter, you back up only specific hives of the Registry. You should keep a full backup of the Registry on hand.

You find the Registry file in the folder %system root%\System32\Config. For most installations the %system root% is typically C:\WINNT. An individual user's Registry data is written to the ntuser.dat file stored in that user's folder at the location C:\WINNT\Profiles\<username>\NTUSER.DAT. When a user logs on to the workstation, a Profile folder is created for the user, with an ntuser.dat file to hold the user's profile. Roaming profiles for a domain are stored as the original copy of the ntuser.dat file on the domain controller. The following CONFIG folder files store direct information on Registry hives:

- DEFAULT
- NTUSER.DAT
- SAM
- SECURITY
- SOFTWARE

- SYSTEM
- USERDIFF
- USERDIFR

Several files are associated with each Registry hive in the CONFIG folder. The first and primary file takes no extension. The CONFIG directory also contains auxiliary files for the Registry, which are the backup, log, and event files. These files have the same names as those listed previously, but take the .LOG, .EVT, or .SAV extension. The System file also has a system.alt file associated with it. The .EVT, or event, files are viewable in the Event Viewer and contain audited events. Log files store changes that can be rolled back. The .SAV files are part of the Last Known Good boot configuration that enables you to restore your Registry based on your last booted session. The Last Known Good option was described earlier in this chapter.

The LOG file is a backup file that enables changes to be rolled back. It is a fault-tolerance feature. Changes are written to the LOG file first. When the data is completely written in the LOG file, updating of the matching Registry hive begins. The data section to be changed is marked, and the data is transferred. When the data transfer is complete, the update flag is reset to indicate successful transfer. Should there be a problem or should your computer malfunction during the transfer, the update is begins again from scratch.

The SYSTEM file is updated in a somewhat different manner because your computer relies on that key to start up. The duplicate system.alt file is used and operates as the replacement for a .LOG file. The entire file is mirrored and replicated. Then, in the event of a crash, the backup file is used and the entire file is replaced.

▼ NOTE

It is unnecessary to back up the entire Registry. Much of the information is transitory and session-dependent. Only specific portions of the Registry need to be protected. The files of greatest importance are the SYSTEM and SOFTWARE files. They are generally small and can fit on a single floppy disk.

To back up the Registry, use the RDISK program described earlier in this chapter and set that option. Do not try to copy the files directly to a disk. You can also back up individual hive files from within the Registry Editor by using the Save Key command on the Registry menu. You can use the Restore Key command to load those backup files.

The hives of the Registry are locked and cannot be accessed to be copied directly. If you have a dual-boot system, or if you boot your system using MS-DOS or some other operating system, these files are not locked and may be copied directly to another drive or volume.

You can view Registry files on a FAT volume from any other operating system. If the file system is an NTFS volume, only a Windows NT or Linux system running a disk access utility can view the files, read them, and copy them. In Windows NT, one program that can do this is NTFSDOS.EXE.

For a temporary copy of a key, use the Restore Volatile command rather than the Restore Key command. This command loads the key in the Registry Editor, but it does not load that key again in a future session after your computer reboots.

Changing the Registry Size

The default size of the Windows NT Workstation Registry is sufficient for most configurations. If you have a large organization and store a lot of user profiles and application data configurations, however, the Registry might run out of room. You might need to alter the allowed size of the Registry. To change the maximum Registry size, complete the following steps:

1. Double-click the System icon in the Control Panel folder.
2. Click the Performance tab, and then click the Change button in the Virtual Memory section to view the Virtual Memory dialog box.
3. Enter a size in the Maximum Registry Size (MB) text box, and then click OK.

The Registry can be somewhat larger than the value entered in the System Control Panel. It is related to the size of your paging file, which is related to the amount of installed RAM in your system. When the Registry exceeds the size you set, it brings your system to a halt with a STOP error. This problem occurs very rarely unless you attempt to reduce the size of the Registry artificially. Keep a maximum Registry size about 2MB larger than the current size in the Virtual Memory dialog box.

Troubleshooting the Registry

Several problems can be directly related to Registry errors. The most common categories of problems are the following:

- Your computer won't boot properly or at all.
- Your computer looks or works differently than it once did.
- Your computer won't shut down correctly.
- You receive the "Blue Screen of Death" resulting from a STOP error.
- A software or hardware component that operated correctly stops working without any physical changes being made to the files or to the device.
- Something stops working after you add new software or hardware, and the two are not known to be incompatible.

Most of these error conditions are at least correctable from backup. The one really frightening error is the STOP error because you can't access your machine. To correct the Blue Screen of Death, try booting from your boot disk and running the Check Disk program to repair the type of errors associated with disk and file problems. The CHDSK.EXE program is located in the <SYSTEM ROOT>\SYSTEM32 directory.

PRACTICE QUESTIONS

IMPLEMENT ADVANCED TECHNIQUES TO RESOLVE VARIOUS PROBLEMS

1. **This question is based on the following scenario. Review the scenario first, followed by the objectives and the proposed solution. Then evaluate the proposed solution by choosing the best answer.**

   Scenario:
   You have a Windows NT Workstation user that calls asking various questions about the Event Viewer application.

   Required Result:
   Teach the user how to filter events in Event Viewer.

   Optional Results:
   Explain to the user which local groups are authorized to view Event Log information.

   Explain to the user how event logs can be exported to other file formats.

   Proposed Solution:
   An Event Viewer filter is enabled by selecting Filter from the Log menu within Event Viewer. You can filter on specific times, specific sources of errors (such as drivers or services), specific categories of errors, or user, computer, or event ids.

   Only Administrators and Power Users are able to view the Application and System Event Logs by default. The Security log is accessible only by members of the Administrators group.

   The only three export file formats are the Event Log format (*.evt), simple text file (*.txt), and comma delimited text (*.txt). The comma delimited text format can then be imported into a database or spreadsheet for further analysis.

   Evaluation of Proposed Solution:
   The proposed solution accomplishes which of the following stated objectives?

   A. The Required Result only

   B. The Required Result and both Optional Results

   C. The Required Result and only one Optional Result

   D. Only one Optional Result

   E. Neither the Required Result nor any Optional Results

2. **There is only one restriction you can place on who can see Event Log information. To whom does that restriction apply?**

   A. Administrators

   B. Users

   C. Guests

   D. Everyone

   E. Power Users

3. **If a Windows NT service fails to start, what tool should you use?**

   A. Performance Monitor

   B. Event Viewer

C. Tracert

D. System Control Panel applet

E. WinMSD

4. This question is based on the following scenario. Review the scenario first, followed by the objectives and the proposed solution. Then evaluate the proposed solution by choosing the best answer.

Scenario:
A user contacts you requesting to know how the Event Logs for a busy computer should be configured.

Required Result:
Instruct the user how to access the settings for the Event Logs.

Optional Results:
Set the log sizes to 2MB each.

Configure the Event Logs to overwrite events more than 14 days old.

Proposed Solution:
From the Logs menu, select the Log Settings option.

In the Maximum Log Size edit box, enter 2MB.

In the Event Log Wrapping section, click the Overwrite Events Older Than radio button. Use the spinner control to change the value to 14 days.

Evaluation of Proposed Solution:
The proposed solution accomplishes which of the following stated objectives?

A. The Required Result only

B. The Required Result and both Optional Results

C. The Required Result and only one Optional Result

D. Only one Optional Result

E. Neither the Required Result nor any Optional Results

5. Select all of the common causes of device problems that trigger events with a stop sign in the System Event Log.

A. Interrupt conflicts

B. Installation of graphics-intensive software packages

C. Initialization failure of new software

D. SCSI problems

E. Open files not written to a tape device

6. The security log indicates a Failure Audit with a _________ and a Success Audit with a __________.

A. Warning Triangle / Exclamation

B. Stop Sign / Exclamation

C. Padlock / Open Padlock

D. Broken Key / Key

E. Padlock / Key

7. Recovery options can be configured by which of the following:

A. REGEDT32

B. System Control Panel applet

C. Services Control Panel application

D. Server applet in Control Panel

E. Directly editing the BOOT.INI file

8. If your Windows NT-based computer manages to boot successfully, yet does not perform correctly, what is the first thing to check?

A. System Event Log

B. Performance Monitor

C. Server applet in Control Panel

D. BOOT.INI

E. WinMSD

9. This question is based on the following scenario. Review the scenario first, followed by the objectives and the proposed solution. Then evaluate the proposed solution by choosing the best answer.

Scenario:
You have a Windows NT workstation that has displayed numerous errors relating to driver initialization, IRQ conflicts, and virtual memory.

Required Result:
Gather more information on the specific errors.

Optional Results:
Determine which interrupt request lines are available.

Reconfigure the virtual memory settings.

Proposed Solution:
Use Event Viewer to check the System and Application Logs for specific errors.

Use the Resources tab in WinMSD to determine which IRQs are free.

Use the Memory tab in WinMSD to view and reconfigure the virtual memory settings.

Evaluation of Proposed Solution:
The proposed solution accomplishes which of the following stated objectives?

A. The Required Result only

B. The Required Result and both Optional Results

C. The Required Result and only one Optional Result

D. Only one Optional Result

E. Neither the Required Result nor any Optional Results

10. Warning events are symbolized in the System log—as displayed in Event Viewer—by which of the following symbols?

A. Stop sign

B. Exclamation mark

C. Question mark

D. An "I" in a blue circle

E. Key symbol

ANSWER KEY

1. D
2. C
3. B
4. C
5. A-D
6. E
7. B-E
8. A
9. C
10. B

ANSWERS & EXPLANATIONS

IMPLEMENT ADVANCED TECHNIQUES TO RESOLVE VARIOUS PROBLEMS

1. Proposed Solution:

- **An Event Viewer filter is enabled by selecting Filter from the Log menu within Event Viewer. You can filter on specific times, specific sources of errors (such as drivers or services), specific categories of errors, or user, computer, or event ids.**
- **Only Administrators and Power Users are able to view the Application and System Event Logs by default. The Security log is accessible only by members of the Administrators group.**
- **The only three export file formats are the Event Log format (*.evt), simple text file (*.txt), and comma delimited text (*.txt). The comma delimited text format can then be imported into a database or spreadsheet for further analysis.**

D. Only one Optional Result

1. CORRECT ANSWER: D

Filters are enabled through the View menu, not the Log menu as suggested by the Proposed Solution. All information presented on the types of available filters in the Proposed Solution is correct. The Proposed Solution does not accomplish the Required Result.

By default, the Event Logs can be viewed by anyone with access to the workstation. Additionally, Event Logs from other machines can be remotely viewed through Event Viewer. The Proposed Solution does not accomplish the first Optional Result.

To restrict who can open the System or Application logs, you can set the following key:

HKEY_LOCAL_MACHINE\System\CurrentControlSet\
Services\EventLog\-<log_name>

The RestrictGuestAccess value of type REG_DWORD is set to 1. When the RestrictGuestAccess is set to 0 or doesn't exist, the default condition is for anyone to be able to access these two logs.

The Event Log supports three types of files for exporting Event Logs: the Event Log (*.evt) format, ASCII text (*.txt), and comma delimited text (*.txt). An Event Log can be exported by selecting the Save As option from the Log menu within Event Viewer. The Proposed Solution accomplishes the second Optional Result.

2. There is only one restriction you can place on who can see Event Log information. That restriction applies to whom?

C. Guests

2. CORRECT ANSWER: C

Setting the following registry key

HKEY_LOCAL_MACHINE\System\CurrentControlSet\
Services\EventLog\-<log_name>

to a value of 1 will restrict members of the Guests local group from accessing the Event Logs. If the above key is set to 0 or is nonexistent, there will be no restrictions on who can view the Event Logs.

3. If a Windows NT service fails to start, what tool should you use?

B. Event Viewer

3. CORRECT ANSWER: B

The majority of Windows NT services and device drivers will create an entry in the System Event Log when they fail to load or initialize.

4. Proposed Solution:

- **From the Logs menu, select the Log Settings option.**
- **In the Maximum Log Size edit box, enter 2MB.**
- **In the Event Log Wrapping section, click the Overwrite Events Older Than radio button. Use the spinner control to change the value to 14 days.**

C. The Required Result and only one Optional Result

4. CORRECT ANSWER: C

Log settings are individually controlled from the Log Settings... option on the Log menu within Event Viewer. When this option is selected, you can control which log the settings will be altered for, regardless of what log is currently being viewed. The Proposed Solution accomplishes the Required Result.

By default, the maximum log size for all Event Logs is set at 512K. This value can be changed through the Maximum Log Size spinner control in the Log Settings dialog box. This value must be expressed in kilobytes and must be an increment of 64K. To set the log size at 2MB, the value entered should be 2,048 kilobytes. The Proposed Solution does not achieve the first Optional Result.

By default, the event log is set to overwrite events older than 7 days. You can change this to any amount of time by using the spinner control provided in the dialog box. Changing this value to 14 days will preserve events for at least 14 days. Events will be overwritten only if the log size exceeds the Maximum Log Size value. The Proposed Solution accomplishes the second Optional Result.

5. Select all of the common causes of device problems that trigger events with a stop sign in the System Event Log.

A. Interrupt conflicts

D. SCSI problems

5. CORRECT ANSWER: A-D

Interrupt conflicts and SCSI controller problems causing a device failure will be denoted with a stop sign icon in the System Event Log. Initialization failures of a new software package or of graphics-intensive software packages will more than likely be written to the Application Log, if the application developer chooses to use the Event Log. The tape device/NT Backup will write warnings to the Event Log for files that were open and not written to tape during a backup.

6. The security log indicates a failure audit with a ________ and a Success Audit with a __________.

E. Padlock / Key

6. CORRECT ANSWER: E

When Auditing is enabled on a system, Success Audits are denoted with a key symbol in the Security Log, and Failure Audits are denoted with a padlock symbol.

7. Recovery options can be configured by which of the following:

B. System Control Panel applet

E. Directly editing the BOOT.INI file

7. CORRECT ANSWER: B-E

The recovery options for Windows NT can be set using the Startup/Shutdown tab in the System Control Panel applet or by editing the boot.ini file and adding the `/crashdebug` switch to the default entry and the Windows NT Workstation Version 4 entries. The preferred method is to use the System applet, because an error in the boot.ini file could cause startup problems.

8. If your Windows NT-based computer manages to boot successfully, yet still is not performing correctly, what is the first thing to check?

A. System Event Log

8. CORRECT ANSWER: A

When a system successfully boots but displays erratic behavior, you should review the System Event Log for errors in service or driver initialization or other general errors.

9. Proposed Solution:

- **Use Event Viewer to check the System and Application Logs for specific errors.**
- **Use the Resources tab in WinMSD to determine which IRQs are free.**
- **Use the Memory tab in WinMSD to view and reconfigure the virtual memory settings.**

C. The Required Result and only one Optional Result

9. CORRECT ANSWER: C

When errors appear in regard to driver loading and initialization, the first resources you should consult are the System and possibly the Application Event Logs. The Proposed Solution accomplishes the Required Result.

WinMSD can be used to provide information about the available/used IRQ lines on the system. The Proposed Solution accomplishes the first Optional Result.

WinMSD can also provide information about the virtual memory configuration for the system; however, WinMSD is a read-only diagnostic tool. The Performance tab in the System Control Panel applet must be used to access and change the virtual memory setting for the computer. The Proposed Solution does not achieve the second Optional Result.

10. Warning events are symbolized in the System log—as displayed in Event Viewer—by which of the following symbols?

B. Exclamation mark

10. CORRECT ANSWER: B

Warning events are identified by an exclamation mark, errors by a stop sign, and information by an "I" in a blue circle. The key symbol is used in the Security Event Log to represent success audits.

FURTHER REVIEW

IMPLEMENT ADVANCED TECHNIQUES TO RESOLVE VARIOUS PROBLEMS

Windows NT comes with several diagnostic tools to help you optimize and tune the system and to correct error conditions. In many ways, the operating system is meant to be *self-tuning* and to require that relatively few settings be altered to make the computer run well. To track errors, Windows has a system of events that are recorded in log files. These events can be tracked and controlled, and they prove very useful in troubleshooting. The following subsections delve into the Event Logs in some detail.

Using Event Viewer to Manage the Event Logs

Events are actions that occur on your system. The system itself generates events and records them in the System and Security log files. Applications record their events in the Application log. There are standard events that you see, and you can audit resources to add additional events. Many application developers use the event system to aid in analyzing their applications. The Event Viewer enables you to view the Event Logs and analyze them.

The log files are a *first-in, first-out (FIFO)* system. When the ultimate limit of a log file is reached, the oldest events are deleted to make room for new events. The default size is 512KB, and the oldest event stored is up to one week old. You can modify these settings from within the Event Viewer.

A prudent administrator makes a habit of checking the Event Logs on a regular basis. Many events occur so frequently that they can overwhelm the Event Logs and make it difficult to determine what other error conditions or trends exist. By analyzing the Event Logs, you can determine what event types are worth keeping and how often they should be noted.

The Event Viewer (like the Performance Monitor) is one of the Windows NT operating system's central diagnostic tools. Learning how to use this tool well will reward the administrator with a smoothly running workstation, a limited number of errors, and a low stress level.

The Event Detail Dialog Box

If you want additional information about an event, double-click on that event to view the Event Detail dialog box. You find the following information generated for an event:

- Date of the event
- Time of the event
- User account that generated the event and information that is recorded in the Security log, when applicable
- Computer on which the event occurred
- Event ID (the actual Event Code)
- Source or component that recorded the error

- Type of error: Error, Information, or Warning
- Category of the event
- Description of the event
- Data describing the event in hexadecimal form

You can find many of the error messages in the documentation and resource kits for Windows NT Workstation. Microsoft also keeps a technical database that contains many of the sources of error messages. You can search the Knowledge Base on the Microsoft Web site (as a premium service) or on The Microsoft Network (MSN) to obtain error information stored in the logs.

Another database is delivered on CD-ROM to programmers as part of their subscription to the Microsoft Developer Network program. This database contains information about not only error conditions, but also internal error codes of interest to programmers. All levels of participation in MSDN result in your receiving this database.

The Event Log is very flexible. You can turn event logging on and off for a number of resources by specifying the auditing properties for that resource. Many developers use the Event Logs to record information specific to their applications.

Find and Search Function

The Event Log is almost an embarrassment of riches. To help you find the particular event you need, the Event Viewer has a find and search function. You can use any of the following filters to limit the search of the Event Log derived from your own computer by using the View menu:

- Computer
- Event date and time
- Event ID
- Event type
- User
- Source of the event

Diagnosing TCP/IP Problems

An amazing number of network problems are related to TCP/IP protocol addressing. Ensure that your workstation has a unique address or uses a DHCP (Dynamic Host Configuration Protocol) service for its TCP/IP assignment. Also check that the subnet address you entered into the TCP/IP Properties dialog box is correct. For more information on troubleshooting and diagnosing TCP/IP configuration problems, see Chapter 4, "Connectivity."

Resource Conflicts

Many configuration errors are resource conflicts. These take the form of duplicate interrupts or I/O assignments or of SCSI devices with duplicate or improper assignments. You might see these problems when you first boot your system, or they might show up later, when a device doesn't work properly.

Check the Event Log to see what error events are listed. Also run the Windows diagnostic program WinMSD (in the Administrative Tools folder) to examine your resource settings. Errors in software can be rolled back using the Last Known Good configuration.

Windows NT ships with several utilities for evaluating a workstation's configuration and performance. A thoughtful administrator, by being proficient in the use of these tools, can solve many problems and prevent others from occurring.

CHAPTER SUMMARY

Troubleshooting is a broad topic, both in the real world and on the certification exam. This topic covers every aspect of Windows NT and ties together most of the topics discussed in other chapters throughout this book. Troubleshooting can cover installation problems (Chapter 2), resource access issues (Chapter 3), network connectivity (Chapter 4), running applications (Chapter 5), and monitoring and optimization (Chapter 6). Many of the tools used to diagnose a particular Windows NT problem have been discussed here and in Chapter 6. One of the most important resources for troubleshooting Windows NT, as well as all other Microsoft operating systems and BackOffice applications, is the Microsoft Technical Information Network, or TechNet. TechNet is an invaluable resource consisting of a library of CDs that is updated monthly. In addition to the troubleshooting aids and a wealth of troubleshooting articles that appear in Microsoft's KnowledgeBase, TechNet also includes all of Microsoft's Resource Kits.

Troubleshooting can be a simple process if you remember one key idea: divide and conquer. When a problem arises, break it into smaller parts and solve each one individually. If you take this approach, your Workstation will quickly be up and running. The same approach should be taken for passing the certification exam. Master each of Microsoft's subobjectives listed on their Web site (`http://www.microsoft.com/train_cert`) in order to master each of the seven objectives encompassed by the certification exam. Achieving certification is not difficult if you pay attention to details, work with the operating system, and study, study, study.

Good luck passing the exam!

Practice Exam 1

1. This question is based on the following scenario.

Scenario:
You have to configure a new computer in the accounting department. In addition to the primary user, several other members of the department will need to use the system from time to time as well. Your organization uses a single NT domain called Biz. You need to decide which file system to implement and which operating system to install on the computer.

Required Result:
You must be able to secure accounting files stored on the system.

Optional Results:
The additional users need to be able to manage their own files and folders on the computer.

You need to be able to configure users and groups for those users.

Proposed Solution:
Install Windows 95 on a FAT partition. Add the computer to the Biz domain. Create accounts for the primary user and additional users on the system.

Evaluation of Proposed Solution:
How would you classify the proposed solution?

A. The proposed solution meets the required results and all of the optional results.

B. The proposed solution meets the required result, but not one of the optional results.

C. The proposed solution meets the required result, but not the optional results.

D. The proposed solution does not meet the required results.

2. Which of the following best describes the use of sysdiff.exe during automated installs?

A. It is used to automate the installation of hardware device drivers.

B. It is used to provide system specific information during setup.

C. It is used to automate the installation of software programs.

D. It is used to query the hardware for Plug and Play configuration during setup.

3. This question uses the same scenario as question 1.

Proposed Solution:
Install Windows NT Workstation on an NTFS partition. Add the computer to the Biz domain.

Create accounts for the primary user and additional users on the system. Create a home directory for each user with appropriate permissions.

Evaluation of Proposed Solution:
How would you classify the proposed solution?

A. The proposed solution meets the required results and all of the optional results.

B. The proposed solution meets the required result, but not one of the optional results.

C. The proposed solution meets the required result, but not the optional results.

D. The proposed solution does not meet the required results.

4. You have been instructed to automate the installation of Windows NT Workstation and several applications on 450 computers at your organization. Which of the following files will you need?

A. UDF

B. Sysdiff.exe

C. Unattend.txt

D. Setup.inf

5. If you want to configure a modem to work with Win32-based applications, which Control Panel applet do you select?

A. Network

B. System

C. Telephony

D. Modems

6. A printer attached to your computer is shared by 10 other users in your department who also run NT. Upon receiving a new driver for your printer, what is the best way to update all of the other users of the printer?

A. Update the driver on your computer and tell everyone to download it and update their computers.

B. Update the driver on your computer and all of the clients manually.

C. Create a new printer and instruct everyone to switch to that printer.

D. Update the driver on your computer.

7. You need to install several network components in your machine. Unfortunately, there is no network adapter physically installed at the present time. What do you do?

A. Install the Dial-Up Networking adapter and then the other components.

B. Install the MS Loopback adapter and then the other components.

C. Install the generic 3Com adapter and then the other components.

D. Install the generic network adapter and then the other components.

8. What is the proper procedure for upgrading Windows 95 to Windows NT Workstation?

A. Install in the same directory as 95 using the winnt.exe program.

B. Install in the same directory as 95 using the winnt32.exe program.

C. Install in the same directory as 95 using the setup.exe program and choosing Upgrade.

D. Install in a different directory and reinstall all applications.

9. The central network printer in your organization is shared by several users. Your manager approaches you and tells you to configure the network so management print jobs print first. How do you accomplish this?

A. Create a separate printer for management and set the priority to 1.

B. Create a separate printer for management and set the priority to 50.

C. Create a separate printer for management and set the priority to 99.

D. Create a separate printer for management and set the priority to 999.

10. To install a MIDI device in your system, which applet would you select from within Control Panel?

A. Devices

B. Sounds

C. Multimedia

D. System

11. What happens to the permissions of a file when you copy it from one directory to another on the same NTFS partition?

A. The permissions of the original file are kept.

B. The permissions of the destination file folder are inherited.

C. The permissions of the copying user are inherited.

D. The permissions are lost.

12. What happens to the permissions of a file when you move it from one directory to another on a different NTFS partition?

A. The permissions of the original file are kept.

B. The permissions of the destination file folder are inherited.

C. The permissions of the moving user are inherited.

D. The permissions are lost.

13. You want to print to a TCP/IP printer on your network. Which of the following pieces of information do you need to accomplish this?

A. The IP address of the print device

B. The IP address of the print server

C. The name of the print device

D. The name of the print server

14. This question is based on the following scenario.

Scenario:
You are the system administrator for ACME construction. Your company has recently experienced a large growth period. Until now, you have been responsible for administering approximately 50 user machines in a single NT domain called ACME. You have now been given the task of installing NT Workstation on 30 new desktop computers and 20 new laptops. All of the desktops are identical, as are all of the laptops.

Required Result:
Automate the installation of the 50 new machines.

Optional Results:
You want to also automate the installation of several Win32-based applications on all of the machines.

You want to configure all of the machines to automatically join the ACME domain during installation.

Proposed Solution:
Create one uniqueness file that will be used to supply the individual user information. Create two answer files that will contain the hardware-specific information. Add the line **OEMPreinstall=Yes** to the [Unattended] section and **JoinDomain=ACME** to the [Network] section. Install NT Workstation on a reference machine. Run `sysdiff.exe /snap` on it, and then install all of the Win32 applications. Rerun `sysdiff.exe` with the `/diff` command line. Add the `sysdiff.exe /apply` to the automated script. Start the installations specifying the answer file and uniqueness files from the command line using an installation image stored on the PDC for the ACME domain.

Evaluation of Proposed Solution:
In which of the following does the proposed solution result?

A. The required result and all of the optional results are met.

B. The required result and only the first optional results are achieved.

C. The required result and only the second optional results are achieved.

D. None of the results are achieved.

15. The advantage of using a printer across the network versus creating a printer locally is:

A. The printer driver does not need to be manually installed.

B. You have more control of print options.

C. Print jobs can be queued locally.

D. There is local spooling of print jobs.

16. Lori and groups she belongs to have the following permissions for the DEV folder and share on the server's NTFS partition:

NTFS:

Developers:	**Change**
Managers:	**Full Control**
Everyone:	**Read**

Share:

Developers:	**Full Control**
Managers:	**Read**
Everyone:	**No Access**

What are Lori's effective permissions to the DEV folder when using the files locally?

A. Full Control

B. Change

C. Read

D. No Access

17. Benjamin, who currently belongs to the users group, would like to view the three different logs on his NT Workstation. What does Ben need to do to accomplish this?

A. Nothing. He will be able to view all of the logs already.

B. Ben must ask the administrator to set the proper permissions on the log files.

C. Ben must be added to the Administrators group.

D. Ben must install the Event Viewer application.

18. To enable auditing for a printer, which auditing events should you audit?

A. User of user rights

B. User and group management

C. File and object access

D. Process tracking

19. Two users, Emily and Jacob, want to access your printer. Emily is a member of the Administration global group, and Jacob is a member of the Marketing global group. Jacob's print jobs need to print first if submitted simultaneously with Emily's. How should you accomplish this?

A. Create a printer and share it. Configure access so Marketing receives a priority of 99 and Administration receives a priority of 1.

B. Create a printer and share it. Configure access so Marketing receives a priority of 1 and Administration receives a priority of 99.

C. Create two printers and share them. Give Marketing access to one with a priority of 99 and Administration access to the other with a priority of 1. Remove all other access from both shares.

D. Create two printers and share them. Give Marketing access to one with a priority of 1 and Administration access to the other with a priority of 99. Remove all other access from both shares.

20. Which of the following logs must you have administrative access to view?

A. Application

B. Security

C. System

D. Device

21. To which of the following groups does Jerrod have to belong in order to share folders on his NT Workstation computer?

A. Administrators

B. Power Users

C. Users

D. System Operators

22. Which of the following NT Workstation tools is used in the process of setting up a roaming user profile?

A. User Manager

B. User Manager for Domains

C. Network in Control Panel

D. System in Control Panel

23. You configure the system to expire all passwords at 30-day intervals. You create a new account for a new employee named Emily, who needs administrative access to the system, and you decide to select the

Password Never Expires option on her account. What happens after 30 days roll around?

A. The password expires, and she is forced to choose a new one.

B. The password expires, but because of the no expire selection, she is locked out and unable to access the account.

C. The password expires, but because of the no expire selection, she is not allowed to log in to change the password and so has to have the administrator change the password for her.

D. The password continues to function.

24. Lori calls you, requesting information on how she can change her NetWare password. She has Client Services for NetWare installed on her NT Workstation, and the NetWare 4.x server is part of an NDS tree. What do you tell her?

A. She needs to run setpass.exe from the NetWare server.

B. She needs to run setpass.exe from the NT Workstation.

C. She needs to select the password option under Client Services for NetWare and change it from there.

D. She needs to press Ctrl+Alt+Delete and click the Change Password button. She should select NetWare or Compatible Network in the domain field and enter a new password.

25. To configure TCP/IP manually on a computer in a routed environment, what parameters do you need?

A. IP address

B. Subnet mask

C. Default gateway

D. Primary WINS server IP address

26. What types of name resolution does WINS provide?

A. NetBIOS to IP

B. NetBIOS to domain

C. Domain to IP

D. Domain to NetBIOS

27. Which of the following are functions of the DHCP protocol?

A. To automatically assign MAC addresses

B. To automatically assign IP addresses

C. To automatically configure key TCP/IP parameters

D. To automatically provide for DNS to WINS connectivity

28. Which of the following protocols are supported on a RAS server for dialing into a network?

A. DLC

B. NetBEUI

C. TCP/IP

D. AppleTalk

29. Your UNIX dial-in box is configured to enable you to dial in with a SLIP

connection. What IP address do you use when connecting to the UNIX box?

A. The IP address assigned when Dial-Up Networking was configured.

B. The IP address assigned by the UNIX box upon dial in.

C. The IP address assigned by the DHCP server on the same subnet as the UNIX box.

D. The IP address assigned by the BOOTP daemon in the UNIX box.

30. **Your corporate network consists of both UNIX and NT Workstation computers. You want to connect to the UNIX systems by their host names, and you want the UNIX boxes to be able to connect to the NT computers by their host names. Your NT system uses TCP/IP and both DNS and WINS servers. What must you do to enable this?**

A. Add the UNIX host names to the DNS servers.

B. Add the NT host names to the WINS servers.

C. Enable the WINS server to perform DNS lookups.

D. Configure the UNIX systems with the IP addresses of the WINS servers.

31. **To access a BTRIEVE application running on a NetWare server, you need to install which of the following?**

A. NWLink

B. Gateway Services for NetWare

C. Client Services for NetWare

D. File and Print Services for NetWare

32. **This question is based on the following scenario.**

Scenario:
You work for a large company that is in the process of creating a company-wide intranet. Currently, your company consists of a departmental structure in which each department has its own NT domain and resources. All of your employees' desktop and laptop systems utilize NT Workstation as the operating system. The intranet will reside on a series of UNIX boxes running the Apache Web server. The IP addresses are assigned to the NT systems by various DHCP servers.

Required Result:
Establish connectivity to the new intranet servers by host name from all of the NT workstations.

Optional Results:
Provide the UNIX systems with the ability to connect to the NT systems by host name.

Provide the UNIX systems with the ability to resolve the host name based upon the IP address of the system connecting for security purposes.

Proposed Solution:
Establish a DNS server. Add all of the UNIX and NT Workstations to the DNS tables. Configure the DHCP servers so they automatically configure the NT Workstations to use the new DNS server for name resolution. Configure the UNIX systems to use the DNS server for name resolution. Add a reverse lookup zone to the DNS server that contains the WINS server address.

Evaluation of Proposed Solution:
In which of the following does the proposed solution result?

A. The required results and all of the optional results are met.

B. The required result and only the first optional result are achieved.

C. The required result and only the second optional result are achieved.

D. None of the results are achieved.

33. Your UNIX dial-in box is configured to enable you to dial in with a PPP connection. What IP address do you use when connecting to the UNIX box?

A. The IP address assigned when Dial-Up Networking was configured.

B. The IP address assigned by the UNIX box upon dial in.

C. The IP address assigned by the DHCP server on the same subnet as the UNIX box.

D. The IP address assigned by the BOOTP daemon in the UNIX box.

34. To connect to your UNIX box from your NT Workstation system, you must use SLIP. You want to automate the process of entering your user name, password, and several other parameters required to log in. How is this best accomplished?

A. Configure Dial-Up Networking to open a terminal window before connecting.

B. Configure Dial-Up Networking to open a terminal window after connecting.

C. Configure Dial-Up Networking to execute the Slip.scp before connecting.

D. Configure Dial-Up Networking to execute the Slip.scp after connecting.

35. To minimize problems, you want to run a 16-bit Windows application so that it is preemptively multitasked and cannot interfere with other 16-bit Windows applications you will be running. How is this best accomplished?

A. By running it in the Win16 NTVDM with its own address space.

B. By running it in the Win32 NTVDM with 16-bit translation enabled.

C. By running it in the Win16 NTVDM with preemptive multitasking enabled.

D. By running it in its own NTVDM.

36. Which of the following statements accurately describes the difference in default behavior between MS-DOS–based applications and Win16-based applications?

A. Each MS-DOS application uses three threads, whereas each Win16 application uses only one.

B. All MS-DOS applications share a common memory space, whereas Win16 applications are given their own memory spaces.

C. Each MS-DOS application is preemptively multitasked, whereas Win16 applications are not.

D. MS-DOS applications can execute only at high priority, whereas Win16 applications can execute only at normal priority or below.

37. What purpose do the autoexec.nt and config.nt files serve?

A. They allow for backward compatibility with Windows 3.1 by providing a method for loading files needed by Win16 applications.

B. They serve as a backup for the autoexec.bat and config.sys files.

C. They serve the same purpose for all NT applications that the autoexec.bat and config.sys did for Windows 3.1 systems.

D. They enable you to configure the startup parameters for NT.

38. You are receiving time-out errors from your Win16 application due to other applications utilizing the bulk of the CPU time. What is the best way to increase the performance of your Win16 application?

A. Run the application in its own memory space.

B. Run the application in its own virtual machine.

C. Run the application with HIGH priority.

D. Run the application with REALTIME priority.

39. Jacob approaches you for assistance in optimizing the paging file on his system. His computer has four physical SCSI drives, with a single partition on each drive. The first drive holds the boot partition. How should Jacob optimize his system?

A. He should use one paging file on the boot disk.

B. He should use one paging file on any disk but the boot disk.

C. He should use three paging files split evenly between the disks.

D. He should use two paging files split between the two disks without the boot partition.

40. This question is based on the following scenario.

Scenario:
You have an NT Workstation system with six 1GB SCSI drives. Each drive is formatted as a FAT partition. The first drive contains both the boot partition and the paging file.

Required Results:
Increase speed of access to files on the drives.

Optional Results:
Optimize the paging file.

Optimize the speed of access to network resources.

Proposed Solution:
Convert all drives to NTFS. Combine the last five drives into one stripe set. Relocate the paging file to the new stripe set partition. Move the most frequently used protocols to the top of the binding order.

Evaluation of Proposed Solution:
Which results does the proposed solution yield?

A. The proposed solution gives the required result and both optional results.

B. The proposed solution gives the required result and the first optional result.

C. The proposed solution gives the required result and the second optional result.

D. The proposed solution does not work.

41. Which of the following Performance Monitor statements are valid?

A. Decreasing the amount of RAM will lower the Pages/sec counter.

B. Increasing the amount of RAM will lower the Pages/sec counter.

C. Decreasing the initial page file size will lower the Pages/sec counter.

D. Increasing the initial page file size will lower the Pages/sec counter.

42. You want to use Performance Monitor to track TCP/IP statistics, but you're unable to locate the counters for doing so. What must you do first in order to track TCP/IP counters in Performance Monitor?

A. Install network monitor agent.

B. Install SNMP.

C. Install network monitor tools and agent.

D. Enable network auditing.

43. Your NT Workstation will no longer boot properly. You suspect that some system files are missing. What is the best way to correct the problem?

A. Boot using the Last Known Good configuration.

B. Boot using the VGA Mode option.

C. Boot from the emergency repair disk and let it fix the problem.

D. Boot from the installation disks and start the emergency repair process.

44. You want to install NT Workstation, but your CD-ROM drive is not on the Hardware Compatibility List. However, you can access your CD-ROM drive well from MS-DOS. How can you install NT Workstation on your system?

A. From MS-DOS, execute the command `winnt.exe /o` from the CD-ROM to create the installation disks.

B. From MS-DOS, copy the \I386 directory to your hard drive, and then execute `winnt.exe /b` from there.

C. From MS-DOS, run `winnt.exe /b` from the CD-ROM.

D. Obtain the NT driver for your CD-ROM from the manufacturer, and install it in MS-DOS so you can access it during the NT installation.

45. The first time you restart after installing a new SCSI controller driver on your system, the computer just hangs with a blank screen part of the way through the startup process. What is the best way to resolve the problem?

A. Boot from the emergency repair disk.

B. Invoke the Last Known Good configuration when prompted.

C. Invoke the VGA Only configuration when prompted.

D. Use the emergency repair process to restore the Registry.

46. **Which of the following will help to reduce disk thrashing caused by excessive page file access?**

    A. Add more memory.

    B. Reduce the size of the page file.

    C. Increase the size of the page file.

    D. Move the page file off of the boot partition.

47. **After Ben installs a new hard drive and creates some new partitions, his computer will no longer boot NT properly. What do you tell him he needs to update to resolve the problem?**

    A. The ntldr file.

    B. The boot.ini file

    C. The bootsect.dos file

    D. The ntdetect.com file

48. **Jacob, the head of security, comes to you for assistance with the following problem. He created a group called Security on his system for his staff to use. He assigned several shares full control access to the Security group. He also assigned no access to the Users group so no one else could access the system. None of the users of his Security group are able to access the system. What do you tell him the problem is?**

    A. Jacob did not correctly grant Log on Locally to the group.

    B. Jacob did not correctly grant Access This Computer from the Network to the group.

    C. Jacob did not add the special Everyone group to the list of members.

    D. The people are also members of the Users group.

49. **After testing a new custom system policy, you find that the computer will no longer boot NT properly. After disabling the system policy on the server, what should you do on the local system?**

    A. Boot from the emergency repair disk.

    B. Boot from the installation disk and start the emergency repair process.

    C. Boot from the Last Known Good configuration.

    D. Boot from the VGA Only configuration.

50. **You recently expanded your network and changed it from one segment into four segments to improve performance. Unfortunately, now none of your users can communicate with segments other than their own. You have been using NetBEUI as your network protocol. What do you need to do to correct the problem?**

    A. Program the router to route NetBIOS traffic.

    B. Program the router to pass RIP broadcasts.

    C. Add the NetBEUI protocol to the router.

    D. Change the network protocol to a routable protocol.

51. You recently split your TCP/IP network into multiple segments, and now many of your computers are not being assigned IP addresses from your DHCP server. What is the best way to resolve the problem?

A. Install the DHCP relay agent on machines on the segments without the DHCP server.

B. Configure the router to pass DHCP assignments.

C. Configure the router to pass NetBIOS broadcasts.

D. Configure the DHCP server with multiple scopes for the new segments.

ANSWERS & EXPLANATIONS

1. **D.** Windows 95 does not support local file system security.
2. **C.** Sysdiff enables you to take a "snapshot" of an existing system before and after installation to create a file that can be used to automate that process later.
3. **A.** The described solution does the job admirably.
4. **A – B – C.** The UDF (uniqueness database file), unattend.txt (answer file), and sysdiff.exe will be needed to accomplish this.
5. **D.** Modems is the correct selection.
6. **D.** If you update the driver on your computer, all of the other NT computers will download and update it automatically the next time they connect.
7. **B.** Microsoft provides the MS Loopback Adapter for precisely this type of scenario.
8. **D.** Windows 95 cannot be upgraded to NT. A new installation must be performed.
9. **C.** A priority of 99 indicates the highest priority available.
10. **C.** The Multimedia applet within Control Panel enables you to control all multimedia devices, such as sound cards.
11. **B.** Copying a file always causes it to inherit the permissions of the target folder.
12. **B.** Because moving a file from one partition to another actually causes the file to be copied and the original deleted, the rules for copying a file apply. That is to say, the permissions of the target folder are inherited.
13. **B – C.** To complete the configuration, you need the name of the print device and the IP address of the print server.
14. **A.** The required and optional results are achieved as desired.
15. **A.** When you connect to a network printer under NT, the remote driver is automatically downloaded to your machine.
16. **A.** Lori gets Full Control because that is the greatest allowed. The No Access option doesn't apply because she is not connecting through the network.
17. **C.** The Administrators group has the permission needed to view all three logs.
18. **C.** File and object access auditing will track printer use.
19. **C.** Two printers are needed to configure two set of priorities. Priority 99 takes precedence over priority 1.
20. **B.** The Security log can only be viewed by administrators.
21. **A – B.** Users must belong to either the Administrators or Power Users group. Power Users group membership is conferred to anyone who tries to share a folder; hence anyone can share a folder.
22. **A – D.** User Manager is used to configure the path to the profile, and System in Control Panel is used to copy the profile to the path.
23. **D.** The Password Never Expires option on individual accounts overrides the general expiration policy.

24. **D.** This procedure will properly change her NetWare password.

25. **A – B – C.** All three are needed in a routed environment.

26. **A.** WINS (Windows Internet Naming Service) provides conversion from NetBIOS names to IP addresses.

27. **B – C.** DHCP can be configured with a scope of IP addresses, which it will automatically assign along with any configuration parameters set in the scope.

28. **B – C.** NetBEUI and TCP/IP are both supported for dial-in; however, NetBEUI can be used to access only a single remote segment.

29. **A.** SLIP does not allow for dynamic IP assignment, so the IP address must be statically configured upon setup.

30. **A – C.** B is unnecessary because the WINS servers will collect the host names of the NT boxes automatically. D isn't possible because UNIX systems cannot use WINS.

31. **A – C.** NWLink provides the protocol, and Client Services for NetWare provides server connectivity.

32. **C.** Adding the NT Workstations to the DNS server does not allow for their dynamic address assignment and will, therefore, be delivering incorrect IP addresses in short order.

33. **B.** PPP allows for dynamic IP address assignment.

34. **D.** You can enter desired prompts and responses into the Slip.scp file for execution after connection to the server.

35. **D.** To meet all of the requirements, you have to execute the application in its own NTVDM.

36. **C.** This statement is true.

37. **A.** The autoexec.nt and config.nt files are provided solely for Win16 compatibility.

38. **C.** HIGH priority will yield the best performance without crippling the system for all of the other applications.

39. **D.** This configuration will yield optimal paging file performance.

40. **A.** The proposed solution does increase file access both locally and across the network. Moving the paging file also improves its performance.

41. **B.** The Pages/sec counter indicates the frequency at which the page file is accessed. Increasing physical RAM is the only valid listed way to reduce this count.

42. **B.** The installation of SNMP adds support for tracking TCP/IP in Performance Monitor.

43. **D.** The first two options aren't available if the system won't boot, and the emergency repair disks are not bootable.

44. **B – C.** Both of these methods will work.

45. **B.** This will cause the computer to boot without loading the new driver.

46. **A.** Although answer D will improve page file performance, it will not serve to reduce the amount of paging.

47. **B.** The boot.ini most likely needs to be updated with the correct ARC of the system partition.

48. **D.** No Access always overrides other permissions.

49. **C.** Because the policy editor is actually making Registry changes, booting from the Last Known Good configuration causes the system to use the previous Registry copy, which should enable you to boot.

50. **D.** Because NetBEUI is not routable, option D is your only viable solution.

51. **A.** Although D will need to be done also, the fact that requests for addresses are not getting to the DHCP server from the remote segments is the problem; forwarding agents will pass them through the router to the DHCP server.

Practice Exam 2

1. **You have a 2GB hard drive upon which you need to store several sensitive files such as payroll. Which of the following are reasons for using NTFS for the file system?**

   A. Only NTFS supports long filenames.

   B. NTFS partitions can be used with several operating systems such as Windows 95.

   C. NTFS typically performs better on volumes greater then 500MB in size.

   D. Only NTFS allows permissions to be assigned to individual files and folders.

2. **You have to set up 40 identical desktops, 50 identical laptops, and 75 identical mini-tower PCs. What is the minimum number of answer and UDF files you need to perform the installation?**

   A. 1 answer file and 3 UDF files.

   B. 3 answer files and 1 UDF file.

   C. 165 answer files and 3 UDF files.

   D. 3 answer files and 165 UDF files.

3. **Which of the following statements best describes the purpose of a uniqueness database file during automated installations?**

   A. It provides information needed to install various software programs.

   B. It provides information needed to configure for individual users or programs.

   C. It provides information needed to install hardware components.

   D. It provides information needed to configure network connectivity.

4. **After installing a new application in your Windows NT Workstation system, you want to add the applications directory to the path. How would you modify the PATH to add that of the application?**

   A. Modify the PATH in the autoexec.nt.

   B. Modify the PATH in the config.nt.

   C. Modify the PATH in the System properties under the Environment tab.

   D. Modify the key \HKLM\System\CurrentControlSet\Microsoft\Environment\Path.

5. **If you move a file from an NTFS partition to a FAT partition, what happens?**

   A. The long filename and permissions are lost.

B. The long filename remains, but the permissions are lost.

C. The long filename is lost, but the permissions remain.

D. Nothing; the long filename and permissions are retained.

6. If you want to replace NT Workstation with DOS on a system that is using NTFS partitions, what is the correct procedure?

A. Run rollback.exe from the command prompt.

B. Run setup.exe from NT distribution disks.

C. Boot from an MS-DOS disk and execute the SYS C: command.

D. Run fdisk.exe, delete all partitions, create FAT partitions, and then install from the MS-DOS distribution disks.

7. To print to an HP Jet-Direct series interface, which protocol do you need?

A. NWLink

B. TCP/IP

C. Appletalk

D. DLC

8. To print to a new Macintosh printer on your network, which network protocol do you need to install?

A. NWLink

B. TCP/IP

C. AppleTalk

D. DLC

9. Your local printer is out of toner. You need to print a report from an MS-DOS–based program that does not support UNC redirection to another printer across the network. Which of the following is the correct action to take?

A. Install the MS-DOS print redirector and configure it to print to the alternate printer.

B. Redirect a physical port to the UNC of the alternate printer, and then print to that port.

C. Use the MS-DOS command `MAP LPT1:=\\`*`servername`*`\`*`printershare`* where `\\`*`servername`*`\`*`printershare`* is the UNC of the alternate printer.

D. Install the MS-DOS printer driver for the alternate printer, and then print using that.

10. One of your client's computers is currently configured to use HPFS and is currently running NT 3.51. The client wants you to upgrade her system to NT 4. What is the best way to accomplish this?

A. Install NT 4, and then convert the file system to FAT.

B. Install NT 4, and then convert the file system to NTFS.

C. Convert the file system to FAT, and then install NT 4.

D. Convert the file system to NTFS, and then install NT 4.

11. **What happens to the permissions of a file when you move it from one directory to another on the same NTFS partition?**

    A. The permissions of the original file are kept.

    B. The permissions of the destination file folder are inherited.

    C. The permissions of the moving user are inherited.

    D. The permissions are lost.

12. **What happens to the permissions of a file when you move it from one directory on an NTFS partition to another on a FAT partition?**

    A. The permissions of the original file are kept.

    B. The permissions of the destination file folder are inherited.

    C. The permissions of the copying user are inherited.

    D. The permissions are lost.

13. **This question is based on the following scenario.**

    Scenario:
    You are the system administrator for ACME construction. Your company has recently experienced a large growth period. Until now, you have been responsible for administering approximately 50 user machines in a single NT domain called ACME. You have now been given the task of installing NT Workstation on 30 new desktop computers and 20 new laptops. All of the desktops are identical, as are all of the laptops.

    Required Result:
    Automate the installation of the 50 new machines.

    Optional Results:
    You want to automate the installation of several Win32-based applications on all of the machines.

    You want to configure all of the machines to automatically join the ACME domain during installation.

    Proposed Solution:
    Create one answer file that will be used to supply the individual user information. Create two uniqueness files that contain the hardware-specific information. Install NT Workstation on a reference machine. Run `sysdiff.exe /snap` on it, and then install all of the Win32 applications. Rerun `sysdiff.exe` with the `/diff` command line. Add the `sysdiff.exe /apply` to the automated script. Start the installations, specifying the answer file and uniqueness files from the command line and using an installation image stored on the PDC for the ACME domain.

    Evaluation of Proposed Solution:
    In which of the following does the proposed solution result?

    A. The required results and all of the optional results are met.

    B. The required result and only the first optional result are achieved.

    C. The required result and only the second optional result are achieved.

    D. None of the results are achieved.

14. **You want to use the same system policy throughout your organization. All of your users log into the domain after starting up NT Workstation. What is the best way to provide them with consistent policies?**

A. Create a system policy and copy it into each user's home directory.

B. Create a system policy for each user in his or her home directory.

C. Create a system policy and copy it into the NETLOGON directory of the PDC.

D. Create a system policy for each user and copy all of them into the NETLOGON directory of the PDC.

15. Which of the following files need to be replicated between domain controllers in an NT domain?

A. Logon scripts

B. System policy for the domain

C. Roaming user profiles

D. Mandatory user profiles

16. Lori and groups she belongs to have the following permissions for the DEV folder and share on the server's NTFS partition:

NTFS:
Developers: Change
Managers: Full Control
Everyone: Read

Share:
Developers: Full Control
Managers: Read
Everyone: No Access

What are Lori's effective permissions to the DEV folder when using the files across the network?

A. Full Control

B. Change

C. Read

D. No Access

17. Which of the following statements about access to a shared folder on an NTFS partition are correct?

A. A user accessing the folder remotely has more-restrictive access than if he were to access it locally.

B. A user accessing the folder remotely has the same access he would if he were to access it locally.

C. A user accessing the folder remotely has less-restrictive access than if he were to access it locally.

D. A user accessing the folder has the same or more-restrictive access than if he were to access it locally.

18. If you want to be notified of successful completion of print jobs when using Client Services for NetWare to print to a NetWare server, which of the following actions should you take?

A. Configure print job notification under the User properties on the NetWare server.

B. Turn on auditing of file and object access.

C. Select the Notify When Printed option on the General properties tab for the printer.

D. Select the Notify When Printed option under Client Services for NetWare options.

19. Grace has just come to you complaining that her roaming user profile has not

worked since you installed the new system profile in the NETLOGON directory of the PDC. What must you or she do to resolve this problem?

A. Grace must log out and log back in to copy the new system policies into the roaming profile.

B. You must alter the system policy file.

C. You must convert her roaming profile to mandatory.

D. Grace must switch from a roaming profile to a local profile.

20. **Both system profiles and mandatory profiles can be used to control desktop settings on user systems. Suppose a user has a mandatory profile, a system policy with an individual user entry, and a group entry to which the user belongs. Which of the following best describes the precedence that applies in this situation?**

A. Individual system policy, group system policy, default user system policy, mandatory user profile

B. Group system policy, individual system policy, default user system policy, mandatory user profile

C. Default user system policy, individual system policy, group system policy, mandatory user profile

D. Mandatory user profile, group system policy, individual system policy, default user system policy

21. **Given the following NTFS permissions for a folder, which statement best describes the access users of the folder will experience?**

Special Access: (RWX) (None)

A. Individuals will have Read/Write/Execute access for existing files and No Access for new files. Creators of new files will have Read access to those files.

B. Individuals will have Read/Write/Execute access for existing files and No Access for new files. Creators of new files will have Read/Write/Execute access to those files.

C. Individuals will have Read/Write/Execute access for existing files and Read/Write/Execute access for new files. Creators of new files will have Read access to those files.

D. Individuals will have Read/Write/Execute access for existing files and No Access for new files. Creators of new files will have Full Control of those files.

22. **Ben is using Client Services for NetWare to print to a printer off a NetWare server. Ben wants to use separator pages to distinguish his many print jobs. How do you tell him to go about setting it up?**

A. In Client Services for NetWare, he needs to select Add Header Page.

B. In Client Services for NetWare, he needs to select Print Banner.

C. Ben needs to configure it on the user settings of his account on the NetWare server.

D. In the properties sheet of the printer, he needs to select Use Separator Page.

23. **Having recently migrated from a NetWare environment, you want to set up individual disk space limitations like you had on your NetWare server. Where do you configure individual disk space limitations for the users in NT?**

    A. Through the user properties in User Manager.

    B. Through the folder properties in File Manager.

    C. Through the System applet in Control Panel.

    D. They can't be restricted in NT.

24. **Tim complains to you that whenever he connects to the corporate RAS server from his NT Workstation from home, the connection drops after only a few seconds. What is the best approach to resolving this problem?**

    A. Use Event Viewer to examine the connection errors in the System log.

    B. Use Event Viewer to examine the connection errors in the Application log.

    C. Watch the connection as Tim connects by using Dial-Up Networking Monitor.

    D. Enable device logging, and then connect and view the log results.

25. **What types of name resolution does DNS provide?**

    A. NetBIOS to IP

    B. NetBIOS to domain

    C. Domain to IP

    D. Domain to NetBIOS

26. **Which of the following NetWare utilities will operate correctly from Windows NT Workstation?**

    A. Capture

    B. Logout

    C. Attach

    D. Syscon

27. **To be able to access both NT Servers and NetWare servers from your NT Workstation computer, which of the following do you need to install?**

    A. NWLink only

    B. NWLink and Client Services for NetWare

    C. NWLink and Gateway Services for NetWare

    D. NWLink and File and Print Services for NetWare

28. **Emily calls you and asks for the proper UNC to type into her system so she can connect to the new Procedures share on the intranet server. She knows that she can get to the intranet server by typing http://www.acme.com in her Web browser, but she doesn't know how to get to the share from her NT workstation box. What do you tell her to use?**

    A. \\procedures\acme.com

    B. \\acme.com\procedures

    C. \\www.acme.com.\procedures

    D. \\procedures\www.acme.com

29. When using your NT Workstation from home to connect to the Internet, you want to prevent malicious persons on the Internet from accessing the information on your computer. What must you do to accomplish this?

A. Disable the Workstation service on your computer.

B. Disable the Server service on your computer.

C. Disable the Browser service on your computer.

D. Disable the Messenger service on your computer.

30. If IP addresses on your NT workstation are assigned by a DHCP server, which of the following name resolution methods will work the best?

A. LMHOSTS file

B. WINS

C. DNS

D. HOSTS file

31. Which service on NT Workstation allows for trap messages to be forwarded to other systems?

A. Messenger

B. Alerter

C. Workstation

D. SNMP

32. This question is based on the following scenario.

Scenario:
You work for a large company that is in the process of creating a company-wide intranet. Currently, your company consists of a departmental structure in which each department has its own NT domain and resources. All of your employees' desktop and laptop systems utilize NT Workstation as the operating system. The intranet will reside on a series of UNIX boxes running the Apache Web server. The IP addresses are assigned to the NT systems by various DHCP servers.

Required Result:
Establish connectivity to the new intranet servers by host name from all of the NT workstations.

Optional Results:
Provide the UNIX systems with the ability to connect to the NT systems by host name.

Provide the UNIX systems with the ability to resolve the host name based upon the IP address of the system connecting for security purposes.

Proposed Solution:
Establish a DNS server. Add all of the UNIX systems to the DNS tables. Add an entry for the WINS server to the DNS records for the primary zone. Configure the DHCP servers so they automatically configure the NT workstations to use the new DNS server for name resolution. Configure the UNIX systems to use the DNS server for name resolution. Add a reverse lookup zone to the DNS server that contains the WINS server address in a record.

Evaluation of Proposed Solution:
In which of the following does the proposed solution result?

A. The required results and all of the optional results are met.

B. The required result and only the first optional result are achieved.

C. The required result and only the second optional result are achieved.

D. None of the results are achieved.

33. Which protocol is best suited to allow remote office connectivity by way of the Internet without sacrificing security?

A. X.25

B. NWLink

C. PPP

D. PPTP

34. To execute a 16-bit Windows application called reports.exe from the command line in its own memory space and in a minimized window, which of the following commands would you use?

A. `net start /min /separate reports.exe`

B. `net start reports.exe /min ➥/separate`

C. `start /min /separate reports.exe`

D. `start reports.exe /min /separate`

35. Which of the following are limitations of MS-DOS applications running under Windows NT?

A. They cannot be preemptively multitasked.

B. They cannot be given their own virtual machine.

C. They cannot be run with a common memory space.

D. They cannot be given direct access to the hardware.

36. Which statement best describes the default method by which Win16 applications are run?

A. Win16 apps are executed as a single thread in a single NTVDM with a shared address space.

B. Win16 apps are executed as separate threads in a single NTVDM with a shared address space.

C. Win16 apps are executed as a single thread in separate NTVDMs with separate address spaces.

D. Win16 apps are executed as separate threads in separate NTVDMs with separate address spaces.

37. By which of the following methods could you start a Win16 application in its own memory space?

A. Start the application using the Run command from the Start menu.

B. Start the application from the command line using the `start` command.

C. Start the application by selecting Run in Separate Memory Space from the application's context menu.

D. Start the application by double-clicking its icon.

38. You want to monitor % Network Utilization in Performance Monitor, but you are unable to locate the counter. What do you need to do to enable the counter?

A. Install network monitor agent

B. Install SNMP

C. Install network monitor tools and agent

D. Enable network auditing

39. This question is based on the following scenario.

Scenario:
You have an NT Workstation system with six 1GB SCSI drives. Each drive is formatted as a FAT partition. The first drive contains both the boot partition and the paging file.

Required Result:
Increase speed of access to files on the drives.

Optional Results:
Optimize the paging file.

Optimize the speed of access to network resources.

Proposed Solution:
Convert all drives to NTFS. Rebuild the paging file on the first NTFS partition. Combine the last five drives into one stripe set. Move the most frequently used protocols to the top of the binding order.

Evaluation of Proposed Solution:
Which results does the proposed solution yield?

A. The proposed solution gives the required result and both optional results.

B. The proposed solution gives the required result and the first optional result.

C. The proposed solution gives the required result and the second optional result.

D. The proposed solution does not work.

40. Which of the following programs enable you to view memory usage statistics in your system?

A. Performance Monitor

B. System Monitor Agent

C. Task Manager

D. Event Viewer

41. Which of the following counters should be monitored to determine if the processor activity is higher than normal?

A. % Usage

B. % Processor Time

C. Usage Peak (bytes)

D. System Object Processor Queue Length

42. Your NT Workstation has begun experiencing a series of STOP errors. How do you configure the system to save STOP error information to a memory dump file?

A. By specifying the Recovery option in Server Manager.

B. By specifying the Recovery option in System properties.

C. By specifying the Recovery option in File Manager.

D. By specifying the Recovery option in Performance Monitor.

43. Lori's computer, which usually dual boots between Windows 95 and NT Workstation, won't boot Workstation anymore. After examining it, you suspect the boot sector. What methods can you use to resolve the problem?

A. Boot from Windows 95 and execute sys.com from \Windows\Command.

B. Boot from Windows 95 and execute winnt.exe to repair the boot sector.

C. Boot from the emergency repair disk and repair the boot sector from there.

D. Boot from the installation disks and start the emergency repair process.

44. Several print jobs submitted by users of the network you administer have become stuck in the print queue. The jobs will not print, and the users are unable to delete them. What is the best way for you, as the administrator, to resolve the problem?

A. Create a new printer and redirect the contents of the first to that queue.

B. Delete all of the files from the physical spool file on the print server.

C. Stop and restart the Spooler service.

D. Make sure the printer is not out of paper.

45. What is the most likely cause of the following error:

```
Windows NT could not start because the
following file is missing or corrupt:

\Winnt\Root\System32\Ntoskrnl.exe.
Please reinstall a copy of the above
file.
```

A. The bootsect.dos file is missing.

B. The boot.ini file is missing.

C. The ntdetect.com file is missing.

D. The ntldr file is missing.

46. Which of the following does running the emergency repair process accomplish?

A. Replace the master boot record.

B. Inspect the boot sector.

C. Verify the system files.

D. Inspect the startup environment.

47. What is the default location of the device.log file after it has been activated?

A. \%winnt_root%\system

B. \%winnt_root%\system\RAS

C. \%winnt_root%\system32

D. \%winnt_root%\system32\RAS

48. After you configure a new system manually with TCP/IP, the computer is able to access some of the local systems but not all of them, and none of the remote systems. What setting is the likely culprit?

A. IP address

B. Subnet mask

C. Default gateway

D. Router

49. Your computer is configured to dual boot between MS-DOS and NT Workstation. Recently, you have been unable to boot to MS-DOS. What do you suspect is the problem?

A. The boot.ini file is missing.

B. The ntldr file is missing.

C. The bootsect.dos file is missing.

D. The ntdetect.com file is missing.

50. Print jobs on Emily's computer have recently started to take significantly more time to print, and sometimes they stall out entirely. Which of the following is the most likely solution to her problem?

A. Increase memory.

B. Increase the page file size.

C. Increase the printer priority.

D. Clean out more hard drive space.

51. You manually configure NWLink on two different PCs and restart both, but the two are still unable to communicate. Both of them are able to communicate with the NetWare server, but they cannot communicate with one another. What is the likely cause of the problem?

A. You haven't loaded Client Services for NetWare.

B. They are using different frame types.

C. You need to load Gateway Services for NetWare.

D. You need to enable SAP broadcasts.

ANSWERS & EXPLANATIONS

1. **C – D.** A is incorrect, because FAT supports long filenames as well. B is incorrect because NTFS is supported only under Windows NT.
2. **B.** You need three answer files, one for each type of hardware configuration, and one UDF file in which you can place individual sections for each user or system.
3. **B.** The uniqueness database file contains the information needed to make each user's PC unique.
4. **C.** Using System properties in Control Panel or the properties sheet for My Computer, you can select the Environment tab and modify the value of PATH from there.
5. **B.** FAT supports long filenames, but not permissions.
6. **D.** MS-DOS is not compatible with NTFS; therefore, you must repartition and reformat the system from scratch.
7. **D.** DLC is used for IBM mainframe and HP Jet-Direct communications.
8. **C.** Macintosh computers communicate using the AppleTalk protocol.
9. **B.** Redirecting a physical port fools the MS-DOS program into thinking it is printing to a physical printer.
10. **D.** Because NT 4 does not support the HPFS file system from OS/2, you must first convert the file system. Like NTFS, HPFS supports permissions and ownership. If you convert to FAT, this is all lost; so NTFS is the better choice.
11. **A.** Moving a file on the same partition causes the file to retain its original permissions.
12. **D.** Because FAT does not support any permissions, all permissions are lost.
13. **D.** The answer file and uniqueness files have been reversed. This causes the installation to fail entirely. Because the answer file is used to specify the hardware information, two are needed. The uniqueness file is used to specify the user information, so only one is needed.
14. **C.** You can create a single policy and have all users apply it by placing it in the NETLOGON directory of the PDC.
15. **A – B.** Logon scripts and policies need to be replicated for users to use them.
16. **D.** Lori gets No Access because that overrides all other permissions.
17. **D.** A user is always given the more restrictive of either local or remote access when accessing remotely.
18. **D.** This option will turn on notification of print job completion.
19. **B.** System policies override local, roaming, or mandatory profiles, so you will have to modify the system policy to include a user entry for Grace with the settings from her roaming profile.

20. **A.** System policies always take precedence over mandatory user profiles. Individual occurs before group, which precedes default profiles (i.e. no others found).

21. **D.** The first RWX stipulates Read/Write/Execute for existing files. The None signifies no access for new files. Creators always have Full Control of their own files.

22. **B.** The Print Banner option will cause NetWare to precede print jobs with a separator page.

23. **D.** NT does not have the ability to limit disk space use on an individual basis.

24. **C.** Using the Dial-Up Networking Monitor will show you information such as what protocols are being established when the connection is made.

25. **C.** DNS (Domain Name Service) provides the resolution of domain names into IP addresses.

26. **D.** Syscon is the only listed tool that will work correctly. The functionality of the rest is built into NT Workstation.

27. **B.** NWLink provides a common protocol, and Client Services for NetWare provides the capability to act as a client to the NetWare server.

28. **C.** \\www.acme.com.\procedures will get Emily to the correct spot.

29. **B.** The Server service allows incoming connections, so disabling it prevents others from connecting to your computer.

30. **B.** WINS is designed specifically to allow name resolution in a dynamic environment.

31. **D.** SNMP allows NT to be configured to send traps to management stations.

32. **A.** Enabling the DNS server to interact with the WINS server allows for the UNIX systems to use WINS, which would otherwise not be possible.

33. **D.** Point-to-Point Tunneling Protocol allows for encrypted communications by way of TCP/IP networks such as the Internet.

34. **C.** This is the correct syntax.

35. **C – D.** MS-DOS applications cannot share the same memory space or have direct access to the hardware.

36. **B.** Each Win16 application is given its own thread in a common NTVDM with shared memory for backward compatibility. It should be noted that each application has its own thread inside the NTVDM; outside the NTVDM, all applications share the same thread.

37. **A – B.** Both these methods enable you to specify the option to execute the application in a separate memory space.

38. **A.** Network monitor agent allows the system to listen to the network and obtain information such as utilization.

39. **C.** The proposed solution does increase file access speed both locally and across the network. It does nothing to help with the paging file, however.

40. **A – C.** These tools both enable you to see memory usage.

41. **B – D.** The % Processor Time shows non-idle activity of the processor, and the

System Object Processor Queue Length indicates the processes using that time.

42. **B.** The Recovery option (on by default) is enabled and disabled through the Startup/Shutdown tab of the System applet in Control Panel.

43. **B – D.** Both of these methods will work.

44. **C.** This is the appropriate response. Although the other items are reasonable, they do not account for the user's inability to delete the job from the queue.

45. **B.** The boot.ini file tells the system where to find the boot information.

46. **B – C – D.** `Fdisk.exe /mbr` needs to be run to fix the master boot record.

47. **D.** C:\Winnt\system32\RAS is the default directory on most systems for this.

48. **B.** An incorrect subnet mask would allow some connectivity by yielding some local systems as local and others as remote.

49. **C.** The bootsect.dos file contains a copy of the original MS-DOS boot sector and is needed to successfully boot MS-DOS.

50. **D.** A lack of hard drive space for spooling the files is the most likely culprit.

51. **B.** The server is probably configured with dual IPX/SPX frame types, and the stations have differing IPX/SPX frame types.

APPENDIX A

Exam Strategies

You must pass rigorous certification exams to become a Microsoft Certified Professional. These closed-book exams provide a valid and reliable measure of your technical proficiency and expertise. Developed in consultation with computer industry professionals who have on-the-job experience with Microsoft products in the workplace, the exams are conducted by two independent organizations. Sylvan Prometric offers the exams at more than 1,400 Authorized Prometric Testing Centers around the world. Virtual University Enterprises (VUE) testing centers offer exams as well.

To schedule an exam, call Sylvan Prometric Testing Centers at 800-755-EXAM (3926) or VUE at 888-837-8616.

This appendix is divided into two main sections. First, it describes the different certification options provided by Microsoft, and how you can achieve those certifications. The second portion highlights the different kinds of examinations and the best ways to prepare for those different exam and question styles.

Types of Certification

Currently Microsoft offers seven types of certification, based on specific areas of expertise:

- **Microsoft Certified Professional (MCP).** Qualified to provide installation, configuration, and support for users of at least one Microsoft desktop operating system, such as Windows NT Workstation. Candidates can take elective exams to develop areas of specialization. MCP is the base level of expertise.
- **Microsoft Certified Professional+Internet (MCP+Internet).** Qualified to plan security, install and configure server products, manage server resources, extend service to run CGI scripts or ISAPI scripts, monitor and analyze performance, and troubleshoot problems. Expertise is similar to that of an MCP, but with a focus on the Internet.
- **Microsoft Certified Professional+Site Building (MCP+Site Building).** Qualified to plan, build, maintain, and manage Web sites by using Microsoft technologies and products. The credential is appropriate for people who manage sophisticated, interactive Web sites that include database connectivity, multimedia, and searchable content.
- **Microsoft Certified Systems Engineer (MCSE).** Qualified to effectively plan, implement, maintain, and support information systems with Microsoft Windows NT and other Microsoft advanced systems and workgroup products, such as Microsoft Office and Microsoft BackOffice. MCSE is a second level of expertise.

- **Microsoft Certified Systems Engineer+ Internet (MCSE+Internet).** Qualified in the core MCSE areas, and also qualified to enhance, deploy, and manage sophisticated intranet and Internet solutions that include a browser, proxy server, host servers, database, and messaging and commerce components. An MCSE+Internet–certified professional is able to manage and analyze Web sites.
- **Microsoft Certified Solution Developer (MCSD).** Qualified to design and develop custom business solutions by using Microsoft development tools, technologies, and platforms, including Microsoft Office and Microsoft BackOffice. MCSD is a second level of expertise, with a focus on software development.
- **Microsoft Certified Trainer (MCT).** Instructionally and technically qualified by Microsoft to deliver Microsoft Education Courses at Microsoft-authorized sites. An MCT must be employed by a Microsoft Solution Provider Authorized Technical Education Center or a Microsoft Authorized Academic Training site.

▼ NOTE

For the most up-to-date information about each type of certification, visit the Microsoft Training and Certification Web site at `http://www.microsoft.com/train_cert`. You also can call or email the following sources:

- Microsoft Certified Professional Program: 800-636-7544
- `mcp@msprograms.com`
- Microsoft Online Institute (MOLI): 800-449-9333

Certification Requirements

The requirements for certification in each of the seven areas are detailed below. An asterisk after an exam indicates that the exam is slated for retirement.

How to Become a Microsoft Certified Professional

Passing any Microsoft exam (with the exception of Networking Essentials) is all you need to do to become certified as an MCP.

How to Become a Microsoft Certified Professional+Internet

You must pass the following exams to become an MCP specializing in Internet technology:

- Internetworking Microsoft TCP/IP on Microsoft Windows NT 4.0, #70-059
- Implementing and Supporting Microsoft Windows NT Server 4.0, #70-067
- Implementing and Supporting Microsoft Internet Information Server 3.0 and Microsoft Index Server 1.1, #70-077

  OR Implementing and Supporting Microsoft Internet Information Server 4.0, #70-087

How to Become a Microsoft Certified Professional+Site Building

You need to pass two of the following exams in order to be certified as an MCP+Site Building:

- Designing and Implementing Web Sites with Microsoft FrontPage 98, #70-055

- Designing and Implementing Commerce Solutions with Microsoft Site Server 3.0, Commerce Edition, #70-057
- Designing and Implementing Web Solutions with Microsoft Visual InterDev 6.0, #70-152

How to Become a Microsoft Certified Systems Engineer

You must pass four operating system exams and two elective exams to become an MCSE. The MCSE certification path is divided into two tracks: the Windows NT 3.51 track and the Windows NT 4.0 track.

The following lists show the core requirements (four operating system exams) for both the Windows NT 3.51 and 4.0 tracks, and the elective courses (two exams) you can take for either track.

The four Windows NT 3.51 Track Core Requirements for MCSE certification are as follows:

- Implementing and Supporting Microsoft Windows NT Server 3.51, #70-043*
- Implementing and Supporting Microsoft Windows NT Workstation 3.51, #70-042*
- Microsoft Windows 3.1, #70-030*

  OR Microsoft Windows for Workgroups 3.11, #70-048*

  OR Implementing and Supporting Microsoft Windows 95, #70-064

  OR Implementing and Supporting Microsoft Windows 98, #70-098
- Networking Essentials, #70-058

The four Windows NT 4.0 Track Core Requirements for MCSE certification are as follows:

- Implementing and Supporting Microsoft Windows NT Server 4.0, #70-067
- Implementing and Supporting Microsoft Windows NT Server 4.0 in the Enterprise, #70-068
- Microsoft Windows 3.1, #70-030*

  OR Microsoft Windows for Workgroups 3.11, #70-048*

  OR Implementing and Supporting Microsoft Windows 95, #70-064

  OR Implementing and Supporting Microsoft Windows NT Workstation 4.0, #70-073

  OR Implementing and Supporting Microsoft Windows 98, #70-098
- Networking Essentials, #70-058

For both the Windows NT 3.51 and the 4.0 tracks, you must pass two of the following elective exams for MCSE certification:

- Implementing and Supporting Microsoft SNA Server 3.0, #70-013

  OR Implementing and Supporting Microsoft SNA Server 4.0, #70-085
- Implementing and Supporting Microsoft Systems Management Server 1.0, #70-014*

  OR Implementing and Supporting Microsoft Systems Management Server 1.2, #70-018

  OR Implementing and Supporting Microsoft Systems Management Server 2.0, #70-086

- Microsoft SQL Server 4.2 Database Implementation, #70-021

  OR Implementing a Database Design on Microsoft SQL Server 6.5, #70-027

  OR Implementing a Database Design on Microsoft SQL Server 7.0, #70-029
- Microsoft SQL Server 4.2 Database Administration for Microsoft Windows NT, #70-022

  OR System Administration for Microsoft SQL Server 6.5 (or 6.0), #70-026

  OR System Administration for Microsoft SQL Server 7.0, #70-028
- Microsoft Mail for PC Networks 3.2-Enterprise, #70-037
- Internetworking with Microsoft TCP/IP on Microsoft Windows NT (3.5-3.51), #70-053

  OR Internetworking with Microsoft TCP/IP on Microsoft Windows NT 4.0, #70-059
- Implementing and Supporting Microsoft Exchange Server 4.0, #70-075*

  OR Implementing and Supporting Microsoft Exchange Server 5.0, #70-076

  OR Implementing and Supporting Microsoft Exchange Server 5.5, #70-081
- Implementing and Supporting Microsoft Internet Information Server 3.0 and Microsoft Index Server 1.1, #70-077

  OR Implementing and Supporting Microsoft Internet Information Server 4.0, #70-087
- Implementing and Supporting Microsoft Proxy Server 1.0, #70-078

  OR Implementing and Supporting Microsoft Proxy Server 2.0, #70-088
- Implementing and Supporting Microsoft Internet Explorer 4.0 by Using the Internet Explorer Resource Kit, #70-079

How to Become a Microsoft Certified Systems Engineer+ Internet

You must pass seven operating system exams and two elective exams to become an MCSE specializing in Internet technology.

The seven MCSE+Internet core exams required for certification are as follows:

- Networking Essentials, #70-058
- Internetworking with Microsoft TCP/IP on Microsoft Windows NT 4.0, #70-059
- Implementing and Supporting Microsoft Windows 95, #70-064

  OR Implementing and Supporting Microsoft Windows NT Workstation 4.0, #70-073

  OR Implementing and Supporting Microsoft Windows 98, #70-098
- Implementing and Supporting Microsoft Windows NT Server 4.0, #70-067
- Implementing and Supporting Microsoft Windows NT Server 4.0 in the Enterprise, #70-068
- Implementing and Supporting Microsoft Internet Information Server 3.0 and Microsoft Index Server 1.1, #70-077

  OR Implementing and Supporting Microsoft Internet Information Server 4.0, #70-087

- Implementing and Supporting Microsoft Internet Explorer 4.0 by Using the Internet Explorer Resource Kit, #70-079

You must also pass two of the following elective exams for MCSE+Internet certification:

- System Administration for Microsoft SQL Server 6.5, #70-026
- Implementing a Database Design on Microsoft SQL Server 6.5, #70-027
- Implementing and Supporting Web Sites Using Microsoft Site Server 3.0, # 70-056
- Implementing and Supporting Microsoft Exchange Server 5.0, #70-076

  OR Implementing and Supporting Microsoft Exchange Server 5.5, #70-081
- Implementing and Supporting Microsoft Proxy Server 1.0, #70-078

  OR Implementing and Supporting Microsoft Proxy Server 2.0, #70-088
- Implementing and Supporting Microsoft SNA Server 4.0, #70-085

How to Become a Microsoft Certified Solution Developer

The MCSD certification is undergoing substantial revision. Listed next are the requirements for the new track (available fourth quarter 1998), as well as the old.

For the new track, you must pass three core exams and one elective exam.

The core exams include the following:

Desktop Applications Development (1 required)

- Designing and Implementing Desktop Applications with Microsoft Visual C++ 6.0, #70-016

  OR Designing and Implementing Desktop Applications with Microsoft Visual Basic 6.0, #70-176

Distributed Applications Development (1 required)

- Designing and Implementing Distributed Applications with Microsoft Visual C++ 6.0, #70-015

  OR Designing and Implementing Distributed Applications with Microsoft Visual Basic 6.0, #70-175

Solution Architecture (required)

- Analyzing Requirements and Defining Solution Architectures, #70-100

Elective Exams

You must also pass one of the following elective exams:

- Designing and Implementing Distributed Applications with Microsoft Visual C++ 6.0, #70-015

  OR Designing and Implementing Desktop Applications with Microsoft Visual C++ 6.0, #70-016

  OR Microsoft SQL Server 4.2 Database Implementation, #70-021*

- Implementing a Database Design on Microsoft SQL Server 6.5, #70-027

  OR Implementing a Database Design on Microsoft SQL Server 7.0, #70-029
- Developing Applications with C++ Using the Microsoft Foundation Class Library, #70-024
- Implementing OLE in Microsoft Foundation Class Applications, #70-025
- Designing and Implementing Web Sites with Microsoft FrontPage 98, #70-055
- Designing and Implementing Commerce Solutions with Microsoft Site Server 3.0, Commerce Edition, #70-057
- Programming with Microsoft Visual Basic 4.0, #70-065

  OR Developing Applications with Microsoft Visual Basic 5.0, #70-165

  OR Designing and Implementing Distributed Applications with Microsoft Visual Basic 6.0, #70-175

  OR Designing and Implementing Desktop Applications with Microsoft Visual Basic 6.0, #70-176
- Microsoft Access for Windows 95 and the Microsoft Access Development Toolkit, #70-069
- Designing and Implementing Solutions with Microsoft Office (Code-named Office 9) and Microsoft Visual Basic for Applications, #70-091
- Designing and Implementing Web Solutions with Microsoft Visual InterDev 6.0, #70-152

Former MCSD Track

For the old track, you must pass two core technology exams and two elective exams for MCSD certification. The following lists show the required technology exams and elective exams needed to become an MCSD.

You must pass the following two core technology exams to qualify for MCSD certification:

- Microsoft Windows Architecture I, #70-160*
- Microsoft Windows Architecture II, #70-161*

You must also pass two of the following elective exams to become an MSCD:

- Designing and Implementing Distributed Applications with Microsoft Visual C++ 6.0, #70-015
- Designing and Implementing Desktop Applications with Microsoft Visual C++ 6.0, #70-016
- Microsoft SQL Server 4.2 Database Implementation, #70-021*

  OR Implementing a Database Design on Microsoft SQL Server 6.5, #70-027

  OR Implementing a Database Design on Microsoft SQL Server 7.0, #70-029
- Developing Applications with C++ Using the Microsoft Foundation Class Library, #70-024
- Implementing OLE in Microsoft Foundation Class Applications, #70-025
- Programming with Microsoft Visual Basic 4.0, #70-065

OR Developing Applications with Microsoft Visual Basic 5.0, #70-165

OR Designing and Implementing Distributed Applications with Microsoft Visual Basic 6.0, #70-175

OR Designing and Implementing Desktop Applications with Microsoft Visual Basic 6.0, #70-176

- Microsoft Access 2.0 for Windows-Application Development, #70-051

  OR Microsoft Access for Windows 95 and the Microsoft Access Development Toolkit, #70-069

- Developing Applications with Microsoft Excel 5.0 Using Visual Basic for Applications, #70-052
- Programming in Microsoft Visual FoxPro 3.0 for Windows, #70-054
- Designing and Implementing Web Sites with Microsoft FrontPage 98, #70-055
- Designing and Implementing Commerce Solutions with Microsoft Site Server 3.0, Commerce Edition, #70-057
- Designing and Implementing Solutions with Microsoft Office (Code-named Office 9) and Microsoft Visual Basic for Applications, #70-091
- Designing and Implementing Web Solutions with Microsoft Visual InterDev 6.0, #70-152

Becoming a Microsoft Certified Trainer

To understand the requirements and process for becoming an MCT, you need to obtain the Microsoft Certified Trainer Guide document from the following site:

`http://www.microsoft.com/train_cert/mct/`

At this site, you can read the document as Web pages or display and download it as a Word file. The MCT Guide explains the four-step process of becoming an MCT. The general steps for the MCT certification are as follows:

1. Complete and mail a Microsoft Certified Trainer application to Microsoft. You must include proof of your skills for presenting instructional material. The options for doing so are described in the MCT Guide.
2. Obtain and study the Microsoft Trainer Kit for the Microsoft Official Curricula (MOC) courses for which you want to be certified. Microsoft Trainer Kits can be ordered by calling 800-688-0496 in North America. Interested parties in other regions should review the MCT Guide for information on how to order a Trainer Kit.
3. Take the Microsoft certification exam for the product about which you want to be certified to teach.
4. Attend the MOC course for the course for which you want to be certified. This is done so you can understand how the course is structured, how labs are completed, and how the course flows.

> **◆ WARNING**
>
> You should consider the preceding steps a general overview of the MCT certification process. The precise steps that you need to take are described in detail on the Web site mentioned earlier. Do not misinterpret the preceding steps as the exact process you need to undergo.

If you are interested in becoming an MCT, you can receive more information by visiting the Microsoft Certified Training Web site at `http://www.microsoft.com/train_cert/mct/` or by calling 800-688-0496.

Study and Exam Preparation Tips

This part of the appendix provides you with some general guidelines for preparing for the exam. It is organized into three sections. The first section, "Study Tips," addresses your pre-exam preparation activities, covering general study tips. This is followed by "Exam Prep Tips," an extended look at the Microsoft Certification exams, including a number of specific tips that apply to the Microsoft exam formats. Finally, "Putting It All Together" discusses changes in Microsoft's testing policies and how they might affect you.

To better understand the nature of preparation for the test, it is important to understand learning as a process. You probably are aware of how you best learn new material. You may find that outlining works best for you, or you may need to see things as a visual learner. Whatever your learning style, test preparation takes place over time. Although it is obvious that you can't start studying for these exams the night before you take them, it is very important to understand that learning is a developmental process. Understanding it as a process helps you focus on what you know and what you have yet to learn.

Thinking about how you learn should help you to recognize that learning takes place when you are able to match new information to old. You have some previous experience with computers and networking, and now you are preparing for this certification exam. Using this book, software, and supplementary materials will not just add incrementally to what you know. As you study, you actually change the organization of your knowledge as you integrate this new information into your existing knowledge base. This will lead you to a more comprehensive understanding of the tasks and concepts outlined in the objectives and of computing in general. Again, this happens as an iterative process rather than a singular event. Keep this model of learning in mind as you prepare for the exam, and you will make better decisions about what to study and how much more studying you need to do.

Study Tips

There are many ways to approach studying, just as there are many different types of material to study. However, the tips that follow should prepare you well for the type of material covered on the certification exams.

Study Strategies

Individuals vary in the ways they learn information. Some basic principles of learning apply to everyone, however; you should adopt some study strategies that take advantage of these principles. One of these principles is that learning can be broken into various depths. Recognition (of terms, for example) exemplifies a more surface level of learning—you rely on a prompt of some sort to elicit recall. Comprehension or understanding (of the concepts behind the terms, for instance) represents a deeper level of learning. The ability to analyze a concept and apply your understanding of it in a new way or novel setting represents an even further depth of learning.

Your learning strategy should enable you to understand the material at a level or two deeper than mere recognition. This will help you to do well on the exam(s). You will know the material so thoroughly that you can easily handle the recognition-level types of questions used in multiple-choice testing. You will also be able to apply your knowledge to solve novel problems.

Macro and Micro Study Strategies

One strategy that can lead to this deeper learning includes preparing an outline that covers all the objectives and subobjectives for the particular exam you are working on. You should delve a bit further into the material and include a level or two of detail beyond the stated objectives and subobjectives for the exam. Then flesh out the outline by coming up with a statement of definition or a summary for each point in the outline.

This outline provides two approaches to studying. First, you can study the outline by focusing on the organization of the material. Work your way through the points and subpoints of your outline with the goal of learning how they relate to one another. For example, be sure you understand how each of the main objective areas is similar to and different from another. Then do the same thing with the subobjectives; be sure you know which subobjectives pertain to each objective area and how they relate to one another.

Next, you can work through the outline, focusing on learning the details. Memorize and understand terms and their definitions, facts, rules and strategies, advantages and disadvantages, and so on. In this pass through the outline, attempt to learn detail rather than the big picture (the organizational information that you worked on in the first pass through the outline).

Research has shown that attempting to assimilate both types of information at the same time seems to interfere with the overall learning process. Separate your studying into these two approaches, and you will perform better on the exam than if you attempt to study the material in a more conventional manner.

Active Study Strategies

In addition, the process of writing down and defining the objectives, subobjectives, terms, facts, and definitions promotes a more active learning strategy than merely reading the material. In human information-processing terms, writing forces you to engage in more active encoding of the information. Simply reading over it constitutes more passive processing.

Next, determine whether you can apply the information you have learned by attempting to create examples and scenarios of your own. Think about how or where you could apply the concepts you are learning. Again, write down this information to process the facts and concepts in a more active fashion.

The hands-on nature of the step-by-step tutorials and exercises at the ends of the chapters provide further active learning opportunities that will reinforce concepts as well.

Common-sense Strategies

Finally, you should follow common-sense practices in studying. Study when you are alert, reduce or eliminate distractions, take breaks when you become fatigued, and so on.

Pre-testing Yourself

Pre-testing allows you to assess how well you are learning. One of the most important aspects of learning is what has been called meta-learning. *Meta-learning* has to do with realizing when you know something well or when you need to study more. In other words, you recognize how well or how poorly you have learned the material you are studying. For most people, this can be difficult to assess objectively on their own. Practice tests are useful in that they reveal more objectively what you have learned and what you have not learned. You should use this information to guide review and further studying. Developmental learning takes place as you cycle through studying, assessing how well you have learned, reviewing, assessing again, until you feel you are ready to take the exam.

You may have noticed the practice exams included in this book. Use them as part of this process.

Exam Prep Tips

Having mastered the subject matter, your final preparatory step is to understand how the exam will be presented. Make no mistake about it—a Microsoft Certified Professional (MCP) exam will challenge both your knowledge and test-taking skills! This section starts with the basics of exam design, reviews a new type of exam format, and concludes with hints that are targeted to each of the exam formats.

The MCP Exams

Every MCP exam is released in one of two basic formats. What's being called exam format here is really little more than a combination of the overall exam structure and the presentation method for exam questions.

Each exam format utilizes the same types of questions. These types or styles of questions include multiple-rating (or scenario-based) questions, traditional multiple-choice questions, and simulation-based questions. It's important to understand the types of questions you will be presented with and the actions required to properly answer them.

Understanding the exam formats is key to good preparation because the format determines the number of questions presented, the difficulty of those questions, and the amount of time allowed to complete the exam.

Exam Formats

There are two basic formats for the MCP exams: the traditional fixed-form exam and the adaptive form. As its name implies, the fixed-form exam presents a fixed set of questions during the exam session. The adaptive format, however, uses only a subset of questions drawn from a larger pool during any given exam session.

Fixed-form

A fixed-form, computerized exam is based on a fixed set of exam questions. The individual questions are presented in random order during a test session. If you take the same exam more than once, you won't necessarily see the exact same questions. This is because two to three final forms are typically assembled for every fixed-form exam Microsoft releases. These are usually labeled Forms A, B, and C.

The final forms of a fixed-form exam are identical in terms of content coverage, number of questions, and allotted time, but the questions themselves are different. You may have noticed, however, that some of the same questions appear on, or rather are shared across, different final forms. When questions are shared across multiple final forms of an exam, the percentage of sharing is generally small. Many final forms share no questions, but some older exams may have a ten to fifteen percent duplication of exam questions on the final exam forms.

Fixed-form exams also have a fixed time limit in which you must complete the exam.

Finally, the score you achieve on a fixed-form exam, which is always reported for MCP exams on a scale of 0 to 1000, is based on the number of questions you answer correctly. The exam passing score is the same for all final forms of a given fixed-form exam.

The typical format for the fixed-form exam is as follows:

- 50–60 questions
- 75–90 minute testing time
- Question review allowed, including the opportunity to change your answers

Adaptive Form

An adaptive form exam has the same appearance as a fixed-form exam, but differs in both how questions are selected for presentation and how many questions actually are presented. Although the statistics of adaptive testing are fairly complex, the process is concerned with determining your level of skill or ability with the exam subject matter. This ability assessment begins by presenting questions of varying levels of difficulty and ascertaining at what difficulty level you can reliably answer them. Finally, the ability assessment determines if that ability level is above or below the level required to pass that exam.

Examinees at different levels of ability will then see quite different sets of questions. Those who demonstrate little expertise with the subject matter will continue to be presented with relatively easy questions. Examinees who demonstrate a higher level of expertise will be presented progressively more difficult questions. Both individuals may answer the same number of questions correctly, but because the exam-taker with the higher level of expertise can correctly answer more difficult questions, he or she will receive a higher score, and is more likely to pass the exam.

The typical design for the adaptive form exam is as follows:

- 20–25 questions
- 90-minute testing time, although this is likely to be reduced to 45–60 minutes in the near future
- Question review not allowed, providing no opportunity to change your answers

Your first adaptive exam will be unlike any other testing experience you have had. In fact, many examinees have difficulty accepting the adaptive testing process because they feel that they are not provided the opportunity to adequately demonstrate their full expertise.

You can take consolation in the fact that adaptive exams are painstakingly put together after months of data gathering and analysis and are just as valid as a fixed-form exam. The rigor introduced through the adaptive testing methodology means that there is nothing arbitrary about what you'll see! It is also a more efficient means of testing, requiring less time to conduct and complete.

As you can see from Figure A.1, there are a number of statistical measures that drive the adaptive examination process. The most immediately relevant to you is the ability estimate. Accompanying this test statistic are the standard error of measurement, the item characteristic curve, and the test information curve.

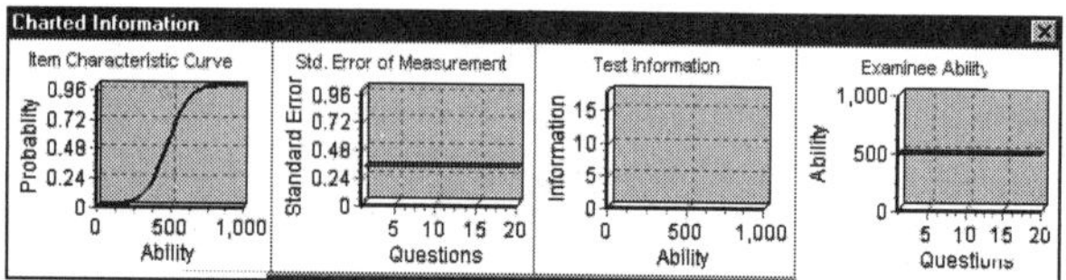

FIGURE A.1
Microsoft's Adaptive Testing Demonstration Program.

The standard error, which is the key factor in determining when an adaptive exam will terminate, reflects the degree of error in the exam ability estimate. The item characteristic curve reflects the probability of a correct response relative to examinee ability. Finally, the test information statistic provides a measure of the information contained in the set of questions the examinee has answered, again relative to the ability level of the individual examinee.

When you begin an adaptive exam, the standard error has already been assigned a target value below which it must drop for the exam to conclude. This target value reflects a particular level of statistical confidence in the process. The examinee ability is initially set to the mean possible exam score: 500 for MCP exams.

As the adaptive exam progresses, questions of varying difficulty are presented. Based on your pattern of responses to these questions, the ability estimate is recalculated. Simultaneously, the standard error estimate is refined from its first estimated value of one toward the target value. When the standard error reaches its target value, the exam terminates. Thus, the more consistently you answer questions of the same degree of difficulty, the more quickly the standard error estimate drops, and the fewer questions you will end up seeing during the exam session. This situation is depicted in Figure A.2.

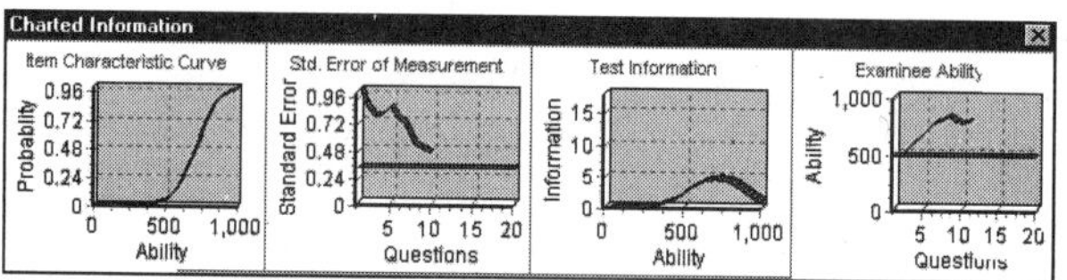

FIGURE A.2
The changing statistics in an adaptive exam.

As you might suspect, one good piece of advice for taking an adaptive exam is to treat every exam question as if it were the most important. The adaptive scoring algorithm is attempting to discover a pattern of responses that reflects some level of proficiency with the subject matter. Incorrect responses almost guarantee that additional questions must be answered (unless, of course, you get every question wrong). This is because the scoring algorithm must adjust to information that is not consistent with the emerging pattern.

New Question Types

A variety of question types can appear on MCP exams. Examples of multiple-choice questions and scenario-based questions appear throughout this book. They appear in the Top Score software as well. Simulation-based questions are new to the MCP exam series.

Simulation Questions

Simulation-based questions reproduce the look and feel of key Microsoft product features for the purpose of testing. The simulation software used in MCP exams has been designed to look and act, as much as possible, just like the actual product. Consequently, answering simulation questions in an MCP exam entails completing one or more tasks just as if you were using the product itself.

The format of a typical Microsoft simulation question is straightforward. It presents a brief scenario or problem statement along with one or more tasks that must be completed to solve the problem. An example of a simulation question for MCP exams is shown in the following section.

A Typical Simulation Question

It sounds obvious, but the first step when you encounter a simulation is to carefully read the question (see Figure A.3). Do not go straight to the simulation application! Assess the problem being presented and identify the conditions that make up the problem scenario. Note the tasks that must be performed or outcomes that must be achieved to answer the question, and review any instructions about how to proceed.

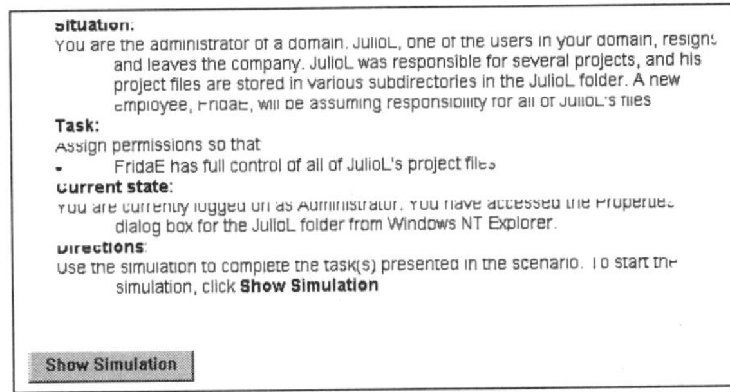

FIGURE A.3
Typical MCP exam simulation question with directions.

The next step is to launch the simulator. Click the Show Simulation button to see a feature of the product, such as the dialog box shown in Figure A.4. The simulation application partially covers the question text on many test center machines. Feel free to reposition the simulation or to move between the question text screen and the simulation using hot keys, point-and-click navigation, or even by clicking the simulation launch button again.

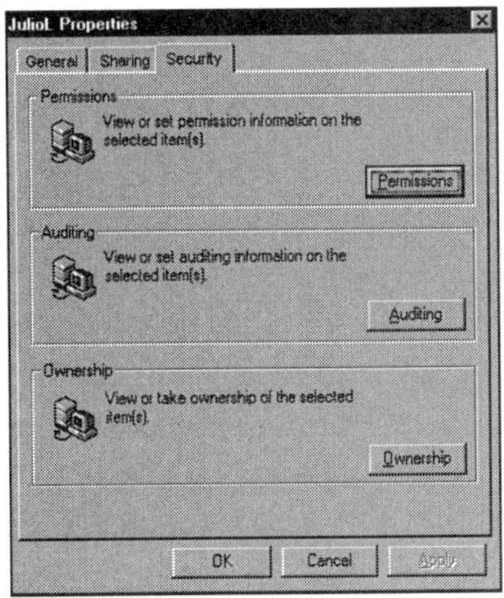

FIGURE A.4
Launching the simulation application.

It is important to understand that your answer to the simulation question is not recorded until you move on to the next exam question. This gives you the added capability to close and reopen the simulation application (using the launch button) on the same question without losing any partial answer you may have made.

The third step is to use the simulator as you would the actual product to solve the problem or perform the defined tasks. Again, the simulation software is designed to function, within reason, just as the product does. But don't expect the simulation to reproduce product behavior perfectly.

Most importantly, do not allow yourself to become flustered if the simulation does not look or act exactly like the product. Figure A.5 shows the solution to the example simulation problem.

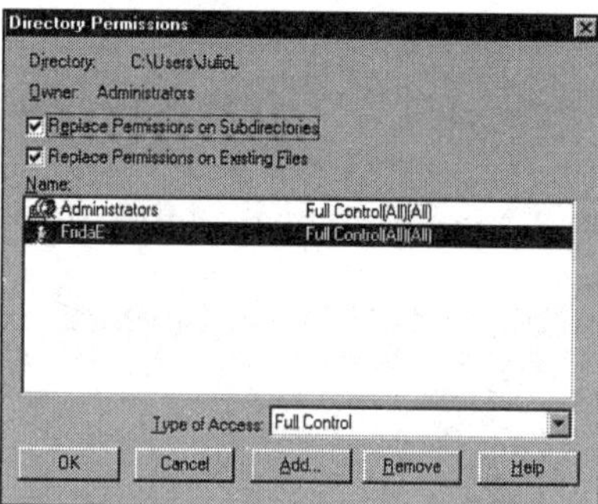

FIGURE A.5
The solution to the simulation example.

There are two final points that will help you tackle simulation questions. First, respond only to what is being asked in the question. Do not solve problems that you are not asked to solve. Second, accept what is being asked of you. You may not entirely agree with conditions in the problem statement, the quality of the desired solution, or the sufficiency of defined tasks to adequately solve the problem. Always remember that you are being tested on your ability to solve the problem as it has been presented.

The solution to the simulation problem shown in Figure A.5 perfectly illustrates both of these points. As you'll recall from the question scenario (refer to Figure A.3), you were asked to assign appropriate permissions to a new user, FridaE. You were not instructed to make any other changes in permissions. Thus, if you had modified or removed Administrators permissions, this item would have been scored as incorrect on an MCP exam.

Putting It All Together

Given all these different pieces of information, the task is now to assemble a set of tips that will help you successfully tackle the different types of MCP exams.

More Pre-exam Preparation Tips

Generic exam preparation advice is always useful. Tips include the following:

- Become familiar with the product. Hands-on experience is one of the keys to success on any MCP exam. Review the exercises and the step-by-step activities in the book.
- Review the current exam preparation guide on the Microsoft MCP Web site. The documentation Microsoft makes publicly available over the Web identifies the skills every exam is intended to test.
- Memorize foundational technical detail as appropriate. Remember that MCP exams are generally heavy on problem solving and application of knowledge rather than just questions that only require rote memorization.
- Take any of the available practice tests. We recommend the ones included in this book and the ones you can create using New Riders' exclusive Top Score Test Simulation software suite, available through your local bookstore or software distributor. Although these are fixed-format exams, they provide practice that is valuable for preparing for an adaptive exam. Because of the interactive nature of adaptive testing, it is not possible to provide examples of the adaptive format in the included practice exams. However,

fixed-format exams do provide the same types of questions as found on adaptive exams and are the most effective way to prepare for either type of exam. As a supplement to the material bound with this book, also try the free practice tests available on the Microsoft MCP Web site.

- Look on the Microsoft MCP Web site for samples and demonstration items. These tend to be particularly valuable for one significant reason: They allow you to become familiar with any new testing technologies before you encounter them on an MCP exam.

During the Exam Session

Similarly, the generic exam-taking advice you've heard for years applies when taking an MCP exam:

- Take a deep breath and try to relax when you first sit down for your exam session. It is very important to control the pressure you may (naturally) feel when taking exams.
- You will be provided scratch paper. Take a moment to write down any factual information and technical detail that you've committed to short-term memory.
- Carefully read all information and instruction screens. These displays have been put together to give you information relevant to the exam you are taking.
- Accept the Non-Disclosure Agreement and preliminary survey as part of the examination process. Complete them accurately and quickly move on.
- Read the exam questions carefully. Reread each question to identify all relevant detail.
- Tackle the questions in the order they are presented. Skipping around won't build your confidence; the clock is always counting down.
- Don't rush, but similarly, don't linger on difficult questions. The questions vary in degree of difficulty. Don't let yourself be flustered by a particularly difficult or verbose question.

Fixed-form Exams

Building from this basic preparation and test-taking advice, you also need to consider the challenges presented by the different exam designs. Because a fixed-form exam is composed of a fixed, finite set of questions, add these tips to your strategy for taking a fixed-form exam:

- Note the time allotted and the number of questions appearing on the exam you are taking. Make a rough calculation of how many minutes you can spend on each question and use this to pace yourself through the exam.
- Take advantage of the fact that you can return to and review skipped or previously answered questions. Mark the questions you can't answer confidently, noting the relative difficulty of each question on the scratch paper provided. When you reach the end of the exam, return to the more difficult questions.
- If there is session time remaining after you have completed all questions (and you aren't too fatigued!), review your answers. Pay particular attention to questions that seem to have a lot of detail or that required graphics.

- As for changing your answers, the rule of thumb here is *don't*! If you read the question carefully and completely, and you felt like you knew the right answer, you probably did. Don't second-guess yourself. If, as you check your answers, one stands out as clearly marked incorrectly, however, you should change it in that instance. If you are at all unsure, go with your first impression.

Adaptive Exams

If you are planning to take an adaptive exam, keep these additional tips in mind:

- Read and answer every question with great care. When reading a question, identify every relevant detail, requirement, or task that must be performed and double-check your answer to be sure you have addressed every one of them.
- If you cannot answer a question, use the process of elimination to reduce the set of potential answers, then take your best guess. Stupid mistakes invariably mean additional questions will be presented.
- Forget about reviewing questions and changing your answers. After you leave a question, whether you've answered it or not, you cannot return to it. Do not skip a question, either; if you do, it's counted as incorrect!

Simulation Questions

You may encounter simulation questions on either the fixed-form or adaptive form exam. If you do, keep these tips in mind:

- Avoid changing any simulation settings that don't pertain directly to the problem solution. Solve the problem you are being asked to solve, and nothing more.
- Assume default settings when related information has not been provided. If something has not been mentioned or defined, it is a non-critical detail that does not factor in to the correct solution.
- Be sure your entries are syntactically correct, paying particular attention to your spelling. Enter relevant information just as the product would require it.
- Close all simulation application windows after completing the simulation tasks. The testing system software is designed to trap errors that could result when using the simulation application, but trust yourself over the testing software.
- If simulations are part of a fixed-form exam, you can return to skipped or previously answered questions and review your answers. However, if you choose to change your answer to a simulation question, or even attempt to review the settings you've made in the simulation application, your previous response to that simulation question will be deleted. If simulations are part of an adaptive exam, you cannot return to previous questions.

Final Considerations

There are a number of changes in the MCP program that will impact how frequently you can repeat an exam and what you will see when you do.

- Microsoft has instituted a new exam retake policy. This new rule is "two and two, then one and two." That is, you can attempt any exam two times with no restrictions on the time between attempts. But after the second attempt, you must wait two weeks before you can attempt that exam again. After that, you will be required to wait two weeks between any subsequent attempts. Plan to pass the exam in two attempts, or plan to increase your time horizon for receiving an MCP credential.
- New questions are being seeded into the MCP exams. After performance data has been gathered on new questions, they will replace older questions on all exam forms. This means that the questions appearing on exams are regularly changing.
- Many of the current MCP exams will be republished in adaptive format in the coming months. Prepare yourself for this significant change in testing format; it is entirely likely that this will become the new preferred MCP exam format.

These changes mean that the brute-force strategies for passing MCP exams may soon completely lose their viability. So if you don't pass an exam on the first or second attempt, it is entirely possible that the exam will change significantly in form. It could be updated to adaptive form from fixed-form or have a different set of questions or question types.

The intention of Microsoft is clearly not to make the exams more difficult by introducing unwanted change. Their intent is to create and maintain valid measures of the technical skills and knowledge associated with the different MCP credentials. Preparing for an MCP exam has always involved not only studying the subject matter, but also planning for the testing experience itself. With these changes, this is now more true than ever.

APPENDIX B

Glossary

A

Account policy Controls the way passwords must be used by all user accounts of a domain or of an individual computer. Specifics include minimum password length, how often a user must change his or her password, and how often users can reuse old passwords. Account policy can be set for all user accounts in a domain when administering a domain and for all user accounts of a single workstation or member server when administering a computer.

Alert view A view in the Performance Monitor in which thresholds for counters are set and then actions are taken when those thresholds are crossed.

Application log A server log accessible from the Event Viewer. This log records messages, warnings, and errors generated by applications running on your NT Server or Workstation.

applications A computer program used for a particular kind of work, such as word processing. This term is often used interchangeably with "program."

ARC-path The Advanced RISC Computing path is an industry standard method of identifying the physical location of a partition on a hard drive. ARC-paths are used in the BOOT.INI file to identify the location of NT boot files.

B

base priority The priority at which a program runs without any user or system intervention.

baseline An initial reading of a computer's performance, which is used as a "normal" reading against which other readings can be compared.

binary compatible A program having the characteristic of being usable by any hardware platform on which NT runs. DOS and WIN16 programs claim to be binary compatible across all hardware-specific versions of NT.

binding A process that establishes the communication channel between a protocol driver (such as TCP/IP) and a network card.

BOOT.INI A file located on the system partition of an NT Server or Workstation that's responsible for pointing the boot process to the correct boot files for the operating system chosen in the boot menu.

BOOTSECT.DOS A file located on the system partition that contains information required to boot an NT System to a non-NT operating system (MS-DOS, Windows 95) if a user requests it.

bottleneck A system resource that is the limiting factor in speed of processing. All systems have a bottleneck of some sort; the question is whether the bottleneck is significant in the context in which a Server finds itself.

built-in user accounts User accounts that are created in the account database automatically and cannot be deleted. Only the Administrator and Guest accounts are built-in.

built-in Windows NT groups Groups that are created in the NT accounts database automatically and cannot be deleted. These accounts include the Administrators group and the Guests group.

C

Chart view A view in the Performance Monitor in which a dynamically updated line graph or histogram is displayed for the counters selected in the view configuration.

Client Services for NetWare (CSNW) Included with Windows NT Workstation, this enables workstations to make direct connections to file and printer resources at NetWare servers running NetWare 2.x or later.

counter A specific component of a Performance Monitor object that has a displayable value. For example, for the object Memory, one counter is Available Bytes.

CSR subsystem The Client Server subsystem. Among its many functions is the execution of 32-bit Windows programs.

D

default performance boost The performance boost normally given to programs running in the foreground to allow better performance to the programs that a user is interacting with. This can be set between 0 and 2.

DETECT A troubleshooting acronym indicating a recommended method for approaching NT problems. The acronym DETECT stands for Discover, Explore, Track, Execute, Check, Tie-up.

device Any piece of equipment that can be attached to a network, such as a computer, a printer, or any other peripheral equipment.

difference file Created by the SYSDIFF program, a file that contains a description of the differences between one installation of NT and another. This difference file is used to create an .INF or an executable, both of which are typically used to install applications in conjunction with an automated NT installation.

DISKPERF A disk statistic monitor that can be turned on or off. It is required that DISKPERF be turned on to monitor disk performance.

DLC A protocol that, in NT, is typically used to communicate with direct interface network printer adapters such as an HP Direct Jet.

Domain Name System (DNS) DNS offers a static, hierarchical name service for TCP/IP hosts. The network administrator configures the DNS with a list of hostnames and IP addresses, allowing users of workstations configured to query the DNS to specify remote systems by hostnames instead of by IP addresses. For example, a workstation configured to use DNS name resolution could use the command PING remotehost instead of PING 1.2.3.4 if the mapping for the system named remotehost was contained in the DNS database.

dual boot A computer that can boot two different operating systems.

Dynamic Host Configuration Protocol (DHCP) A protocol that offers dynamic configuration of IP addresses and related information through the DHCP Server service running on an NT Server. DHCP provides safe, reliable, and simple TCP/IP network configuration, prevents address conflicts, and helps conserve the use of IP addresses through centralized management of address allocation.

E

Emergency Repair Disk (ERD) A floppy disk containing configuration information for a specific NT Server or Workstation. This disk is created and updated using the RDISK utility and can be used in conjunction with the three NT Setup disks to recover from many NT system failures resulting from file and/or Registry corruption.

Event Viewer An administrative utility used to look at event logs. Three logs are provided to the Event Viewer: System log, Security log, and Application log.

extended partition Created from free space on a hard disk, an extended partition can be subpartitioned into zero or more logical drives. Only one of the four partitions allowed per physical disk can be an extended partition, and no primary partition needs to be present to create an extended partition.

F

FAT (File Allocation Table) A table or list maintained by some operating systems to keep track of the status of various segments of disk space used for file storage. Also referred to as the FAT file system, this method is used to format hard drives in DOS, Windows 95, and OS/2, and can be used in Windows NT.

File Delete Child A phenomenon resulting from the presence of the POSIX subsystem that allows someone to delete a file to which he or she has no access (NTFS permission) if he has Full Control to the folder in which the file is located.

FORCEDOS A switch used to ensure that OS/2 applications run in an NT Virtual DOS machine instead of in an OS/2 subsystem. This must be used to run OS/2 applications on non-Intel platforms because RISC platforms do not have the OS/2 subsystem.

G, H

hard links A POSIX compatibility feature that allows multiple filenames to point to the same file. Unlike shortcuts, which are files that point to other files, hard links actually are multiple filenames on the same file.

Hardware Compatibility List (HCL) The Windows NT Hardware Compatibility List lists all hardware devices supported by Windows NT. The most current version of the HCL can be downloaded from the Microsoft Web page (microsoft.com) on the Internet.

hardware profile A grouping of hardware devices that make up the current recognized NT hardware. An NT user can use different hardware profiles based on the needs of different situations.

High Performance File System (HPFS) Native to the OS/2 operating system, this file system was once supported by NT but is no longer in NT 4.0.

hive A section of the Registry that appears as a file on your hard disk. The Registry subtree is divided into hives (named for their resemblance to the cellular structure of a beehive). A hive is a discrete body of keys, subkeys, and values that is rooted at the top of the Registry hierarchy. A hive is backed by a single file and a .LOG file, which are stored in the %SystemRoot%\system32\config folder or the %SystemRoot%\profiles\username folder. By default, most hive files (Default, SAM, Security, and System) are stored in the %SystemRoot%\system32\config folder. The %SystemRoot%\profiles folder contains the user profile for each user of the computer. Because a hive is a file, it can be moved from one system to another; however, it can be edited only by using Registry Editor.

I, J, K

instances Multiple occurrences of the same object in Performance Monitor. For example, if a computer has two processors, each is recognized as a separate instance of the Processor object and can be monitored separately.

IPC mechanism A method, provided by a multitasking operating system, by which one task or process is enabled to exchange data with another. Common IPC mechanisms include pipes, semaphores, shared memory, queues, signals, and mailboxes.

L

LastKnownGood configuration A set of Registry settings that contains the hardware configuration of an NT computer during its last successful login. LastKnownGood can be used to recover from incorrect hardware setup as long as logon does not occur between when the configuration was changed and when LastKnownGood was invoked.

local group For Windows NT Workstation, a group that can be granted permissions and rights only for its own workstation. However, it can contain user accounts from its own computer and (if the workstation participates in a domain) user accounts and global groups both from its own domain and from trusted domains.

For Windows NT Server, a group that can be granted permissions and rights only for the domain controllers of its own domain. However, it can contain user accounts and global groups both from its own domain and from trusted domains.

Local groups provide a way to create handy sets of users from both inside and outside the domain, to be used only at domain controllers of the domain.

Log view The Performance Monitor view in which the configuration of a log is determined. Logs have no dynamic information; however, the resulting file can be analyzed using any of the other Performance Monitor views.

M

Master Boot Record (MBR) The place on the disk where the initial computer startup is directed to go to initiate operating system boot. The MBR is located on the primary partition.

multithreaded A program that has multiple execution strands or threads. On a multiprocessor system, multiple threads can be executed simultaneously and can, therefore, speed execution of the program as a whole.

N

NDIS Acronym for Network Driver Interface Specification, the Microsoft/3Com specification for the interface of network device drivers. All network adapter card drivers and protocol drivers shipped with Windows NT Server conform to NDIS.

NetBEUI A network protocol usually used in small, department-size local area networks of 1 to 200 clients. Because it is non-routable, it is not a preferred WAN protocol.

network monitor An administrative utility installed on an NT computer when the Network Monitor Tools and Agent service is installed. The network monitor provided with NT allows you to capture and analyze network traffic coming into and going out of the local network card. The SMS version of network monitor runs in a promiscuous mode that allows monitoring of traffic on the local network.

/NoSerialMice A BOOT.INI switch that prevents NT from checking for serial mice on COM ports. This is frequently used to prevent NT from inadvertantly shutting down a UPS connected to the COM port.

NT Virtual DOS Machine (NTVDM) Simulates an MS-DOS environment so that MS-DOS–based and Windows-based applications can run on Windows NT.

NTBOOTDD.SYS The driver for a SCSI boot device that does not have its BIOS enabled. NTBOOTDD.SYS is stored on an NT system partition and is required to create a fault-tolerant boot disk.

NTCONFIG.POL A file that defines an NT system policy.

NTDETECT.COM The program in the NT boot process that's responsible for generating a list of hardware devices. This list is later used to populate part of the HKEY_LOCAL_MACHINE subtree in the Registry.

NTFS An advanced file system designed for use specifically within the Windows NT operating system. It supports file system recovery, extremely large storage media, long filenames, and various features for the POSIX subsystem. It also supports object-oriented applications by treating all files as objects with user-defined and system-defined attributes.

NTFS permissions Local permissions on NTFS volumes that allow for the restriction of both local and network access to files and folders.

NTHQ A program that executes from a floppy disk and that automatically checks the hardware on a computer against the HCL for NT compatibility.

NTLDR The program responsible for booting an NT system. It is invoked when an NT computer is started, and it is responsible for displaying the boot menu (from the BOOT.INI file) and starting the NTDETECT.COM program.

NTOSKRNL.EXE The program responsible for maintaining the core of the NT operating system. When NTLDR has completed the boot process, control of NT is handed over to the NTOSKRNL.

NWLink A standard network protocol that supports routing and can support NetWare client-server applications (when NetWare-aware Sockets-based applications communicate with IPX\SPX Sockets-based applications).

NWLink frame type The type of network package generated on a network. In NT configuration, this refers to the type of network packages sent by a NetWare server that an NT client is configured to accept.

O, P, Q

object A specific system category for which counters can be observed in Performance Monitor. Objects whose counters are frequently monitored are Memory, Processor, Network, and PhysicalDisk.

OS/2 An operating system, originally developed by Microsoft, which is currently owned and maintained by IBM.

OSLOADER.EXE On a RISC-based machine, the program that's responsible for the function of the NTLDR on an Intel-based machine.

Peer Web Server (PWS) A service that can be installed on NT Workstation, which allows the workstation to publish files over the Internet. Its features include WWW, FTP, and Gopher protocol support.

Performance Monitor An administrative application used to monitor object counters on an NT computer to determine bottlenecks in the system and to increase overall efficiency.

Point-to-Point Protocol (PPP) A set of industry-standard framing and authentication protocols that is part of Windows NT RAS, which ensures interoperability with third-party remote access software. PPP negotiates configuration parameters for multiple layers of the OSI model.

Point-to-Point Tunneling Protocol (PPTP) PPTP is a new networking technology that supports multiprotocol virtual private networks (VPNs), enabling remote users to access corporate networks securely across the Internet by dialing into an Internet service provider (ISP) or by connecting directly to the Internet.

POSIX An NT emulation of the UNIX operating system. The POSIX subsystem was implemented in NT to allow UNIX programs to execute and thus fulfill the requirements for some government contracts.

preemptive multitasking A multitasking environment in which the operating system decides how long a certain process will have exclusive use of the processor. Windows NT is a preemptive multitasking environment.

primary partition A partition is a portion of a physical disk that can be marked for use by an operating system. There can be up to four primary partitions (or up to three if there is an extended partition) per physical disk. A primary partition cannot be subpartitioned.

print device The actual hardware device that produces printed output.

print server The computer that provides the support for the sharing of one or more printers.

printer The software interface between the operating system and the print device. The printer defines where the document will go before it reaches the print device (to a local port, to a file, or to a remote print share), when it will go, and various other aspects of the printing process.

printer pool Consists of two or more identical print devices associated with one printer.

printer priorities Refers to the relative importance put on certain printers. When one printer that prints to a print device has a higher priority than another printer printing to the same print device, the print jobs of the former will be printed before those of the latter; these print jobs will "jump queue" to take a preeminent place in the print queue while waiting to be printed.

process When a program runs, a Windows NT process is created. A process is an object type that consists of an executable program, a set of virtual memory addresses, and one or more threads.

Program Information File (PIF) A PIF provides information to Windows NT about how best to run MS-DOS applications. When you start an MS-DOS application, Windows NT looks for a PIF to use with the application. PIFs contain such items as the name of the file, a startup directory, and multitasking options.

R

RDISK.EXE A program used to create and update Emergency Repair Disks and the /REPAIR folder on an NT system.

recovery disk A floppy disk that contains the files required by NT to begin the boot process and to point to the boot partition. The files required for an Intel system are: BOOT.INI, NTDETECT.COM, NTLDR, and NTBOOTDD.SYS (if the hard drive is SCSI with BIOS disabled).

REGEDIT.EXE One of two Registry editors available in NT. This one has the same interface as the Registry editor available in Windows 95 and provides key value searching.

REGEDT32.EXE One of two Registry editors available in NT. This one has a cascaded subtree interface and allows you to set Registry security.

Remote Access Service (RAS) A service that provides remote networking for telecommuters, mobile workers, and system administrators who monitor and manage servers at multiple branch offices. Users with RAS on a Windows NT computer can dial in to remotely access their networks for services such as file and printer sharing, electronic mail, scheduling, and SQL database access.

Report view A view in the Performance Monitor that displays current counter values in a single-page format.

S

scheduling printing The process by which certain print jobs are sent to printers that are available only at certain times of the day. By doing this, the load on printers can be kept to a minimum during times when many people require access to the same printer for small print jobs.

Security Identifier (SID) A unique name that identifies a logged-on user to the security system. Security IDs (SIDs) can identify one user or a group of users.

Security log Records security events and can be viewed through the Event Viewer. This helps track changes to the security system and identify any possible breaches of security. For example, depending on the Audit settings in User Manager or User Manager for Domains, any attempts to log on to the local computer may be recorded in the Security log. The Security log contains both valid and invalid logon attempts, as well as events related to resource use (such as creating, opening, and deleting files).

/Separate A switch used on WIN16 programs run from a command prompt that forces execution of that program in a separate NT Virtual DOS machine.

service A process that performs a specific system function and often provides an application programming interface (API) for other processes to call. Windows NT services are RPC-enabled, meaning that their API routines can be called from remote computers.

shared folder A folder on a computer to which access has been given to network users through sharing.

/SOS A BOOT.INI switch indicating that during NT Server or Workstation boot, the list of loading drivers should be displayed. This switch is used for troubleshooting and is normally configured as part of the [VGA] boot option.

source compatible A program having the characteristic of only being usable on the hardware platform for which it was compiled. Windows 32-bit programs are source compatible because they need different versions for every hardware platform.

Spooler service Software that accepts documents sent by a user to be printed and then stores those documents and sends them, one by one, to available printer(s).

spooling A process on a server in which print documents are stored on a disk until a print device is ready to process them. A spooler accepts each document from each client, stores it, and then sends it to a print device when it is ready.

subnet mask A 32-bit value that allows the recipient of IP packets to distinguish the network ID portion of the IP address from the host ID portion.

symmetric multiprocessing A multiprocessor architecture that allows any process to use any processor, thus ensuring the most effective execution of multithreaded processes. NT uses symmetric multiprocessing. This is an improvement over asymmetric multiprocessing systems in which one processor is used exclusively by the operating system, whether it uses the full capabilities of the processor or not.

SYSDIFF A program that is used to create difference files representing the differences between one NT installation and another. *See also* difference file.

System log The System log contains events logged by the Windows NT components and can be viewed through Event Viewer. For example, the failure of a driver or other system component to load during startup is recorded in the System log.

T

Task Manager Task Manager enables you to start, end, or run applications; end processes (either an application, application component, or system process); and view CPU and memory use data. Task Manager gives you a simple, quick view of how each process (application or service) is using CPU and memory resources. (Note: In previous versions of Windows NT, Task List handled some of these functions.)

TCP/IP An acronym for Transmission Control Protocol/Internet Protocol, TCP/IP is a set of networking protocols that provide communications across interconnected networks made up of computers with diverse hardware architectures and various operating systems. TCP/IP includes standards for how computers communicate and conventions for connecting networks and routing traffic.

U

unattended answer file A file that defines the basic installation characteristics for NT. In essence, it answers the questions that a user would be asked during an interactive installation.

UNC (Universal Naming Convention) name A full Windows NT name of a resource on a network. It conforms to the *servername**sharename* syntax, where *servername* is the server's name and *sharename* is the name of the shared resource. UNC names of directories or files can also include the directory path under the sharename, with the following syntax:

*servername**sharename**directory**filename*

uniqueness database file (UDF) A file that defines the unique characteristics of a number of computers. UDFs are used in unattended NT installations to ensure that the features that must be unique (computer name, for instance) are provided without manual user intervention.

user profile Configuration information can be retained on a user-by-user basis and is saved in user profiles. This information includes all the user-specific settings of the Windows NT environment, such as the desktop arrangement, personal program groups and the program items in those groups, screen colors, screen savers, network connections, printer connections, mouse settings, window size and position, and more. When a user logs on, the user's profile is loaded and the user's Windows NT environment is configured according to that profile.

V, W, X, Y, Z

WINDIFF A program that enumerates all the differences between two folders or files. This program will show information as specific as line-by-line differences between files or as general as a list of files in two folders that differ.

Windows Internet Name Service (WINS) A name resolution service that resolves Windows NT networking computer names to IP addresses in a routed environment. A WINS server handles name registrations, queries, and releases.

Windows Microsoft Diagnostic (WinMSD) A program that displays hardware configuration information for the purposes of diagnostics and general system reporting.

Windows on Windows (WOW) A WIN16 emulation that runs inside of an NT Virtual DOS machine and allows the execution of WIN16 programs in the 32-bit NT environment.

WINNT.EXE The program used to install Windows NT from a non-NT platform.

WINNT32.EXE The program used to install or upgrade Windows NT from an NT platform.

APPENDIX C

Fast Facts

Now that you have thoroughly read through this book, worked through the exercises and gotten as much hands-on exposure to NT Server as you could, you've now booked your exam. This chapter is designed as a last minute cram for you as you walk out the door on your way to the exam. You can't re-read the whole book in an hour, but you will be able to read this chapter in that time.

This chapter is organized by objective category, giving you not just a summary, but a rehash of the most important point form facts that you need to know. Remember that this is meant to be a review of concepts and a trigger for you to remember wider definitions. In addition to what is in this chapter, make sure you know what is in the glossary because this chapter does not define terms. If you know what is in here and the concepts that stand behind it, chances are the exam will be a snap.

PLANNING

Remember: Here are the elements that Microsoft says they test on for the "Planning" section of the exam.

- Plan the disk drive configuration for various requirements. Requirements include: choosing a file system and fault tolerance method
- Choose a protocol for various situations. Protocols include: TCP/IP, NWLink IPX/SPX Compatible Transport, and NetBEUI

Minimum requirement for installing NT Server on an Intel machine is 468DX/33, 16MB of RAM, and 130MB of free disk space.

The login process on an NT Domain is as follows:

1. WinLogon sends the user name and password to the Local Security Authority (LSA).
2. The LSA passes the request to the local NetLogon service.
3. The local NetLogon service sends the logon information to the NetLogon service on the domain controller.
4. The NetLogon service on the domain controller passes the information to the domain controller's Security Accounts Manager (SAM).
5. The SAM asks the domain directory database for approval of the user name and password.
6. The SAM passes the result of the approval request to the domain controller's NetLogon service.

7. The domain controller's NetLogon service passes the result of the approval request to the client's NetLogon service.
8. The client's NetLogon service passes the result of the approval request to the LSA.
9. If the logon is approved, the LSA creates an access token and passes it to the WinLogon process.
10. WinLogon completes the logon, thus creating a new process for the user and attaching the access token to the new process.

The system partition is where your computer boots and it must be on an active partition.

The boot partition is where the WINNT folder is found and it contains the NT program files. It can be on any partition (not on a volume set, though).

NT supports two forms of software-based fault tolerance: Disk Mirroring (RAID 1) and Stripe Sets with Paritiy (RAID 5).

Disk Mirroring uses two hard drives and provides 50% disk space utilization.

Stripe sets with Parity uses between 3 and 32 hard drives and provides a (n-1)/n*100% utilization (n = number of disks in the set).

Disk duplexing provides better tolerance than mirroring because it does mirroring with separate controllers on each disk.

NT Supports 3 file systems: NTFS, FAT, and CDFS (it no longer supports HPFS, the OS/2 file system nor does it support FAT32, a file system used by Windows 95).

The following table is a comparison of NTFS and FAT features:

Table C.1 shows a quick summary of the differences between file systems:

TABLE C.1 FAT VERSUS NTFS COMPARISON

Feature	*FAT*	*NTFS*
File name length	255	255
8.3 file name compatibility	Yes	Yes
File size	4 GB	16 EB
Partition size	4 GB	16 EB
Directory structure	Linked list	B-tree
Local security	No	Yes
Transaction tracking	No	Yes
Hot fixing	No	Yes
Overhead	1 MB	>4 MB
Required on system partition for RISC-based computers	Yes	No
Accessible from MS-DOS/ Windows 95	Yes	No
Accessible from OS/2	Yes	No
Case-sensitive	No	POSIX only
Case preserving	Yes	Yes
Compression	No	Yes
Efficiency	200 MB	400 MB
Windows NT formattable	Yes	Yes
Fragmentation level	High	Low
Floppy disk formattable	Yes	No

The following is a table to summarize the protocols commonly used by NT for network communication:

TABLE C.2 PRIMARY PROTOCOL USESES

Protocol	*Primary Use*
TCP/IP	Internet and WAN connectivity
NWLink	Interoperability with NetWare
NetBEUI	Interoperability with old Lan Man networks

The main points regarding TCP/IP are as follows:

- Requires IP Address, and Subnet Mask to function (default Gateway if being routed)
- Can be configured manually or automatically using DHCP server running on NT
- Common address resolution methods are WINS and DNS

INSTALLATION AND CONFIGURATION

Remember: Here are the elements that Microsoft says they test on for the "Installation and Configuration" section of the exam.

- Install Windows NT Server on Intel-based platforms.
- Install Windows NT Server to perform various server roles. Server roles include: Primary domain controller, Backup domain controller, and Member server.
- Install Windows NT Server by using various methods. Installation methods include: CD-ROM, Over-the-network, Network Client Administrator, and Express versus custom.
- Configure protocols and protocol bindings. Protocols include: TCP/IP, NWLink IPX/SPX Compatible Transport, and NetBEUI.
- Configure network adapters. Considerations include: changing IRQ, IObase, and memory addresses and configuring multiple adapters.
- Configure Windows NT server core services. Services include: Directory Replicator, License Manager, and Other services.
- Configure peripherals and devices. Peripherals and devices include: communication devices, SCSI devices, tape device drivers, UPS devices and UPS service, mouse drivers, display drivers, and keyboard drivers.
- Configure hard disks to meet various requirements. Requirements include: allocating disk space capacity, providing redundancy, improving security, and formatting.
- Configure printers. Tasks include: adding and configuring a printer, implementing a printer pool, and setting print priorities.
- Configure a Windows NT Server computer for various types of client computers. Client computer types include: Windows NT Workstation, Microsoft Windows 95, and Microsoft MS-DOS-based.

The Hardware Compatibility list is used to ensure that NT supports all computer components.

NT can be installed in 3 different configurations in a domain: Primary Domain Controller, Backup Domain Controller, and Member Server.

Two sources can be used for installation files: CD-ROM or network share (which is the hardware specific files from the CD copied onto a server and shared).

Three Setup diskettes are required for all installations when a CD-ROM is not supported by the operating system present on the computer at installation time (or if no operating system exists and the computer will not boot from the CD-ROM).

WINNT and WINNT32 are used for network installation; WINNT32 for installations when NT is currently present on the machine you are installing to and WINNT when it is not.

The following table is a summary of the WINNT and WINNT32 switches:

TABLE C.3 WINNT AND WINNT32 SWITCH FUNCTIONS

Switch	*Function*
/B	Prevents creation of the three setup disks during the installation process
/S	Indicates the location of the source files for NT installation (e.g., /S:D:\NTFiles)
/U	Indicates the script file to use for an unattended installation (e.g., /U:C:\Answer.txt)
/UDF	Indicates the location of the uniqueness database file which defines unique configuration for each NT machine being installed (e.g., /UDF:D:\Answer.UDF)
/T	Indicates the place to put the temporary installation files
/OX	Initiates only the creation of the three setup disks
/F	Indicates not to verify the files copied to the setup diskettes
/C	Indicates not to check for free space on the setup diskettes before creating them

To remove NT from a computer you must do the following:

1. Remove all the NTFS partitions from within Windows NT and reformat them with FAT (this ensures that these disk areas will be accessible by non-NT operating systems).
2. Boot to another operating system, such as Windows 95 or MS-DOS.
3. Delete the Windows NT installation directory tree (usually WINNT).
4. Delete pagefile.sys.
5. Turn off the hidden, system, and read-only attributes for NTBOOTDD.SYS, BOOT.INI, NTLDR, and NTDETECT.COM and then delete them. You might not have all of these on your computer, but if so, you can find them all in the root directory of your drive C.
6. Make the hard drive bootable by placing another operating system on it (or SYS it with DOS or Windows 95 to allow the operating system that does exist to boot).

The Client Administrator allows you to do the following:

- Make Network Installation Startup disk: shares files and creates bootable diskette for initiating client installation.
- Make Installation Disk Set: copies installation files to diskette for installing simple clients like MS-DOS network client 3.0.
- Copy Client-Based Network Administration Tools: creates a folder which can be attached to from Windows NT Workstation and Windows 95 clients to install tools for administering an NT Server from a workstation.

MANAGING RESOURCES

Remember: Here are the elements that Microsoft says they test on for the "Managing Resources" section of the exam.

- Manage user and group accounts. Considerations include: managing Windows NT groups, managing Windows NT user rights, administering account policies, and auditing changes to the user account database.
- Create and manage policies and profiles for various situations. Policies and profiles include: local user profiles, roaming user profiles, and system policies.
- Administer remote servers from various types of client computers. Client computer types include: Windows 95 and Windows NT Workstation.
- Manage disk resources. Tasks include: copying and moving files between file systems, creating and sharing resources, implementing permissions and security, and establishing file auditing.

Network properties dialog box lets you install and configure the following:

- Computer and Domain names
- Services
- Protocols
- Adapters
- Bindings

When configuring NWLink ensure that if more than one frame type exists on your network that you don't use AutoDetect or only the first frame type encountered will be detected from then on.

The following table shows you three TCP/IP command-line diagnostic tools and what they do:

TABLE C.4 TCP/IP COMMAND LINE DIAGNOSTIC TOOLS

Tool	*Function*
IPConfig	Displays the basic TCP/IP configuration of each adapter card on a computer (with/all displays detailed configuration information)
Ping	Determines connectivity with another TCP/IP host by sending a message that is echoed by the recipient if received
Tracert	Traces each hop on the way to a TCP/IP host and indicates points of failure if they exist

Network adapter card configuration of IRQ and I/O port address may or may not be configurable from the Network Properties dialog box; it depends on the card.

To allow NT computers to participate in a domain, a computer account must be created for each one.

Windows 95 clients need special profiles and policies created on a Windows 95 machine and then copied onto an NT Server to participate in domain profile and policy configuration.

Windows 95 clients need printer drivers installed on an NT Server acting as a print controller to print to an NT controller printer.

Typical services tested for NT Server are listed and described in the following table:

TABLE C.5 NT SERVER SERVICES AND THEIR FUNCTIONS

Service	*Function*
DNS	Provides TCP/IP address resolution using a static table and can be used for non-Microsoft hosts
WINS	Provides TP/IP address resolution using a dynamic table and can be used for Microsoft hosts
DHCP	Provides automatic configuration of TCP/IP clients for Microsoft clients

continues

TABLE C.5 CONTINUED

Service	*Function*
Browser	Provides a list of domain resources to Network Neighborhood and Server Manager
Replicator	Provides import and export services for automated file distribution between NT computers (Servers can be export and import, Workstations can only be import)

REGEDT32.EXE and REGEDIT are used to view and modify registry settings in NT.

The five registry subtrees are:

- HKEY_LOCAL_MACHINE. Stores all the computer-specific configuration data.
- HKEY_USERS. Stores all the user-specific configuration data.
- HKEY_CURRENT_USER. Stores all configuration data for the currently logged on user.
- HKEY_CLASSES_ROOT. Stores all OLE and file association information.
- HKEY_CURRENT_CONFIG. Stores information about the hardware profile specified at startup.

REGEDT32.EXE allows you to see and set security on the registry and allows you to open the registry in read-only mode, but does not allow you to search by key value.

NT checking for serial mice at boot may disable a UPS. To disable that check, place the /noserialmice in the boot line in the BOOT.INI file.

The SCSI adapters icon in the Control Panel lets you add and configure SCSI devices as well as CD-ROM drives.

Many changes made in the disk administrator require that you choose the menu Partition, Commit Changes for them to take effect.

Although you can set drive letters manually, the following is how NT assigns letters to partitions and volumes:

1. Beginning from the letter C:, assign consecutive letters to the first primary partition on each physical disk.
2. Assign consecutive letters to each logical drive, completing all on one physical disk before moving on to the next.
3. Assign consecutive letters to the additional primary partitions, completing all on one physical disk before moving on to the next.

Disk Administrator allows for the creation of two kinds of partitions (primary and extended) and four kinds of volumes (volume set, stripe set, mirror set, and stripe set with parity). The following table is a summary of their characteristics:

TABLE C.6 PARTITION CHARACTERISTICS

Object	*Characteristics*
Primary partition	Non-divisible disk unit which can be marked active and can be made bootable.
	Can have up to four on a physical drive.
	NT system partition must be on a primary.
Extended partition	Divisible disk unit which must be divided into logical disks (or have free space used in a volume) in order to function as space storage tool.
	Can have only one on a physical drive.
	Logical drive within can be the NT boot partition.
Volume Set	Made up of 2-32 portions of free space which do not have to be the same size and which can be spread out between 1 and 32 disks of many types (IDE, SCSI, etc.).
	Can be added to if formatted NTFS.
	Cannot contain NT boot or system partition.

Object	*Characteristics*
	Removing one portion of the set destroys the volume and the data is lost.
	Is not fault tolerant.
Stripe Set	Made up of 2-32 portions of free space which have to be the same size and which can be spread out over between 2 and 32 disks of many types (IDE, SCSI, etc.).
	Cannot be added to and removing one portion of the set destroys the volume and the data is lost.
	Is not fault tolerant.
Mirror Set	Made up of 2 portions of free space which have to be the same size and which must be on 2 physical disks.
	Identical data is written to both mirror partitions and they are treated as one disk.
	If one disk stops functioning the other will continue to operate.
	The NT Boot and System partitions can be held on a mirror set.
	Has a 50% disk utilization rate.
	Is fault tolerant.
Stripe Set with Parity	Made up of 3-32 portions of free space which have to be the same size and must be spread out over the same number of physical disks.
	Maintains fault tolerance by creating parity information across a stripe.
	If one disk fails, the stripe set will continue to function, albeit with a loss of performance.
	The NT Boot and System partitions cannot be held on a Stripe Set with Parity.
	Is fault tolerant.

Disk Administrator can be used to format partitions and volumes either FAT or NTFS.

If you have any clients who access a shared printer that are not using NT or are not using the same hardware platform as your printer server, then you must install those drivers when you share the printer.

By assigning different priorities for printers associated with the same print device you can create a hierarchy among users' print jobs, thus ensuring that the print jobs of some users print sooner than others.

By adjusting the printer schedule you can ensure that jobs sent to particular printers are only printed at certain hours of the day.

A printer has permissions assigned to it. The following is a list of the permissions for printers.

- No Access. Completely restricts access to the printer.
- Print. Allows a user or group to submit a print job, and to control the settings and print status for that job.
- Manage Documents. Allows a user or group to submit a print job, and to control the settings and print status for all print jobs.
- Full Control. Allows a user to submit a print job, and to control the settings and print status for all documents as well as for the printer itself. In addition, the user or group may share, stop sharing, change permissions for, and even delete the printer.

Printer pools consist of one or more print devices that can use the same print driver controlled by a single printer.

MS-DOS users must have print drivers installed locally on their computers.

The assignment of permissions to resources should use the following procedure:

1. Create user accounts.
2. Create global groups for the domain and populate the groups with user accounts.

3. Create local groups and assign them rights and permissions to resources and programs in the domain.
4. Place global groups into the local groups you have created, thereby giving the users who are members of the global groups access to the system and its resources.

The built-in local groups in a Windows NT Domain are as follows:

- Administrators
- Users
- Guests
- Backup Operators
- Replicator
- Print Operators
- Server Operators
- Account Operators

The built-in global groups in an NT Domain are as follows:

- Domain Admins
- Domain Users
- Domain Guests

The system groups on an NT server are as follows:

- Everyone
- Creator Owner
- Network
- Interactive

The built-in users on an NT server are as follows:

- Administrator
- Guest

The following table describes the buttons on the User Properties dialog box and their functions:

TABLE C.7 BUTTONS ON THE USER PROPERTIES DIALOG BOX

Button	*Function*
Groups	Enables you to add and remove group memberships for the account. The easiest way to grant rights to a user account is to add it to a group that possesses those rights.
Profile	Enables you to add a user profile path, a logon script name, and a home directory path to the user's environment profile. You learn more about the Profile button in the following section.
Hours	Enables you to define specific times when the users can access the account. (The default is always.)
Logon To	Enables you to specify up to 8 workstations from which the user can log on. (The default is all workstations.)
Account	Enables you to provide an expiration date for the account. (The default is never.) You also can specify the account as global (for regular users in this domain) or domain local.

The following table is a summary of the account policy fields:

TABLE C.8 ACCOUNT POLICY FIELDS

Button	*Function*
Maximum Password Age	The maximum number of days a password can be in effect until it must be changed.
Minimum Password Age	The minimum number of days a password must stay in effect before it can be changed.
Minimum Password Length	The minimum number of characters a password must include.
Password Uniqueness	The number of passwords that NT remembers for a user; these passwords cannot be reused until they are no longer remembered.
Account Lockout	The number of incorrect passwords that can be input by a user before the account becomes locked. Reset

Button	*Function*
	will automatically set the count back to 0 after a specified length of time. In addition the duration of lockout is either a number of minutes or forever (until an administrator unlocks it).
Forcibly disconnect remote	In conjunction with logon hours, this checkbox enables forcible disconnection of authorized users from server when logon hours come to a close.
Users must log on in order to	Ensures that a user whose password has expired cannot change his or her password but has to have it reset by an administrator.

Account SIDs are unique; therefore, if an account is deleted, the permissions cannot be restored by recreating an account with the same name.

Local profiles are only available from the machine on which they were created, whereas roaming profiles can be accessed from any machine on the network.

A mandatory profile is a roaming profile that users cannot change. They have the extension .MAN.

Hardware profiles can be used with machines that have more than one hardware configuration (such as laptops).

The System Policy editor (POLEDIT) has two modes, Policy File mode and Registry Mode.

The application of system policies is as follows:

1. When you log in, the NT Config.pol is checked. If there is an entry for the specific user, then any registry settings indicated will be merged with, and overwrite if necessary, the user's registry.
2. If there is no specific user entry, any settings for groups that the user is a member of will be applied to the user.
3. If the user is not present in any groups and not listed explicitly then the Default settings will be applied.
4. If the computer that the user is logging in on has an entry, then the computer settings are applied.
5. If there is not a computer entry for the user then the default computer policy is applied.

Windows 95 policies are not compatible with NT and therefore Windows 95 users must access a Windows 95 policy created on a Windows 95 machine and copied to an NT machine and named Config.Pol.

The Net Use command line can be used to map a drive letter to a network share; using the /persistent switch ensures that it is reconnected at next logon.

FAT long file names under NT have 8.3 aliases created to ensure backward compatibility. The following is an example of how aliases are generated from 5 files that all have the same initial characters:

Team meeting Report #3.doc	TEAMME~1.DOC
Team meeting Report #4.doc	TEAMME~2.DOC
Team meeting Report #5.doc	TEAMME~3.DOC
Team meeting Report #6.doc	TEAMME~4.DOC
Team meeting Report #7.doc	TEAMME~5.DOC

A long file name on a FAT partition uses one file name for the 8.3 alias and then one more FAT entry for every 13 characters in the name.

A FAT partition can be converted to NTFS without loss of data through the command line

CONVERT <drive>: /FS:NTFS

NTFS supports compression as a file attribute that can be set in the file properties.

Compression can be applied to a folder or a drive and the effect is that the files within are compressed and any file copied into it will also become compressed.

Compression can be applied through the use of the COMPACT.EXE program through the syntax

COMPACT <file or directory path> [/switch]

The available switches for COMPACT are as follows:

TABLE C.9 COMPACT SWITCHES

Switch	*Function*
/C	Compress
/U	Uncompress
/S	Compress an entire directory tree
/A	Compress hidden and system files
/I	Ignore errors and continue compressing
/F	Force compression even if the objects are already compressed
/Q	Display only summary information

Share-level permissions apply only when users access a resource over the network, not locally. The share-level permissions are:

- No Access. Users with No Access to a share can still connect to the share, but nothing appears in File Manager except the message You do not have permission to access this directory.
- Read. Allows you to display folder and file names, display file content and attributes, run programs, open folders inside the shared folder.
- Change. Allows you to create folders and files, change file content, change file attributes, delete files and folders, do everything READ permission allows.
- Full Control. Allows you to change file permissions and do everything change allows for.

Share-level permissions apply to the folder that is shared and apply equally to all the contents of that share.

Share-level permissions apply to any shared folder, whether on FAT or NTFS.

NTFS permissions can only be applied to any file or folder on an NTFS partition.

The actions that can be performed against an NTFS object are as follows:

- Read (R)
- Write (W)
- Execute (X)
- Delete (D)
- Change Permissions (P)
- Take Ownership (O)

The NTFS permissions available for folders are summarized in the following table:

TABLE C.10 NTFS FOLDER PERMISSIONS

Permission	*Action permitted*
No Access	none
List	RX
Read	RX
Add	WX
Add & Read	RXWD
Change	RXWD
Full Control	RXWDPO

The NTFS permissions available for files are summarized in the following table:

TABLE C.11 NTFS FILE PERMISSIONS

Permission	*Action permitted*
No Access	none
Read	RX
Add & Read	RX
Change	RXWD
Full Control	RXWDPO

If a user is given permission to a resource and a group or groups that the user is a member of is also given access, then the effective permission the user has is the cumulation of all of the user permissions. This applies unless any of the permissions are set to No Access in which case the user has no access to the resource.

If a user is given permission to a shared resource and is also given permission to that resource through NTFS permissions, then the effective permission is the most restrictive permission.

The File Child Delete scenario manifests itself when someone has full control to a folder but is granted a permission which does not enable deletion (Read or No Access, for example). The effect is that a user will be able to delete files inside the folder even though sufficient access does not appear to be present.

To close the File Child Delete loophole, do not grant a user Full Control access to a folder but instead, use special Directory permissions to assign RXWDPO access, this eliminates the File Child Delete permission.

Access Tokens do not refresh and a user needs to log off and log back on if changed permissions are to take effect.

MONITORING AND OPTIMIZATION

Remember: Here are the elements that Microsoft says they test on for the "Monitoring and Optimization" section of the exam.

- Monitor performance of various functions by using Performance Monitor. Functions include: processor, memory, disk, and network.
- Identify performance bottlenecks.

Performance monitor has 4 views: chart, alert, log, and report.

The subsystems that are routinely monitored are: Memory, Disk, Network, and Processor.

Disk counters can be enabled through the command line:

Diskperf -y

Or

Diskperf -ye (for RAID disks and volumes)

TROUBLESHOOTING

Remember: Here are the elements that Microsoft says they test on for the "Troubleshooting" section of the exam.

- Choose the appropriate course of action to take to resolve installation failures.
- Choose the appropriate course of action to take to resolve boot failures.
- Choose the appropriate course of action to take to resolve configuration errors.
- Choose the appropriate course of action to take to resolve printer problems.
- Choose the appropriate course of action to take to resolve RAS problems.
- Choose the appropriate course of action to take to resolve connectivity problems.
- Choose the appropriate course of action to take to resolve fault tolerance problems. Fault-tolerance methods include: tape backup, mirroring, stripe set with parity, and disk duplexing.

The acronym DETECT can be used to define the troubleshooting process and stands for:

- Discover the problem.
- Explore the boundaries.
- Track the possible approaches.
- Execute an Approach.
- Check for success.
- Tie up loose ends.

An NTHQ diskette can test a computer to ensure that NT will successfully install on it.

The following list identifies possible sources of installation problems:

- Media errors
- Insufficient disk space
- Non-supported SCSI adapter
- Failure of dependancy service to start
- Inability to connect to the domain controller
- Error in assigning domain name

The files involved in the boot process are identified in the following table for both Intel and RISC machines:

TABLE C.12 FILES INVOLVED IN THE BOOT PROCESS

Intel	*RISC*
NTLDR	OSLOADER.EXE
BOOT.INI	NTOSKRNL.EXE
NTDETECT.COM	
NTOSKRNL.EXE	

In the NT boot process (in BOOT.INI) ARC paths define the physical position of the NT operating system files and come in two forms:

Scsi(0)disk(0)rdisk(0)partition(1)\WINNT
Multi(0)disk(0)rdisk(0)partition(1)\WINNT

SCSI arc paths define hard drives which are SCSI and which have their bios disabled. The relevant parameters are:

- SCSI: the SCSI controller starting from 0
- DISK: the physical disk starting from 0

- PARTITION: the partition on the disk stating from 1
- \folder: the folder in which the NT files are located

MULTI arc paths define hard drives which are non-SCSI or SCSI with their bios enabled. The relevant parameters are:

- MULTI: the controller starting from 0
- RDISK: the physical disk starting from 0
- PARTITION: the partition on the disk stating from 1
- \folder: the folder in which the NT files are located

Partitions are numbered as follows:

1. The first primary partition on each disk gets the number 0.
2. Each additional primary partition then is given a number, incrementing up from 0.
3. Each logical drive is then given a number in the order they appear in the Disk Administrator.

Switches on boot lines in the boot.ini file define additional boot parameters. The following table lists the switches you need to know about and their function:

TABLE C.13 BOOT.INI FILE SWITCHES

Switch	*Function*
/basevideo	Loads standard VGA video driver (640x480, 16 color)
/sos	Displays each driver as it is loaded
/noserialmice	Prevents autodetection of serial mice on COM ports which may disable a UPS connected to the port

A recovery disk can be used to bypass problems with system partition. Such a disk contains the following files (broken down by hardware platform):

TABLE C.14 FILES ON A FAULT-TOLERANT BOOT DISKETTE

Intel	*RISC*
NTLDR	OSLOADER.EXE
NTDETECT.COM	HAL.DLL
BOOT.INI	*.PAL (for Alpha machines)
BOOTSECT.DOS	(allows you to boot to DOS)
NTBOOTDD.SYS	(the SCSI driver for a hard drive with SCSI bios not enabled)

An Emergency repair disk can be used to recover an NT system if the registry becomes corrupted and must be used in conjunction with the three setup diskettes used to install NT.

The RDISK programs allows you to update the \REPAIR folder which in turn is used to update your repair diskette.

The Event Viewer allows you to see three log files: System Log, Security Log, and Application Log.

The Windows NT Diagnostics program allows you to see (but not modify) configuration settings for much of your hardware and environment.

The course of action to take when a stop error occurs (blue screen) can be configured from the System Properties dialog box (in the Control Panel) on the Startup/Shutdown tab.

To move the spool file from one partition to another, use the Advanced Tab on the Server Properties dialog box; this can be located from the File, Server Properties menu in the printers dialog box.

Common RAS problems include the following:

- User Permission: user not enabled to use RAS in User Manager for Domains.
- Authentication: often caused by incompatible encryption methods (client using different encryption than server is configured to receive).
- Callback with Multilink: Client configured for callback but is using multilink; server will only call back to a single number, thereby removing multilink functionality.
- Autodial at Logon: Shortcuts on desktop referencing server-based applications or files cause autodial to kick in when logon is complete.

User can't log in may be caused by a number of factors including:

- Incorrect user name or password
- Incorrect domain name
- Incorrect user rights (inability to log on locally to an NT machine, for example)
- Netlogon service on server is stopped or paused
- Domain controllers are down
- User is restricted in system policies from logging on at a specific computer

The right to create backups and restore from backups using NT Backup is granted to the groups Administrators, Backup Operators, and Server Operators by default.

NT Backup will only backup files to tape, no other media is supported.

The following table summarizes the backup types available in NT backup:

TABLE C.15 BACKUP TYPES AVAILABLE IN NTBACKUP

Type	*Backs Up*	*Marks?*
Normal	All selected files and folders	Yes
Copy	All selected files and folders	No
Incremental	Selected files and folders not marked as backed up	Yes
Differential	Selected files and folders not marked as backed up	No
Daily Copy	Selected files and folders changed that day	No

The local registry of a computer can be backed up by selecting the Backup Local Registry checkbox in the Backup Information dialog box.

Data from tape can be restored to the original location or to an alternate location and NTFS permissions can be restored or not, however, you cannot change the names of the objects being restored until the restore is complete.

Backup can be run from a command line using the NTBACKUP command in the syntax:

Ntbackup backup path [switches]

Some command line backup switches are shown in the following table:

TABLE C.16 NTBACKUP COMMAND LINE SWITCHES

Switch	*Function*
/a	Append the current backup to the backup already on the tape
/v	Verify the backed up files when complete
/d *text*	Add an identifying description to the backup tape
/t option	Specify the backup type. Valid options are: normal, copy, Incremental, differential, and daily

To recover from a failed mirror set you must do the following:

1. Shut down your NT server and physically replace the failed drive.
2. If required, boot NT using a recovery disk.
3. Start the Disk Administrator using the menu Start, Programs, Administrative Tools (Common), Disk Administrator.
4. Select the mirror set by clicking on it.
5. From the Fault Tolerance menu choose Break Mirror. This action exposes the remaining partition as a volume separate from the failed one.
6. Reestablish the mirror set if desired by selecting the partition you desire to mirror and a portion of free space equal in size and choosing the menu Fault Tolerance, Establish Mirror.

To regenerate a stripe set with parity, do the following:

1. Shut down your NT server and physically replace the failed drive.
2. Start the Disk Administrator using the menu Start, Programs, Administrative Tools (Common), Disk Administrator.
3. Select the stripe set with parity by clicking on it.
4. Select an area of free space as large or larger than the portion of the stripe set that was lost when the disk failed.
5. Choose Fault Tolerance, Regenerate.

Hopefully, this has been a helpful tool in your final review before the exam. You might find after reading this that there are some places in the book you need to revisit. Just remember to stay focused and answer all the questions. You can always go back and check the answers for the questions you are unsure of. Good luck!

Index

Symbols

A

B

C

D

E

N

O

P

Q-R

S

V

W-Z

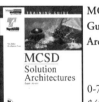

MCSD Training Guide: Microsoft Visual Basic 6, Exam 70-176

0-7357-0031-1, $49.99, Q1/99

TRAINING GUIDES

FIRST EDITIONS

Your Quality Elective Solution

MCSE Training Guide: Systems Management Server 1.2, 1-56205-748-0

MCSE Training Guide: SQL Server 6.5 Administration, 1-56205-726-X

MCSE Training Guide: SQL Server 6.5 Design and Implementation, 1-56205-830-4

MCSE Training Guide: Windows 95, 70-064 Exam, 1-56205-880-0

MCSE Training Guide: Exchange Server 5, 1-56205-824-X

MCSE Training Guide: Internet Explorer 4, 1-56205-889-4

MCSE Training Guide: Microsoft Exchange Server 5.5, 1-56205-899-1

MCSE Training Guide: IIS 4, 1-56205-823-1

MCSD Training Guide: Visual Basic 5, 1-56205-850-9

MCSD Training Guide: Microsoft Access, 1-56205-771-5

TESTPREPS

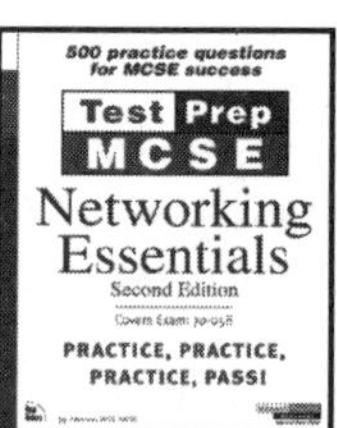

MCSE TestPrep: Networking Essentials, Second Edition

0-7357-0010-9, $19.99, 11/98

MCSE TestPrep: TCP/IP, Second Edition

0-7357-0025-7, $19.99, 12/98

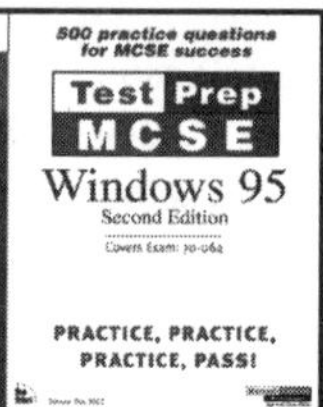

MCSE TestPrep: Windows 95, Second Edition

0-7357-0011-7, $19.99, 11/98

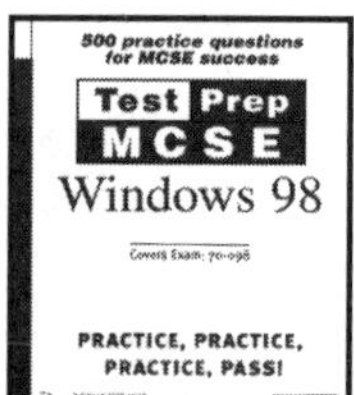

MCSE TestPrep: Windows 98

1-56205-922-X, $19.99, Q4/98

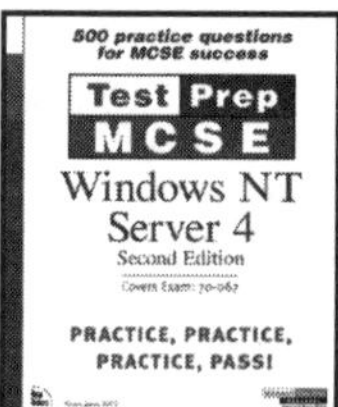

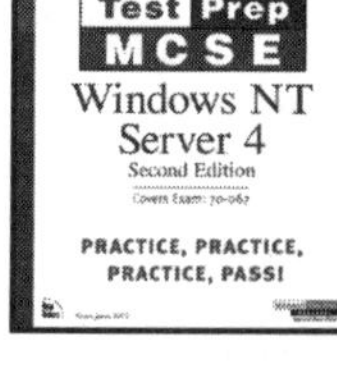

MCSE TestPrep: Windows NT Server 4, Second Edition

0-7357-0012-5, $19.99, 12/98

MCSE TestPrep: Windows NT Server 4 Enterprise, Second Edition

0-7357-0009-5, $19.99, 11/98

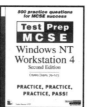

MCSE TestPrep: Windows NT Workstation 4, Second Edition

0-7357-0008-7, $19.99, 11/98

TESTPREPS

FIRST EDITIONS

Your Quality Elective Solution

MCSE TestPrep: SQL Server 6.5 Administration, 0-7897-1597-X

MCSE TestPrep: SQL Server 6.5 Design and Implementation, 1-56205-915-7

MCSE TestPrep: Windows 95 70-64 Exam, 0-7897-1609-7

MCSE TestPrep: Internet Explorer 4, 0-7897-1654-2

MCSE TestPrep: Exchange Server 5.5, 0-7897-1611-9

MCSE TestPrep: IIS 4.0, 0-7897-1610-0

FAST TRACK SERIES

The Accelerated Path to Certification Success

Fast Tracks provide an easy way to review the key elements of each certification technology without being bogged down with elementary-level information.

These guides are perfect for when you already have real-world, hands-on experience. They're the ideal enhancement to training courses, test simulators, and comprehensive training guides. *No fluff, simply what you really need to pass the exam!*

LEARN IT FAST

Part I contains only the essential information you need to pass the test. With over 200 pages of information, it is a concise review for the more experienced MCSE candidate.

REVIEW IT EVEN FASTER

Part II averages 50–75 pages, and takes you through the test and into the real-world use of the technology, with chapters on:

1) Fast Facts Review Section
2) The Insider's Spin (on taking the exam)
3) Sample Test Questions
4) Hotlists of Exam-Critical Concepts
5) Did You Know? (real-world applications for the technology covered in the exam)

MCSE Fast Track: Networking Essentials

1-56205-939-4, $19.99, 9/98

MCSE Fast Track: TCP/IP

1-56205-937-8, $19.99, 9/98

MCSE Fast Track: Windows 98

0-7357-0016-8, $19.99, Q4/98

MCSE Fast Track: Internet Information Server 4

1-56205-936-X, $19.99, 9/98

MCSE Fast Track: Windows NT Server 4

1-56205-935-1, $19.99, 9/98

MCSD Fast Track: Solution Architectures

0-7357-0029-X, $19.99, Q1/99

MCSE Fast Track: Windows NT Server 4 Enterprise

1-56205-940-8, $19.99, 9/98

MCSD Fast Track: Visual Basic 6, Exam 70-175

0-7357-0018-4, $19.99, Q4/98

MCSE Fast Track: Windows NT Workstation 4

1-56205-938-6, $19.99, 9/98

MCSD Fast Track: Visual Basic 6, Exam 70-176

0-7357-0019-2, $19.99, Q4/98

How to Contact Us

IF YOU NEED THE LATEST UPDATES ON A TITLE THAT YOU'VE PURCHASED:

1) Visit our Web site at www.newriders.com.

2) Click on the DOWNLOADS link, and enter your book's ISBN number, which is located on the back cover in the bottom right-hand corner.

3) In the DOWNLOADS section, you'll find available updates that are linked to the book page.

IF YOU ARE HAVING TECHNICAL PROBLEMS WITH THE BOOK OR THE CD THAT IS INCLUDED:

1) Check the book's information page on our Web site according to the instructions listed above, or

2) Email us at support@mcp.com, or

3) Fax us at (317) 817-7488 attn: Tech Support.

IF YOU HAVE COMMENTS ABOUT ANY OF OUR CERTIFICATION PRODUCTS THAT ARE NON-SUPPORT RELATED:

1) Email us at certification@mcp.com, or

2) Write to us at New Riders, 201 W. 103rd St., Indianapolis, IN 46290-1097, or

3) Fax us at (317) 581-4663.

IF YOU ARE OUTSIDE THE UNITED STATES AND NEED TO FIND A DISTRIBUTOR IN YOUR AREA:

Please contact our international department at international@mcp.com.

IF YOU WISH TO PREVIEW ANY OF OUR CERTIFICATION BOOKS FOR CLASSROOM USE:

Email us at pr@mcp.com. Your message should include your name, title, training company or school, department, address, phone number, office days/hours, text in use, and enrollment. Send these details along with your request for desk/examination copies and/or additional information.

We Want to Know What You Think

To better serve you, we would like your opinion on the content and quality of this book. Please complete this card and mail it to us or fax it to 317-581-4663.

Name ______________________________

Address ______________________________

City ______________ State ________ Zip ______________

Phone ______________ Email Address ______________

Occupation ______________________________

Which certification exams have you already passed? ______________________________

Which certification exams do you plan to take? ______________________________

What influenced your purchase of this book?

- ❑ Recommendation
- ❑ Cover Design
- ❑ Table of Contents
- ❑ Index
- ❑ Magazine Review
- ❑ Advertisement
- ❑ Reputation of New Riders
- ❑ Author Name

How would you rate the contents of this book?

- ❑ Excellent
- ❑ Very Good
- ❑ Good
- ❑ Fair
- ❑ Below Average
- ❑ Poor

What other types of certification products will you buy/have you bought to help you prepare for the exam?

- ❑ Quick reference books
- ❑ Testing software
- ❑ Study guides
- ❑ Other

What do you like most about this book? Check all that apply.

- ❑ Content
- ❑ Writing Style
- ❑ Accuracy
- ❑ Examples
- ❑ Listings
- ❑ Design
- ❑ Index
- ❑ Page Count
- ❑ Price
- ❑ Illustrations

What do you like least about this book? Check all that apply.

- ❑ Content
- ❑ Writing Style
- ❑ Accuracy
- ❑ Examples
- ❑ Listings
- ❑ Design
- ❑ Index
- ❑ Page Count
- ❑ Price
- ❑ Illustrations

What would be a useful follow-up book to this one for you? ______________________________

Where did you purchase this book? ______________________________

Can you name a similar book that you like better than this one, or one that is as good? Why? ______________________________

How many New Riders books do you own? ______________________________

What are your favorite certification or general computer book titles? ______________________________

What other titles would you like to see New Riders develop? ______________________________

Any comments? ______________________________

Fold here and Scotch tape to mail

Place
Stamp
Here

New Riders
201 W. 103rd St.
Indianapolis, IN 46290